# WHITE-COLLAR CRIME: THEORY AND RESEARCH

*Books in this series:*

1. The Rights of the Accused: In Law and Action
   STUART S. NAGEL, *Editor*
2. Drugs and the Criminal Justice System
   JAMES A. INCIARDI and CARL D. CHAMBERS, *Editors*
3. The Potential for Reform of Criminal Justice
   HERBERT JACOB, *Editor*
4. The Jury System in America: A Critical Overview
   RITA JAMES SIMON, *Editor*
5. The Juvenile Justice System
   MALCOLM W. KLEIN, *Editor*
6. Criminal Justice and the Victim
   WILLIAM F. McDONALD, *Editor*
7. Modeling the Criminal Justice System
   STUART S. NAGEL, *Editor*
8. Corrections and Punishment
   DAVID F. GREENBERG, *Editor*
9. The Future of Policing
   ALVIN W. COHN, *Editor*
10. Preventing Crime
    JAMES A. CRAMER, *Editor*
11. The Prosecutor
    WILLIAM F. McDONALD, *Editor*
12. The Costs of Crime
    CHARLES M. GRAY, *Editor*
13. White-Collar Crime: Theory and Research
    GILBERT GEIS and EZRA STOTLAND, *Editors*

Volume 13. **Sage** Criminal Justice System Annuals

# WHITE-COLLAR CRIME
## Theory and Research

GILBERT GEIS
and
EZRA STOTLAND
*Editors*

SAGE Publications Beverly Hills London

*For information address:*

SAGE Publications, Inc.
275 South Beverly Drive
Beverly Hills, California 90212

SAGE Publications Ltd
28 Banner Street
London EC1Y 8QE, England

Printed in the United States of America

**Library of Congress Cataloging in Publication Data**
Main entry under title:

White-collar crime.

(Sage criminal justice system annuals ; v. 13)
Bibliography: p.
Includes index.
1. White collar crimes—Addresses, essays, lectures. 2. White collar crimes—United States—Addresses, essays, lectures. I. Geis, Gilbert. II. Stotland, Ezra, 1924- III. Series.
HV6635.W45 364.1'68 79-26672
ISBN 0-8039-1404-0
ISBN 0-8039-1405-9 pbk.

SECOND PRINTING, 1982

## CONTENTS

# INTRODUCTION

The course of research and theorizing on the subject of white-collar crime has had a staccato history. The topic had its scientific birth under highly favorable circumstances, constituting the subject of the presidential address of Edwin H. Sutherland to the American Sociological Society in Philadelphia in 1939. Sutherland subsequently expanded his address into the classic, though severely flawed, monograph, *White-Collar Crime,* published a decade later. Sutherland, then 66-years old, largely confined himself thereafter with regard to white-collar crime scholarship to defending the position that it was *real* crime, a view that would be challenged by Paul W. Tappan's jesuitical and unconvincing claim that only persons convicted in criminal courts could be regarded as having committed crimes.

Sutherland's rather hit-and-run pattern of work on white-collar crime (in contrast to cumulative, paradigmatic research) has been duplicated ever since his time. Criminological scholars generally complete a book or an article or two, perhaps with their dissertation providing source material, and then move to another substantive area. Marshall Clinard took advantage of his wartime appointment to the Office of Price Administration to study black market crimes, while Frank Hartung looked at price violations in the meat industry during the same period. Donald Cressey interviewed embezzlers incarcerated in federal prisons, and Donald J. Newman examined public attitudes toward pure food violations; the latter work was published during the early 1950s. Thereafter, investigations by criminologists of white-collar crime virtually ceased. Introductory sociology and social problems textbooks almost invariably mentioned the subject: it was too pedagogically provocative to overlook. In addition, Sutherland's original presidential address has been very widely reprinted. But there the matter remained. Perhaps it was the political mood of the times, perhaps the successful putsch to suzerainty by the quantitative forces in social science that helped force the subject into the shadows. White-collar crime is not a topic that readily lends itself to the kind of studies favored by behavioral science journals; nor were there during this period nearly the number of diverse outlets for monographic works on criminal justice topics that now exist.

The first significant change appeared in 1967, with the inclusion of a small section on white-collar crime within the report of the Assessment Task Force of the President's Commission on Law Enforcement and Administration of Justice. Several reviewers of the commission's work, including Ralph Nader, noted critically that only a minute segment of the very considerable output of the commission attended to white-collar crime. These critics failed to appreciate that the commission's terms of reference solely concerned traditional street crimes, the kinds of events that had made criminal behavior a paramount political issue during the 1964 presidential campaign. Only at the insistence of Lloyd Ohlin, the Assessment Task Force director, was the subject of white-collar crime addressed at all. Ohlin believed that fairness required that an inventory of illegal activity in the United States must embrace upperworld as well as street crime.

From that time on, at first gradually but then with increased momentum, there has been a revival of work on white-collar crime, with more activity during the past five years than during the previous twenty-five. The diversity and quality of the work included in the present book testifies, we believe, to the exciting renaissance of concern with white-collar crime. In particular, as the essays in this volume demonstrate, scholars are bringing to bear upon the substantive domains of white-collar crime sophisticated constructs and insights from neighborhood intellectual areas, such as organizational and economic theory.

The roster of recent work on white-collar crime includes an overview by John Conklin (an academician) titled *Illegal But Not Criminal.* Four volumes of readings on the topic have appeared in print in the past four years. In addition, the Law Enforcement Assistance Administration (LEAA) granted more than a million dollars to a consortium of scholars at Yale University to conduct white-collar crime research. The group has focused particularly on decision-making processes within federal regulatory agencies.

In 1975, the presidential address by Stanton Wheeler to the Society for the Study of Social Problems dealt primarily with white-collar crime. Wheeler called on criminologists to turn greater attention to the study of "the more affluent but perhaps more acquisitive members who are located closer to the core of American society, and whose study may tell us more about the kind of society we are to become." Two years later, in his presidential address to the Society for the Psychological Study of Social Issues, Ezra Stotland chided psychologists for their neglect of white-collar crime issues and urged them "to participate in the growing national effort to fight white-collar crime."

A number of specialized prosecutorial units concentrating on forms of white-collar crime have been funded by LEAA from 1973 to the present. Some critics maintain that these units tend to focus on fly-by-night petty fraud to the neglect of more complicated but more meretricious acts of larger corporations. Certainly this is true of the emphasis of the Chamber of Commerce of the United States, whose pamphlet on white-collar crime discusses not wrongdoing among the powerful business groups that traditionally support the chamber, but the petty shenanigans of lower-level con artists. The work of the Committee on Economic Offenses of the American Bar Association's Section on Criminal Justice is more sophisticated than that of the Chamber of Commerce: Reporting early in 1977, that committee offered ten recommendations, including stepped-up federal efforts aimed at detecting and convicting white-collar offenders, centralized data collection, continued funding of the special state prosecution units, expansion of reciprocal pretrial discovery in white-collar crime cases, and "greater emphasis on punishing economic crime offenders following their convictions." The committee report insisted that "the most effective punishment for the economic crime offender is incarceration"; further, the committee thought that such punishment would meet criteria of equal justice and produce both special and general deterrence. At the same time, its report "recognized" the value of "social sentences" for white-collar crime offenders, sentences which require an offender to make contributions to the victim or to the community, such as by means of participation in a restitution program or through voluntary work or charitable contributions.

The upsurge of concern about white-collar crime is illustrated by a flurry of recent national meetings. The only previous academic conference on the subject was held in Columbus, Ohio, in 1975; failure to secure funding led to cancellation of a planned follow-up gathering. But in 1978, conferences on white-collar crime were convened in Washington under the sponsorship of LEAA; in New York, hosted by Peat, Marwick, Mitchell & Co., an accounting firm; and in Seattle, under the aegis of the Battelle Research Center. The following summer the United Nations gathered scholars from all over the world to discuss economic offenses, and in the fall the Temple Law School conducted a symposium on white-collar crime, later publishing the proceedings in the *Temple Law Quarterly.* Finally, in the winter of 1980, the State University College at Potsdam, New York, conducted a three-day meeting focused on white-collar crime. These sessions were complemented by hearings of the Subcommittee on Crime of the Committee on the Judiciary of the U. S. House of Representatives, which in mid-1978, under the chairmanship of John Conyers, began what were planned to be several years of hearings on the subject of white-collar crime.

Economic malaise, caused by high inflation rates, recurring energy crises, and high unemployment, were contributing to more skeptical and critical stances toward business integrity in the United States, a condition encouraged by the rapid growth of a Marxist criminology with its derogation of capitalistic enterprise. Political liberals also began calling for closer attention to corporate behavior. Tom Wicker of the *New York Times,* for example, noted that huge corporations were the most glaring examples of contemporary institutional forces that have been "little scrutinized and mostly unchallenged in print and on the airwaves." The absence of satisfactory media monitoring of corporations becomes particularly troublesome if one accepts R. H. Tawney's observation that "the man who employs governs. He occupies what is really a public office."

Work in other Anglo-Saxon jurisdictions on white-collar crime also has been proceeding at a much more rapid pace than in earlier times. In Canada, Colin Goff and Charles Reasons recently published a criminological examination of the enforcement of the anti-combines act, the first full-length study of white-collar crime done in the country. The work is complemented by a monograph by Andrew Hopkins dealing with similar legislation in Australia. In Britain, Frank Pearce's *Crimes of the Powerful* is a Marxist treatise on white-collar crime that largely builds its case on American studies.

In Europe, criminological and legal work in West Germany traditionally has placed great emphasis on *wirtschaftskriminalität,* but the marked tendency is to concentrate on immediate practical enforcement and prosecutory issues rather than attempting to gain a more general and theoretical understanding of the class of behavior. Georges Kellens of Liege has almost single-handedly carried the burden of research on white-collar crime in the French-speaking nations. In the Soviet Union, the lingering presupposition that all crime represents a vestigal capitalistic aberration has checked any public probes into what might prove to be embarrassing ideological revelations. However, the Soviet position that crimes of the marketplace—such as black market operations—are far more serious than street offenses, since they directly threaten the socioeconomic system, represents a distinctively different emphasis than that found in America. In Asia and Africa, material regarding white-collar law-breaking focuses almost exclusively on corruption. In those countries, the arguments in the academic community about corruption are likely to center on its functional or dysfunctional significance for economic, personal, and social existence.

The absence of centralized statistical portraits of the extent and correlates of white-collar crime has seriously handicapped research and public policy progress. The *Uniform Crime Reports,* with their many shortcomings, nonetheless regularly concentrate attention on the offenses included within them, almost all of which are street crimes. The appearance of the *UCR* statistics allows statements to be made (and challenged) about the characteristics of criminals; the increase or decrease in the number of offenses known to the police; ecological variations in reported behaviors; and the manner in which criminal justice authorities are responding, and what success they are having, in regard to crimes to which the *UCR* attends.

It is not beyond argument, of course, that some statistics can produce more damage than enlightenment. Countries which do not much publicize criminal activity, such as the Soviet Union, perhaps lull their populations into a desirable sense of security. A news correspondent has reported from Moscow that "some of the fearlessness here stems from ignorance . . . because violence is rarely publicized . . . just as some of the fear in New York City may be exaggerated by detailed reporting in the radio, television, and press." At the same time, ignorance may produce malaise. "We are afraid because we don't know," one Russian is quoted as saying. The issue of publicity about criminal activity requires much more attention than it has heretofore received.

That a public accounting such as that provided by the *Uniform Crime Reports* does not exist for white-collar crime tells us something about our priorities, though the complexities involved in cataloguing white-collar offenses most likely has contributed to the situation. In 1972, Michael Brintnall and others at Battelle developed a three-dimensional classification system for the Economic Crime Project of the National District Attorney Association. However, in 1978 a further step toward analyzing and cataloguing major data sources on white-collar crime got underway. This work, conducted by Albert J. Reiss and Albert D. Biderman, involves examination of administrative records and agency audits for 30 federal offices to determine how they generate information on white-collar crime. The focus will be on the manner in which events coming to the agencies' attention are classified and counted, with special attention to the accuracy and completeness of the counts, and on the effect of proactive (seeking out violations) and reactive (responding to complaints) strategies in making an agency aware of white-collar offenses. Legal, administrative, and management decisions also are to be reviewed to discover their role in conditioning definitions of events as white-collar crimes.

The difficulties noted in regard to establishing a data bank on white-collar crime include the rapid manner in which acts that might be so classified are redefined by legislative mandate, a matter that is much more salient than with "street" offenses. Also, acts that victimize organizations or those for which organizations are prosecuted pose more formidable classification obstacles than the traditional one-on-one criminal acts. Issues also arise concerning the proper unit count for a white-collar offense: A single fraud scheme involving the use of the mails often contains a large number of counts, each referring to a single letter. Further, some criminal acts, such as safety violations, may represent long-term, ongoing events that could continue up to the point that the court adjudicates the charge. If victimization counts are sought, proper definitional questions can be even more complicated. Are the victims of an advertising fraud those who see the advertisement, those who are influenced by it, or those who are persuaded but would not have been were the advertisement true? Or are the victims the competitors who lost or who might have lost business? These are but a few of the knotty issues that must be resolved before a satisfactory continuing inventory can be rendered of the extent and characteristics of white-collar crime.

Much of the earlier writing on white-collar crime devoted an inordinate amount of attention to problems of definition. Definitions of phenomena, of course, can serve a variety of purposes: They may create a climate of sensible agreement about what is being considered, and they can serve to establish homogeneous classifactory relationships that encourage fruitful investigation. But definitions also inevitably represent somewhat arbitrary conclusions superimposed upon individualistic "real" matters. In short, definitions both clarify and obfuscate, and they sometimes do both at the same time, lighting up one segment of a situation at the expense of pushing another into the shadows. In the present volume, we deliberately have avoided the conceptual and terminological issues involved in white-collar crime definitions. Instead, we relied on an intuitively satisfying understanding of white-collar crime as a broad term that encompasses a wide range of offenses, abuses, and crimes whose outer boundaries are as yet ill-drawn and perhaps not precisely definable. Within this broad range can be included sets of more precisely and conceptually strong definitions. These definitions no doubt will develop in the interplay between research and theory of the nature that is included within the present volume.

A primary, although not exclusive, purpose in this book has been to show that systematic methodologically sound research can be done in an area which many scholars have avoided because of fears of not being able to conduct work measuring up to the best standards. We do not, however, mean to confine the realm of scholarly research to quantitative investigations. Case studies and historical analyses can make as much of a contribution as quantitative inquiries. As Clinard and Hartung demonstrated in the early days of white-collar crime work, sound and significant combinations of theory and quantitative investigation can be rendered with white-collar crime as the substantive focus. In preparing this volume, we were pleased to find that this tradition is now enjoying a rebirth. The article by Schrager and Short reanalyzing survey research data as it pertains to white-collar crime opens up what could prove to be a particularly productive line of work. In a similar genre is the report by McGuire and Edelhertz on the consequences of a program to protect older persons against consumer fraud; the study of the deterrent value of convictions by Stotland, Brintnall, L'Heureux, and Ashmore; and the interpretation of price-bidding data by Maltz and Pollack.

We also found that a number of other themes and concerns run through and across the chapters in this book, some of which may indicate the emergence of somewhat different emphases regarding white-collar crime.

One theme evident in several papers is a stress on control of white-collar crime: that is, an interest in the legal definitions of crime, as well as issues of deterrence. We see this interest in law enforcement in the work of Maltz and Pollack, who show how statistics can be brought into the courtroom in white-collar crime cases; in the chapter by Sorensen, Grove, and Sorensen on how auditors can detect fraud; in the case studies of Sutton and Wild, in which they are concerned with legalistic precision as a factor limiting the prosecutability of white-collar criminals; in the report by McGuire and Edelhertz on the effectiveness of consumer protection agencies; in the chapter by Stotland et al. on the deterrent effect of prosecution of persons who perpetrate home repair frauds; and, finally, in Parker's work on methods for preventing computer frauds.

A second theme regards development, enactment, and functioning of laws denoting white-collar offenses. Writers want to discover the value of such laws to the business community as well as to the rest of society. This issue is handled historically by Carson in regard to the English factory laws, contemporaneously by Shover in regard to strip mining, and cross-culturally by Reasons and Goff, with particular attention to antitrust law. The role of laws and regulations in the conduct of business is also dealt with by Gross and by Sutton and Wild.

A third theme relates to corporate involvement in white-collar crime, with special attention to the atmosphere of the corporation as a force engendering law violation among an organization's personnel. Gross analyzes this matter in terms of historical, legal, and sociological considerations, while Vaughan deals with the corporation as both a victim and a perpetrator of criminal acts.

A final theme is the concern with victims of white-collar crime. Schrager and Short report on public evaluations of the seriousness of white-collar crime as these relate to the degree of the physical impact and harm caused by the proscribed acts. McGuire and Edelhertz survey victimization of elderly persons, and Vaughan deals with the question of how corporate personnel view their firm as the victim of the government.

We would like to express our deep indebtedness to Carol Wyatt, Linda Hunt, and Margaret Thomlinson for their great help in preparing the manuscripts, and to Tom Clay for particular editorial assistance during the final stages of the book's preparation.

To our wives, Robley and Pat, for their love and support throughout, we are profoundly grateful.

Finally, we would note that both editors disclaim major responsibility for errors of omission or commission. The order in which our names appear was decided by the toss of a coin.

*Gilbert Geis*
*Ezra Stotland*

*Chapter 1*

# HOW SERIOUS A CRIME? PERCEPTIONS OF ORGANIZATIONAL AND COMMON CRIMES

LAURA SHILL SCHRAGER and
JAMES F. SHORT, Jr.

> Modern sin takes its character from the mutualism of our time. Under our present manner of living, how many of my vital interests I must entrust to others! Nowadays the water main is my well, the trolley car my carriage, the banker's safe my old stocking, the policeman's billy my fist. My own eyes and nose and judgment defer to the inspector of food, or drugs, or gas, or factories, or tenements, or insurance companies [Ross, 1907:3].

The nature of modern mutualism was a prominent concern for early sociologists. It is a pervasive theme of *The Division of Labor in Society* ([1893]1964), in which Durkheim saw the increasing interdependence of individuals and of social functions reflected in the growth of administrative and commercial law. By 1902, when he attached a new preface to the second edition of the book, Durkheim was convinced that the "anomic state" of "occupational ethics" was the cause "of the incessantly recurrent conflicts, and the multifarious disorders of which the economic world exhibits so sad a spectacle" (p. 2). He argued that regulation was the only way to control abuses of power and guarantee individual freedom: "I can be free only to the extent that others are forbidden to profit from their physical, economic, or other superiority to the detriment of my liberty" (p. 3). It greatly disturbed him that "the most blameworthy acts are so often absolved by success that the boundary between what is permitted and what is prohibited, what is just and what is unjust, has nothing fixed about it, but seems susceptible to almost arbitrary change by individuals" (p. 2).

At the same time, Ross (1907) was confronting this problem in the United States. He found that the increasingly complicated forms of interdependence within society created vulnerabilities which were

AUTHORS' NOTE: *We are grateful to Peter H. Rossi for making available to us the data collected under grant 72NI-99-0035-G from the Law Enforcement Assistance Administration. The chapter has profited, also, from his comments and from critical readings by Michael Allen, Donald Comstock, and Sam Schrager.*

being exploited by a new class he labeled "criminaloid." The hallmark of criminaloid practices was that, even though they were often technically illegal, they had "not yet come under the effective ban of public opinion" (p.48). Since the perpetrators "are not culpable in the eyes of the public and in their own eyes" (p. 48), they did not perceive their actions to be criminal. Their behavior therefore took place in a perilously ambiguous realm—frequently quite harmful in its effects on individuals and on the social order, yet unrecognized as such by the public. Ross lamented this indifference and advanced a number of reasons for it, including the unintended nature of any resultant physical injury, the impersonality of the relation between victim and offender, and the offender's high status. Ross' views were accepted by subsequent American theorists working within the white-collar crime perspective articulated by Sutherland (1949). They depict white-collar crime as a serious problem, the seriousness of victimization caused by corporations often exceeding that attributable to common criminals; yet, at the same time, they concede the paradox that the public is not aroused by illegal corporate acts.

The assertion of public apathy regarding harmful organizational acts has not been tested to a major degree, however. The purpose of this chapter is to examine this assumption of indifference, using data from a survey of public perception of the seriousness of a variety of white-collar and common crimes.

We are specifically interested in organizational crimes, which are a subset of white-collar crimes. In an earlier paper we proposed a working definition of organizational crimes as "illegal acts of omission or commission of an individual or a group of individuals in a legitimate formal organization in accordance with the operative goals of the organization, which have a serious physical or economic impact on employees, consumers or the general public" (Schrager and Short, 1977:411-412). A primary purpose of this definition is to focus attention on the objective impact of illegal organizational actions. This is based on the recognition that organizational illegality, like common illegality, has an extremely wide range of possible consequences. The physical impact of an illegal organizational act, for example, may be nonexistent. It may also be catastrophic, as when the collapse of the unlawfully maintained dam at Buffalo Creek, West Virginia, in 1972, killed over 125 persons (Stern, 1976:3); or when the collapse of the cooling tower as a result of safety violations at Willow Island, West Virginia, in 1978, caused 51 deaths (Kennedy, 1978). The degree of importance of impact in the public's evaluation of the seriousness of organizational offenses is the empirical question we will begin to test here. This question will be examined both with respect to differentiating among types of organizational illegality and in comparing organizational to common crime.

Although the economic harm caused by organizational illegality is often recognized to far exceed the costs of common crime (New York *Times*, 1977), little as yet is known about the physical harm caused by organizational offenses. The state of statistics in this area is comparable to that for common crime before the development of the *Uniform Crime Reports.* There are government compilations about the extent of regulatory offenses but not about the consequences of such violations. It is estimated that each year occupational accidents account for approximately 14,200 deaths and 2 million disabling injuries, occupational disease for as many as 100,000 deaths, and consumer products for about 30,000 deaths and 20 million serious injuries (National Safety Council, 1976:25; U.S. Department of Labor, 1972:11; National Commission on Product Safety, 1970:1). Yet, we do not know to what extent and in what ways these injuries and deaths are caused by violations of law. Evidence cited by Ashford (1976:108-115) suggests that more than one-half of worker accidents are caused by illegal safety violations or dangerous—but legal—conditions.

The dearth of statistics on the physical impact of illegal organizational offenses mirrors the emphasis in prosecutions of organizational offenses on violations of regulations and procedures rather than on impact. Organizational activity is regulated by laws which are remedial in nature, designed to reduce the likelihood of harmful behavior through enforcement of standards rather than by prosecution of actions which have harmful consequences. For example, a violation of the Occupational Safety and Health Administration regulations which causes a death is liable for sanctions that are only slightly more harsh than those for repeated violations of standards which have no physical consequences (Schrager and Short, 1977: 408-409). The law clearly minimizes the importance of impact in the prosecution of organizational illegality.

One source of the failure to stress physical impact in legal definitions and prosecutions appears to be the "indirectness of intention" characteristic of these crimes. The aim of harmful activity is not to cause physical injury, but rather to further organizational goals, such as short-term monetary gain. Officials of the Buffalo Mining Company maintained an illegal dam not because they wished to jeopardize human lives but because they were reluctant to spend the time and money necessary to make the dam meet legal safety standards (Stern, 1976). In the commission of common crime, an offender typically is held personally liable for inadvertent physical consequences flowing from his or her illegal activity, as when a mugger precipitates a heart attack resulting in death. Yet, the intent of most muggers is similarly economic gain rather than physical injury. The haziness of the intention to cause physical harm may lead to a reduction in charges against a mugger, but rarely to the drastic separation of considerations of impact from the determination of penalties which characterizes organizational crime.

The separation between the objective impact of organizational crimes in society and the low stress placed on impact in legal processing requires explanation. The conflict approach to white-collar crime points to the importance of the power of organizational interests in shaping the definition, enforcement, and administration of laws regulating their behavior (Quinney, 1970). The consensus approach sees existing laws and enforcement as reflections of the lack of public concern for organizational illegality (Wilson, 1975). Kadish (1963:435-440) contrasts the two positions, choosing the consensus view that the power of corporations to reduce the use of criminal sanctions for violations of economic regulations matters less than the fact that such behavior "is not generally regarded as morally reprehensible in the common view" (1963:436). Thus, disagreement about the significance of white-collar crime often pits consensus theorists, who seize upon the presumed moral neutrality of public opinion, against conflict theorists, who respond somewhat defensively that organizations are highly successful in shaping public opinion. Past research findings showing that the public is not very disturbed by white-collar crime have clearly been critical in determining the focus of the debate. Unfortunately, both sides have been willing to draw conclusions from evidence which is fundamentally incomplete and increasingly out of date.

The ambiguities in studies of the perceived seriousness of white-collar crimes stem in part from failure to investigate crimes with physical impact, to obtain adequate samplings of public opinion, and to separate evaluation of offenses from evaluation of offenders. The two most frequently cited studies illustrate the interpretative problems. Aubert (1952) surveyed Norwegian businessmen about their attitudes toward violations of price and rationing regulations and found that they tended to condemn violations in general but to defend many specific offenses. The choice of businessmen as a sampling frame drastically limits the generalizability of these findings. Evidence cited by Clinard (1952:333-334), for example, indicates that the general public is likely to regard such offenses far more seriously than will a sample of businessmen. Moreover, all the violations considered were economic, and there is no reason to suspect that their objective impact would have been severe. Newman (1953) compared actual court decisions involving violations of the Food, Drug and Cosmetics Act with penalties proposed for these cases by a sample drawn from the general public. Seventy-eight percent of the penalties proposed by the public were harsher than the actual court decisions; however, they more nearly resembled sentences commonly meted out for serious traffic violations than those for common crimes such as burglary. There are a number of difficulties in interpreting these findings: scenarios presented to the sample depicted organizations as the offenders, and the responsibility of individuals was not specified; the most severe physical impact reported was acute nausea and intestinal disorders. The researchers did not make the more appropriate comparison of penalties proposed for white-collar crimes with those imposed for common crimes which would require specification of common criminals who were first-time offenders and previously had been upstanding citizens.[1]

The 1974 study by Rossi, Waite, Bose, and Berk provides an opportunity to reexamine public evaluation of the seriousness of white-collar crimes. Rossi et al. included organizational offenses with both physical and economic impact in their survey of the perceived seriousness of 140 crimes. Their published analysis does not differentiate organizational crimes by type of impact or distinguish them from white-collar crimes such as embezzlement or tax evasion. Reanalysis of the data, concentrating on the organizational crimes, makes possible investigation of several important dimensions in public attitudes toward organizational offenses. Not surprisingly, secondary analysis of these data has major limitations, since the questions included in the survey were selected according to criteria which were not sensitive to the specific issues we wish to examine. On the other hand, possible biases which might have been introduced had we designed the study are thereby eliminated.

We wish to know, first, whether people are sensitive to the seriousness of impact of organizational offenses. Such sensitivity is clearly true for common crimes, in both public and legal judgments, but it has not been investigated with respect to organizational crime. While Rossi and his associates (1974:227) concluded that white-collar crimes "are not regarded as particularly serious offenses," their published results (pp. 228-229) suggest the importance of impact in ratings of organizational crime. Our hypothesis, drawing on earlier work (Schrager and Short, 1977), may be stated as follows:

*Hypothesis 1: Individuals consider organizational crimes with physical impact to be more serious than those with economic impact.*

Second, we wish to examine the criteria used by individuals in evaluating organizational crimes. It is commonly asserted that a single criterion of seriousness underlies the ratings of all types of crimes for all people (Sellin and Wolfgang, 1964). In contrast, we hypothesize that persons differ in their responses to various components of crimes, particularly that of impact. The Rossi et al. (1974) data provide an opportunity to investigate the importance of impact and of type of crime in regard to how people judge common and organizational offenses. We anticipate that individuals sensitive to the physical impact of a common crime will also be sensitive to the physical component of an organizational crime; likewise, sensitivity to economic impact will be similar for organizational and common offenses.

*Hypothesis 2: There will be a strong association between ratings of common and organizational crimes with economic impact, and between ratings of common and organizational crimes with physical impact.*

Our position on the importance of impact leads also to the hypothesis that the type of crime, organizational or common, is a weaker criterion in crime seriousness ratings than is impact. Individuals giving higher ratings to organizational crimes with physical impact, for instance, are not expected to be particularly sensitive to organizational offenses with economic impact.

*Hypothesis 3: Associations between crimes with economic and those with physical impact will be weaker than associations between common and organizational crimes with similar impact. This will be true within both the organizational and common crime subsets.*

Finally, we are concerned with how individuals rate organizational and common crimes having similar impact. A finding of substantial similarity in the seriousness ratings of common and organizational crimes would directly challenge the widespread assumption of the normative ambiguity of organizational offenses.

*Hypothesis 4: Organizational crimes are rated as seriously as common crimes with comparable impact.*

## SAMPLE AND METHOD

The Rossi et al. (1974) study was based on a sample drawn from the Baltimore, Maryland, area. Predominantly white and black census tracts were separately stratified into three groups on the basis of median income, and one tract was randomly chosen from each income group for whites and two tracts from each income category for blacks. Depending on the desired number of interviewees from each tract, a variable number of blocks were then selected. Interviewers proceeded from house to house with no call-backs. They were instructed to interview an equal number of male and female respondents and to split their hours between daylight weekday hours and evening and weekend hours. This sampling procedure introduces sampling bias toward older, nonworking, and less active members in the sampling area. See Rossi et al. (1974) for a fuller description of the sample and method.

The interview consisted of a small number of questions on (1) perception of the crime problem; (2) victimization during the previous year; (3) background characteristics such as age, occupation, and education; and (4) a rating task for 80 crimes. Twenty crimes were rated by all respondents. An additional 60 crimes were rated according to the respondent's placement in one of two groups. Thus, all 200 respondents rated crimes 1 through 20, half (100) rated crimes 21 through 80, and half (100) rated crimes 81 through 140. Each crime was sorted into one of nine categories on a continuum from most (9) to least (1) serious.

## FINDINGS

The first hypothesis refers to the perceived seriousness of organizational crimes with physical versus economic impact. Table 1 lists the organizational crimes rated by respondents. In this survey the only actual physical outcome mentioned was death. Within the table, crimes which specify actual physical impact are distinguished from those with only the potential for causing physical harm. All offenses with physical impact in the survey also have an economic impact, but the reverse is not true. Group one rated organizational offenses with primarily economic impact, while group two responded to a good mixture of offenses with both economic and physical impact.

Ratings given these crimes by each sampling group were analyzed using the sign test, the results of which are listed in Tables 2 and 3. The sign test assesses whether an individual rated one offense higher than another, without making assumptions as to the normality or interval-level nature of the variables which would be necessary with a statistical test such as the t-test. Tied ratings were coded so that they were treated as failures, except when both crimes were given the maximum rating of nine. The sign test represents a clear measure based on the number of individuals who rated one crime more seriously than another. Ratings for economic offenses were compared with those for physical offenses, and ratings for crimes with potential physical impact were compared with all offenses.

*Table 1* List of All Organizational Crimes and Type of Impact

| *Crime* | *Type of Impact* |
|---|---|
| Sampling Group One: | |
| 25.[a] Causing the death of an employee by neglecting to repair machinery | Physical |
| 27. Manufacturing and selling autos known to be dangerously defective | Potential physical |
| 53. Lending money at illegal interest rates | Economic |
| 54. Knowingly using inaccurate scales in weighing meat for sale | Economic |
| 55. Knowingly selling worthless stocks as valuable investments | Economic |
| 63. Fixing prices of a consumer product like gasoline | Economic |
| 64. False advertising of a headache remedy | Economic |
| 75. Refusal to make essential repairs to rental property | Economic or potential physical |
| 79. Overcharging on repairs to automobiles | Economic |
| Sampling Group Two: | |
| 85. Causing the death of a tenant by neglecting to repair heating plant | Physical |
| 86. Manufacturing and selling drugs known to be harmful to users | Potential physical |
| 90. Knowingly selling contaminated food which results in a death | Physical |
| 113. Overcharging for credit in selling goods | Economic |
| 114. Knowingly selling defective used cars as completely safe | Potential physical |
| 123. Fixing prices of machines sold to businesses | Economic |

[a]Crimes are numbered as in the Rossi et al. (1974) data file.

The hypothesis that individuals consider organizational crimes with physical impact to be more serious than those with economic impact is consistently supported ($p < .01$). The percentage of respondents who rated a physical organizational crime more seriously than an economic organizational crime ranged from a low of 63 to a high of 85.

The ratings given crimes with the potential for causing physical harm further illustrates the importance of impact in the evaluation of organizational crimes. Manufacturing and selling harmful drugs (86) was rated significantly higher than selling defective autos (114), and both these crimes were rated higher than overcharging for credit (113) and fixing prices (123). Thus, the organizational crimes in group two with the potential for causing physical harm appear to have been evaluated as more serious than economic offenses, but as

*Table 2* Percentages in Sampling Group One†

| | *Physical Impact* | *Potential Physical Impact* | |
|---|---|---|---|
| | *Employee Death* 25 | *Manufacture Defective Cars* 27 | *Rental Repairs* 75 |
| Economic Impact: | | | |
| 53. Illegal interest | 63**[b] | 56 | 30*** |
| 54. Meat scales | 78*** | 69*** | 40* |
| 55. Worthless stocks | 68*** | 58 | 8*** |
| 63. Gas price-fixing | 79*** | 73*** | 48 |
| 64. False advertising | 85*** | 74*** | 48 |
| 79. Overcharging repairs | 76*** | 67** | 36** |
| Potential Physical Impact: | | | |
| 27. Manufacture defective cars | 48 | | |
| 75. Rental repairs | 77*** | 66** | |

†Respondents in sampling group one rating physical and potentially physical organizational crimes higher than economic crimes and associated significance level of sign tests. See (a) below.
[a]Ns vary from 92 to 96 counting ties and from 85 to 94 dropping cases tied on the maximum value of nine.
[b]The table values refer to the percentage of persons rating the column crime (e.g., employee death) more seriously than the row crime (e.g., illegal interest.)

Significance levels (one-tailed test) * .05 level
** .01 level
*** .001 level

*Table 3* Percentages in Sampling Group Two†

| | *Physical Impact* | | *Potential Physical Impact* | |
|---|---|---|---|---|
| | *Tenant Death* 85 | *Food Death* 90 | *Harmful Drugs* 86 | *Sell Defective Used Cars* 114 |
| Economic Impact: | | | | |
| 113. Overcharging for credit | 67***[b] | 82*** | 83*** | 59* |
| 123. Machine price-fixing | 73*** | 84*** | 87*** | 68*** |
| Potential Physical Impact: | | | | |
| 86. Harmful drugs | 1*** | 47 | | |
| 114. Sell defective used cars | 55 | 76*** | 70*** | |

† Respondents in sampling group two rating physical and potentially physical organizational crimes higher than economic crimes and associated significance level of sign tests. See (a) below.
[a]Ns vary from 95 to 98 counting ties and from 88 to 95 dropping ties, except for the comparison of 86 and 90 which has only 68 cases after cases tied on the maximum value of nine are dropped.
[b]The table values refer to the percentage of persons rating the column crime (e.g., tenant death) more seriously than the row crime (e.g., overcharging for credit.)

Significance levels (one-tailed test) * .05 level
** .01 level
*** .001 level

less than or equal in seriousness to physical offenses. In the case of crimes from group one, those with potential physical impact (27 and 75) were rated as more serious than (27) or equal (75) in seriousness to most of the economic offenses. Crimes implying potential injury thus appear to be rated according to the extent of harm that might be caused and its probability of occurrence. The act of manufacturing and selling drugs known to be harmful to users (86) suggests both likely and serious physical impact and was considered a very serious organizational offense. Refusal to make essential repairs to rental property (75), on the other hand, involves only a faint suggestion of physical harm and was not judged to be very serious.

The second and third hypotheses address the strength of the patterning of individuals' responses to crimes according to the criteria of impact and type (that is, organizational versus common crime status). These hypotheses require examination of the relevance of the physical and economic components in ratings of both the organizational and common crime subsets of the Rossi et al. crimes. To investigate this possibility, principal axis factor analyses with varimax rotation were performed on all organizational crimes and on a representative selection of common crimes rated by group two. (The analyses for this and the following sections are limited to data from this group because of the limited sample of organizational crimes with physical impact rated by group one.)

The organizational crimes generated two factors, with physical crimes loading mainly on the first factor and economic crimes on the second; this supported the distinctiveness of the physical and economic dimensions in evaluations of organizational crimes, as stated in hypothesis three. Causing the death of a tenant (85) loaded heavily on both factors and was eliminated from further analyses in this and the following section. Selling defective used cars (114) loaded on the economic factor, suggesting that the physical danger implied in this crime was not a primary element in its seriousness rating. A factor analysis of common crimes also generated two factors. Crimes which loaded on the first factor included all burglary and robbery offenses. The second factor consisted of most of the crimes which resulted in death stemming either from direct assault or from indirect or negligent injury. Economic offenses, largely against businesses and entailing no physical danger, loaded heavily on the third factor. (See Table 4 for a listing of the crimes for each of these factors; see Schrager, 1977, for a full report of these factor analyses.)

The scores on items composing each of the factors identified in the factor analyses were summed for each respondent. These composite scores then were divided into quartiles or quintiles for each factor. The strategy for testing response patterning was to measure the associations among respondents' composite scores on the organizational and common crime factors. A measure of ordinal association, gamma, was chosen as an appropriate statistic for this purpose. Gamma values for all possible comparisons are listed in Table 4. A high and positive gamma value indicates that respondents who rate highly items composing one composite measure, relative to other respondents, also are likely to rate items relatively high on the other composite measure.

Three strong associations among the composite measures emerge in Table 4: (1) physical organizational crimes with common crimes involving death through assault or negligence; (2) economic organizational crimes with economic common crimes involving no potential physical threat; and (3) economic common crimes with burglary and robbery offenses. The first two relationships offer strong support for our second hypothesis: *crimes with the same type of impact are rated*

*Table 4* Gammas Among Organizational and Common Crime Composites and Their Associated Significance Levels for Group Two[a]

| | *Physical Organizational Crimes*[b] | *Death Common Crimes*[c] | *Economic Organizational Crimes*[d] | *Economic Common Crimes*[e] | *Burglary/Robbery Common Crimes*[f] |
|---|---|---|---|---|---|
| Physical Organizational Crimes | — | .50** | .27 | .23 | .13 |
| Death Common Crimes | | — | .26 | .17 | .19 |
| Economic Organizational Crimes | | | — | .58** | .23 |
| Economic Common Crimes | | | | — | .56** |
| Burglary/Robbery Common Crimes | | | | | — |

[a]Ns vary from 84 to 93.
[b]Physical organizational crimes include manufacturing and selling drugs known to be harmful to users and knowingly selling contaminated food which results in a death.
[c]Death common crimes include impulsive killing of an acquaintance, killing a pedestrian while exceeding the speed limit, killing someone during a serious argument, and deliberately starting a fire which results in a death.
[d]Economic organizational crimes include overcharging for credit in selling goods, knowingly selling defective used cars as completely safe, and fixing prices of machines sold to businesses.
[e]Economic common crimes include shoplifting a book in a bookstore, passing worthless checks involving less than $100, using stolen credit cards, and using false identification to obtain goods from a store.
[f]Burglary/robbery common crimes include mugging and stealing $25 in cash, burglary of a home stealing a color TV set, armed street holdup stealing $200 cash, and burglary of an appliance store stealing several TV sets.

Significance levels (one-tailed) *.05 level
**.001 level

*by respondents in a similar fashion.* As assessment of hypothesis three is constrained because the composite measures are based on factor analyses designed to achieve orthogonality. Thus, low associations between the composites within each class of crimes are to be expected. Nevertheless, the third strong relationship from Table 4 suggests overlapping in evaluations of economic and robbery/burglary common crimes. All other gamma values are low, both within each class and between the organizational and common crime subsets, offering tentative support for hypothesis three: Sharing of organizational or common crime characteristics is not reflected in the similarity of seriousness ratings. The dominance of type of impact over class of crime in respondents' evaluations is further suggested by the strong association of economic organizational crimes with economic common crimes, together with their weak associations with robbery and burglary offenses, thus indicating that absence of physical threat is a crucial factor in how economic organizational crimes are rated.

The fourth hypothesis refers to the relative seriousness ratings given organizational and common crimes with similar impact. Mean seriousness ratings of items included in the composite measures were computed for each respondent. The ratings on these measures were then compared using sign tests, and the results are reported in Table 5. Only two comparisons were *not* significant at the .05 level: (1) economic organizational with economic common crimes, and (2) physical organizational with assaultive and negligence common crimes causing death. Thus, organizational and common crimes with economic and physical impact, respectively, are ranked in a similar manner, and approximately equally in seriousness.

Two issues arise in the apparent evaluation of economic organizational crimes. First, the economic losses from the "average" economic organizational crime included in this study doubtless exceed the "average" for the economic common crimes; thus, there may be a discounting of the seriousness of economic organizational crimes. Second, burglary and robbery offenses are considered to be more serious than economic organizational offenses, despite their shared economic impact. The seriousness ratings of burglary/robbery crimes cannot be attributed solely to economic threat or loss, however, for robbery is classified as a violent crime in the F.B.I. Uniform Crime Report system, and burglaries, far more than shoplifting, bad checks, or the use of false identification and stolen credit cards, pose the threat of confrontation between perpetrator and victim, and so the possibility of violence. For this reason, burglary and robbery offenses are more appropriately compared with physical organizational or death common crimes.

*Table 5* Comparative Mean Ratings †

| | *Physical Organizational Crimes*[b] | *Death Common Crimes* | *Economic Organizational Crimes* | *Economic Common Crimes* | *Burglary/ Robbery Common Crimes* |
|---|---|---|---|---|---|
| Physical Organizational Crimes | — | 48[c] | 7** | 14** | 26** |
| Death Common Crimes | | — | 9** | 9** | 26** |
| Economic Organizational Crimes | | | — | 53 | 78** |
| Economic Common Crimes | | | | — | 88** |
| Burglary/Robbery Common Crimes | | | | | — |

† Given items of composite measures by respondents in group two and associated significance level of sign tests. See note a.

[a]Ns vary from 84 to 94 counting ties and from 77 to 90 dropping ties.

[b]See notes (b) through (f) in Table 4 for a listing of items included in the composites.

[c]The table values refer to the percentage of persons with a mean seriousness rating for the items in the column crime composite (e.g., death common crimes) higher than for the items in the row crime composite (e.g., physical organizational crimes.)

Significance levels (two-tailed test) **less than .001

## DISCUSSION

The Rossi et al. (1974) data consistently support the importance of impact in the public's evaluation of the seriousness of organizational crimes. Individuals not only consider organizational crimes with physical impact to be far more serious than those with economic impact, but they also rate physical organizational crimes as equal in seriousness to a range of common crimes which theorists such as Nettler (1974) and Wilson (1975) consider central to the "crime problem." People appear to evaluate both common and organizational offenses in terms of impact. They respond to the physical dimension of both common and organizational crimes in a similar manner, and the same was found for the economic dimension. Further research which clearly specified the extent of economic and physical impact for both common and organizational crimes would help in advancing our understanding. We need to explore the importance of victimization, both potential and actual, in evaluations of the seriousness of organizational crimes.

The proper relation between the law and public perception is beyond the scope of our concerns in this chapter. We are not arguing that the public accurately measures seriousness or that public perceptions should be the sole basis for legal responses. Crimes often have impacts far beyond immediate apparent harms. The crimes of Watergate, for example, were neither physically harmful nor very serious economically. Yet, they aroused a nation, challenged its legal system, and threatened its social fabric. Dangerousness and impact are extremely complex matters, and the crimes presented in this study and the judgments elicited from respondents encompass only a small part of this complexity. The proper roles of intention and responsibility in the definition and prosecution of organizational crimes likewise pose complex moral and legal problems that we do not explore. These problems are exacerbated by the role of large-scale organizations in modern societies. The welfare of large numbers of citizens is deeply affected by the performance of the large corporations which produce goods and services and supply jobs, and by governments whose responsibilities extend even more broadly to the common welfare. Our purpose here is to examine the public's evaluation of the seriousness of organizational crimes and the criteria used in making the judgments. Such understanding is a prerequisite for discussion of the relation between public opinion and legal definition and processing.

Toward this goal, the comparison of organizational and common crimes with economic impact in the Rossi et al. data illuminates the normative status of those organizational crimes which have received primary attention in past research. The common crimes included in the economic common crime composite measure are *not* central foci of public concern about crime, nor were they generally rated as seriously as the average crime in the Rossi sample. (The average rating given all crimes was 6.27 versus 5.27 for the economic common crimes.) Findings presented in this study indicate that these crimes are considered approximately *equal* in seriousness to economic organizational crimes. By concentrating on offenses with diffuse economic impact similar to those included in this study, research on organizational crime has largely ignored those crimes which are considered most serious by the general public—those with physical impact. It thus appears that the generalizability of findings from past studies on economic crimes to the entire realm of organizational crime is very limited.

The conclusion that organizational offenses are regarded with "normative neutrality" is, in part, an artifact of research methodology and of failures in conceptualization. Our analysis supports the position of Kadish (1963) of low reprobation toward many economic organizational offenses, but it also points to the high degree of public concern for illegal actions with serious adverse physical impact. The focus within white-collar crime research on diffuse economic offenses has resulted in a distorted image of public evaluation of organizational crimes.

Geis and Monahan (1976) argue that the distinction commonly made between deaths caused by commercial or organizational actions and deaths due to common crime obscures the similarity in their impact and in the moral culpability of those responsible. Our analysis indicates that the general public does not draw a firm line between deaths from these two different causes. This sample from the Baltimore area does not support the "social ethic that winks at white-collar violence committed at a distance while swiftly condemning crime in the street" (Geis and Monahan, 1976:343). Respondents judged white-collar and street crimes with serious physical consequences as equally heinous, even though these two types of crimes are handled very differently within the law. Geis and Monahan (1976:342) hope "to persuade readers that definitions of what constitutes violence provide telling information about the distribution and employment of power." But the Baltimore respondents do not appear to define violence in ways that legitimate its use by powerful groups in society.

The divergence of public conceptualization about the seriousness of organizational offenses from legal definitions raises important questions. Among them are the following: (1) Does the legal emphasis on violation of regulations rather than on impact defuse public reaction to organizational offenses? (2) How do people respond to ambiguity of individual responsibility in specific organizational offenses? (3) How does public sentiment on sentencing differ from legal penalties, and what consequences do such disjunctions have for public belief in legal justice? (4) How does knowledge of adverse consequences of organizational behavior affect public opinion?

As to the last of these questions, the manipulation of knowledge about harmful impacts of organizational activity has become an important arena of social conflict. The findings in our study indicate that there should be strong public support for the goals of agencies such as the Occupational Safety and Health Administration, the Environmental Protection Agency, and the Consumer Product Safety Commission agencies, which are particularly concerned with reducing the physical consequences of organizational activity. Many corporations are actively campaigning against the efforts of these regulatory agencies (Tirman, 1978). Corporations appear able to muster public opposition to regulators and regulations through an appeal to economic impact, as in the Pittsburgh area, where residents recently voted for relaxation of air pollution standards which they believed endangered the jobs of thousands of steelworkers. Most were more fearful of the immediate economic threat such standards seemed to pose than of higher but more remote risks to their health

(Oregonian, 1977). On the other hand, studies are beginning to establish that even the economic interests of the public and of corporations may conflict: economists at Carnegie-Mellon, for example, estimate that the $10 billion clean-up tab required to meet the 1971 smokestack pollution standards would be overshadowed by a $20 billion savings in health costs, not to mention a 7 percent reduction in illness and death (cited in Tirman, 1978:732).

The delayed and diffuse effects of many organizational offenses in contrast to those of common crime serve to hinder the development of personal knowledge. One whose home has been burglarized will notice the crime, but cancer sufferers whose disease is the result of illegal industrial pollution or those who are injured because of safety violations may be unaware that illegal actions have caused their suffering. Still, a worker who handles hazardous materials, or a person living close to a proposed nuclear power plant, is likely to be more sensitive than others who are not directly affected to information on the potential harm of these organizational activities, regardless of their legal status.[2] It is to be expected that people will try to reduce threats to their personal safety in their environment, even mobilizing to do so. Thus, as knowledge about the social impact of organizational behavior expands, tensions between the interests of organizations and the public may be expected to increase. Predictably, culpable or potentially culpable organizations will attempt to counter with more sophisticated evidence on the deleterious effects of regulating their behavior. Findings from the natural and social sciences become weapons used by opposing parties in their advocacy of acceptable levels and types of risk.

As social scientists, we would do well to reflect upon the role we play in the process of defining social problems. It may be comforting to believe that we merely measure the existing state of opinion in society at large. In the case of white-collar crime it seems evident that we have failed to ask the proper questions that would delineate the dimensions on which seriousness is judged. The consequences of this error are compounded when we then proceed to infer lack of public concern about the phenomenon, and therefore transfer to the public responsibility for the lack of attention given these offenses. However inadvertently, social scientists have furthered the view that the leniency of prosecution of organizational crime and the paucity of knowledge about it are directly related to a lack of public abhorrence. Study of the definition, control, impact, and causes of organizational illegality can provide key insights into the social transformations and conflicts generated by industrial development and the continually expanding mutualism which was of such concern to our forebears. But this cannot be realized unless social scientists critically examine the assumptions on which much of this research proceeds and what interests these assumptions might serve.

## NOTES

1. Other studies have been peripherally interested in normative beliefs of the general public on economic organizational crime (Ennis, 1967; McIntyre, 1967). More work has been done on violation and victimization rates (Ball, 1960; Best and Andreasen, 1977; Hartung, 1950), but the findings do not indicate public opinion on the seriousness of illegal organizational acts.

2. In an earlier analysis (Schrager, 1977) an attempt was made to explore the association between ratings of organizational crimes and background characteristics of individuals in the Rossi sample. Information directly linking individuals to exposure to hazardous organizational activities was lacking and the findings were inconclusive, but the data suggested that subgroups in the population may differ in sensitivities to some types of organizational crimes.

## REFERENCES

ASHFORD, N. A. (1976) Crisis in the Workplace: Occupational Disease and Injury. Cambridge: MIT Press.

AUBERT, V. (1952) "White collar crime and social structure." American Journal of Sociology 58 (November):263-271.

BALL, H. V. (1960) "Social structure and rent-control violations." American Journal of Sociology 65 (May):598-604.

BEST, A. and A. R. ANDREASEN (1977) "Consumer responses to unsatisfactory purchases: A survey of perceiving defects, voicing complaints, and obtaining redress." Law and Society Review 11:701-742.

CLINARD, M.B. (1952) The Black Market. New York: Holt, Rinehart & Winston.

DURKHEIM, E. |1893|/(1964). The Division of Labor in Society. New York: Free Press.

ENNIS, P. H. (1967) Criminal Victimization in the United States: A Report of a National Survey. Washington, DC: U.S. Government Printing Office.

GEIS, G. and J. MONAHAN. (1976) "The social ecology of violence." Pp. 342-356 in T. Lickona (ed.) Moral Development and Behavior. New York: Holt, Rinehart & Winston.

HARTUNG, F. E. (1950) "White-collar offenses in the wholesale meat industry in Detroit." American Journal of Sociology 56 (July): 25-32.

KADISH, S. H. (1963) "Some observations on the use of criminal sanctions in enforcing economic regulations." University of Chicago Law Review 30 (Spring):423-449.

KENNEDY, E. (1978) "The tragedy at Towner No. 2." New York Times Magazine (December 3):54-57ff.

McINTYRE, J. (1967) "Public attitudes toward crime and law enforcement." Annals of the American Academy of Political and Social Science 374:34-46.

National Commission on Product Safety (1970) Final Report. Washington, DC: U.S. Government Printing Office.

National Safety Council (1976) Accident Facts. Chicago: National Safety Council.

NETTLER, G. (1974) Explaining Crime. New York: McGraw-Hill.

New York Times (1977) "Business roundup: That costly white collar mob." (January 2):F15.

NEWMAN, D. J. (1953) "Public attitudes toward a form of white collar crime." Social Problems 4 (January):228-232.

Oregonian (1977) "Pittsburgh voters choose jobs over clean air." (November 10):C1.

QUINNEY, R. (1970) The Social Reality of Crime. Boston: Little, Brown.

ROSS, E. A. (1907) Sin and Society. Boston: Houghton Mifflin.

ROSSI, P., E. WAITE, C. E. BOSE, and R. E. BERK (1974) "The seriousness of crimes: Normative structure and individual differences." American Sociological Review 39 (April):224-237.

SCHRAGER, L. S. (1977) "Seriousness of organizational crime." M.A. thesis. Pullman: Washington State University.

——— and J. F. SHORT, Jr. (1977) "Toward a sociology of organizational crime." Social Problems 25 (April):407-419.

SELLIN, T. and M. E. WOLFGANG (1964) The Measurement of Delinquency. New York: John Wiley.

STERN, G. M. (1976) The Buffalo Creek Disaster: The Story of the Survivors' Unprecedented Lawsuit. New York: Random House.

SUTHERLAND, E. H. (1949) White Collar Crime. New York: Dryden.

TIRMAN, J. (1978) "Mobil-izing for action: Business wars on the regulators." The Nation 227:730-733.

U. S. Department of Labor (1972) President's Report on Occupational Health and Safety. Washington, DC: U. S. Government Printing Office.

WILSON, J. Q. (1975) Thinking About Crime. New York: Vintage.

*Chapter 2*

# THE VICTIM OF WHITE-COLLAR CRIME: ACCUSER OR ACCUSED?

MARILYN E. WALSH and
DONNA D. SCHRAM

Ever since Edwin H. Sutherland (1940:1-12) introduced the concept of white-collar crime into criminological and sociological thought, the subject has aroused considerable argument and debate. Central to the controversy is the discomfiting picture of unequal justice accorded the white-collar criminal when compared with the conventional offender. Generally, those who are poor and powerless evoke a harsh response, while the wealthy and powerful are either trivially dealt with or virtually ignored. Were it not for this "double standard" in the criminal justice system, Sutherland's concept of white-collar crime might have become a long-forgotten criminological curiosity. Instead, the concept has fueled a continuing debate between those who view the system's response as deferential and those who see it as merely differential.

Discussions of white-collar crime have focused on arguments over its definition, assessments of its impact, and disputes about the nature and importance of the white-collar criminal's socioeconomic status. The now familiar arguments represent attempts to account for the uneven use of the criminal sanction in white-collar versus common crimes.

## VICTIMS OF WHITE-COLLAR CRIME AND THE MISSING DIALOGUE

Largely missing from discussions of the criminal justice system's response to white-collar crimes is a consideration of the part played by the victims of such crimes in influencing the level and kinds of sanctions imposed on offenders. There appear to be two reasons for this. First, Sutherland (1945) somewhat preempted consideration of the white-collar crime victim when he rather unequivocally stated that three factors contributed to the lack of investigation and prosecution of white-collar offenders: "the status of the businessman, the trend away from punishment, and the relatively unorganized resentment of the public against white-collar criminals"

(p. 137). It might be argued that for Sutherland "the public" was the victim of white-collar crime and thus he did consider the importance of those victimized (p. 139). However, this remains unclear, since his greater concern for the lack of "organized resentment" on the part of "the public" seems to have less to do with its role as victims and more to do with its embodiment of "the moral sentiments of the community."

Consideration of the individual victim was complicated by Sutherland's choice of white-collar crimes on which to focus. By singling out for emphasis the crimes of corporations, he selected a group of crimes in which victimization was difficult to define except in terms of generic classes of harmed persons or the public at large. And while he could well describe the victimizers, those specifically victimized remained remote. Sutherland himself recognized this, noting:

> The effects of a white-collar crime . . . are diffused over a long period of time and perhaps over millions of people, with no person suffering much at a particular time [1945:132-139].

Sutherland also recognized that the broad implication of such remote and ill-defined victims was to make moral culpability (or criminal intent) difficult to establish (1945:132-139).

Given Sutherland's preoccupation with white-collar crime as a theoretical construct, it is not surprising that he spent little time focusing on its victims. It is surprising, however, that since Sutherland little systematic attention has been paid to the white-collar crime victim, the way(s) in which that victim is perceived, and the impact of such perceptions on the treatment received by the white-collar offender.[1] Geis (1975) acknowledges this lack and notes that, from most accounts, victims appear to respond indifferently to their experiences.

> [There is] need for research to determine the truth and the limits of rhetoric that is being put forward in regard to white-collar crime. It has been said, for instance, that "when the people are too smart to be good fool the people who are too good to be smart, then the society begins to crumble." . . . Are the white-collar crime victims in fact "people who are too good to be smart"? *We ought to examine propositions such as this as best we can, and determine as well attitudes toward victimization held by those offended against and those who do the offending* [Geis, 1975:101; italics added].

The failure to "examine propositions" concerning and to "determine attitudes toward" the white-collar crime victim is particularly surprising for three reasons. First, expansions of the white-collar crime concept, after Sutherland, have embraced crime areas in which specific victims are readily identifiable for analysis. At the same time, the emergence of the American consumer movement and the rise of class action suits have provided numerous case examples of white-collar crimes in which individual victims and groups of victims can be segregated for study.

Second, the period since Sutherland's first contribution of the white-collar crime concept has been marked by another major development in criminological thought—the emergence of the subdiscipline of victimology. One might have expected the growth of this field—with its primary emphasis on victims, the patterns of their interactions with offenders, and the ramifications of those interactions—to have had an impact on the white-collar crime literature. Quinney (1974), in commenting on the narrow range of crimes to which study of the criminal-victim relationship has been limited, notes:

> Criminologists are reluctant to consider that victims are present in less dramatic offenses. Perhaps they refuse to admit there is in fact a victim in other types of crimes—in consumer fraud—for example [1974:105].

Finally, and perhaps most intriguing about the lack of attention given the white-collar crime victim, is the fact that white-collar crimes are not alone in being offenses about which the serious issue of a double standard has been raised. In attempting to account for the double standard in white-collar crime enforcement, students of the subject, then, might have been expected to seek corollary criminological contexts in the hope of finding instructive insights. Had they done so, they would soon have run headlong into the most vociferous of controversies about the injustice of American justice and about the system's unwillingness to sanction offenders commensurate with the seriousness and harmfulness of their conduct. We refer, of course, to the debate concerning the crime of forcible rape, a double standard debate centering primarily on victims, their credibility, and their unsatisfactory treatment by the criminal justice system.

## DOUBLE STANDARD ISSUES IN THE RAPE CONTEXT

The crime of rape has attracted considerable research interest. This research has confirmed that perpetrators of the offense frequently escape sanction altogether or receive minor penalties associated with lesser offenses.[2] More important, however, research on rape has indicated that the reluctance to impose sanctions in rape cases is primarily accounted for *not* by offender attributes but rather by a set of public attitudes and beliefs about the rape victim which transcend the facts of individual rape cases. These attitudes and beliefs about the victim can be distilled into three larger issues which surround and serve to obfuscate the true dimension of the crime: (1) ambivalence toward the conduct complained of by the victim; (2) the degree of victim involvement in the crime; and (3) ambivalence toward the victim's demand for redress (Chappell, et al., 1978).

For the white-collar crime scholar, these are not familiar double standard arguments. By far the most popular and prevalent explanation for the double standard in white-collar crime has had little to do with its victims. Instead, offender attributes, in particular the power and status of the white-collar offender, are generally believed to contribute to leniency in white-collar crime sanctioning practices. This has remained true despite the fact that the status portion of Sutherland's definition of white-collar crime and his tendency to force analytical similarities among unrelated acts based on the status identity of perpetrators have been regarded—even by strong proponents of the white-collar crime concept (Geis, 1968:15, and Mannheim, 1967:469-476, most notably)—as the weakest part of his conceptualization.

The issues of a double standard toward victims of rape should not, however, be totally unfamiliar to the white-collar crime scholar. Indeed, it is for this reason that a comparative analysis of such issues as framed in the rape context can be instructive.

## RAPE AND WHITE-COLLAR CRIME—INSTRUCTIVE PARALLELS

The double standard issues in rape—ambivalence toward the conduct, victim involvement, and ambivalence toward the claim for redress—are discussed below in both the rape and the white-collar crime contexts. Two dimensions of these issues must be stressed at the outset, however. First, an important dimension of these double standard issues is their degree of interdependence. Though each will be discussed separately, they should be viewed as interacting in a way that progressively improves the offender's position and denigrates that of the victim. And while each issue by itself may be potent enough to affect negatively the sanction invoked in a given case, when taken in combination they tend to make a double-standard-like outcome not only likely but inescapable.

The reason why it is the victim's rather than the offender's position that is progressively eroded relates to the fact that each issue is to some degree determined by the victim or by beliefs held about the victim. Victim involvement in the crime, for example, is obviously victim-based. It may be less clear, however, that ambivalence toward the proscribed conduct is also victim-based. This is because it is our attitudes about the victim that confirm our ambivalence toward the conduct. Absent the victim and her complaint, the conduct presents few problems for us. Once the victim comes forward, however, we are forced to confront and contend with unsettled attitudes we have about the complained-of conduct. The various ways in which beliefs about victims serve to shape each of these double standard issues make them especially valuable tools for analysis.

**Ambivalence Toward The Proscribed Conduct**

For an act to be considered criminal, two requirements must be satisfied. First, the act must be construed as "unacceptable"; that is, a violation of the statutes of a legal jurisdiction. Second, the perpetrator must undertake to commit the act for an unlawful purpose or, in more legal terms, the offender must perform the act with criminal intent. Thus, it is not solely the illegality of an act which makes it criminal and subject to sanctions; criminal intent must also be demonstrated.

In cases of most common crimes, these two requirements are easily met. Burglary and armed robbery, for example, are almost universally seen as unacceptable acts. Likewise, criminal intent is readily established precisely because the parameters of such acts are so well defined. It is difficult to imagine a perpetrator performing a breaking and entry or a hold-up in the absence of an intent to commit a crime. These requirements, however, are not so easily established for rapes and many forms of white-collar crime.

Instead of there being a clear consensus about the unacceptability of the conduct in rape and white-collar crimes, there is a tendency to view the conduct as associated with otherwise acceptable behavior. Thus, rape may be identified as behavior distinguished from approved conduct only by its location on the more aggressive end of a continuum of demonstration of sexual prowess. Similarly, many frauds and larcenies by trick or false pretenses can be viewed as excesses in what is normally accepted, aggressive salesmanship or shrewd economic behavior.

The tendency to identify the rapist's and the white-collar offender's conduct not only as a variation on otherwise approved behavior, but also as more associated with approved than disapproved conduct, produces a decided ambivalence toward these offenses which reflects on judgments about the offender. Thus, Stotland (1977) has observed that society often reacts to many white-collar criminals and their needs with admiration rather than disapproval.

> Some people admire the skill of the con man. After Angelo Ponzi was exposed as a fraud, he was treated as a celebrity by the very police officers who arrested him. In fact he was cheered publicly by thousands of people. . . . Our use of language bespeaks the same tendency: we talk of con-*artists* and the *sharp* trader, of the *smart* thing to do. We speak of the *skill* of the defrauders, of their *imagination,* rather than of their sneakiness [Stotland, 1977:187].

While the rapist does not receive the same degree of general social admiration as the white-collar offender, his conduct may be met with a curious mixture of connotations. It has been suggested, for example, that rapists be charged not with rape but with attempted rape since this would be a more damaging comment on their sexual skills and prowess (Chappell et al., 1978).

The tendency to confuse the offender's conduct in rape and white-collar crime with otherwise approved behavior is enhanced further by the contexts in which the behavior is seen to arise. Edelhertz (1970), for example, has observed:

> A further complication with respect to proving criminal intent arises from the fact that most white-collar crimes arise in the non-criminal contexts, and are often only illegal appendages attached to otherwise proper execution of a previously legitimate role [1970:48].

The variety of situations in which rape is alleged can readily be identified as social settings in which it is similarly possible to view the crime as an "illegal appendage attached to the execution of an [otherwise] legitimate role." Witness the following account of a rape incident (Schram, 1978:15-23):

> _______ and me had just been listening to music. We had drunk a little wine and he started pulling at my sweater. He told me to take my clothes off and lay on the rug or he would break my arm off. I told him that I had not ever done it before and I was afraid I would have a baby. He said what the hell did I come over there for if I did not want a screw. Girls just did not come over and drink his wine and think they could leave when they wanted to.

The offender's conduct in this instance may be viewed as merely "an extension" of the otherwise "legitimate roles" of male host and aggressor.

Since neither the conduct nor the context of the rapist's and white-collar offender's crime is clearly identifiable as criminal in nature, the use of the criminal proscription and the penal sanction is viewed by society with considerable ambivalence. This ambivalence is further enhanced by two factors: There is a perceived unfairness inherent in punishing someone for conduct that might otherwise be praised, and the lack of settled opinion about the conduct as clearly antisocial appears to require that a separate judgment be made each time the issue is raised. As Friedmann (1972) has noted, "[The] purpose of the penal law [is] to express a formal social condemnation of forbidden conduct, buttressed by sanctions calculated to prevent it" (p. 119). Conduct which is clearly forbidden, such as breaking into another person's house or assaulting someone and taking his wallet, will result in little or no equivocation. However, where there is conduct which is not generically forbidden, but rather taboo only under certain circumstances, there arises a question not only about the necessity for formal condemnation, but also about the propriety of invoking a sanction.

When confronted with behaviors that ordinarily may be perfectly legal, it is little wonder that decision makers in rape and white-collar crime cases are often significantly impressed by the unfairness implicit in their sanctioning responsibility. Thus, Kadish (1963) concludes that the moral neutrality and the lack of "moral opprobrium" associated with much white-collar crime conduct accounts for the "reluctance of jurors to find guilt" and the "reluctance of judges to impose strong penalties" in such cases. Unfairness may also be inferred from a historical failure to sanction. Stotland (1977), for example, notes:

> If laws are passed but not enforced fully, the moral uncertainty is even greater. Within the General Electric Company there was a general understanding that the anti-trust laws were unjust. This understanding was no doubt enhanced by the fact that up till the time that case was prosecuted, no one had been sent to prison for violating those laws [1977:191].

The more impressed a decision maker is with the unfairness of invoking the sanction at all, the more likely he or she will be to find evidence mitigating guilt. This was precisely the reasoning which led Judge Archie Simonson of Madison, Wisconsin, to issue his now infamous opinion in vacating the rape conviction of a juvenile. Noting that sex stories carried in the newspapers, nude dancing in bars, and young women appearing in public in revealing clothing were common in Madison, Simonson (New York *Times*, 1977:A9), said:

> This community is well-known to be sexually permissive. . . . Should we punish a 15- or 16-year old boy who reacts to it normally?

Thus, for Simonson the provocative circumstances surrounding this case, in the absence of clearly forbidden conduct, made imposition of a sanction seem not only inappropriate but downright unfair.

The sanctioner in rape and white-collar crime cases is asked to make two separate judgments: one as to the criminality of the offender's conduct itself, and one as to his guilt or innocence in the case at hand. The dual judgments required have the net effect of shifting attention away from the complained-of *act* and toward the *circumstances* surrounding it. The only way an otherwise acceptable act can be deemed unacceptable is under unacceptable circumstances. Both rape and white-collar crime present great difficulties for decision makers in this regard. Merton (1957) makes this point for white-collar crimes in his discussion of innovation as a mode of adaptation:

> [P]ressure toward innovation [on top economic levels] not infrequently erases the distinction between business-like strivings this side of the mores and sharp practices beyond the mores. As Veblen observed, "it is not easy in any case . . . to say whether it is an instance of praiseworthy salesmanship or a penitentiary offense" [1957:141].

Based on the circumstances surrounding the act, a rape case often presents a situation in which the distinction between acceptable and unacceptable behavior becomes blurred for those reviewing it after the fact. In a recent reversal of a rape conviction in California, for example, the appeals judge wrote:

> [The] lone female hitchhiker in the absence of an emergency situation, as a practical matter, advises all who pass by that she is willing to enter the vehicle with anyone who stops and in so doing advertises that she has less concern for the consequences than the average female. Under such circumstances it would not be unreasonable for a man to believe that the female would consent to sexual relations [Crime Control Digest, 1977:1, 7].

In this case, the circumstances surrounding the act were seen to imbue it with a legitimacy. For the appeals judge this rape, far from being unacceptable, was deemed reasonable—under the circumstances.

Commentators who have noted the ambivalence toward white-collar crime conduct have not generally identified it as being of the "circumstantial" character exemplified in rape. Rather, for most commentators ambivalence toward white-collar crime conduct is seen as derived primarily from some evolutionary or developmental defects, such as the fact that statutes governing business and economic matters are of relatively recent origin. Johnson (1968), for example, points out that "moral sentiments are not developed as rapidly as legal norms. The latter, therefore, lack the support of strong public mores as is the case for conventional crimes" (p. 265). Similarly, Friedmann (1972) notes that "transition from a laissez-faire to a regulated . . . economy has led to the condemnation and criminality of actions which in a system of economic individualism were legitimate and perhaps praiseworthy" (p. 194). Kadish (1963) also makes this argument, noting that the nature of conduct restrained under this "new legislation" is conduct that is not criminal "under traditional categories of crime, and apart from the regulatory proscription, closely resembles acceptable aggressive business behavior" (p. 425).

While this line of argument is attractive, it contains two basic flaws. First, if recency of enactment of laws truly accounted for a lack of social condemnation of or moral opprobrium toward sanctioned conduct, then we should be showing considerable ambivalence toward invoking sanctions in such areas as the possession and use of controlled substances, theft of credit cards, and air piracy. The second weakness of this argument is that it fails to account for the many forms of white-collar crime that are not of recent statutory origin, but are mere elaborations of well-established crime categories such as larceny by trick, by false pretenses, and common law fraud. Edelhertz (1970:4), for example, lauds Sutherland's perceptiveness in noting that "white-collar" legislation "established a unique legal structure with complex administrative proceedings, injunctions and cease and desist orders, to meet [what is essentially] common law fraud." Even Kadish (1963) concedes:

> Certainly the use of criminal sanctions to protect interests of economic character is not a contemporary departure. The extension of the classic larceny offense by courts and legislatures to embrace fraud, embezzlement, and similar varieties of misappropriation . . . is a well-documented chapter in the history of the criminal law [1963:425].

And while Kadish attempts to distinguish what he terms "newer economic regulatory offenses" from these "traditional and expanded property offenses" (1963:425), his characterization of the former as morally neutral behaviors fails to account for society's ambivalence in sanctioning the latter. Nor does Kadish explain how it is that securities fraud, which falls within his class of "newer offenses," is morally neutral, while fraud is a "traditional property offense [designed to] protect private property interests against the acquisitive behavior of others."

It is quite clear from an examination of the simplest forms of white-collar crimes, of the frauds and swindles documented daily in the local newspaper, that society's ambivalence toward such conduct derives neither from statutory recency nor from a lack of moral opprobrium based on this recency. Instead, it is an ambivalence whose history is nearly as old as the crimes themselves. Witness, for example, the comments of John Gay and Ambrose Bierce in the eighteenth and late nineteenth centuries, respectively. MacHeath, the highway robber in Gay's (1960:79) *The Beggar's Opera,* compares himself to other robbers in high positions of government and trade. The only difference MacHeath can find is in the sanctions each receives.

> Since laws were made for every degree,
> To curb vice in others, as well as me,
> I wonder we han't better company upon Tyburn tree!
> But gold from law can take out the sting
> And if rich men, like us, were to swing,
> 'Twould thin the land, such numbers to string
> upon Tyburn tree!

Bierce (quoted in Merton, 1957), commenting on nineteenth-century American society, observed: "The American people will be plundered as long as the American character is what it is; as long as it is tolerant of successful knaves" (p. 143).

Neither society's tolerance of "successful knaves" nor its lack of consistency in curbing all robbers appears to be any more recent than the traditional ambivalence with which it has dealt with the crime of rape. Even more instructive is the following question posed by an eighteenth-century British chief justice: "When A got money from B by pretending that C had sent for it, shall we indict one man for making a fool of another?" (Geis and Edelhertz, 1973:992). For this chief justice at least, a sanction for the fraudulent act complained of was no more justified—under the circumstances—than it was in the rape case before the appeals court judge in California. Ambivalence toward white-collar crime conduct, it seems, is no more recent and no less situational than the ambivalence associated with rape. The issue of victim involvement, to which we next turn, is particularly enlightening in this respect.

## The Element of Victim Involvement In Rape And White-Collar Crime

The issue of a victim's involvement in his or her own victimization is one which has consistently intrigued social scientists. Studies (Drapkin and Viano, 1974, 1975) of the dynamics of this involvement in various crime areas have yielded such interesting concepts as victim participation, victim precipitation, and victim proneness. For the victimologist, different degrees of victim involvement tend to blur the usual distinctions between offender and victim and alter perception of the criminal act. Despite the fact, however, that for the victimologist "the reality of life . . . points to a scale of graduated inter-activities between perpetrator and victim which elude the formal boundaries set up by statutes and the artificial abstractions of legal science" (von Hentig, 1974:51), the criminal law generally finds the distinction between victim and offender neither elusive nor artificial.

Instead, the criminal law is primarily concerned only with the offender's conduct, and while certain acts of victim provocation or participation may tend to mitigate culpability, victim actions rarely nullify or excuse guilt. Nor is it generally considered unfair to invoke sanctions against offenders where there has been victim involvement in the crime. Thus, society does not find it difficult or unfair to sanction the burglar for his conduct, despite the fact that the victim may have "cooperated" with the offender by leaving his residence unlocked. Similarly, the mugger's conduct does not evoke an ambivalent response, even though his victim may have "provocatively" ventured alone down a darkened street.

The same cannot be said for rape and for many forms of white-collar crime. On the contrary, where these crimes are concerned, the usual rules seem to become the exception. This is because victim involvement in these crimes is viewed not as an extraneous factor but as an essential element of the completed act. Von Hentig (1974) notes:

> The felony of [larceny by] false pretenses as a rule includes the cooperation of the victim. By means of the false pretenses the defrauded person is tempted to act in the direction of his detriment. *As in rape, abduction and seduction, the personal qualities of the victim have played a large role in the requirements of the statutes* [1974:49-50; italics added].

Von Hentig suggests that in both rape cases and cases of theft by fraud and deceit, *because the victim might be presumed to have cooperated in order for the crime to occur,* the statutory proofs required to sustain the charge will hinge on a showing of the blamelessness of the *victim's* conduct. The victim cannot logically suggest that cooperation was not forthcoming, since the fact of cooperation is already presumed. Instead, then, the victim must be able to show that the cooperation he or she provided was not freely given, but was induced by some act(s) on the part of the offender: in fraud, by the use of deceit, guile, or false pretenses; in rape, by the use or threat of force.

The fact that proof of the corpus delicti in both rape and fraud cases is as likely—if not more likely—to turn on the behavior of the victim as on the offender's behavior tends to obfuscate and often nullify the offender's guilt. The tendency to weigh and balance the relative behaviors of *both* parties forces a determination of the criminality of the offender's conduct to be based on an assessment of what might be termed the "contributory negligence" of the victim (Kalven and Zeisel, 1966:246-254). The inappropriate introduction of a civil law concept into a criminal matter allows criminal culpability to be nullified, for while victim cooperation is not excusatory in criminal law, contributory negligence does excuse in tort. The analysis by the California appeals court in the hitchhike rape noted earlier is a perfect example of the inappropriate application of offender culpability. The victim's behavior in that case was perceived to be sufficiently negligent as to render the offender's conduct not only blameless but "reasonable."

In white-collar crime where Edelhertz (1970:15-16) has noted "reliance by the perpetrator on the ignorance or carelessness of the victim" is an essential element, adoption of a negligence concept has the same effect as in rape. Thus, the more careless, cooperative, or negligent the victim's behavior can be characterized, the less culpable and more acceptable the perpetrator's conduct becomes. In its most extreme form, the negligence concept can be seen to shift responsibility for the act away from the offender to the victim. As an English court centuries ago noted (Geis and Edelhertz, 1973:992): "[there is] no remedy for the man who trusted the word of a liar."

The issue of victim involvement in cases of rape and white-collar crime has one further dimension shared by both—the assumption of his or her own guilt by the crime victim. The idea of crime victims developing a sense of guilt associated with their victimization is closely associated with rape, but similar characterizations of white-collar crime victims are not unknown. In recent testimony before the U.S. House of Representatives (U.S. Congress, 1976) concerning con games and swindles directed at the elderly, John Murphy of the New York Police Department made the comparison directly:

> [W]hen we get a victim down at the office, a victim in her seventies, she comes in and she will sit there. First of all she has

> tremendous shame that she was conned. *It is almost like a crime of rape.* She will sit down and start telling the story and she is embarrassed and shaken. When you realize they just lost their life savings or that crutch that helps them stave off poverty; when you see the realization hitting them that they are going to have to move . . . you can see a dead person in front of you, as brutal as it sounds [1976:14].

The picture Murphy draws of the guilt and shame of the victim of a con game or swindle is one well documented for rape (Burgess and Holmstrom, 1974:9, 1975:322-326, 1976:413-418; McCombie, 1976:137-158; Notman and Nadelson, 1976:408-413; Sutherland and Scherl, 1970:503-511). The rape literature suggests that many of the victim's feelings concerning herself and the crime, once considered a result of individual personality factors, can instead be accounted for by the interactions she experiences following the crime. The more supportive and understanding these interactions, the less guilt the victim may feel. The more accusatory and insensitive these interactions, the greater the victim's tendency to take on and retain shame and guilt. Indeed, much of the movement to reform rape enforcement practices has consisted of attempts to deal directly with the feelings of guilt and shame expressed by rape victims and to modify attitudes of criminal justice system personnel which have been found to induce or enhance such feelings in victims (Still, 1975:183-187; Bard and Ellison, 1974:68; Lovis, 1974:2-6). Studies of rape (Schram, 1978) have also suggested that the failure to report victimization, once viewed as an admission of responsibility on the part of the victim, can largely be accounted for by the negative treatment "expected" by the victim at the hands of the criminal justice system and others.

The victim of white-collar crime has received practically no research attention compared with the rape victim. While we know that some white-collar crime victims express personal feelings akin to those of the rape victim, we do not know the general strength of such feelings among these victims as a group, nor the intensity with which they are individually experienced. However, we do know that, like the rape victim, white-collar crime victims may not be able to expect the best treatment by the criminal justice system, which may tell them that their complaint is "a civil matter" (Edelhertz et al., 1977:8-9; Galton, 1975:15-30; University of Pennsylvania Law Review, 1968:277-322), or by society, which continues to view both the behavior they complain of and their own "involvement" in the victimization in an ambivalent or skeptical fashion.

Even well-meant criminal justice system attention to the plight of the white-collar crime victim, as with the rape victim, may contribute to victim discomfiture and "guilt." Thus, in both instances, as part of the case evaluation process, investigators and prosecutors may closely question victims with respect to their character, motives, and possible contributory fault—in order to assess future trial problems.

Despite this, there has been a tendency where the white-collar crime victim is concerned to attribute underreporting of crimes to an "indifference" to victimization, or to some admission of having "asked for" a fraudulent experience (Geis, 1975:97-99). These are not unlike the motives once assumed for the rape victim which are now, on the basis of extensive research, largely discredited. In victimization studies (Ennis, 1967:46), nonreporting victims of fraud have identified two factors as the primary reasons for their failure to report: (1) the matter was not a concern of the police; and (2) the police would not be effective. This may be "indifference" or it may be a realistic view of how their complaints would fare. A fraud prosecutor notes:

> People who are victimized by white-collar criminals are embarrassed. . . . Even when we get the witnesses, sometimes we decide not to prosecute. Unless the offense is outrageous, there's a danger that the criminal will receive a light sentence. Some judges just don't consider such a person a serious menace to society [Katz, 1970:43, 62].

Victims whose losses are not "outrageous" enough to warrant the system's attention may feel justifiably discouraged from reporting their experiences.

Finally, in testimony received in the House of Representatives regarding fraud victimization of the elderly (U.S. Congress, 1976), witnesses touched on a facet of underreporting behavior among white-collar crime victims especially reminiscent of the rape victim. One witness noted:

> Once the victim loses her savings . . . she is very embarrassed and ashamed to come forward. Also, at her age she worries that possibly her family will think she is becoming senile . . . cannot take care of herself [1976:221].

Some white-collar crime victims apparently learn quickly what many rape victims have known for some time: the fact of victimization may reflect more negatively on the victim than on the offender. Just how this process operates is the subject to which we now turn.

## Rape, White-Collar Crime, And The Unworthy Victim

Unlike the victims of most crimes, victims of rape and many face-to-face white-collar crimes do not arouse the general sympathy reserved for those who have suffered harm, loss, or injury. Instead, these victims are often viewed with a mixture of skepticism, suspicion, and disbelief. The general incredulity with which these victims are regarded seems to derive from two widely held beliefs: (1) that victimization from fraud and rape does not happen except to those of questionable character, and (2) that only those who have shown an exceptional disregard for simple rules of conduct become victims of rape and fraud. Each of these items deserves separate attention.

The idea that a rape victim's own questionable character led to her assault is well documented (Brownmiller, 1975). Extensive discussions of the mode of dress, choice of places to socialize, and prior sexual history of rape victims have been used to "explain" the crime of rape and excuse the rapist's conduct. Certain white-collar crime victims have received similar attention. Maurer (1949), for example, observes that the swindler "prospers only because of the fundamental dishonesty of his victim" (p. 2). Similarly, MacDonald (1939) quotes a con man: "An honest man will not allow himself to be a party in any scheme in order to gain sudden riches. A man must have larceny in his mind to become a perfect victim" (p. 2).

The shifting of blame for victimization from the offender back to the victim has the effect of glossing over the dynamics of the crime. A person simply does not become a fraud victim all by himself/herself—fundamental dishonesty and a larcenous mind notwithstanding. Instead, as Maurer (1949:2) also notes: "swindlers' techniques are adapted to the qualities of the victim." Most fraud victims are neither dishonest nor greedy; they are people whose most outstanding quality is that they have particular needs around which fraud artists can adapt their techniques. Thus, bogus medical cures are rarely sold to the healthy; debt consolidation schemes cannot be foisted upon the affluent; and the sale of fraudulent dance studio contracts works most successfully with the lonely and isolated.

There remains a prevailing notion that just as "nice girls don't get raped," so it follows that "you can't cheat an honest man." And lest it be thought that such ideas are located merely in "old saws" and aphorisms, consider the following, more erudite restatement by von Hentig (1974:51):

> Are we not permitted to say that in some cases criminality is a self-consuming process of antisocial elements in which criminals prey on criminaloids, . . . oversexed on oversexed, and dishonest individuals on dishonest?

The second widely held belief attached to victims of rape and white-collar crimes concerns their disregard for the basic rules of sensible conduct. By not complying with the rules, these victims are frequently viewed as having "asked for" their victimization. Thus, it may be held that one of the reasons nice girls don't get raped is that nice girls don't hitchhike or they don't tempt normal boys by wearing provocative clothing. Similarly, even the most elementary understanding of *caveat emptor* should tell a person to "get something in writing" before consummating a transaction or to "read before you sign" when money is involved. Those who choose to disregard such admonitions do so at their own risk. Stotland (1977) observes that in some white-collar crime situations the stereotypic view of the world "as a game among sharp practitioners" tends to deny that victims are really victims at all. Instead, they may be viewed merely as "losers" or those "outsmarted" in the complex game of life. Similarly, rape victims may be considered among those who do not know how to "play the game." Because of their apparent failure to observe some basic rules of conduct, these victims may be callously regarded as "fair game" for those who would exploit their "foolish" conduct.

Most damaging to the victims of rape and white-collar crime, however, is not their reputed carelessness or stupidity—many crime victims, after all, are careless. Instead, it is the effect such perceived carelessness has on the credibility of their claims that most hurts the victims of rape and white-collar-type crimes. We hold these victims to a higher standard of care and conduct than we do other crime victims, at the same time conferring on their victimizers an advantage when this standard is not met. This is not a criterion applied to other crimes.

Von Hentig (1974:50), comparing rape and theft by false pretenses, observed:

> *The victim could be held unworthy of being protected by the law,* either [by] not being a female "of previous chaste character" or [by] succumbing to false pretenses which would not deceive "a man of ordinary intelligence and caution."

Without an exemplary record of conduct, then, these victims are seen as unworthy of society's protection. Unless they can prove otherwise, they lack the *right* to demand that the formal condemnation of society be placed upon those who victimized them. It is in this sense that the victims of rape and white-collar-type crimes stand accused—charged with being neither careful enough, chaste enough, smart enough, nor honest enough to deserve the attention of society or to warrant its condemnation of others in their behalf.

## THE DOUBLE STANDARD IN WHITE-COLLAR CRIME—A REEXAMINATION

It has been the thesis of this chapter that at least some of the explanation for the double standard in the sanctioning of white-collar crimes can be attributed to ambivalent attitudes toward and perceptions of the victims of these crimes. By this we have not meant to suggest that other arguments advanced to explain the double standard—such as the status of the offender, the difficulty of establishing criminal intent in individual cases, or the general trend away from punishment—have no merit. Nor have we meant to imply that ambivalent attitudes toward victims in any way justify this double standard. What we have tried to suggest is that systematic attention to the white-collar crime victim and attitudes and beliefs about this victim may prove as fruitful in explanatory value as have parallel investigations of offender attributes and of public attitudes toward offenders.

The analogy of the crime of rape has been a useful starting point in this respect, since it provides a valuable framework within which to examine societal ambivalence toward the sanctioning of certain behaviors and the sources of that ambivalence. While rapes and white-collar crimes are quite distinct victimization events, they appear to share some dynamics and public attitudes that are strikingly similar.

This is not to say that white-collar crime is like rape, for comprehended within the former concept is a far broader and more complex range of conduct. A review of similarities does suggest, however, that for many white-collar crimes in which direct victim-offender interaction has occurred the public and the criminal justice system have a tendency to view the offender's conduct, the victim's involvement, and the victim's claim for redress from a set of perspectives not very different from that traditionally adopted in the crime of rape.

The rape analogy can be troublesome and disturbing, especially if we believe that the victim of white-collar crime now has a sympathetic place in the public consciousness. As evidence of this, we might point to the rise of the consumer movement and to the publicity surrounding recent white-collar crime scandals in the public and private sectors. We might also believe that the once troublesome doctrine of *caveat emptor* now is viewed as an anachronistic philosophy that need no longer be taken seriously. The rape analogy calls all this into question, asking:

- Just how worthy in the public's view is the white-collar crime victim?

- Just how defunct is the doctrine of *caveat emptor?*
- And finally, are we truly any more willing than was the eighteenth-century British Chief Justice to "indict one man for making a fool of another"?

Recent lobbying efforts by feminist groups and findings provided by the research community focused attention on the plight of rape victims, attempting to win for them a more sensitive and just response by society. The rape analogy raises issues in white-collar crime enforcement that need similar exploration and attention, asking us to address directly the ambivalence shown toward victims of fraud and deceit.

## NOTES

1. In Geis' (1968) collection of readings on white-collar crime—for example, the section on victims—consists primarily of articles discussing public attitudes and responses toward white-collar offenses and of materials prepared to educate the public, rather than reports on attitudes toward individual victims and their victimization experiences. The victim-related work that has been done has been in the form of victimization studies which have confirmed that only a small proportion of white-collar crimes are reported.

2. Schram (1978) notes that less than 2 percent of the rape reports examined in a recent study resulted in a conviction for rape.

## REFERENCES

BARD, M. and K. ELLISON (1974) "Crisis intervention and investigation of forcible rape." The Police Chief 41 (May):68-74.

BROWNMILLER, S. (1975) Against Our Will: Men, Women and Rape. New York: Simon and Schuster.

BURGESS, A. W. and L. L. HOLMSTROM (1974) "Rape trauma syndrome." American Journal of Psychiatry 131 (September):981-986.

——— (1975) "Assessing trauma in the rape victim." American Journal of Nursing 75 (August):322-326.

——— (1976) "Coping behavior of the rape victim." American Journal of Psychiatry 133 (April):413-418.

CHAPPELL, D., C. LeGRAND, and J. REICH (1978) Forcible Rape: An Analysis of Legal Issues. Washington, DC: U.S. Government Printing Office.

Crime Control Digest (1977) 11, 30:1-7.

DRAPKIN, I. and E. VIANO [eds.] (1974) Victimology: A New Focus. Theoretical Issues in Victimology (Vol. 1); Society's Reaction to Victimization (Vol. 2). Lexington, MA: D.C. Heath.

——— (1975) Victimology: A New Focus. Crimes, Victims and Justice (Vol. 3); Violence and Its Victims (Vol. 4); Exploiters and Exploited (Vol. 6). Lexington, MA: D.C. Heath.

EDELHERTZ, H. (1970) The Nature, Impact and Prosecution of White-Collar Crime. Washington, DC: U.S. Government Printing Office.

——— E. STOTLAND, M. WALSH, and M. WEINBERG (1977) The Investigation of White-Collar Crime: A Manual for Law Enforcement Agencies. U.S.

Department of Justice, LEAA. Washington, DC: U.S. Government Printing Office.

ENNIS, P. H. (1967) Criminal Victimization in the United States: A Report of a National Survey (Field Survey II). Washington, DC: U.S. Government Printing Office.

FRIEDMANN, W. (1972) Law in a Changing Society. New York: Columbia University Press.

GALTON, E. R. (1975) "Police processing of rape complaints: A case study." American Journal of Criminal Law 4 (Winter):15-30.

GAY, J. (1960) The Beggar's Opera. Lincoln: University of Nebraska Press.

GEIS, G. [ed.] (1968) White-Collar Criminal: The Offender in Business and the Professions. New York: Atherton.

_____ (1975) "Victimization patterns in white-collar crime." In I. Drapkin and E. Viano (eds.), Victimology: A New Focus. Exploiters and Exploited (Vol. 5). Lexington, MA: D. C. Heath.

_____ and H. EDELHERTZ (1973) "Criminal law and consumer fraud: A sociolegal view." American Criminal Law Review 11 (Summer):989-1010.

JOHNSON, E. H. (1968) Crime, Correction and Society. Homewood, IL: Dorsey.

KADISH, S. H. (1963) "Some observations on the use of criminal sanctions in enforcing economic regulations." University of Chicago Law Review 30 (Spring):423-449.

KALVEN, H. and H. ZEISEL (1966) The American Jury. Chicago: University of Chicago Press.

KATZ, H. (1970) "The white-collar criminal." Washingtonian 5 (May):40-43, 62.

LOVIS, C. (1974) "Rape: The ultimate invasion of privacy." FBI Law Enforcement Bulletin (May):2-6.

McCOMBIE, S. L. (1976) "Characteristics of rape victims seen in crisis intervention." Smith College Studies in Social Work 46 (March):137-158.

MacDONALD, J.C.R. (1939) Crime in Business. Stanford: Stanford University Press.

MANNHEIM, H. (1967) Comparative Criminology. Boston: Houghton Mifflin.

MAURER, D. W. (1949) The Big Con. New York: Pocketbooks.

MERTON, R. K. (1957) Social Theory and Social Structure. New York: Free Press.

New York Times (1977) (May 27): IA-9.

NOTMAN, M. T. and C. C. NADELSON (1976) "The rape victim: Psychodynamic considerations." American Journal of Psychiatry, 133 (April):408-413.

QUINNEY, R. (1974) "Who is the victim?" Pp. 103-110 in I. Drapkin and E. Viano (eds.), Victimology: A New Focus. Lexington, MA: D. C. Heath.

SCHRAM, D. (1978) Forcible Rape: Final Project Report. Washington, DC: U.S. Government Printing Office.

STILL, A. (1975) "Police enquiries in sexual offenses." Journal of Forensic Science Society 15 (July):183-188.

STOTLAND, E. (1977) "White-collar criminals." Journal of Social Issues 33:179-196.

SUTHERLAND, E. H. (1940) "White-collar criminality." American Sociological Review 5 (February):1-12.

_____ (1945) "Is 'white-collar crime' crime?" American Sociological Review 10 (April):132-139.

SUTHERLAND, S. and SCHERL, D. (1970) "Patterns of response among victims of rape." American Journal of Orthopsychiatry 40 (April):503-511.

U.S. Congress, House, Select Committee on Aging (1976) Confidence Games Against the Elderly. Washington, DC: U.S. Government Printing Office.

University of Pennsylvania Law Review (1968) "Police discretion and the judgement that a crime has been committed: Rape in Philadelphia." 117 (December):277-322.

von HENTIG, H. (1974) "Remarks on the interaction of perpetrator and victim," Pp. 45-53 in I. Drapkin and E. Viano (eds.), Victimology: A New Focus. Lexington, MA: D. C. Heath.

*Chapter 3*

# ORGANIZATION STRUCTURE AND ORGANIZATIONAL CRIME

EDWARD GROSS

The doctrine of criminal responsibility would seem to be applicable only to biological persons—those who can be credited with motives and opportunities. Yet, to an increasing extent, we are finding organizations being labeled "criminal" and an increased willingness of courts to find them guilty to the point of imposing penalties. Of course, an organization cannot itself commit crimes: it needs agents who act for it. Such persons often cover themselves with elaborate excuses. Geis (1967:144) quotes an executive of a large firm, accused of conspiracy to violate the law, replying to an attorney's question on whether he felt he was doing anything illegal: "Illegal? Yes, but not criminal. I assumed that criminal action meant damaging someone, and we did not do that." However self-justifying such claims may be, members of organizations do try to dissociate themselves from the organization if they can. Perhaps the organization was up to no good, they say, but "I at least acted from purer motives." Courts will try to handle this dilemma by punishing both persons *and* organizations, but a theoretical problem remains of disentangling the two.

In discussing theories of corporate criminality, Goff and Reasons (1978: chap. 2) divide them into two broad classes: "kinds of people" theories and "kinds of environment" theories; yet, both are found wanting. It is difficult to explain much of corporate crime by pointing to the personal characteristics of executives (compensation for feelings of inferiority or hostility) let alone trying to apply such notions to the corporation itself. It is also difficult to learn much from environmental theories, which call attention to the role of poverty, broken homes, or prejudice against minorities. It is our claim that what we speak of as "organizational crime" must be seen as a transaction between corporate persons (that is, corporations) and the law, in the process of which the corporate person plays a key role in dealing with law, as it does with any other element of its environment. Corporate persons do not so much deliberately break the law as they run afoul of the law. To show this, we shall first develop an explanation of the utility of seeing organizations as corporate persons, show how such persons may be said to engage in crime, and then describe the conditions under which such crime occurs. Those conditions will be shown to be a market which is created by the corporate persons which, for various reasons, becomes disorderly. Crime then follows from the need to create an orderly market, though it is often revealed when that market itself becomes disorderly.

In order to explain how such a state of affairs comes into existence, we shall have to proceed through the following steps:

(1) describe the emergence of corporate persons;
(2) show how biological persons were separated from corporate persons; and
(3) show how the separated biological persons then set about creating an environment in which corporate persons could operate with maximum freedom. That environment will be seen to have two elements: (a) a set of norms (laws) which facilitate organizational ability to attain their goals and (b) a network of other corporate persons, small enough in number such that a common, mutually beneficial set of assumptions can be worked out and be enforced.

Crime is hence seen as an organizational contingency, with its own set of calculable costs, reflecting either a breakdown in the environment or a minimal set of "frictional" costs. We shall conclude by claiming that the network of corporate actors forms a *criminaloid conspiracy* (a conspiracy to control the environment), which has tendencies to result in crime. Thus, biological persons do not, for the most part, seek to commit crimes (they prefer not to commit them), but come to see crime as occasionally inevitable in the search for larger goals.

## THE EMERGENCE OF CORPORATE PERSONS

Although the organizational form reached its highest development in the case of the corporation, the form has had such success that it has been copied by governments, churches, universities, social work agencies, and football franchises. Hence, our description must be regarded as generalizable to all organizations that found the corporate model attractive.

In law, a distinction is made between what are called "natural" persons and "juristic" persons.[1] The former refers to what I am calling "biological" persons, since the legal term is not quite the same. A biological person is simply any living person with arms and legs, heart, brain, and so forth, whereas "natural" persons can exclude inmates of mental hospitals and, historically, in fourteenth-century Europe, also excluded monks, Jews, and serfs. "Juristic" persons include intangible entities such as corporations, churches, trade unions, and even towns. Such persons have no fixed life span and could conceivably live forever, but they can be destroyed, as when a court brings an injunction against one or when one goes bankrupt. Unlike biological persons, juristic persons cannot be imprisoned for crimes, but they can be punished in other ways, as by fines or constraints on their freedom of behavior. At the same time, although the law has created these "persons," they cannot, of course, act autonomously; agents must act for them. Hence, when we speak of corporate "actors" it must be recognized that there are always biological persons who act, in the manner of puppeteers, to put the show on. The modern corporation came into existence around the fifteenth century, but its origins must be sought even further back, sometime in the twelfth century in Europe. Although the presence of such juristic persons can be traced back to Roman law, what began to change by the twelfth century was the willingness of the law to allow such corporate actors a great deal of latitude to the point where they themselves began to maneuver to act in their own right. Interestingly, this new latitude was first evident not in private corporations (which hardly existed), but in churches and towns.

We can illustrate this process using an example provided by Coleman (1974). In Germany in the middle ages, a landowner often built a church on his land, arranged for a priest, and sought to have the church serve his household. Others might be allowed to worship there also. In time, the priest might begin to argue that the landowner did not have full rights to the church and the land on which it stood: Slaves or serfs for some generations might have worked the church land and devoted their lives to church matters. As the landowner's rights were challenged, he often retreated before the spiritual claims of the church and satisfied himself with the role of "patron" of the church. But having given up his rights, the question now arose as to whom such rights did belong—not to the priest surely, since he might die or be transferred by his bishop to another church. The question became increasingly important as church rights grew and as the church came to have independent income acquired through bequests by those who did not intend to leave their valuables or rights to income to the landowner. Such resources, further, could be and were sold by the church to others, and such income was further invested in other lands or buildings. But who owned the church property? A temporary expedient was to declare that the owner was the saint for whom the church was named. Hence, many centuries after their deaths, St. Peter and St. Paul became extensive property owners. In that situation, the priest was declared the "guardian" of St. Paul's property. But such a gimmick gradually was allowed to wither. In effect, the church came to be regarded as a helpless infant, the priests, its guardians; and, as often happens with guardians, some had to be taken to court or otherwise chastised for taking advantage of their trust—the infant had to be protected from its guardians. Thus, the law had succeeded in creating a new kind of person, corporate in nature, which was separated from those who were its agents, the guardians. Such a change occurred in the development of boroughs both in England and in Europe.

Another important change was the emergence of financial trusts. In England, a biological person might dispose of his personal property in any way allowed by law, but land was protected by the rule of primogeniture and went to the eldest son, a device which enabled the lord to impose inheritance taxes. To thwart the lord, the concept of the trust was introduced: the landholder, while still alive, conveyed his land to a set of trustees who became the owners. The transfer included a condition whereby the trustees were obligated to do as the owner wished with the land before *and* after he died. The land would become a legal possession of the trust, which never transferred ownership and hence paid no transfer or inheritance tax. The genius of this invention was that if one or all of the trustees died they would be replaced, but the trust would go on indefinitely. In a sense, the corporation itself becomes man's way of overcoming death. Biological persons die, but a corporation can live forever.

Once the concept of separate legal persons had been developed, it was seized upon and applied to independent organizations, which, in America, grew rapidly. Some states, eager to attract corporations for economic reasons, made the laws easy on them. The predictable result was an enormous explosion in the growth of corporations. Other countries exhibited similar expansion, often with active connivance of national governments. In the process, the private corporation developed some special features; these deserve separate treatment.

## THE SEPARATION OF BIOLOGICAL AND CORPORATE PERSONS

The early privately owned factories in England and Europe were run by single individuals or families, who conceived themselves entrepreneurs and invested their own or their family's money, hired their own workers, bought their own supplies, and sold the output. Such a person (or family) was clearly limited in the amount of money he had and in the scale of his enterprise. When he went broke (as he often did) or died, his company usually died with him, leaving his workers or dependents without income. However, this arrangement was adequate to cottage industry or the putting out system which reached its high point in England between the fifteenth and eighteenth centuries. The entrepreneur traveled around the country depositing supplies of wool, cotton, or other raw materials and returned later to pick up the spun or woven cloth. But there were deficiencies in this arrangement: Cottage work was hard to supervise, embezzlements were frequent, and there was frequent turnover of workers. More important, the scheme was simply unequal to handling the demands of the emerging state, international trade, and the burgeoning appetites of the new middle class. These agencies and persons created huge new markets for products—gunpowder, ships, uniforms, coins, and ships for the state; for the wealthy classes, luxuries such as porcelain, glass, soap, silk, velvet, and spices. But obtaining such products required large amounts of capital and involved heavy risks. For example, masts for the navy's ships required extensive voyages, some as far as to the western coasts of North America. There was a demand for furs for warmth and luxury, requiring trips to northern Canada or Hudson's Bay. To satisfy such demands required large ships, warehouses, wharves, and, most important, the ability to invest large sums of money and wait (perhaps for two or three years) until the ships returned with their precious cargo. Hence, the traditional market mentality of the bazaar, requiring a quick turnover, was not equal to such a venture. There was also considerable risk from storms, pirates, and competition from the ships of Spain, Russia, France, and Holland. Clearly, if a single person were to risk his own money (even if he had enough to do it) and the ship were lost or pirated, he would be ruined. Therefore, a method had to be developed for gathering large sums of money while limiting the risk to any one investor. This method (perhaps invented by Italian bankers) was the joint-stock company, or limited liability corporation, which was built on the already established concept of the corporate person as a legal entity.

In this new organization, the state granted to a group of persons the right to form a corporation: a charter, which enabled the corporation to sue or be sued in its own name, irrespective of the particular individuals who ran it or invested in it. The organization had a continuous life. Those who did invest in it, the legal owners, were not responsible for its debts: the corporation was liable, as a juristic person, for its own debts. The investor risked only the loss of that which he had invested. Through this means one could gather together many investors, each contributing small amounts of money which in total could provide enough to finance the huge enterprises that were now called for. At the same time, individual investors could finance very risky adventures, if they wished, with small individual loss if the risk proved ill-advised.

These developments have reached a high point in the case of the giant corporation, which may have a large number of stockholders. The most widely held U.S. stock is American Telephone and Telegraph, with over a half-billion shares held by close to three million stockholders. Other organizations are not far behind: Exxon has a quarter of a billion shares with about 800,000 stockholders; Boeing has 21 million shares held by 84,000 stockholders; and Penney's has 53 million shares held by 70,000 stockholders.

We come now to a paradox and a controversy. Not only is the number of stockholders large, but many of them are not biological persons—instead, they are banks, pension funds, insurance companies, and mutual funds. The paradox is that most of these persons and institutions have very little interest in the conduct of "their" corporation: What they want is a good return on their money, better than they can get from any other corporation. This is doubly so for the institutions, since often persons have put their money into those institutions solely for skilled management. Hence, the stage is set for a situation in which a corporation may be engaged in illegal action about which the stockholders are ignorant. Even if the illegality were discovered by the stockholders, some may continue to hold the stock as long as the company appears in no danger of serious loss. This is a theme to which we shall return below.

There is a controversy about the fact and impact of the separation of ownership and control. The above argument (first offered by Berle and Means, 1932) suggests that managers of corporations are largely freed from close control by the owners; hence, they are free to engage in innovative behavior, including crime, if they feel it would further their own careers. Galbraith (1967), for example, asserts that as long as the managers keep the stockholders satisfied with a good return on equity and manage to pay the company's creditors, then they may enjoy autonomy from control. Indeed, the managers themselves control the agenda at the annual meetings of stockholders and have a large, even decisive, say in who constitutes the board of directors. Other researchers have questioned this argument: Some have disputed the facts themselves, claiming that such dispersal conceals the reality of control by a small number of families and the use of pyramiding and other devices to maintain control (Zeitlin, 1974; Villarejo, 1961a, 1961b; Lundberg, 1969; Burch, 1972). On the other hand, a careful study by Larner (1970) reaffirms the original Berle-Means (1932) findings (at least for data up to 1963) and concludes that the separation of ownership has gone even further. In addition, a study by Blumberg (1975) shows a strong tendency for ownership to become even more impersonal by being transferred to large investment banks, which end up managing very high proportions of the stock in major corporations. Larner (1970) raises this important theoretical question: Whatever the facts about separation of ownership from control, do managers behave any differently than they would if they were owners? He finds that they do not. They remain committed to profit goals, a consequence Larner attributes to the fact that managers often hold stock themselves and because they cannot help their early socialization—they consider "profit" to be the major criterion of organizational success and hence as quite consistent with efforts to advance their own careers. Still, whatever the outcome of this debate, it remains true that the separation of the corporation from its owners has been completed. Even if the owners are small in number and concentrated in a small number of families—as the critics argue—they are still entirely separate from the corporations they own (if they do). The corporation can be found in violation of the law (and fined) and every one of the owners can go about their other business unscathed (except for possible financial loss).

## ORGANIZATIONS AS ACTORS

Yet, most persons have difficulty with the concept of the organization as an actor: there must be live biological persons behind the operation. Aside from shell corporations, that is, of course, true. But what must be understood is that organizations, though inventions of biological persons and thus totally dependent upon the continuous activity of such actors, nevertheless may take on lives of their own. This fact follows from the concept of organizational structure, a structure that has two aspects: one from within the organization, where it influences the behavior of biological participants, and one from the outside, where we speak of the market or environment within which the organization acts in a corporate manner. First, we must explicate the sense in which we can speak of structure at all—and that we will do for the organization from "within."

It is customary for persons to speak of organizations as actors by using sentences such as the following: The railroad hauls freight. The church held an evening service. The university is accused of discriminating against minorities. The government has broken off diplomatic relations with a foreign power. Haworth (1959) raises the question of whether these statements are to be taken literally or to be seen as simply a sort of shorthand for the sum of the behaviors of many individuals. The question is vital to understanding "organizational" crime. Is such a concept meaningful, or are we merely giving a name to the criminal acts of several biological individuals?

If we take the above statements about organizations, in a sense they are "reducible" to statements about particular persons. When we say the railroad hauls freight, we are also saying that a man sits in the locomotive and pulls levers, others load freight onto the cars, still others make out waybills, and others wave lanterns. But if that is all we mean by "reducible," we are saying something that is certainly true and also trivial. We are saying no more than that no organization can run without persons, but persons alone are not enough. Suppose one goes down to the freight yard in midmorning and observes individuals doing what we have described. We would feel justified in asserting: The railroad is hauling freight. Suppose one returns a couple of hours later. Now the same persons are observed eating sandwiches; others will be seated on piles of goods and drinking coffee; some will be absent, having gone to nearby restaurants; a few will be smoking. One may make many comments about this activity *except:* The railroad is eating lunch. Although this statement sums up several individual actions, the latter activity is not coordinated—or at least not coordinated centrally. Haworth (1959) goes further: We may speak of an organization as acting when what is meant is that the organization is *responsible* for the outcome, so that if the outcome is desirable, the organization—and not its members—receives credit, and if undesirable, harmful, or criminal, the organization—and not its members—will be blamed. Responsibility is felt to inhere in the organization rather than its members for two reasons: (1) What happens represents the outcome of the *pattern* or activities which make up its form; and (2) the quality of the outcome depends minimally on the peculiar qualities of the persons who make it possible. They are following or enacting the patterns. That is, what makes up the organization *is* the peculiar arrangement or pattern of activities and jobs. The engineers, trainmen, switchmen, and repairmen are so arranged that there is high probability that whatever happens can be attributed to that arrangement. If one were to arrange the workers differently, something different would happen. In contrast, having lunch is less dependent on any particular arrangement—people are freer to follow their impulses. A structure still exists, of course (one always does), but the structure is not one the railroad is responsible for.

Hence, we *can* say that railroads haul freight, hospitals cure, or universities discriminate against women if the arrangement of activities is such that there is a high probability that those activities will occur. To take the example of discrimination against women (since it may involve a legal violation), Chubin (1974) presents data on sex differences in career patterns among American sociologists. It has been asserted that "old-boy networks" tend to discriminate against the hiring of women since such networks are made up largely of men. The attempt is made, then, to do away with such discrimination by widening the search through national advertising, open competition for positions, and other devices. But Chubin also shows that women with Ph.D.s are proportionally underrepresented in Ph.D. granting departments and overrepresented in private industry or government jobs and in nonsociology jobs (such as administration) in academic organizations. How does that happen, in violation of pressures and laws designed to prevent such discrimination? Most academic sociologists would sincerely deny any deliberate intent to produce such discrimination. But at the same time, many departments have a conception of "minimum progress" in graduate school: Persons are expected to move along at a certain rate (complete general examinations, prepare a thesis prospectus, and so on). If they move too slowly, they receive warnings of increasing degrees of severity and may even be dropped from graduate school. Such persons are not likely to be considered the top choices when jobs at academic institutions are talked about. Chubin (1974) shows that women who received their Ph.D.s in the 1930s took a median of one year longer than did men, whereas those who received their degrees in the 1950s took a median of seven-tenths of a year longer. Perhaps the gap is closing, but it is still considerable. It is quite possible then, that women, who may take longer because of family responsibilities, end up taking longer to take the degree, and as a result receive stern letters telling them they are failing to make "minimum progress" and hence may not be recommended for jobs in academic institutions. We can conclude that the minimum progress requirement, however desirable it may be for other reasons and even though it is not intended to discriminate against anyone, still has the effect of penalizing women. In that sense, we can say the university (or that part of it represented by that rule) does discriminate against women, and not that particular sociologists (who are members of departments) discriminate.

## ORGANIZATIONAL RESPONSIBILITY: THE MORAL QUESTION

We have argued thus far that it is possible to assign responsibility for an organizational outcome to the organization itself (rather than the persons who work in the organization) if the structure is such that the result is a reasonable expectation. Such a structural argument has been made in many contexts. For example, Merton, (1957) in a classic statement on anomie, argued that if a society emphasizes success but also prevents a given group from access to the means for achieving success by legitimate means, then it sets the stage for the attainment of success by illegitimate means. Such deviance is built into the social structure. No one is forced, by such a structure, to be a deviant, but it should hardly be surprising if some persons become deviant. When we apply the argument to organizations, we must consider a troubling question. If the outcome can be attributed to the structure of the organization, and hence we can hold the organization "responsible," don't the biological persons who participate also share in that responsibility? Can they be dissociated, as Haworth (1959) proposes, in the sense that if replaced by others, the replacements would carry on in much the same way? Such a view would seem to make of biological individuals automatons or mechanical units who simply do whatever is required. Yet, it can hardly be true that those biological individuals are at least not aware of the outcome and of the fact that unless they participated, it would not happen. What if the structure is such that the outcome is something evil or illegal? Suppose, for example, a company produces a drug that has harmful side-effects. Or, to take the most striking case, what about killing persons in an unjust war? After all, an army is an organization so arranged as to maximize the likelihood that men will kill others, and do so willingly. Can those persons who plan wars and carry them out dissociate themselves from the outcome? It is one thing for a truck driver who may be carrying a load of sugar (which has been claimed to have harmful effects); perhaps he can shrug his shoulders and say: "All I do is drive the truck. People don't have to eat sugar." But can soldiers say the same thing? To make the matter concrete, could Eichmann make a similar argument about his arrangements to transport millions of Jews to concentration camps and gas chambers, or could Calley say the same thing about his involvement in the My Lai massacre in the Vietnam war?

The sociological answer is in terms of the concept of socialization. All organizations develop ways of integrating persons into organizations. However carried out, this integration of persons clearly involves more than teaching or learning skills or other accomplishments. Many organizations create new self-images in the recruit. For example, Dornbusch (1955), writing of Coast Guard Academy recruits, states: "If a cadet falters on the parade ground, he is told, 'You're marching like a reserve.' Swabs are told to square their shoulders while on liberty, 'or else how will people know you're not a reserve?'' Referring to later transformations of identity, he quotes one cadet: "I used to be shy. Now I'm reserved." Such identity shifts are facilitated by new interaction patterns and new involvements.

The university freshman finds available a choice of subcultures—collegiate, intellectual, sports, political—all of which can fashion (or squelch) ambitions and perspectives. Caplow (1964) points out that socialization involves not simply the development of new relationships but the abandonment of old.

> The bride is no longer a maiden; a new chief is expelled from the peer group. The extent and importance of the old relationships that are abandoned usually determines what kind of socialization process is necessary. In those cases in which socialization takes a drastic form, the severity of the new experience is explained not so much by the difficulty of learning a new part as by the difficulty of forgetting the old [1964:171].

Goffman (1961) has described in detail that process of eliminating prior status in the case of mortification of new mental patients in hospitals. In many organizations, this destruction of the past is often accomplished by sequestration, in which persons are sent off to retreats, or entire days or longer periods are wholly given over to a rite of passage.

As identities and interactions shift so may values, as illustrated by Merriam and Mack's (1960) study of the jazz community, or the way in which nurse trainees change their view of their work from a lay conception to a more technical one (Psathas, 1968). Westley (1970) has called our attention to the fact that the police operate in a world which is often hostile to the police activity itself, a fact which pushes them into isolation and secrecy. Such secretiveness leads, he finds, to a willingness to condone violence and not to inform on one another even when engaged in clearly illegal acts. Van Maanen (1978), in studies of the British police, confirms this finding and points out also that such isolation, as well as the frequency with which those arrested by police escape punishment, leads to a sense of moral superiority and a willingness to condone "street justice" in direct violation of the law.

We can, perhaps, begin to understand the willingness of persons to participate in one of the greatest frauds of the last decade, the Equity Funding scandal (to which we shall return). Here we note only that this fraud required the actual manufacture of completely bogus insurance policies, policies totaling in value close to $1 billion. When the auditors asked to see certain policy files:

> What the conspirators did, in the main, was wait for the auditors to request certain policy files and then, at night time, "fraud parties" feverishly forged sets of files for delivery to the auditors. This involved filling out medical forms, policy applications, credit checks, and other documentation for each policy

> issued. Later, when the bogus policies were created in huge numbers, a separate "mass marketing" office staffed by young women would whip out forged documents in assembly-line fashion.
>
> When [a lawyer, an employee] first was asked to help out at the "parties," he says, it was like "someone asking you to help move a sofa from here to there. I didn't think anything of it; it was something the company needed done, that's all" [Blundell, 1978:171].

Can socialization processes explain the Eichmann and Calley cases? Certainly, both insisted that they were simply obeying orders; Eichmann repeatedly called himself a "Kleinmensch," a mere underling who hardly knew what was going on. But the evidence suggested that he did his job willingly and could hardly have been ignorant of what was to happen to the people he was shipping off in freight cars. What of the *Enola Gay,* the B-29 that dropped the atomic bomb on Hiroshima? How can one explain the willingness of a man to press a button that will kill 50,000 persons? Can one blame that on socialization? Perhaps. Training seeks to deindividualize the enemy, to develop a sense of loyalty to the platoon or the company. A soldier insists that unless he carries out orders, his own buddies may be killed. The enemy is redefined. To Eichmann, the Jews were defined as enemies of the state, or as mere vermin. Calley spoke of the Viet Cong as "gooks." Terms are employed which dehumanize and hence legitimize destructive acts. Of course, not all organizations engage in such intensive socialization, but then not all organizations have to—only those demanding evil or criminal acts from their members. In the end, we would conclude that organizations, conceived of as patterns or structures, require that persons shall be competent to carry out or implement those patterns, and be willing to. The evidence, alas, suggests that they succeed in finding or producing such persons.

## CRIMINOGENIC ORGANIZATIONS

The structure of organizations we have described is of such a nature as to allow for possible criminal activities. This is not to say that they are inevitably criminal. As we noted above, even the biological person, however much he may be tempted by criminal opportunities, does not *have* to commit a criminal act. Still, one can see a relationship between opportunities and rate of crime. Organizations in their modern form have additional features which make crime more than merely a possibility. Gross (1978) has related this potentiality to the performance emphasis found in complex organizations. Organizations are judged and evaluated by their relative performance success.[2] At the same time, they often find themselves in hostile or difficult environments, surrounded by fierce competitors, or constrained by regulations which interfere with their performance. Yet, pressures remain—pressures from stockholders who desire profits or an increase in the value of their shares; employees who desire to keep their jobs; executives who seek to advance their careers by successful operation of organizations; labor unions whose members' ability to continue to pay dues would be abridged by any cessation of employment; and the multitude of concerns and agencies in the community at large, from fund-raising organizations to social work agencies to city governments, all of which rely on taxes or the continued flow of resources from the organizations. The stakes are very high and executives who run the organizations will experience almost irresistible pressures to do everything possible to keep the organization moving toward attaining its many goals. If "everything possible" occasionally means breaking the law, then the likelihood of doing so increases. For example, Straw and Szwajkowski (1975), studying data on violations of antitrust laws and the Federal Trade Commission Act between 1968 and 1972, report an inverse relationship between what they call the "munificence" of the environment and the likelihood that the organization will be cited for unfair market practices and restraint of trade. When these organizations faced difficulty in meeting their profit goals, then, they resorted to crime in order to do so.

Further, organizations have certain features which make their criminogenic tendencies very difficult to overcome. First is the performance emphasis that we have alluded to. While biological individuals also are pressured to perform and occasionally commit crimes to succeed, they are not forever performing or competing. However, performance, for organizations, is their very excuse for existence, and they have built-in mechanisms to make sure they stay on track. Accounting departments, personnel departments, time-and-study departments, and research divisions generate a constant stream of reports which exist to "keep tabs" on how successfully the organization is moving toward its goals (Churchill and Cooper, 1964). Even the Catholic Church has been the subject of a management study (Management Audit, 1956). Further, as Thompson (1967) pointed out, organizations engage in a variety of strategies for "reducing uncertainty"—that is, for eliminating anything that might get in the way of efficient goal attainment. Techniques include buffering through building up inventories, smoothing peak loads through special inducements to customers, anticipation of future demands, and rationing of services if need be. If these fail, other devices are available: A subsidiary can be set up in a foreign country where the laws are more liberal and what would be criminal in one country is not criminal there. Ultimately, crime may develop a "cost," a loss of income through fines, which must be calculated and taken into account in the same manner as any other cost. Still another feature of organizational structure may conduce or make crime more likely—namely, the fact that an organization is made up of departments and divisions, each of which has its own goals. Department managers are held responsible for their departments and are judged by how close they come to preset targets. Berliner (1957) shows how that kind of expectation leads the Soviet manager to make use of *blat* (influence through friends and contacts) as well as to overproduce products with high ruble value and underproduce those with low value. But since other departments or organizations are dependent on such departments, there will be inevitable shortages and surpluses, so that such violations or subterfuges turn out to be costly and come to be treated as sabotage. So too, a part of the famous electric parts manufacturing case occurred (in the case of General Electric) by a decision to break up the company into "profit centers" whereby each unit became a more or less autonomous company, with each president assigned responsibility for a high level of profit. Although warned about the antitrust laws, each unit was shielded from corporate headquarters. Producing units may hardly even take into account the possibility that such headquarters may be faced with antitrust action. Further, each unit is encouraged and rewarded for tending to its *own* affairs and letting headquarters deal with corporate policy as well as with relationships or impacts of the units.

Organizations, then, often find it difficult to meet their goals, but the structure of organizations often enables responsibility for task objectives to be delegated, with some units passing off onto other units the risky consequences of questionable behavior, but in which the legal violations may come to be simply one of the costs of doing business, a risk to be endured. The structure we have described so far is internal to the organization. We must now call attention to the way in which the organization seeks to transform the environment itself, to impose a structure on it, which further facilitates criminal behavior.

## THE ENVIRONMENTS OF MODERN ORGANIZATIONS

Two aspects of the environment are of special importance in understanding organizational crime—the legal environment and the concentration of control into a small number of leading organizations which come to dominate a market.

**The Legal Environment**

It is important to see law as a part of the environment within which organizations operate. Further, many laws have been constructed with the deliberate intention of controlling organizations so that they cannot harm the public interest, or so that activities considered important will not be interrupted. In that sense, the law is much more a looming presence for organizations than it is for most citizens. But just as organizations seek to reduce uncertainty in their present environments, they seek also to reduce uncertainty in the future, and the best way to do so is through the creation of laws which introduce stability into the organization's environment. In this sense, laws have two functions. First, if obeyed, they prevent or control violence in the pursuit of organizational goals. Hence, in the emergence of modern society, regular business and the conduct of government depended on elimination of piracy, free-booting, terrorism, and other interruptions which made the conduct of regular affairs perilous. Central governments sought, through impositions of laws and their enforcement, to create an atmosphere in which contracts would be honored and organizational resources themselves would be secure from theft.

The second function of law has been described by Weber (1968) as the coming of "formal rationality." Weber saw rationalization as a broad social movement which came into being with the Protestant Reformation and the coming of the modern world. The gist of his discussion is clear in his phrase, *"die Entzauberung der Welt"* (the disenchantment of the world), by which he meant that magical and irrational explanations were increasingly rejected. Even the Catholic Church now subjects would-be saints or others who claim supernatural experiences to examinations by psychiatrists and to other modern tests of sanity and credibility. Whereas in former times the future might be gleaned through consultation of oracles, or the guilt or innocence of a man might be decided by trial by fire or water, modern society and the courts seek rational means of coming to conclusions. But Weber went even further. The law underwent a special development in that it represented an appeal to *formal* rationality. By that he meant that a decision must depend only on the content of the law itself, or on its derivability, by strict legal principles, from previous laws. The major feature that a law represented, then, was calculability: If a law was clearly stated, then one could count on it. The contrast was with traditional law (or with substantive rationality). In traditional law, appeals were made to "the way things always were" as justification for a ruling, and interpretations were made orally by wise men or elders who would seek to show that the law was always adaptable to modern conditions. Substantive considerations might enter at any time—that is, appeals to ethical, political, utilitarian, hedonistic, feudal, or egalitarian ideals. A poor man might appear before a judge with evidence overwhelmingly showing his guilt. Yet, the judge might, on the basis of "justice for the poor," let him off. Such arbitrary rulings made the law a personal thing, or placed its enforcement in the hands of men who might follow ethical or expediential rules as the times or circumstances seem to require them. The significant contribution of formal rationality in law, then, became its predictable character, and as such it fitted well the coming of modern organizations and the stable atmosphere required for successful operation of giant enterprises. When a firm sought to operate in complex markets with products that required research and development, and where the organization's stockholders or citizens might have to wait for years before receiving returns, stability and predictability became essential. As such, the modern organizational executive is far from pleased with a situation in which there are few government controls. In spite of the frequent criticism by business conservatives of "government interference," they could hardly operate for an hour without such interference. Instead, the executives and their legal staffs prefer an environment rich with laws, planted from coast to coast. Such laws provide a means for predicting with accuracy the risks of alternative plans. Some will be ruled out as illegal; others are as likely to result in illegalities. However, it is also possible to predict the cost to the organization of legal violations and to take those costs into account in planning organizational activity.

Thus, the legal environment becomes a means for stabilizing an otherwise unpredictable future. The organization becomes heavily dependent on its legal staff to interpret the law, to warn the organization of possible violations, and, if no laws exist, to assist in drafting laws (such as those against spreading rumors) which protect existing organizations to ensure that operations proceed normally.

### The Structural Environment

Our discussion thus far perhaps has implied that something called "the organization" exists and constructs an environment suitable to itself. This is hardly the case. Instead, we must call attention to the emergence of organizational sets—that is, sets of organizations of a particular kind which are visible to one another (Caplow, 1964:201). Examples include the psychology departments of major universities; the Methodist churches in a moderate-sized city; the Returned

Services League branches (a war veterans organization) in Melbourne, Australia; the leading manufacturers of plant equipment and machinery in the United States; the symphony orchestras in most urbanized countries; or the athletic teams within a league which play one another on a regular basis.[3] Although our concern is with large-scale organizations, we call attention to the generality of the concept of set, since the generalizations we seek to present are drawn from such sets. In particular, the major feature of an organizational set for our purposes is as follows: The members of an organizational set, visible to one another and engaged in similar activities, compare themselves with one another, thus generating a well-understood status order. That is, the organizations themselves become stratified. A common pattern is for the set to exhibit a tiny group of from two to five recognized leading organizations, a small number of solidly established competitors who concede that they are second best (at least temporarily) but only to the leaders, and a much larger group of distinctly inferior producers or competitors who are often viewed with hostility by their superiors. At the very bottom of the structure life becomes precarious, entry is easy but mortality is high, and there is even some question as to whether these minor members are in the same organizational set with those higher up. This phenomenon appears to be quite general, and is evident, for example, in sports leagues, universities (ivy league, top state universities, regional universities, junior colleges), as well as business and manufacturing organizations.

Such a structure appears to be a historical development which represents a "solution" to the problem of competition by a large number of organizations for a limited field or market. An example is the period in the United States from the late 1890s to the depression of 1904, during which about 3,000 independent firms disappeared, mainly through mergers. The striking thing about these mergers was that almost 74 percent involved at least five firms; 26 percent, ten or more firms. In this way, many of the giants that still dominate manufacturing were formed: Standard Oil, General Electric, Westinghouse, National Lead, U.S. Rubber, Pittsburgh Plate Glass, and United Fruit. The motive was not simply greed, the image of the robber barons notwithstanding. Something of the process is suggested by the story of the biggest of the mergers, namely the formation in 1901 of United States Steel Corporation, which combined an estimated 785 plants. As Scherer (1970:165) writes:

> During the late 1890's, a series of mergers consolidated more than 200 formerly independent iron and steel makers into 20 much larger rival entities. Most of these new firms were

> confined to just a few facets of steel making, and after their formation many mapped out programs of integrating vertically to cover the whole spectrum from ore mining through fabrication. Charles Schwab, then president of Carnegie Steel, foresaw that this would lead to excess capacity and sharp price competition. He communicated his views to J. P. Morgan, who organized a merger among 12 of the prior consolidations and for his labor realized promotional profits estimated at $62.5 million. The end product was U.S. Steel, which at the time of its creation controlled roughly 65 per cent of all domestic blast furnace and finished steel output.

This type of solution—a cartel or something approximating it, is not simply an effort to dominate but to stabilize a market and, whatever the profits to Morgan or the company, provides to users of steel a predictable source of products at stable prices. Note that not all steel firms are included—in fact, most (162 in 1963) are not. The process that eventually results is illustrated by the following examples (figures for 1963): four firms account for 91 percent of sales of cathode ray picture tubes, but 148 firms are in that business; four firms account for 72 percent of sales of soap and detergents, but there are 641 firms in that business; four firms account for 43 percent of sales of farm machinery and equipment, but there are 1,481 firms in that business. The tendency is for the market to be broken up into segments, with strong product differentiation, different degrees of vertical integration—segmentation which is analogous to sports leagues. A small firm further down does not try to compete with U.S. Steel or Bethlehem Steel; it produces a special type of steel for a special market. Thus, Control Data seeks to dominate not the mass routine business market that IBM dominates, but the highly sophisticated market represented by the universities and the government space program. Firms, like sports teams, are careful not to take on opponents that are not in their league.

The implications of stratified organization sets for crime are as follows. (1) The fact that the numbers *within* any stratum (especially at the top) are small means that a conspiracy is an ever-present possibility and a continual temptation. The organizations not only know of one another's existence, their own success depends further on a continuous monitoring of one another's behavior. "Price leadership" is well known among the leaders in an industry; such a process results in identical prices without direct collusion. Bethlehem Steel, for example, simply announces one day in a news conference that it is raising the price of various grades of steel by so many dollars. This is a signal to U.S. Steel, Republic Steel, and the other members of the stratum, who, if they choose, immediately announce they are raising their prices by the same amount. If they reject the signal, Bethlehem Steel withdraws the announced increase. In this manner, the companies seek, without collusion, to make certain that the competition that does go on will be about steels of different qualities, specialized and tailor-made products for special customers, through competition on delivery dates, or other special features which are basically noncomparable. The companies seem to have tacitly recognized that once they get into a battle about prices, they can easily destroy each other. Evidence for this conclusion is suggested by the occasional "price wars" that break out between gasoline service stations or the "bread wars" that surface from time to time among supermarkets. Typically, if your competitor lowers his price, you have no recourse but to lower yours. There appears to be no point of stability in this game until the price reaches zero. Such games appear to function to attract trade, to lead to free advertising (since they make good newspaper copy), and to be severely limited in time. If they continue, no one can survive.[4]

But if mutual visibility can lead to such consistent behavior without collusion, even better controls over the market are possible by direct contact. The most striking cases in recent years have been the conspiracy among the manufacturers of electrical equipment, the collusion among plumbing equipment manufacturers, and a similar set of conspiracies among folding box manufacturers. Of course, the fact of visibility includes visibility to the Securities and Exchange Commission, the Department of Justice, and other organizations which are supposed to monitor such organizations. Thus, a conspiracy is only possible, not inevitable.

(2) The fact that organizations in the upper strata are small in number is by no means necessary for criminal activity to occur. In lower strata, the numbers may be larger but collusion is possible there too—it is only more difficult to coordinate. The one element that must be present is that *all* serious competitors at any level must be included in the conspiracy or the cartel. This then becomes feasible through stratification, since stratification breaks up the hundreds of potential competitors into smaller clusters of genuine competitors—persons in the same "business," doing business with the same set of customers, engaged in similar activities, working in the same market. They are genuinely comparable organizations who have a stake in that market and who stand, at all times, in danger of being destroyed by overaggressive competition from fellow competitors. Indeed, the electrical equipment manufacturer conspiracy fell apart, from time to time, because some (especially small companies) broke away or refused to abide by price agreements. Conspiracies often come to light when one of its members "blows the

whistle" (often because he is unsatisfied with his allotted share of the market) or because a potential competitor is left out altogether.

(3) Once sets form, and once the outlines of strata become clear, a new form of interorganizational behavior becomes possible; namely, relations among organizations in completely different sets and different strata. Perhaps the most striking illustration is the Equity Funding Corporation of America fraud which came to light in 1973, which forms a worthy successor (in the literature) to the electrical equipment fraud. This fraud was *not* an intercompany conspiracy, but was hatched largely inside one company. It was not brilliant, but rather slipshod; a sad commentary on the looseness of controls over corporate behavior. Equity Funding arose in the growth-mad years of the 1960s when stock prices seemed destined to go forever upward. Originally it was a combined insurance and mutual fund operation: Persons who were sold insurance were also sold shares of mutual funds. The company then offered to lend customers the money to pay for their insurance premiums, using the mutual fund shares as collateral for the loan. Customers were told they might keep their insurance policies, for example, 10 years, at which time they might cash them in for whatever cash value they had earned. Of course, now customers would have to pay off the loan that had been paying the premiums all those years (plus interest on the loan), but the hope was that, in the meantime, the value of the mutual fund shares would have gone up, enough to pay off the loan, and perhaps even make a profit. Equity Funding was highly successful in marketing this "concept" (which was not original with them) and, from the company point of view, it brought in money—from sales of mutual fund shares. Such a scheme can succeed only as long as share values go up. But there was an additional motive for the company to give an impression of success: the fact that the value of the company shares would also go up. The top executives themselves owned many shares and realized huge profits through dividends and stock sales. Further, being associated with a successful company was itself rewarding in the many practical and fringe benefits it provided. In addition, with a good stock earnings record, the company was able to buy other companies—including insurance companies and foreign corporations—by the exchange of stock. Finally, such earnings records enabled the company to borrow money more easily from banks with which to purchase other companies and to finance the company's operations. The network began to spread, reaching out into other organization sets composed of banks, insurance companies, mutual fund companies, securities sales organizations, and foreign corporations. As sales of insurance-cum-mutual funds lagged, the company began the first of its frauds—simply inflating the

company's reported earnings, largely through recording nonexistent commission income (from nonexistent sales) in the company's books and records. Over the years, some $85 million in bogus income was reported in that way.

As time went by, it became difficult to conceal this apparent income, since it brought no money into the company. For example, it was to be expected that some of the nonexistent policyholders would redeem their policies (for cash value) or pay off their loans and enjoy the proceeds of the inflation in value of the mutual fund shares; there would be some decrease in the funding totals. To finance this process, the company borrowed money to pay off such redemptions or sales. Some such money was borrowed legitimately,[5] but most was simply invented and laundered through foreign corporations as presumed commissions from sales earned abroad. This foreign structure included corporations (some real, some wholly imaginary) in Liechtenstein, Panama, Italy, the Netherlands, the Antilles, and the Bahamas.

These devices proved insufficient to generate the "income" desired and the company moved into a new phase—insurance fraud. The company had been handing over its policies for "reinsurance" to bona fide insurance companies. This frequently used device meant that the company handed over the burden of paying off due policies to other companies, contenting itself with the income from sales and the commission from reinsurance. But then it began buying insurance companies and using them to create bogus reinsurance, a process involving relations with such reinsurers as Pennsylvania Life Insurance Company, United Presidential, Phoenix Mutual, Ranger, Great Southern, and Kentucky General. Eventually the company carried out the most celebrated part of the fraud, the wholesale manufacture of entirely nonexistent policies (called "Y" business) by a group of men and women who filled out false medical statements and other supporting documents as required. This became a mass operation, resulting in the creation of imaginary policies running into extremely high figures. Covering up these fraudulent entries required further transactions between organizations, the issuance of bogus bonds and depositing such bonds as collateral for loans, as well as the total obfuscation (to put the kindest face on it) of auditors. It is claimed also by Dirks and Gross (1974:249) that the New York Stock Exchange was lax in making sure that its usual requirements for listing had been met before Equity Funding Corporation was admitted to the Exchange. In addition, the structure of the insurance industry itself continued to emphasize the safety of insurance and its value at a time when inflation was rapidly eroding the value of its payouts to policyholders.

We have here a picture of a vast network of organizations which was available to the thieves who engineered Equity Funding. The very complexity of that network enabled the perpetrators to escape discovery for such a long period. Even the insurance watchdogs of Illinois, New York, and California were unable to discover the fraud until very late, partly because each of them was limited to fraud within its own borders, and the company found that it could shift evidence of fraud from state to state and abroad as necessary. There was no overarching authority—certainly not at the international level—which could force a revelation of the fraud.

In that context, the organizational sets involved are independent, each paying attention to its own affairs. The insurance industry is separate from the mutual fund industry; the banks are separate from the mutual fund industry; the stockholders of any one company do not have regularized involvement with the stockholders of another company, let alone the policyholders of insurance companies. Each industry is insulated from every other. It is this insulation that enables a single organization to make its way through this tidy set of sets, acting as a link among strata in various of these domains. Ultimately, Equity Funding fell apart because of a disgruntled employee who told his story to a security dealer, and both of them had great difficulty in securing public action to stop the fraud. Relationships between sets are so complex and intertwined that there has not yet been created a set of controls to monitor those relationships. Yet, the fraud itself was not complex—only the interorganizational relationships.

## CONCLUSION

There is something quasi-biological about organizational crime. We do not see organizations as merely hurting biological persons—polluting the air, poisoning the water, or killing miners. In addition, organizations seem to be lethal to one another. Equity Funding gobbled up a purchased subsidiary solely for the value of its assets. Mergers enable the survivors to dominate a market, and, as the organizations themselves become organized into sets, the top stratum comes to dominate the entire industry, where firms further down serve as subcontractors for the affairs of firms at the top. Hence, organizations become satellites of other organizations and can hardly be expected to resist or expose crime which threatens their own likelihood of survival. Clearly, our ability to understand, let alone control, organizational crime requires going beyond theories of individual deterrence and punishment. We shall have to study organizations themselves and the organizational world they have created.

Do such organizational networks as we have described "cause" crime? If we are using "cause" in the same sense as it is used when we say that a mixture of chemicals "causes" an explosion, then the answer is certainly no. But the situation is not so much different from the analysis of the causation of crime on the part of biological individuals. No matter how close the correlation between crime and personal or environmental influences, no one *has* to commit crime (although the costs of not doing so may rise to unacceptable levels). Similarly, all we have described is the construction of an organizational world in which organizational crime becomes possible. In that sense we conceive of it as a criminaloid conspiracy—an arrangement put together deliberately to enable organizations to dominate markets and to stabilize competition to acceptable, predictable levels. Sometimes the mere construction of such a tidy world is itself a crime (where the public good is felt to require more competition or freedom to deviate than such a conspiracy allows). At other times, those organizations which upset a stable arrangement (for example, fair trade laws) become defined as criminal, in that the uncertainty and unpredictability that their activity creates may lead to public harm. Crime, then, is an ever-present possibility, perhaps endemic to the structure itself; sometimes petty, often destructive, frequently disturbing to public conceptions of proper behavior. But whatever its effect, organizational crime should be no surprise.

## NOTES

1. Our discussion for the next few paragraphs draws upon that analysis of Coleman (1974: chap. 1).

2. The concept of "performance" is here offered in place of speaking simply of "goals" because of the criticisms of the goal concept. For example, Yuchtman and Seashore (1967) prefer to evaluate organizations in terms of their ability to exploit their environment in "the acquisition of scarce and valued resources." Whether this terminology really avoids the need to speak of goals is something we cannot deal with here (for example, the word "valued" clearly suggests some focus, if not goals). It seems difficult to avoid some concept related to valued accomplishments. Even "performance" is not entirely satisfactory, since one must ask, further, what kind of performances are desired and what is the priority in which they are pursued.

3. Space forbids our pausing to explain why organizations form themselves into sets, but we can note some major factors in passing: the transmission of an institutional model for newcomers, the allocation of personnel and resources, the evaluation of innovations, the training and evaluation of one another's members, and the control of outputs (as when a soccer league makes sure that games occur only between equally matched teams).

4. One might raise a question as to whether mere visibility (without actual collusion) is necessarily illegal but perhaps only bad public policy. Yet, such "price leadership" behavior is at present the target of the Shenefield Commission (Shenefield is Assistant Attorney General for anti-trust) and the Congress under Senator Edward Kennedy. The attempt is being made to attack concentration as such (called

"monopoly power") as being *"presumed* to be maintained by illegal conduct" without having to prove intent or actual collusion. See Ehrbar (1979).

5. Presumably, entirely bogus accounts could have been created from the start, but there was much irrationality in behavior, including a lingering sense that there should be *some* real money from time to time. Further, genuine loans shored up contacts with banks and other institutions.

## REFERENCES

BERLE, A. A. and G. C. MEANS (1932) The Modern Corporation and Private Property. New York: Macmillan.

BERLINER, J. S. (1957) Factory and Managers in the USSR. Cambridge: Harvard University Press.

BLUMBERG, P. I. (1975) The Megacorporation in American Society. Englewood Cliffs, NJ: Prentice-Hall.

BLUNDELL, W. E. (1978) "Equity Funding: 'I did it for the jollies." Pp. 153-185 in J. M. Johnson and J. D. Douglas (eds.), Crime at the Top. Philadelphia: Lippincott.

BURCH, P. H., Jr. (1972) The Managerial Revolution Reassessed. Lexington, MA: D. C. Heath.

CAPLOW, T. (1964) Principles of Organization. New York: Harcourt Brace and Jovanovich.

CHUBIN, D. (1974) "Sociological manpower and womanpower: Sex differences in career patterns of two cohorts of American doctorate sociologists." American Sociologist 9 (May):83-91.

CHURCHILL, N. C. and W. W. COOPER (1964) "Effects of auditing records: Individual task accomplishment and organizational objectives." In W. W. Cooper, H. J. Leavitt, and M. W. Shelly II (eds.), New Perspectives on Organizational Research. New York: John Wiley.

COLEMAN, J. S. (1974) Power and the Structure of Society. New York: Norton.

DIRKS, R. L. and L. GROSS (1974) The Great Wall Street Scandal. New York: McGraw-Hill.

DORNBUSCH, S. M. (1955) "The military academy as an assimilating institution." Social Forces 33 (May):316-321.

EHRBAR, A. F. (1979) "'Bigness' becomes the target of the trust-busters." Fortune 26 (March):34-40.

GALBRAITH, J. K. (1967) The New Industrial State. Boston: Houghton Mifflin.

GEIS, G. (1967) "White-collar crime: The heavy electrical equipment antitrust cases of 1961." Pp. 139-150 in M. B. Clinard and R. Quinneys (eds.), Criminal Behavior Systems: A Typology. New York: Holt, Rinehart & Winston.

GOFF, C. and C. E. REASONS (1978) Corporate Crime in Canada. Scarborough, Ontario: Prentice-Hall.

GOFFMAN, E. (1961) Asylums. Garden City, NY: Doubleday.

GROSS, E. (1978) "Organizational crime: A theoretical perspective." Pp. 55-85 in N. Denzin (ed.) Studies in Symbolic Interaction, Vol. I. Greenwich, CT: JAI Press.

______ and P. W. GRAMBSCH (1974) Changes in University Organization 1964-1971. New York: McGraw-Hill.

HAWORTH, L. (1959) "Do organizations act?" Ethics 70 (October):59-63.

KIESCHEL, W. III (1979) "The crime at the top in Fruehauf Corp." Fortune (January 29):32-35.

LARNER, R. J. (1970) Management Control and the Large Corporation. New York: Junellen.

LUNDBERG, F. (1969) The Rich and the Super-rich. New York: Bantam.

Management Audit (1956) The Roman Catholic Church. Special Audit No. 137, Vol. V, No. 15.

MERRIAM, A. P. and R. W. MACK (1960) "The jazz community." Social Forces 38 (March):211-221.

MERTON, R. K. (1957) "Social structure and anomie." Pp. 31-160 in R. K. Merton, Social Theory and Social Structure. New York: Free Press.

PSATHAS, G. (1968) "The fate of idealism in nursing school." Journal of Health and Social Behavior 9 (March):52-64.

SCHERER, F. M. (1970) The Industrial Market Structure and Economic Performance. Chicago: Rand McNally.

STRAW, B. M. and E. SZWAJKOWSKI (1975) "The scarcity-munificence component of organizational environments and the commission of illegal acts." Administrative Science Quarterly 20 (September):345-354.

THOMPSON, J. D. (1967) Organizations in Action. New York: McGraw-Hill.

VAN MAANEN, J. (1978) "The asshole." In P. K. Manning and J. van Maanen (eds.), Policing. Santa Monica, CA: Goodyear.

VILLAREJO, D. (1961a) "Stock ownership and the control of the corporation, part I." New University Thought 2 (Autumn):33-77.

——— (1961b) "Stock ownership and the control of the corporation, part II." New University Thought 2 (Winter):47-65.

WEBER, M. (1968) "Economy and society." In G. Roth and C. Wittich (eds.). New York: Bedminster Press.

WESTLEY, W. A. (1970) Violence and the Police. Cambridge: MIT Press.

YUCHTMAN, E. and S. E. SEASHORE (1967) "A system resource approach to organizational effectiveness." American Sociological Review 32 (December): 891-903.

ZEITLIN, M. (1974) "Corporate ownership and control: The large corporation and the capitalist class." American Journal of Sociology 79 (March):1073-1119.

*Chapter 4*

# CRIME BETWEEN ORGANIZATIONS: IMPLICATIONS FOR VICTIMOLOGY

DIANE VAUGHAN

## INTRODUCTION

On July 28, 1977, Revco Drug Stores, Inc., one of the nation's largest discount drug chains, was found guilty of a computer-generated double-billing scheme that resulted in the loss of over a half-million dollars in Medicaid funds to the Ohio Department of Public Welfare. This was the largest case of Medicaid provider fraud in the state's history. Discovery of the fraud was accidental: A claims analyst in the welfare department's fraud and abuse investigation unit was examining computer-generated lists of Medicaid prescriptions for a single Revco store. The analysis was in response to a request from the Ohio State Pharmacy Board, which was investigating an unrelated matter. The analyst discovered an irregularity in the computer printouts—the prescriptions did not flow in the usual ascending numerical order. Instead, lower prescription numbers were occurring within a sequence of ascending numbers. Closer examination revealed that the last three digits of certain six-digit prescription numbers were being transposed. A pattern appeared: A prescription was recorded as a claim, and three days later the identical prescription appeared again with the last three digits transposed.

Four separate Ohio organizations participated in the investigation that followed: the Department of Public Welfare, the State Pharmacy Board, the State Highway Patrol, and the Economic Crime Unit of the Franklin County Prosecutor's Office. During the year-long investigation, which was conducted in utmost secrecy, these organizations verified that false prescriptions were being generated from Revco's corporate headquarters in Cleveland and being submitted as Medicaid claims. The welfare department had reimbursed Revco for these false prescriptions. The evidence was confirmed by the seizure of original prescriptions in a simultaneous execution of search

AUTHOR'S NOTE: *The author wishes to thank Professors Ronald G. Corwin, Simon Dinitz, Peter M. Gerhart, and Richard J. Lundman for their comments on early drafts of this chapter.*

warrants in five Revco pharmacies around the state. The case concluded with the entry of no contest pleas by the corporation and by two executives involved. The executives were fined; Revco was fined and ordered to make restitution to the welfare department.

The Revco case is indicative of a significant phenomenon: crime between organizations. This aspect of white-collar crime has implications for traditional victimology. Where once both criminal and victim were individuals, in this case both roles are played by complex organizations. The Revco case will be used in this chapter to document problems in traditional victimology and to suggest an expanded framework useful in the study of crime between organizations. The details of the case will be examined, the limits of the traditional victimology framework identified, and alternatives will be suggested.[1]

## BACKGROUND OF THE CASE

The investigation of the Revco case uncovered the following explanation of the crime. In the spring of 1975, corporate headquarters had moved to a new location. In the subsequent reorganization of departments, boxes of Medicaid claims were found. These claims, dating from 1973, had been submitted to the Ohio Department of Public Welfare for processing and reimbursement. However, the claims had been rejected by the welfare department's computerized screening system, a system which detects errors in claims. When claims are rejected, reimbursement is withheld until the error in the claims is corrected and the claim successfully resubmitted. Revco personnel had not done the manual examination necessary to correct the rejected claims, and so they piled up. The prescriptions that the claims represented had been given to Medicaid recipients by Revco pharmacists. Hence, the boxes of rejected Revco claims signified outstanding accounts receivable: Over 50,000 claims had been rejected by welfare department computers, representing more than a half-million dollars in accounts receivable.

Two executives of the company knew of these rejected claims and assumed responsibility for doing something about them. According to Revco officials, the two embarked on a plan to bring the company's accounts receivable back into balance. To examine each claim individually and legitimately correct the errors would demand personnel and time, and the cost of correction would exceed the value of the claim. Therefore, a temporary staff of six clerical people was hired to alter the rejected claims to render them acceptable to the welfare department computer.

The two executives possessed particular skills that enabled them to direct this project with minimal risk of being detected by the welfare department computer system. One had been former director of Revco's computer system and was knowledgeable not only about Revco's own system, but about welfare department computer billing and screening systems as well. The other executive was a licensed pharmacist with knowledge of drugs and drug dosages.

Rather than correct the rejected claims for resubmission to the state, clerical workers at Revco headquarters were instructed to manually rewrite about the same number of claim forms as the number of rejected claims. They rewrote "model claims"—claims which already had been accepted by the state and paid. Dates were changed, and the last three digits of the six-digit prescription numbers were transposed. No attempt was made to alter amounts of the individual claims. The two executives believed that because of the large number of claims involved, the amount would average the same as the rejected claims. When the backlog of rejected claims had been rewritten, the temporary staff was terminated. The plan, devised in March 1975, was completed by December 1976. The two executives accepted total responsibility for the falsified claims, stating that their actions had been without the knowledge of any other persons employed by Revco.

Fourteen months after the investigation began, Revco entered a plea of no contest to ten counts of falsification, a misdemeanor of the first degree. The two Revco executives also entered pleas of no contest to falsification. Both Revco and the executives were sentenced according to a negotiated plea agreement. The maximum fine of $5,000 per count was imposed on the corporation. In addition, Revco was to make restitution in the amount of $521,521.12 to the Department of Public Welfare. The two executives were fined $1,000 on each of two counts.

## REVCO: CRIMINAL OR VICTIM?

Headlines reported the conclusion of the case: "Revco Stores, Two Officials Found Guilty" (Columbus *Dispatch,* July 28, 1977); "Revco Convicted of Using False Billings to Collect on Ohio Medicaid Prescriptions" (*Wall Street Journal,* August 1, 1977). That Revco did, indeed, falsify prescriptions is indisputable. Yet, at no time did the corporation admit to criminal behavior. In fact, throughout the case, in public statements and correspondence, Revco assumed the role of the victim, not the offender.

Corporate officials stated that there had been a series of frustrating difficulties between Revco and the welfare department's Medicaid program since 1971. Revco placed the responsibility for these problems with the welfare department. A history of the interaction between the two organizations was compiled by Revco and presented to representatives of the prosecutor's office and State Highway Patrol (Revco Drug Stores, Inc., Inter-Office Communication: May 18, 1977). Twenty-two incidents over a four-year period were listed to substantiate Revco's point that the corporation had repeatedly been victimized by the welfare department. The first entry, in November 1971, stated:

> We are informed by this date that there is a severe backlog of claims and that the state is about to run out of money for Medicaid. Communications during this period of time from this date [sic] were extremely poor. There were times when mailings were not made because the state lacked the necessary funds for postage.

Welfare's initiation of a new computer billing system in 1972 was intended to resolve these reimbursement problems. Instead, according to Revco, there was increased confusion. Difficulties such as system breakdown, backlogs of claims, and infrequent reimbursement accompanied the phasing-in of the new system. These transition dilemmas meant the state was often behind in paying providers' claims.

The Revco listing of Medicaid problems mentioned rejects as early as 1974. Revco received a memo from the welfare department concerning continuing problems with rejects because Revco claims failed to pass the computer prepayment screening. The memo noted the state was revamping its reject system and many pharmacies were having problems with making correct submissions to the state.

In order to alleviate these problems, the welfare department computer experts required major providers to install a presubmission edit system of their own to screen claims before sending them on for reimbursement. The intent was to catch errors in matters such as keypunching, drugs allowable, and identification numbers so they could be corrected. This would reduce the number of claims rejected by welfare department computers. Revco was one of the providers that installed such a system.

However, analysis of claims rejection rates of Revco compared with other providers indicated Revco's presubmission screening system was not functioning properly—errors were not being detected. Therefore, the percentage of claims rejected by welfare department computers was higher for Revco than for other providers with similar screening systems. Average rejection rates for other providers varied from 2.0 percent to 6.0 percent per month, while a 12-month summary of Revco's claims indicated that from June 1976 to May 1977, 24.04 percent of Revco's claims were being rejected. A 22-month summary (July 1975 through April 1977) revealed the range of monthly rejections for the period was 5.4 percent to 56.3 percent (Ohio Department of Public Welfare, Intra-Office Communication, July 1977).

According to welfare department computer experts, the responsibility for this problem lay with Revco (Interview, Ohio Department of Public Welfare, Division of Data Services, July 18, 1978). The company had been advised by the welfare department that its presubmission edit system was inadequately programmed, which was resulting in higher than average rejection rates. Suggested changes in Revco's screening system that would reduce rejections were not made. The reasoning behind this omission is not known to me, due to Revco's unwillingness to cooperate with this research. However, one might speculate that cost and complexity were relevant factors.

The maintenance of a reliable presubmission screening system is expensive. Once installed, the provider's system requires constant adjustment: The information needed by the welfare department frequently changes. Allowable claims vary. Recipient eligibility requirements may be altered. New drugs on the market require constant revision of the drug formulary, a listing of disallowable drugs. In July 1978 the then-current drug formulary contained 90 computer-printed pages of disallowable drugs. A welfare department listing of reasons for rejected claims covered eight pages, and "disallowable drug" was but one of many. A welfare department computer specialist, speaking of the Revco rejections, stated, "We complicate the problem by the amount of data we need" (Interview, Ohio Department of Public Welfare, July 18, 1978).

Not only is such a system costly for a provider to maintain, but it is by function preventive, and therefore prospective. At the time the pile-up of rejected Revco claims was discovered, an improved screening system would not have eliminated the outstanding accounts receivable from past rejections. According to Revco officials, the Revco executives responsible for the falsifications saw the rejected claims as another in a long line of inconveniences caused Revco by the welfare department. Prescriptions had been filled in "good faith" (Interview, Revco Drug Stores, Inc., February 1978). Reimbursement was withheld. The rejects would be costly to correct, because of a "cold audit trail." Revco officials admitted correction was theoretically possible, but not practical. The rejected claims were "rewritten" to "expedite the money the state owed us." Submitting false claims was seen as a solution to a "business problem" (*Wall Street Journal,* August 1, 1977), not as a crime.

## ORGANIZATIONS AS VICTIMS: THE LIMITS OF TRADITIONAL VICTIMOLOGY

Traditional victimology developed as a consequence of interest in street crime, which involves interaction among individuals. The explanatory framework generated was, of necessity, micro-level.[2] Research that followed focused on individuals as actors. It was grounded on belief in (1) the existence of some clear victim and (2) the possibility of unraveling the victim-offender interaction to reveal hidden dimensions of the crime. The concept of "victim-precipitation" developed as the major tool for analyzing the victim-offender interaction.

These basic characteristics of traditional victimology are inadequate for understanding crime between organizations. The nature of the actors has changed from individuals to complex organizations, and the question of who is victim and who is offender cannot be easily answered. In addition, the complexity of interorganizational crime puts the utility of victim-precipitation as an analytical tool in serious doubt.

Even within the traditional victimology framework there has been difficulty in distinguishing victim from offender. Mannheim (1965:672) admitted that:

> the distinction between criminal and victim, which in former days appeared as clear-cut as that of black and white, actually often becomes vague and blurred in individual cases. The longer and the more deeply the actions of the persons involved are scrutinized, the more doubtful will it occasionally be who is to blame for the tragic outcome.

The Revco case confirms the existence of this traditional dilemma at the organizational level. Both Revco and the Ohio Department of Public Welfare defined themselves as victims. Admittedly, how much of Revco's insistence on their own victimization is rationalization, how much is "real," and how much legal defense is open to speculation. There is no question that the corporation violated the law. Yet, corporate officials amply documented a past history of difficulties with the welfare department. The company assertion was that the criminal behavior was victim-precipitated: Revco was not to blame.

Use of the concept victim-precipitation in traditional victimology has focused on the overt and objectively ascertainable behavior of the parties during the course of the victim-offender interactions. Levine (1978:85) states:

> The dominant conception of victim precipitation depicts the interaction between victim and offender as being an extremely mechanical, uninterpreted process. The victim accidentally (or with only partially conscious intent) provides a behavioral stimulus or set of stimuli which trigger an automatic reaction from the offender. The implication is thus that precipitation is simply a certain range of conduct produced by actors in certain public settings.

Though originally useful as a sensitizing concept, "victim-precipitation" has been criticized as lacking utility as an explanatory and empirical tool. Silverman (1974) noted that operational definitions have varied with the type of crime studied. Further, the determination of whether or not the act was victim-precipitated has been based on a subjective decision, either by the offender or the researcher, as to what constituted a provocative act. In short, when used to interpret victim-offender interaction at the individual level, the concept has been ambiguous, at best. The changed nature of the actors and the act itself at the organizational level underscores the limitations in applying this concept to crime between organizations.

First, in traditional victimology, the victim-offender interaction is often discrete in time and space. When crime occurs between organizations, such distinctions are seldom possible. Organizational crime is more accurately conceived as longitudinal rather than cross-sectional. The interaction which culminated in the false billings in the Revco case had been ongoing between the two organizations for six years. The crime itself—the creation and submission of the false billings to the welfare department—occurred over a 21-month period. Furthermore, the "location" of the crime was dispersed rather than spatially confined. Organizations, unlike ordinary actors, have the capacity to be in more than one place at one time. Revco, for example, was located not only at corporate headquarters in Cleveland, but in 159 retail outlets around the state. The Ohio Department of Public Welfare was similarly scattered around the state. When and where the act was committed became obscured because of the unique nature of organizations as actors.

Second, the traditional victimological approach assumes the victim-offender interaction is characterized by behavior that is overt and objectively ascertainable. This implies that the crime is committed in some public way—public in the sense that if a witness were present, the act could be seen and interpreted: a blow is struck, a gun is fired. When organizations occupy the role of victim and offender, the interaction does not occur in a way that can be comparably defined as "public." The visibility of crime between organizations is limited. The interaction leading up to the crime in the Revco case was conducted through phone calls, correspondence, interdepartmental memos, and private meetings. Rather than a single incident there were many, and in multiple forms. Only a part of this became permanent written record. The crime itself was concealed in the numeric codes of computer tapes, printouts, and claims analyses. Rather than a single occurrence, there were many instances of false submissions. Yet, there were no outward indicators that a crime was being committed. The actual loss to the welfare department was so thoroughly buried by the two organizations' computer technology that discovery was accidental.

In large measure, the victim-offender interaction at the organizational level is invisible, hidden within the private confines of each separate organization. The crime itself is much more difficult to detect; the victim-offender interaction is much more difficult to unravel. The likelihood of a witness from the general public to help "solve" the crime is scant. The structure of organizations and the nature of the act itself seriously limit the possibility of witnesses to organizational crime. Even within the organizations involved, the existence of a witness to clarify matters is rare. In the Revco case, the crime was conceived and carried out within one subunit of the large organization, transferred onto computer tapes, and passed from one organization to another in this form. Thus, it was even hidden from the view of many members of the local organizations.

Even when insiders witness the crime, they seldom admit knowledge or involvement. In the Revco case, corporate officials claimed the plan to falsify Medicaid claims was devised and carried out by two executives without knowledge of other corporate officers. Whether $500,000 in outstanding accounts receivable could accumulate without attracting attention among other corporate executives is a matter for speculation. Whether six temporary clerical personnel could be hired to falsify claims over a 15-month period and the nature of their work remain unknown is also a matter for speculation. Use of the legal concept of the "reasonable person" would suggest commission of the crime could not have occurred without knowledge of other executives. Yet, Revco officials consistently denied knowledge of the false billings. Delegation of responsibility within the organizational structure makes responsibility for decision-making difficult to determine and thus handicaps interpretation of victim-offender interaction.

Untangling victim-offender relationships at the organizational level is further complicated by the inability to penetrate organizational boundaries. Granted, law enforcement representatives usually have greater success at this than do sociologists; however, both are handicapped in sorting out the facts. Since discovery of illegal organizational behavior is more likely to occur after the fact, analysis of victim-offender relationships are retrospective by definition. Documents tracing the interaction record only selected aspects of the case. Evidence in written form and on computer tapes can be destroyed. Organizational membership changes. The possibility of clarifying the victim-offender relationship is remote.

In sum, in any crime, understanding the victim-offender interaction is an important element of explanation. However, analysis of victim-offender interaction when both roles are played by organizations is beset with problems. Admittedly, Revco's accusation of victim-precipitation gains support from the obvious complexity of welfare department rules, computer data needs, government inefficiency, and bureaucratic delays. However, Revco could have dealt with the problem in ways other than falsifying claims. Would the cost to Revco, for example, have been any greater had the six temporary clerical workers been instructed to actually correct the rejected claims rather than alter the other claims to make up the shortage? The sociologists' need to know is handicapped by the nature of crime between organizations and the characteristics of the organizations themselves. Victim-precipitation, a core concept of traditional victimology, has only limited utility.

Crime between organizations is a macro-level phenomenon. If victimology is to be expanded to include organizations, an explanatory framework is necessary that extends *beyond* the concept of victim-precipitation. The following section suggests a macro-level approach for understanding organizations as victims.

## ORGANIZATIONS AS VICTIMOGENIC

Certain social structural arrangements exist which contribute to crime between organizations. They exist within the environment in which organizations operate, and within the organizations themselves. Though the conditions and combinations of these factors that result in crime between specific organizations cannot yet be unraveled, they exist in general form for all organizations. Therefore, if crime of one organization against another is to be understood, these factors need to be identified. They are: organizational characteristics, environmental conditions, and a supporting ideology. The interplay of these factors creates an environment in which organizations can be understood as victimogenic: susceptible to being victimized by crime.

## Organizational Characteristics

Studies have supported a link between certain organizational characteristics and organizational victimization by individual offenders. Smigel and Ross (1970) pointed out:

> The size, wealth and impersonality of big business and government are attributes which make it seem excusable, according to many people, to steal from these victims.

Smigel (1955) found a direct relationship between public attitudes toward stealing and organizational size. In general, the findings indicated "the larger and more bureaucratic the victim, the greater the willingness to approve stealing" (1955:29).

Large organizations are frequently thought of as highly impersonal institutions. Fattah (1976) points out:

> Acts causing immediate and concrete harm to a real, specific and personalized victim are likely to evoke stronger moral resistance than acts in which the victim is totally absent, impersonal, anonymous or unidentifiable, or where the victim is only an abstraction [176:33].

The intangibility of the harm legitimates the act. Hence, taking from the government or a large corporation evokes fewer moral scruples than do crimes against more visible victims, such as persons or families.

In addition to Smigel's research relating to victimization of organizations, Cameron's work on shoplifting (1964) indicated a relationship between organizational characteristics, such as the development of self-service, and subsequent victimization. Also, Hollinger's (1978) study of employee deviance against the formal work organization found a relationship between property and production deviance and formal organizational sanctions.

Research on this topic has been scant. However, organizational characteristics would seem to encourage the crime of one organization against another, as well. For instance, in the Revco case, the Ohio Department of Public Welfare clearly symbolizes the "size, wealth, and impersonality" that Smigel and Ross (1970) mention. Because size is frequently accompanied by geographic expansion and product diversification, opportunity for crime is likewise expanded.

Internal structure also presents increased opportunity for crime between organizations. For example, division of labor is necessary for task efficiency. The delegation of responsibility associated with this division in hierarchical organizations creates subunits with varying autonomy. Autonomy of subunits makes overall control difficult. An outside organization may be transacting fraudulent business with an autonomous organizational subunit, with no countervailing intra-organizational authority present to detect the illegal behavior. Specialization further complicates this problem. In an organization with highly specialized subunits, one subunit may be incapable of detecting ongoing fraud in another due to lack of transferable expertise.

The technology of an organization also presents opportunities for crime between organizations. An organization's technology is a reflection of the general environmental system in which the organization operates. The advent of computer and other electronic equipment has come to dominate the daily operation of nearly all large organizations, regardless of their major function. The Revco case is but one illustration of the possibilities for crime created by the widespread use of computers.

Computers are a direct link with organizational resources. Theft can be accomplished without breaking and entering. Large amounts can be taken in minutes, or resources can be slowly drained away over long periods. Organizations, alert to the dangers of electronic crime, work to make their systems "theft-proof" by designing special edit systems to detect fraud. Yet, these are not infallible. In the Revco case, the false billings were submitted over a 21-month period. Though the welfare department had a highly sophisticated system, the fraud went undetected by the computer. Only when the data were painstakingly analyzed by human eyes was the fraud discovered.

Commission of crime is also facilitated by such characteristics as technology and internal structure. For example, delegation of responsibility within the offender organization further encourages crime by the very fact that personal responsibility is diffused (Conklin, 1977:64). Determining where within an organization a decision was made is difficult. Conklin aptly states:

> The delegation of responsibility and unwritten orders keep those at the top of the corporate structure remote from the consequences of their decisions and orders, much as the heads of organized crime families remain "untouchable" by the law [1977:65].

Generally, it would seem that as organizations have increased in complexity, more opportunities for crime have been generated. Increased size, impersonality, wealth, geographic dispersion, product diversification, division of labor, hierarchical authority systems, specialization, and complex technologies are all organizational attributes that facilitate crime between organizations.

**Environmental Conditions**

There has been a growing awareness that understanding complex organizations and their behavior requires examination of the environment in which organizations function (see, for example, Terreberry, 1968, and Turk, 1970). Because crime between organizations does not occur in a vacuum, it is insufficient to focus only on organizational characteristics. Factors in the environment that promote crime of one organization against another are also important.

The economic environment of business organizations includes an ideology emphasizing the principles of free competition and profit maximization (Conklin, 1977:41). These notions in practice are sometimes in conflict. The desire for competitive advantage causes excesses that work against the principles of free competition. The theory behind an open competitive marketplace is that if a society is allowed free competition, unrestrained by either government or the private sector, resources will be allocated in an optimal manner. However, the emphasis on profit-making in business organizations reflects the fact that survival in this competitive atmosphere is of more immediate concern than the more diffuse goal of optimum allocation of resources.

In the corporate world, prestige is measured by organizational wealth. The annual publication of "*Fortune's* Top Five Hundred" indicates membership in the elite of an organizational stratification system. How organizations are ranked within this stratification system is monitored through quarterly reports, earnings and dividends, and stock market transactions. The key to social mobility within this system is increased profit. Levine (1978:88) suggests:

> Advanced industrial societies, characterized by highly refined systems of social stratification, generate a set of victimization opportunities associated with social relationships based on the social standings of the parties. An integral feature of such relationships are interests in the acquisition, maintenance and defense of personal and mutual status, social esteem, and public reputation.

Thus, restraint-of-trade actions such as price-fixing and discriminatory price-cutting, theft of trade secrets, false advertising, and bribery and payoffs to ensure market share could be described as "reputational victimization"; that is, victimization of one organization by another that offers the potential of increased profit and therefore upward mobility in the organizational stratification system (Levine, 1978:88).

Organizational norms reinforce actions that result in profits. Frequently, profit-making, the most valued business skill, is pursued at the cost of honesty. The following memorandum, issued by General Electric to company employees, is illustrative; it lists the performance norms by which managers are judged:

1. Profitability
2. Market position
3. Productivity, or the effective utilization of human, material resources
4. Product leadership
5. Personnel development
6. Employee attitudes
7. Public responsibility
8. Balance between short-range and long-range goals [Conklin, 1977:42].

If one can assume that these criteria are listed in descending order of importance, the discrepancy in rank between profitability and public responsibility supports the point. Shover (1976), reflecting on achievement of organizational goals, noted, "many times organizations become so preoccupied with the achievement of goals that they virtually give their employees—or demand—carte blanche powers to use 'innovative' procedures to assure those goals are attained" (1976:15).

These norms supporting profitability at the cost of integrity seem to be common across organizations. In the 1961 heavy electrical equipment antitrust conspiracy, defendants testified that price-fixing in their specific industry was "an established way of life" (Geis, 1967:144). One official stated that price-fixing "had become so common and gone on for so many years that I think we lost sight of the fact that it was illegal" (1967:144). In other instances, inter-organizational norms emerge supporting unethical behavior that interferes with free competition, though no legal violation occurs. In 1975 and 1976, bribes and questionable payments to foreign countries were discovered to have become a routine part of commercial practice for many firms. Payments were made not to "outcompete" foreign competitors, but rather to gain an edge over other U.S. manufacturers. The Council on Economic Priorities noted the frequency of this practice by labeling it the "norm of bribery" (1976:3). Daniel J. Haughton, ousted as chairman of Lockheed Aircraft after the corporation admitted $22 million of political payments, said, "I didn't do anything wrong. We did it playing the rules of the game as they were then" (*New York Times Magazine,* September 26, 1976:47).

The potential of increased profit and upward mobility are made more attractive by the low risk of legal sanctions (see, for example,

Stone, 1975; Nader et al., 1976; and Conklin, 1977). In a credit economy, organizational transactions are characterized by trust and intangible exchange. Hence, crime between organizations has low visibility. Those cases that become known are generally treated with leniency. The community respectability of businessmen, their media influence, political concerns of prosecuting authorities, statutory limitations, and the existence of regulatory agencies which seek compliance rather than punishment also are related to low risk of sanctions. A recent development has further minimized risk of sanctions. Difficulty in detection has resulted in the organization of specialized private departments for dealing with the loss, its discovery, and treatment of the accused. This tendency for organizations to develop their own systems of private dispositions frequently results in failure to stigmatize offenders publicly.

A number of environmental conditions have been suggested here as factors that facilitate crime between organizations. The contributing factors suggested are: the conflict between free competition and profit maximization; an organizational stratification system with wealth as its base; norms which support profit maximization; and low risk of sanction. All are structural in nature; all contribute to an explanation of the fraudulent transaction perpetrated by Revco on the Ohio Department of Public Welfare.

The Revco case is an instance of crime between two organizations ranked very differently in the organizational stratification system. Though both Revco and the Ohio Department of Public Welfare are complex organizations, they are clearly unequal adversaries in one major respect. One is a public agency; the other represents private enterprise. While private enterprise and profit-making are highly valued in this society, governmental agencies seldom receive similar respect; they are generally held in low esteem. Stereotyped imagery of red tape, indolent civil service employees, bureaucratic delays, inefficiency, absence of public accountability, and incompetence defines most public agencies as low status organizations. In this sense, government agencies are peculiarly vulnerable to victimization.

Revco, listed in *Fortune's* Top Five Hundred, is among the "corporate elite." Conklin (1977:45) has noted that the profit drive in the pharmaceutical industry is especially strong. The interaction between profit and the drive for public reputation was clear in the Revco case. The 50,000 rejected claims represented outstanding accounts receivable, which cut corporate profits. The false billings were an attempt to bring accounts receivable back into balance, thus presenting an improved image of the corporation on paper. The act itself was supported by internal norms that rewarded profitability.

The concern with profits and social standing was displayed throughout the case in corporate requests for minimal publicity and speedy settlement.

Risk of sanction was low for several reasons. The crime itself involved little hazard of detection because of the intangible nature of the exchange between Revco and the welfare department, and because of the special skills possessed by the persons responsible. Also, as a government agency, the welfare department has no public audience to which it must be accountable for financial matters, in the sense that private enterprise must be accountable to owners. This further lessens the possibility of detection of the crime. Finally, barriers to punishment, as noted earlier, existed in the environment, minimizing risk of sanction.

### A Collective Definition: Organizations as Legitimate Targets

Witness the behavior of a man who took his car to the auto service department of a major retail chain. While waiting many hours on the premises for his auto to be repaired, he watched the mistreatment and actual damage of cars of other customers. His own car was repaired. However, work in excess of that agreed to was done, and, over objections, he was forced to pay. The next day, he walked into a retail outlet of the same store, picked up a set of jumper cables from the shelf, and walked out without paying. The sense of mistreatment and inability to right the wrong resulted in the commission of an illegal act against the organization (Interview, The Ohio State University, 1977).

Dynes and Quarantelli (1974) first explored this phenomenon in their study of organizations as victims in mass civil disturbances. Organizations were selectively looted by ghetto residents. Widespread looting was not explainable by objective characteristics of the selected organizations. However,

> other factors appear to be more influential in the selective process than whether the objects of attack do or do not actually have certain objectionable features. More important is how organizations, especially classes of them, come to be perceived. In essence, what appears to be involved is best described as a collective definitional process [Dynes and Quarantelli, 1974:71].

Certain stores came to symbolize economic exploitation to the looters. This collective definition was followed by a redefinition of property rights related to these organizations. Perceived exploitation resulted in a reversal of traditional definitions of property and the emergence of a normative definition of the right to use organizational resources. Though Dynes and Quarantelli offer the explanation within a particular historical-geographic context, they suggest that the process of collective definitions and redefinitions is not restricted in time or space. Certain types of organizations come to symbolize economic exploitation, whether or not they actually exhibit it (1974:72).

Increased media exposure of organizational criminality may be generating a collective definition of large organizations as exploitative. Cases such as the recent General Services Administration scandal and instances of industrial espionage, price-fixing, and tax evasion at the corporate level probably are no longer shocking to the average citizen. Not only are these crimes between organizations constantly before the public, but crimes of organizations that directly harm individuals fill the headlines. The notorious Equity Funding, Beech Aircraft, Firestone Tire, and Ford Pinto cases have elevated public sensitivity to abuses of power which ultimately affect the economic and physical well-being of individuals.

The addition of criminality to the stereotyped notion of organizations as impersonal bureaucracies which are inefficient and do not serve the public well may be contributing to a "rip-off mentality" among certain segments of the American public (Conklin, 1977).

Increasingly, individuals *and* organizations are using illegitimate means to gain access to organizational resources that remain elusive when pursued by legitimate means. The individual who took the jumper cables and Revco present parallel examples. In both cases, there was interaction with an organization which was viewed as possessing resources owed the other. In the jumper cable case, the auto service organization did more work than required and the individual was forced to pay. He perceived that the organization held resources he deserved. In the Revco case, the pharmacy company similarly believed the Ohio Department of Public Welfare was in possession of funds legitimately due Revco. In both cases, illegitimate means were used to acquire resources. Though legitimate means were available, they were unsatisfactory alternatives. In the jumper cable example, redress was not attainable through normal bureaucratic procedures. In Revco's case, use of legitimate means worked against the pharmacy's profit-making interest. These examples indicate the presence of emergent normative definitions of the right to use organizational resources.

The interplay among collective definitional processes, perceived exploitation, and redefinition of property rights offers considerable insight into crimes between organizations. The notion is that organizations are exploitative and therefore can be exploited. Given the contribution of tangible organizational characteristics and environmental conditions discussed previously, this provides the missing element in understanding crimes between organizations: a legitimating ideology. These three factors have been suggested here as contributing to organizational crime, thus making organizations victimogenic.

In addition, one other issue of importance to victimology must be addressed.

## Organizations as Surrogate Victims

In crime between organizations, each actor will behave in such a way as to maximize the best interests of the organization per se. Yet, an organization also represents the interests of other categories of actors, and those other interests must also be considered (see Blau and Scott, 1962; Ermann and Lundman, 1978). The Revco double-billing scheme was to benefit that organization by increasing profit and rank. Simultaneously, the act would protect the interests of stockholders by maintaining stock prices and dividends; employees would benefit by maintenance of corporate stability, which would assure employment security; customers would benefit by continued competitive prices; the public-at-large would benefit by any action that would contribute to a stable economy.

As the organization committing the crime represents multiple categories of actors, so does the victim organization. The Ohio Department of Public Welfare specifically represents the interests of Medicaid recipients. However, as a governmental agency, the welfare department also represents the public-at-large. Similarly, employees, as organizational members, are relevant. Because these various categories of actors are related to an organization, victimization results in multiple victims. In the Revco case, the welfare department was the direct victim. Financial loss to the welfare department was immediate. However, the loss was dispersed among the other categories of actors which the organization represents. Welfare fraud imposes costs which affect services to recipients, salaries to employees, and taxes to the general public. Though not involved in the interaction with Revco, these other classes of actors become indirect victims.

Crime between organizations is distinguished from crime between individuals in that victimization is both direct and indirect and multiple victims are involved. The victimized organization emerges in the role of surrogate victim. Directly victimized, it represents the interests of others who are indirect victims because they also suffer harm. However, these other victims are not visible to the organization committing the crime, nor are they aware harm has been done. Hence, they have neither the ability nor the inclination to complain or take action. The organization then becomes a surrogate victim in two ways. First, it is the direct victim, while the other categories of actors which also suffer harm are removed from the crime itself. Second, in negotiating with agencies of social control, the surrogate victim acts not only in its own interests, but in behalf of these invisible victims as well.

This latter fact has implications for sanctions imposed on organizations as offenders. In the Revco case, the welfare department had the power to terminate Revco's contract as a Medicaid provider. Though this was considered, termination was not invoked because it would result in hardship and inconvenience for Medicaid recipients. In the event of termination, recipients would have to turn to other pharmacies for prescription services. Because of age, ill-health, and disability, mobility of many Medicaid recipients is limited. These interests of Medicaid recipients were in conflict with the interests of the public-at-large to control organizational crime by imposition of sanctions. Not wishing to victimize its own clients, welfare chose not to impose this potential sanction on Revco.

Use of other sanctions was similarly curtailed because of concern for the interests of other categories of actors. The Economic Crime Unit, the prosecuting authority in the case, is a commonweal organization representing the interests of the public-at-large, which includes public investors in the stock market. As a result, the ECU conducted the entire case so as to minimize economic impact on the stock market in general and Revco stockholders in particular. The concern for stockholders as a potential class of victims meant the corporate offender was dealt with in ways that minimized negative sanctioning. Awareness of the impact of press releases on the market resulted in tight control of information and minimal publicity. Along with other factors, concern with disturbing the market also encouraged the decision for speedy resolution of the case. This meant proceeding by bill of information rather than indictment and a negotiated plea rather than a trial. Financial impact on stockholders was minimized. However, Revco received this same benefit. The decline in profits that might have resulted from extended publicity was restricted to a short period.[3]

The need for organizations to balance the interests of others does not end with Revco, the welfare department, and the prosecuting authority. Other organizations were involved in the case: the State Highway Patrol and the State Pharmacy Board. As commonweal organizations, they too were charged with protecting the interests of the public-at-large. Primarily social control organizations, each had a vested interest in the final sanctions imposed. The compromises made by the prosecuting authority in behalf of investors were in direct conflict with the interests represented by these other organizations. Though the prosecuting authority also represents the public-at-large, the official role of this organization requires that the divergent interests of various segments of the public be taken into account.

The fact that all organizations represent not only their own interests but those of others has several implications for crimes committed by organizations against other organizations. First, when an organization is victimized, there are multiple victims. The organization, the direct victim, is surrogate for its beneficiaries, the indirect victims. As these other categories of actors are incapable of acting in their own behalf, the organization, as surrogate victim, assumes this function. Second, the criminal and victim organizations may be dealt with by one or more social control organizations. The involvement of multiple organizations means additional interests must be balanced. The interests of all these categories of actors cannot be served simultaneously. Because sanctions against the offender have the potential to *create* additional classes of victims, some interests are compromised in behalf of others. Thus, the potential deterrent impact of the sanctions is mitigated.

## CONCLUSIONS

Revco's computer-generated double-billing scheme against the Ohio Department of Public Welfare has yielded information that supports the inadequacy of traditional victimology for understanding organizations as victims. The traditional approach emphasized micro-analysis, primarily using "victim-precipitation" as an analytical concept. However, understanding the crime of one organization against another is handicapped by this approach because of the nature of the offender and the complexity of the crime.

Instead, a macro-level explanation which moves beyond reliance on the concept of victim-precipitation was suggested. Such structural factors as organizational characteristics, environmental conditions, and supporting ideologies were discussed as conducive to crime between organizations. In the sense that these structural factors exist for all organizations, organizations are victimogenic; that is, particularly susceptible to victimization.

Understanding crime between organizations has been further limited by the traditional focus on direct victimization of one victim by an offender. Analysis of the Revco case revealed that victimization at the organizational level is both direct and indirect, and impact is diffused among multiple victims. The victim organization, in fact, emerges as a surrogate victim. The real victims are indirect victims and as such are incapable of recognizing harm or taking action. The need to balance interests of various other categories of actors complicates imposition of sanctions. Hence, the major consequence of the existence of multiple victims in crime between organizations is that the deterrent impact of sanctions is lessened.

These findings suggest the following: (1) Traditional victimology has inhibited understanding of crimes against organizations, and should be broadened to include the study of organizations as victims; and (2) within the structural explanation offered for the victimization of one organization by another, there is a framework for the explanation of organizational crime in general. This deserves to be pursued.

## NOTES

1. Traditionally, organizations have been viewed as hostile environments for research when the topic is corporate crime (see, for example, Lundman and McFarlane, 1976). This case of Medicaid provider fraud proved no exception. Revco refused to cooperate with the researcher. Therefore, information concerning the case had to be obtained from other sources. Interviews were conducted in all social control organizations investigating the case. This interview data was supported through use of documents, reports, correspondence, minutes of meetings, personal notes, and intra- and interorganizational memos located in the files of these various organizations. Newspaper articles and official public documents related to the case also were used. Because access to the corporation was denied, documents from Revco to the various policing organizations were especially important. One interview was held between the researcher and a Revco official at corporate headquarters. Information from this interview was included and identified.

2. There has been research in victimology which uses a structural approach (Dadrian, 1974). However, micro-analysis has predominated the field.

3. For an extended analysis of the impact on the stock market and Revco's profits during this period, see Vaughan (1979).

## REFERENCES

ADAMS, G. and S. Z. ROSENTHAL (1976) The Invisible Hand: Questionable Corporate Payments Overseas. New York: Council on Economic Priorities.

BLAU, P. M. and W. R. SCOTT (1962) Formal Organizations. San Francisco: Chandler.

CAMERON, M. O. (1964) The Booster and the Snitch. New York: Free Press.

CONKLIN, J. E. (1977) Illegal but Not Criminal: Business Crime in America. Englewood Cliffs, NJ: Prentice-Hall.

DADRIAN, V. (1974) "The structural-functional components of genocide: A victimological approach to the Armenian case." Pp. 123-136 in I. Drapkin and E. Viano (eds.) Victimology: A New Focus. Lexington, MA: D.C. Heath.

DYNES, R. R. and E. L. QUARANTELLI (1974) "Organizations as victims in mass civil disturbances," Pp. 67-77 in I. Drapkin and E. Viano (eds.), Victimology: A New Focus. Lexington, MA: D.C. Heath.

ERMANN, M. D. and R. J. LUNDMAN [eds.] (1978) Corporate and Governmental Deviance: Problems of Organizational Behavior in Contemporary Society. New York: Oxford.

FATTAH, E. (1976) "The use of the victim as an agent of self-legitimization: Toward a dynamic explanation of criminal behavior." Victimology: An International Journal 1 (Spring):29-53.

GEIS, G. (1967) "The heavy electrical equipment antitrust cases of 1961," Pp 139-150 in M. Clinard and R. Quinney (eds), Criminal Behavior Systems. New York: Holt, Rinehart & Winston.

HOLLINGER, R. C. (1978) "Employee deviance against the formal work organization." Presented at the American Society of Criminology Annual Meetings, Dallas, Texas.

LEVINE, K. (1978) "Empiricism in victimological research: A critique." Victimology: An International Journal 3:77-90.

LUNDMAN, R. J. and P. T. McFARLANE (1976) "Conflict methodology: An introduction and preliminary assessment." Sociological Quarterly 17 (Fall):503-512.

MANNHEIM, H. (1965) Comparative Criminology. Boston: Houghton-Mifflin.

NADER, R., M. GREEN, and J. SELIGMAN (1976) Taming the Giant Corporation. New York: Norton.

SHOVER, N. (1976) "Organizations and interorganizational fields as criminogenic behavior settings: Notes on the concept of organizational crime." Knoxville: University of Tennessee. (unpublished)

SILVERMAN, R. A. (1974) "Victim-precipitation: An examination of the concept," Pp 99-109 in I. Drapkin and E. Viano (eds.), Victimology: A New Focus. Lexington, MA: D.C. Heath.

SMIGEL, E. O. (1955) "Public attitudes toward stealing as related to the size of the victim organization." American Sociological Review 21 (June):320-327.

SMIGEL, E. O. and H. L. ROSS (1970) Crimes Against Bureaucracy. New York: Van Nostrand Reinhold.

STONE, C. (1975) Where the Law Ends: Social Control of Corporate Behavior. New York: Harper & Row.

TERREBERRY, S. (1968) "The evolution of organizational environments." Administrative Science Quarterly 12 (March):590-613.

TURK, H. (1970) "Interorganizational networks and urban society." American Sociological Review 35 (February):1-19.

VAUGHAN D. (1979) Crime Between Organizations: A Case Study of Medicaid Provider Fraud. Ph.D. dissertation. Columbus: The Ohio State University.

Von HENTIG, H. (1948) The Criminal and His Victim. New Haven, CT: Yale University Press.

*Chapter 5*

# THE CRIMINALIZATION OF CORPORATE BEHAVIOR: FEDERAL SURFACE COAL MINING

NEAL SHOVER

It is generally accepted that criminologists should devote some of their analytic attention to efforts to enact criminal laws—that is, the criminalization of conduct. The few case studies that have been carried out on criminalization efforts tend to focus on behaviors characteristic of "nuts, sluts and perverts." An adequate understanding of the criminalization process requires analysis of a wider range of behaviors—and, therefore, groups—to which the criminal designation has been applied. This chapter is best viewed as an effort in this direction.

In 1977, President Carter signed the Surface Mining Control and Reclamation Act (Public Law 95-87). The act created an Office of Surface Mining Reclamation and Enforcement (OSM) in the Interior Department, and empowered that office to promulgate regulations for the conduct of surface coal mining. The act also provided both civil and criminal penalties against those who violate provisions of the law or the regulations. What were the political and social processes that led to enactment of the legislation? Do pluralist or radical interpretations of the criminalization process best fit the material? These are issues to be addressed in the body of this chapter.

## SOURCE MATERIALS

A variety of materials were employed. First, I went through all congressional hearings and reports on surface coal mining legislation between 1968 and 1977—more than 10,000 pages in all. Second, I reviewed the major coal industry journals for the nine-year period of 1968-1977. These are *Coal Age,* the *Mining Congress Journal,* and *Mining Engineering.* I also examined issues of journals which represent organizations of smaller mine owners and operators, primarily the *National Independent Coal Leader.* Third, I corres-

AUTHOR'S NOTE: *A number of colleagues read and commented on an earlier draft of this chapter. I am especially grateful to Gilbert Geis and Richard Lundman for their extensive and helpful suggestions.*

ponded with organizations which actively supported or opposed federal surface coal mining legislation, such as the National Audubon Society, the Sierra Club, the National Coal Association, and the National Independent Coal Operators. I also wrote to members of both the House and Senate who appeared to be knowledgable about the history of federal legislative efforts. Finally, I interviewed five persons who I believed were familiar with the legislation's development; these were presidents of two medium-sized coal companies, two individuals engaged in efforts to regulate surface coal mining, and the director of a regional organization of coal operators.

## THEORY

There has been considerable discussion in sociology in recent years about the comparative merits of two different views of the criminalization process: *pluralism* and *radicalism.* Here we only can touch on the differences between them.

While pluralists and radicals are alike in arguing that groups or strata in the population endeavor to create and apply law to promote and protect their own interests, they part company on their view of the structural origins and consequences of these conflictive processes. Pluralists liken the political process to an arena in which diverse groups of citizens struggle to win state support for—that is, laws sympathetic to—their material and symbolic interests. Pluralists assume a diverse and almost random pattern in the origins of these conflicts, with the composition of the competing groups cross-cutting ethnic, regional, religious, and social class boundaries, and shifting one issue to the next. In other words, common interests unite members of unlike groups to such an extent that it is unrealistic to speak of citizens consistently pursuing *class* interests. In the pluralist view, there is sufficient countervailing power among conflicting groups to assure that no single stratum or group consistently wins and employs state power to enhance its interests. On the contrary, the state represents a multiplicity of groups and interests and devises laws and policies which balance and harmonize them. The political process is one of conflict and compromise which assures that, in the long run, government programs and laws "emerge" which serve the interests of the entire citizenry.

Radicals dispute pluralists' claim that class interests and allegiances are inconsequential in the crisscross of groups competing to capture portions of the state's power. Nor do they share pluralists' view of the state as a benign, neutral arbiter of clashing group interests. Instead, radicals argue that, at least under a capitalist system of ownership, control, and production, the class which controls the means of production and the bulk of wealth constitutes a politically dominant stratum. Members of this class enjoy unrivaled access to state power, meaning that they are able to shape law and state programs to their advantage. Radicals contend that there are few effective political checks on such class power—certainly no countervailing forces of the kind envisioned by pluralists. As a result, the state in capitalist societies functions to preserve and enhance capitalist beliefs and structures, and the law is employed to this end (Miliband, 1969).

The debate between pluralists and radicals as to the nature of law and the criminalization process has generated a great deal of heat, but it has shed rather little light on these issues. There would seem to be several reasons for this intellectual impasse. First, the existing data base—that is, empirical studies of criminalization efforts—is heavily skewed toward research which examines the criminalization of underclass behavior (Galliher and Pepinsky, 1978). Second, advocates of the two competing paradigms have vulgarized their opponents' positions and, in the process, have debated what amounts to caricatures. Criminalization process and outcome variables alike have been discussed as *dichotomies* when, in truth, they are much more complex. Particular legislative efforts, for example, have been written about as though they unambiguously can be categorized *either* as favorable or antithetical to elite interests. Reality is not so easy to compartmentalize. Consider the Surface Mining Control and Reclamation Act of 1977. It is 87 pages long and contains 88 different sections. There are probably more than 1,000 provisions in the act. Given this complexity, it becomes difficult to collapse what may be a continuous variable (*degree* of favorableness to elite interests) into a dichotomous format (favorable *or* unfavorable to elite interests). Finally, some of the parties to the debate have focused too narrowly on *criminological* studies and issues. In doing so, they have failed to see the importance for their efforts of larger issues, such as theoretical analyses of the role of the state in industrial societies. Also, analysis of a diversity of studies in the sociology of law may help us to develop a more *general* understanding of the criminalization process than we would be able to gain by restricting ourselves only to criminalization studies.

Studies of the origins of regulatory legislation seem to hold great potential for helping us to move beyond some of the facile analyses and sloganeering of recent polemics over the "true" nature of criminalization and criminal law. This analysis of strip mining legislation seeks to contribute to such an end.

## BACKGROUND

### Coal and America's Coal Industries

A decade ago, surface mining accounted for approximately 40 percent of the coal mined in the United States. By 1976 this had increased to 56 percent, and it is expected to increase even more in coming years. Compared with the problems of deep mining, the process of surface coal mining is simplicity itself. In surface mining, according to the idyllic description of the National Coal Association,

> the coal is produced . . . from seams lying fairly close to the earth's surface. The earth and rock above the coal seam—the overburden—are removed and placed to one side; the exposed coal is broken up, loaded into trucks and hauled away. Bulldozers then grade the overburden to the desired shape, the surface is planted with seeds or young trees, and the land is restored to productive use [*Coal Facts:*11].

There are a number of reasons for strip coal mining's growing importance. Unit production costs are lower than those for deep-mined coal. The average surface miner produces approximately three times the coal produced by the average deep miner (*Coal Data* 1976, 1977:11-16). Other reasons for the increasing use of surface mining include the higher recovery rate; the U.S. Bureau of Mines estimates that surface mining recovers an average of 80 percent of the coal in a seam while deep mining recovers approximately 57 percent (U.S. Congress, Senate, 1972:957). The dramatic increase in the size and handling capacity of heavy equipment also has made surface mining more attractive to the industry, especially in midwestern and western areas where terrain and topography permit the use of extremely large machinery (some of the machines used today are as tall as a ten-story building). Finally, surface coal mining is less hazardous to miners than is deep mining.

The United States, for the moment, has abundant coal reserves, approximately 80 percent of which—given present technology and cost consideration—can be recovered only by deep mining. Still, the United States is estimated to have 45 billion tons of strippable coal reserves (U. S. Bureau of Mines, 1971). Little wonder that spokespersons for the coal industry have taken to calling the United States the "Saudi Arabia of coal." Given this state of affairs, one can understand why plans for coal gasification and liquefaction and slurry pipelines have proliferated in recent years.

Excluding anthracite, which is found exclusively in Pennsylvania, there are three primary grades of coal: bituminous, sub-bituminous, and lignite. The quality of a type of coal is determined chiefly by the amount of BTUs it produces, bituminous coal being of highest quality. Although significant portions of America's coal reserves are located in western states, this coal is of lower quality than mid-western and Appalachian coal. Most western coal is owned by the federal government, though significant portions are held by tribes of native Americans and by the railroads. North Dakota's case is unusual, but it illustrates just how much coal underlies the western states; it is estimated that from one-third to one-half of the entire state has strippable lignite beneath the surface, with the overburden ranging from less than 10 feet to no more than 100 feet.

Despite being somewhat lower in quality, western coal possesses a number of distinct advantages over coal mined in other regions. It costs less per ton to recover (Katell and Hemingway, 1971) and it is lower in sulfur content, making it a preferred fuel for electric utilities because of $SO_2$ emission standards. Also, because western coal seams are much thicker than coal seams in other parts of the United States, the *stripping ratio* is much lower. (This is the ratio of the thickness of the overburden to the thickness of the coal seam.) Stripping ratios in Appalachia and the midwest are approximately 15:1, while the ratio varies in western states from a low of 1.5:1 in parts of Wyoming to a maximum of 18:1 in parts of Montana; the average stripping ratio in western coal seams is approximately 8:1 (U.S. Bureau of Mines, 1971). Finally, the terrain in western states generally is more hospitable to coal strippers; it does not present the steep slopes and narrow valleys which are common in the Appalachian coal fields. For a variety of reasons, therefore, the locus of American coal mining has been shifting to western coalfields during the past 15 years.

In some respects, we can speak of two American coal industries: a large number of small mines and mining companies and a small number of large mines which are owned by the largest coal companies or by the electric utilities. The division between these two industries is, roughly, coextensive with the geographical division between the eastern-midwestern and western coal fields. In 1975, 255 surface mines (only 6.6 percent of all surface mines) produced two-thirds of all the surface-mined coal in the United States. At the same time, 2,837 mines (73.2 percent of the total) produced only 12.7 percent of all the coal surface-mined in the United States. As can be seen, a rather small number of surface mines produces most of the coal mined in the United States. Most small surface mines are located in the Appalachian region, while the largest surface mines are found in the western states.

Western coal production has been increasing and this increase is expected to continue. For example, the Western Energy Company began mining at Colstrip, Montana, in 1968 when 150,000 tons were mined. By 1972 production had increased to 5,501,000 tons and projections were for a production level of between 12 and 13 million tons annually by 1980 (Schmechel and Hodder, 1973). The country's largest coal mine in 1975 was the Decker Coal Company's mine in southern Montana which produced 9.2 million tons. Atlantic-Richfield's Black Thunder Mine in Wyoming's Powder River Basin is expected to produce 20 million tons per year by 1982 (*Coal Age,* August 1976:87, 116).

Over the past 15 years a majority of America's largest coal companies have been purchased by major oil companies. This has occurred at the same time that the locus of coal mining is shifting to the western states. Mining coal on federal lands in the west requires leases from the Department of the Interior and the larger companies have been quick to acquire federal leases. The chairman of Texas Utilities Company told a congressional committee in 1977 that "as you go to the West, it is a new venture and the big boys have gone there, and they have covered themselves with the leases and documents and what not that are necessary, and it has taken the big boys to do it"(U.S. Congress, House, 1977:56).

The shift to western coalfields is responsible in part for changing capital and investment problems of the coal industry. Historically, the primary means of financing the development of mines—in the east—has been for operators to utilize internal cash flows to cover development costs. Since western mining operations tend to be more capital-intensive than eastern mines, little of the financing needed for western development is expected to come from internal investment. Indeed, some of the financing may come from international investment (U.S. Dept. of Interior, 1979).

## Surface Coal Mining: Environmental and Social Effects

The legacy of strip coal mining is immediately apparent to the air traveler over the Appalachian coalfields. In Appalachia *contour mining* is common. In this process, a bench is cut in the side of a mountain to expose a coal seam and then the contour of the mountain is followed, sometimes for miles, in the stripping operation. Traditionally, the trees, rock, and earth which cover the coal seam were "placed to one side" by pushing them over the mountain. In other regions of the country *area mining* is more common; this involves digging a trench to reach the coal seam, with the initial overburden placed to the side of the trench. As subsequent cuts are made, the overburden from the preceding cut are pushed back into the trench from which the coal has been taken. Regardless of the type of surface mining,

> the layers above the coal bed are turned upside down, in effect burying the fertile top soil. At the very least, the surface productivity of the land is ruined. Replacing the rich, humus-laden surface soil is a collection of rocks and boulders, pieces of coal, slate and pyrites. The spoil, whether heaped beside the cuts or pushed over the sides of mountains, is loose and vulnerable to erosion. The loose coal and pyrite, furthermore, are for the first time in millions of years exposed to the air. They begin to oxidize and combine with water to produce a highly acidic runoff. Aside from reshaping the land that has been stripped, the surface mining process produces a sort of fallout that carries the damage of the strippers far beyond the mine site itself [Stacks, 1972:35-36].

In mountainous regions, the fallout can be substantial. Soil banks erode under the onslaught of prolonged rainfall, producing sedimentation and mudslides. Streams become acidic and choked with sediment and silt so that the water—which now runs off the mountain slopes more rapidly because there is less vegetation to hold it—spills out of the stream banks, creating flooding. Streams and lakes become filled with highly acidic mud and water which kills aquatic life.

In Appalachia especially, but in other regions as well, the manner in which stripping has occurred has also damaged dwellings and other property. Blasting cracks house foundations and walls and exposes residents to dangerous flyrock or rock slides. Family cemeteries have been destroyed. Erosion and slides have filled yards and wells with mud and acidic water.

By the mid-1960s the detrimental effects of strip mining no longer could be ignored. Pressures were mounting for regulation or abolition of strip coal mining. At least 28 states enacted or amended strip mining legislation between approximately 1965 and the early 1970s. The initial federal bill was introduced in 1940, but Congress took no action until 1968 when hearings first were held.

## FEDERAL LEGISLATIVE EFFORTS

### The Protagonists

Federal surface coal mining legislation was supported by affected-landowner, environmental, conservation, sportsperson, and Appalachian regional groups. Group members pointed to the destructive impact of surface mining. They also disputed its economy, and charged that actually the mining industry had been permitted to socialize most of the harmful costs of its operations. Legislative proposals ranged from total prohibition of strip mining to severe restrictions on the places where and the conditions under which it could be conducted.

Arrayed against this coalition was the coal industry and those dependent upon it, manufacturers of heavy equipment and the electric utilities—who consume nearly 80 percent of domestically mined coal. In their nine-year effort to frustrate federal legislation, the industry consistently put forth the same set of objections, though it occasionally shifted or modified tactics to take account of developments on the legislative front.

## 90th Congress (1968): Hearings

In 1968 testimony before the Senate Interior Committee, coal industry representatives opposed *any* federal effort to regulate strip coal mining. Although the industry would later modify its opposition, the 1968 testimony contains most of the claims and tactics found subsequently.

Industry representatives were quick to admit that strip mining had produced serious environmental and property damage. This admission was made only in passing, as though it were not worthy of extended comment. The industry claimed that the problems belonged to the past, had been created by a few irresponsible operators—most if not all of whom were no longer mining coal—and would never happen again. The American Mining Congress's (AMC) representative claimed that the problems "have been recognized and are being dealt with by the States in which they exist. [T]here is no indication that additional controls are needed" (U.S. Congress, Senate, 1968:99). In addition, the

> establishment of [federal] guidelines or standards is especially difficult because every mining operation is to some extent unique, and what would be inconsistent with good mining practices in the desert country of the sparsely settled areas of the West might be unacceptable in the East where rainfall and the nature of alternative land uses create far different conditions [1968:104].

The mining industry, the AMC representative assured the senators, has been

> actively engaged for years, on its own initiative and in cooperation with State and local governments, to minimize to every practicable extend the undesirable side effects of mining operations. Where land reclamation is desirable and feasible, the concerted efforts of our industry are increasingly directed to programs designed to bring about land reclamation [1968:97].

Similarly, the vice-president of Consolidation Coal Company (one of the nation's largest) assured the committee that

> the industry today has the technical and engineering staffs to reclaim strip mined land—and they are doing the job—emphatically so! Remarkable progress has been made in the art of land reclamation in the last few years. This progress has been made under local and state supervision, and it is now in good hands [1968:135].

The same witness acknowledged that the coal industry "may have made some mistakes in the past," but, he assured the committee, it is "our considered judgment that a Federal law would only slow down the progress we're now making" (1968:138). An official of the National Coal Association, like other industry representatives, argued that "the principal surface coal mining operators are meeting the obligation to reclaim the land . . . therefore, you have before you reliable evidence to support the conclusion that there is no need for Federal intervention to control the surface mining of coal" (1968:139). During questioning by Senator Len Jordan (Idaho) the witness again distinguished between classes of mine operators:

> We don't say we can defend everything that has been done by a stripper anywhere. . . We are just saying that the major companies at the present time, and the industry as a whole, are all convinced that we have to do this job and we are trying to do it. We are asking for that opportunity [1968:142].

In 1968, and every year thereafter, industry representatives raised the specter of economic retrogression, increasing dependence on foreign fuels, and, possibly, a damaged military defense posture. The coal industry's stand was that federal legislation would be "unnecessary, undesirable, and impractical" (1968:98). Nevertheless, Senator Jordan asked one of the industry's representatives if it would help write an acceptable bill:

> Could not you people in the mining industry suggest amendments to this bill. . . What amendments would you suggest that . . . would provide for some of the things that you think this bill lacks [1968:108]?

The witness again stressed the industry's "opposition to the total concept of Federal Control." He did suggest, however, that the federal government might spend monies on research:

> Research efforts by the Federal Government to aid and supplement the research of the mining industry will far better serve the public interest than the vast system of Federal

> regulatory control as envisioned in [the bills]. Cooperative research is an appropriate use of Federal resources [1968:105].

Those who testified in favor of some type of federal surface mining statute were divided, especially on the question of the adequacy of state reclamation laws. Harry Caudill, a former Kentucky legislator and the author of *Night Comes to The Cumberlands* and *My Land Is Dying,* urged the senators to "view with caution and skepticism industry claims that present State laws are working well and that voluntary efforts are handling the problems satisfactorily" (1968:92). Others were less critical of state efforts. One witness, for example, told the committee that "new and strong state laws are all fairly recent, and the time to see whether they are going to be sufficient without further public action has not yet passed" (1968:338).

This tendency to defer to state regulation was supported by the states themselves. Oklahoma's governor informed the committee by letter that "all segments of the mining industry in Oklahoma have shown their willingness to cooperate in implementation of our reclamation law. I see no reason to add additional burdens to the State by passing Federal reclamation legislation" (1968:287). Georgia's chief geologist assured the senators that "in the light of the legislation to control surface mining passed by the 1968 session of the Georgia General Assembly, we see no need or justification for [federal legislation]" (1968:326).

There were two points which, although they did not figure prominently in the 1968 hearings, later would assume much more importance. First, a number of senators and witnesses suggested that the states were reluctant to develop strong regulatory programs for fear of harming local mining industries. It was said that the coal industry threatened relocation to less restrictive states in order to water down state control efforts. By equalizing the regulatory costs, it was argued, a federal law would eliminate any competitive advantage a state with weak laws might have. Nonetheless, Wyoming's governor told the committee that "surface mining regulation should not be used to equalize competitive situations. It should be limited to its stated purpose—to conserve natural resources" (1968:351). The western governors recognized that, in the words of Montana's Tim Babcock, they were standing "on the threshold of development of great coal deposits" (1968:346). Wyoming's Stanley Hathaway told the committee that states with similar problems resulting from surface mining should be

> allowed the opportunity to cooperate regionally in solving their problems. . . . States could cooperate in developing legislative objectives. . . . Rehabilitation standards could be adopted.

> Duplication in research work could be avoided. Above all, by common agreement and action any competitive advantage to one state over another resulting from regulations could be prevented [1968:352].

A second issue raised almost in passing in the 1968 Senate Interior Committee hearings appears in a written statement provided the committee by the National Association of Manufacturers (NAM). It notes that "a perpetual, overhanging possibility of federal intervention with a set of differing regulations . . . would make realistic planning—from both the operational and economic standpoints—practically impossible" (1968:307). The NAM was suggesting that the uncertainty about federal regulatory legislation could prove to be damaging to the mining industry, quite apart from the substance of regulations themselves.

**Interim Events**

The Senate Interior Committee did not report a bill in the 90th Congress and further hearings were not held until 1971. In the interim, the states made various efforts to deal with surface mining problems. There was a dramatic increase in the pace and volume of state regulatory legislation. West Virginia had enacted the nation's first surface coal mining law in 1939, but it was not until the mid- to late 1960s that most states became seriously involved in surface mining regulation. Between 1965 and 1977, 38 states either enacted or amended their strip mining laws. Tennessee, a coal producing state, is not atypical in this regard; its initial law was passed in 1967.

Because my analysis concentrates on legislative efforts at the federal level, I have not dealt with conflict between mine operators and environmental groups at the state and local level; nor did I try to collect any data on these conflicts. However, if Tennessee is typical at all, conflict at the congressional level has been matched by conflict at the local level. In 1972 a group of citizens in the coalfields of east Tennessee formed SOCM (Save Our Cumberland Mountains) in order to resist what they believed were the unchecked abuses of coal companies. Still in existence, the group has gathered and published data on the operations of coal firms, agitated for stronger state and federal laws, and urged various state and federal agencies fully to enforce existing laws. SOCM has, for instance, used media exposés and court suits to make the state of Tennessee enforce its coal truck weight limits and has threatened legal action to force the Tennessee Valley Authority to cease permitting overweight coal trucks to unload at its steam plants. In 1974 coal operators in east Tennessee formed their own organization, FACT (Facts About Coal in Tennessee), with the avowed intention of combating SOCM's efforts. Both groups have been extremely active on strip mining issues at the state level. In other Appalachian states, new organizations of strip mining companies were established during the late 1960s and early 1970s. Many of these organizations adopted names suggestive of an environmental consciousness: for example, the West Virginia Surface Mining and Reclamation Association. Representatives of these various groups crossed swords with environmental groups not only at the state level, but at the federal level as well; many of them testified before congressional committees considering federal regulations. Further, examination of those testifying before Congress indicates that comparable local conflict was taking place in some of the western states where coal mining only recently has been conducted on a large scale.

The states also made a limited effort to cope with strip mining problems cooperatively by establishing the Interstate Mining Compact Commission. The Compact was conceived in 1964 at the Southern Governors' Conference to prod the mining industry "to utilize techniques designed to minimize waste of our natural resources" and take action "to assure adherence to sound standards and procedures by the mining industry" (Annual Report 1978, 1979:6). The Compact required four members before it became operational, but this was not accomplished until 1971 when Oklahoma joined—having been preceded by Kentucky, Pennsylvania, and North Carolina. Currently there are 14 member states, all but two (Texas and Oklahoma) located in either the midwestern or Appalachian regions. None of the western states with large coal reserves has elected to join the Compact. During the Commission's organizational period, it noted:

> Many states have failed to pass adequate legislation for the protection of their lands and water and because of this the federal government has now undertaken the task of writing a law that will apply nationwide. Had the Compact become active a few years earlier, there would be no need for federal legislation in this field for it is required that each state pass adequate surface mining legislation in order to become a member of the Compact [Untitled, n.d.:3-4].

The Compact movement was a case of too little too late and may have foundered on the problem of regional competition for coal markets. Some states apparently felt they had little to gain by tough regulations when their reclamation problems and existing environmental problems were not as severe as those in other regions, chiefly in Appalachia. In any case, the western states generally have not elected to join the Compact.

Certainly, midwestern and eastern coal operators fear western competition. A 1974 study notes that "Midwestern coal markets have declined in recent years. . . . A part of the regional demand for Midwestern coal has been transferred to the Northern Great Plains where extensive low-sulfur coal reserves are currently being developed." This movement, along with the "emerging Midwestern market for coal-based synthetic fuels, indicates a need for coordinated programs to develop the region's coal reserves" (Carter et al., 1974:5). The president of the Harlan County (Kentucky) and National Independent Coal Operators' Associations worries about western coal invading traditional markets for eastern coal. He suggests forming an "operators' league to promote the use of Appalachian coal," saying that "if we don't unite our efforts together [sic] and offset some of the Western strippers," the Eastern coal industry may be severely damaged (*National Independent Coal Leader,* April 1977:21).

## 92d and 93d Congresses: Hearings and Legislation

By 1971 any hope that the states could and would regulate surface mining had all but disappeared. In the 92d Congress (1971-1972) and 93d Congress (1973), approximately 20 bills to regulate strip mining were introduced. Committees of both the House and Senate held hearings. A witness for Save Our Kentucky, a citizens' group opposing strip mining, told the House committee that

> Kentucky's reclamation attempts have been a wholesale failure. Reclamation is a fiction. It is the grandest lie perpetuated upon the American public. The so-called reclamation which the strippers practice does not even merit the description of repair work [U.S. Congress, House, 1972:541].

Replacing 1968's cautiously optimistic view for reclamation was the firm conviction by legislation supporters that strip mining would have to be banned entirely or, failing that, the job of regulating it turned over to the federal government. The former deputy director of West Virginia's Department of Natural Resources told the Senate committee

> the surface mining industry in Appalachia is not amenable to social control. . . . In a word, State regulation is no match for the surface mine industry, at least in West Virginia, and I suspect from superficial observations the same can be said elsewhere [U.S. Congress, Senate, 1972:285, 287].

The witness doubted that a federal law would make any appreciable difference, but he noted such a law would have some advantages:

> [A]t least it offers escape from the depressing game of economic blackmail which has so frequently reduced State legislatures and State regulatory bodies to virtual impotence [U.S. Congress, Senate, 1972:287].

Environmental, conservation, and affected-landowner groups were not completely united during the 1971-1973 hearings; their proposals took both "hard" and "soft" positions. The "hard" position called for an end to all strip mining commencing from six to eighteen months after enactment of legislation. The "soft" position advocated a ban on strip mining only in areas or locations where the possibility of adequate reclamation could not be conclusively demonstrated, such as on mountain slopes of 14 degrees or more. A variant of the "soft" position called for the abolition of certain *types* of strip mining, primarily contour stripping in mountainous regions. Supporters of both "hard" and "soft" positions maintained that deep mining could be stimulated sufficiently quickly to minimize any temporary decrease in coal production.

The coal industry, especially its largest producers, reversed the stand it had taken in 1968 when it opposed all federal legislation—it now supported the establishment of minimum federal *guidelines* for regulating surface mining. The states would be given the opportunity to develop regulations consistent with the guidelines and, after a time, the federal government would be empowered to enforce federal regulations in states which failed to develop an acceptable regulatory program. The president of the National Coal Association (NCA) told the Senate Committee that

> [t]he *responsible companies* of the coal industry now support reasonable Federal legislation which will enable the States to do a more effective job of regulating surface mining and reclamation. We believe fair and reasonable regulation, uniformly enforced, can and will allow the continued production of coal for the national interest and will assure that all operators—including *some who might otherwise shirk their duty, to the detriment of the whole industry* and the Nation—follow good reclamation practice [1972:315; italics added].

Although less enthusiastic, the National Independent Coal Operators' Association supported the NCA's position (U.S. Congress, Senate, 1972:775-777). On the other hand, the Tri-County Independent Coal Operators (Virginia)—which, presumably, represented smaller operators—continued to oppose federal legislation, generally making the same arguments the entire industry had advanced in 1968, that the states were adequate to the task (1972:619-623).

The industry's "support" of federal legislation hardly could be called enthusiastic. In fact, it appears that it was pushed into publicly endorsing the concept of federal controls only by the extreme measures advocated by strip mining opponents. Moreover, the industry asserted that it would support only "workable, reasonable, and realistic" legislation. These words were to be repeated many times over the next six years as the industry nominally continued to support federal legislation, but only its own kind of legislation.

The 1971-1973 hearings were critical for the coal industry. Although our reconstruction of motives and objectives necessarily is speculative, the record suggests that the largest coal producers were primarily concerned with protecting, if not enhancing, the value of their western coal leases. They pursued this objective by working to defeat the call for the abolition of strip mining. They sought to allay the concerns of western lawmakers who did not want their states to become another Appalachia, used their nominal support for federal legislation to pressure "irresponsible" elements in the industry to put more effort into reclamation, and to establish the importance of *flexible* and *general* federal guidelines.

In emphasizing its support for "fair, realistic, and reasonable" federal legislation, the coal industry advanced eight key points in its 1971-1973 congressional testimony:

(1) Because of the immense diversity in mining conditions and problems in the 50 states, federal regulations would have to be broad and flexible rather than specific and rigid.

(2) The environmental abuses of strip mining were a product of the past and were produced by a small percentage of operators, those on the fringe of the industry. Comparable abuses could not and would not occur again.

(3) They would not occur again because the "science" of reclamation now was so much more developed than in earlier times. In fact, developments in reclamation technology were taking place at such a fast pace that virtually all land would be reclaimable in the future.

(4) A total ban on strip mining would reduce coal production, make the United States more dependent on foreign fuels, and lead to electric power shortages.

(5) A total ban on strip mining would produce rising unemployment and have a severe economic effect in areas dependent on coal mining.

(6) A rapid or substantial conversion to underground mining could not prevent these consequences because the lead time required to open deep mines was too long.

(7) A return to deep mining would consign increasing numbers of miners to death or injury, because deep mining, as conducted traditionally, is more hazardous than strip mining.

(8) The federal government should play a larger part in supporting and conducting coal-related research.

It is not possible here to convey fully the extent of the industry's persistence in calling for flexibility in the guidelines. Nor is it possible to document the extensive disagreement over details of the various federal proposals. The industry generally avoided taking a rigid stance on any single aspect of the debated bills. For example, various bills called for the segregation of soil strata during a mining operation so they could be put back in the same order in which they were removed. Hanna Coal Company's president told the Senate Committee:

> If the land is to be revegetated, the most important consideration of the reclaimer is to create a good growing medium for vegetation. Reclaimers have discovered that often the topsoil—where it exists—has become worn with time and usage and that a previously unexposed layer will contain better nutrients for maintaining healthy growth. More often than not, a mixture of several layers of earth uncovered in mining will provide the best growing medium.
>
> We have found in some cases that the upper strata are the best and should become the future growing surface. Each case is different, however, and for this reason I would suggest that any legislation drafted by this committee reject the idea that, replacing topsoil after mining necessarily insures good reclamation [U.S. Congress, Senate, 1972:320].

The industry, it must be noted, called for flexibility only in those areas which would increase its options in planning and conducting mining activities. It opposed flexibility in legislative provisions which would have decreased its own operating options or increased uncertainties or unpredictability. The industry, for example, urged a narrow, inflexible provision for public comment on mining permit applications and for citizen suits against coal operators. While many environmental groups favored entrusting enforcement responsibilities to the Environmental Protection Agency, fearing that the Interior Department had too much of a protectionist relationship with the coal industry, the industry insisted that the Interior Department was the "logical" place for surface mining enforcement responsibilities. Similarly, industry representatives generally opposed the inclusion of criminal sanctions in federal legislation:

> [W]e believe most emphatically that criminal sanctions in a Federal surface mining statute would be most inappropriate. It will not be possible to meet the due process requirements of the law. Moreover, in matters affecting mined land where every operation is necessarily unique, it is most unfair to suggest that operators should be subject to criminal sanctions when the regulations issued pursuant to the act will be couched in generalized language. The proper enforcement mechanism in such situations is by way of injunction, the terms of which will explicitly define the impact of the regulation in a specific mining operation [1972:283].

Examination of the legislative record clearly indicates that opposition to criminal penalties was not a major concern of the coal industry. The matter received only peripheral attention; nor was the industry completely united on the issue. The NCA did not actively oppose the provision for criminal sanctions, suggesting only that they be reserved for cases in which a person "*knowingly* authorized, ordered or carried out" a violation of the law (1972:411; italics in original).

The importance of allaying western lawmakers' anxieties cannot be underestimated. This was made doubly important by the fact that an overwhelming majority of committee members in both the House and the Senate were from western states; in 1972, 77 percent of the House committee members were westerners while 100 percent of the Senate committee members were from the west. Arizona's Senator Paul Fannin told Tennessee's Senator Howard Baker that he had seen the damage done by stripping in Appalachia and "I don't want that to happen to my State" (1972:586). Also, some western lawmakers' constituents resisted the encroachment of coal strip mining. A Montana witness told the Senate committee:

> We do not want our beautiful State of Montana ruined, nor other Western States, in order to decrease the air pollution in the East when the true motive behind strip mining is a higher margin of profit for the coal companies. This greed and irresponsibility of the coal companies will lead to the destruction of our area and others like it [1972:646].

The coal industry was successful in the 1971-1973 session in defeating the call for a ban on strip mining and, in general, appeared to convince western lawmakers that their region was sufficiently different from Appalachia that they need not worry. A resident of the

Hopi-Navajo reservation in New Mexico praised Peabody's Black Mesa project, which prompted Utah's Senator Frank Moss to remark:

> I am somewhat reassured to hear from the Peabody representative here today, as well as you, that there is restoration work going on and that there will be no permanent damage on Black Mesa after the coal is removed" [1972:471].

And if he ever had any doubts about the coal operators' intentions and integrity, Wyoming's Senator Clifford Hansen put them aside during the hearings:

> We are proud of the fact in Wyoming we have had our own land restoration law for some time and it has been accepted in good faith by the mining industry. They have been very cooperative and as a matter of fact they have suggested a number of measures that have since been written into law that I think reflect the kind of rapport that must exist between industry and legislators if we hope to come up with workable laws.
>
> It is one thing to hear from people not involved in the business. I don't say those persons shouldn't be heard. I do say it is crucially important that an affected industry be heard also [1972:449].

After hearing the testimony, Arizona's Senator Paul Fannin said:

> I will pay tribute to Department of the Interior when this is all completed in 30 years. The land there will be in much better condition than when it started. In fact, as it goes along, they will have a productivity they do not have now. They will have facilities that are not available now [1972:586].

Finally, perusal of the committee reports suggests the industry was legislatively successful in its efforts to portray the abolition of strip mining as catastrophic:

> The Committee is aware of the critical energy situation facing the nation and the very significant role that coal plays in the energy supply picture. This was a significant factor in directing the Committee's attention to means for regulation and control of coal mining surface activities rather than outright prohibition. The latter would create an intolerable situation in the presently overstrained energy supply picture [1972a:19].

The committee further expressed its concern about the economic and employment problems which would result from a ban on strip mining, and declared its belief that reclamation not only was possible but that first-rate reclamation work was being conducted.

Although the House did pass a bill (H.R.6482), the 92d Congress did not enact surface coal mining legislation.

### 93d and 94th Congresses: Legislation and Vetoes

Gerald Ford's opposition to legislation regulating strip mining was well known. Consequently, the coal industry could stall as long as Ford occupied the White House. Between 1971 and 1977—when a bill was finally signed—the industry supported the concept of federal controls but worked to defeat any specific bill. Its 1971-1973 testimony and the oil embargo of 1973 had served to put advocates of strong strip mining controls in a defensive position. In 1974, the bill which passed the 93d Congress (S.425) was modified to deal with the industry's contentions that regulation led to increases in unemployment. Bill S.425 contained a section providing extra unemployment benefits for anyone put out of work by surface mine shutdowns resulting from federal controls. The same section gave preference in contracts for reclamation work to former mine operators or employees who possessed the requisite heavy equipment (U.S. Congress, Senate, 1974). Still, the industry was not entirely happy. For one thing, the bill contained provisions permitting the Secretary of the Interior to designate lands or areas unsuitable for mining. The industry position opposed any flat prohibition on mining in designated areas or terrain conditions.

In 1974 Congress passed S.425 and sent it to the White House. President Ford vetoed the bill on December 30, 1974. Congress responded by passing a similar bill (H.R.25) in 1975 which Ford vetoed on May 20 of that year. Ford gave four principal reasons for the action: (1) the unemployment the bill would cause, (2) higher electric bills for consumers, (3) America's resulting increasing dependence on foreign oil, and (4) the resulting decrease in coal production (U.S. Congress, House, 1975).

### 95th Congress: The Surface Mining Control and Reclamation Act of 1977

Relevant congressional committees had been angered by Ford's stated rationales for vetoing H.R.25 and they seemed determined to pass similar legislation early in the 95th Congress. Added to the fact that Congress had already enacted strip mining legislation twice, this resoluteness assured passage of another statute. The Surface Mining Control and Reclamation Act of 1977 was the second bill introduced in the House and the seventh bill introduced in the Senate—that is, H.R.2 and S.7.

Between 1973 and 1977 Congress held no hearings on strip mining legislation and the president vetoed the bills it passed. Developments generally strengthened the industry's interpretations of the nation's energy problems and the need to do nothing to handicap surface mining. Other developments, however, made the industry more willing to accept federal controls.

Data suggest that the climate of uncertainty surrounding federal coal mining regulations was making it difficult for the industry to attract external capital and, thus, to plan mining ventures. Colorado's Governor Richard Lamm indicated that in the west,

> One of the problems we have . . . is the whole question of predictability. If we can have better predictability about where coal development or energy development is going to take place, we have a number of coal leases in Colorado, and we are getting production on less than 10 percent of our coal leases . . . and what we would like to know is to have some overall idea about where the impact is going to take place so that we can react to it and anticipate [U.S. Congress, House, 1977:101-102].

These remarks were echoed by Atlantic-Richfield's representative, who testified that "what we need is to understand the rules and to be able to obey them from this point forward. . . . We need to understand what the risks are, and what the ground rules are" (U.S. Congress, House, 1977:61). Of course, considerable mining planning had been conducted during the period when strip mining legislation was debated. Protection of these plans and capital investments was a major plea by the industry by 1977.

As a presidential candidate, Jimmy Carter had stated that he would have signed the second bill Ford had vetoed. According to *Coal Age* (December 1976:21), part of Carter's reason for pledging to do so was his belief that "substantial increases in coal production and utilization will only come with a stable regulatory climate. The veto of the strip mining bill merely prolonged the climate of uncertainty." The industry realized that it no longer could count on a sympathetic president's veto of any bill it opposed.

Finally, it could be argued that western coal developers by now *needed* federal legislation for other reasons as well. Much of western coal, as noted, is owned by the federal government, even though private parties own the surface rights. Federal regulation of some kind would be required for the mining of federally owned coal. In 1976, the Interior Department secretary issued regulations for surface coal mining on federal lands (known as the "211 regs"). This move, by itself, meant that western mine operators would now be operating under some kind of federal controls.

For various reasons, then—a new president, the industry's difficulty attracting capital because of regulatory uncertainty, and the fact that the entire issue of federal controls had become moot—by 1977 the coal industry was ready to "capitulate." At the same time, Congress was concerned with writing a bill with which "the industry [can] live."

Although by 1977 passage of legislation was a foregone conclusion, there remained groups and individuals who wanted to contest issues which were then moot. They had not heard the message that Congress no longer was considering a total ban on strip mining. The president of Save Our Cumberland Mountains told the House subcommittee "we feel that the only sensible thing is to start a regulated phase out of strip mining" (U.S. Congress, House, 1977:29). Others wanted to contest the issue of whether mined land could be reclaimed, apparently not realizing that Congress had already accepted the industry's assurances that the "science of reclamation" was progressing daily. A Montana cattle rancher called this a "dangerous premise," arguing that

> reclamation research is a new form of alchemy. Although old-time alchemists abandoned the idea of turning base metals into gold, the present-day reclamation alchemists are now faced with transforming money and spoil material into diverse vegetative forage.
>
> The saddest aspect . . . is that the reclaimers and researchers and the general public desperately want to believe the new alchemic theory, because it rationalizes the advisability of strip mining [1977:51].

Members of the House and Senate subcommittee assured industry representatives that they wanted to write a bill which would permit the industry to *increase* coal production. Arizona's Representative Morris Udall told a utility company representative:

> I want to assure you that I believe the Nation has got to increase the production of coal over the next decade. It is our insurance policy against the Arabs. . . . I want to write [a bill] that lets more coal be mined and lets it be mined at a reasonable cost . . . but this uncertainty is paralyzing the country [1977:49].

Although the entire coal industry opposed the 1977 bill (H.R.2), at least nominally, a clear split in interest between eastern and western coal producers became evident. (Many believe that federal controls do not work as heavy a burden on the larger coal producers as on the smaller mine operators.) These two segments of the industry differed in the adamance and extent of their opposition to H.R.2. Western witnesses made statements of opposition almost in an obligatory fashion, but then went on to offer detailed amendments. Eastern witnesses were more vociferous—even defiant—in their statements of opposition.

Eastern and western industry representatives were united, however, in their calls for amendments to three sections in H.R.2: provisions for *public hearings* and *citizen suits,* and requirements for determining the *hydrological consequences* of surface mining. At the same time, western witnesses were concerned about prohibitions on mining on *alluvial valley floors,* provisions for acquiring *surface owner consent* to mine, and restrictions on the length of mining *permits* and the permit renewal process. While these issues did not concern eastern operators, they were more concerned about the provision that mined land be returned to its *approximate original contour.* Generally, eastern operators were fearful that (1) the bill effectively would make it impossible to mine much eastern coal and (2) would make it too costly for small operators to comply. Western operators expressed few, if any, concerns in these areas.

In their testimony, the coal industry and utilities consistently sought to increase their options under the forthcoming bill while limiting others' options. Industry saw citizen suits and public hearings on applications for mining permits as potential sources of harassment and, therefore, delay and unpredictability. With respect to citizen suits, Congressman Udall reassured a witness:

> One of the most utter frustrations of people who fear coal mining in Appalachia is that there is no one to talk to. The legislature has been bought off, in their view, and at the county courthouse the judge and all the lawyers are on the side of the coal companies.
>
> If they had some place to be heard and take out the frustrations, a lot of times that helps. You give your wife the right to complain and sometimes she won't complain. They don't have a forum to be heard, and that is the philosophy behind the citizen suit provisions, to legitimize and *standardize* some kind of forum through which people who haven't been heard on the strip mining provisions could be heard [1977:50; italics added].

Bill H.R.2 was passed by Congress on August 3, 1977, and the president signed it. As passed, the act contains a number of provisions clearly beneficial to the coal industry; for example, federal funds for coal research, for training graduate mining engineers and other technical personnel, and for providing assistance to operators of small mines to help them meet regulatory costs and requirements. There are very few rigid requirements in the act; flexibility and variances generally are permitted. Consequently, some of the most difficult problems faced by lawmakers have been transformed into administrative problems, to be worked out between regulators and the industry. While there surely are some provisions in the act which the coal industry would have preferred were absent—such as a coal severance tax—the bill, as President Carter noted when he signed it, does not seem overly restrictive.

## IMPLICATIONS

Studies such as this of the criminalization of corporate or white-collar conduct demonstrate how difficult it can be to assess the comparative merits of pluralist and radical perspectives on the criminalization process. Nevertheless, this is my principal task in the remainder of the chapter.

### Interpretation

What kinds of data would support a radical interpretation of the Surface Mining Control and Reclamation Act? Perhaps the strongest support would be evidence that the coal industry *initiated* or actively *supported* federal regulatory legislation. Historically, other industries adopted such a stance toward state regulation. Kolko (1965), for instance, has shown that, far from opposing it, the railroads were among the strongest supporters of railroad regulation at the turn of the century. They looked to the federal government and the newly created Interstate Commerce Commission to help them solve problems which they had been unable to deal with by themselves: specifically, destructive competition, rate fluctuation, severe state regulation, and powerful shippers. But the railroads wanted and got controls on their own terms. Consequently, they were able to use "political means to solve economic problems while maintaining the essential theory of social priorities and values of a capitalist economy" (Kolko, 1965:238). However, there is no indication that coal operators took a similarly active part in promoting federal regulation of their industry, at least in the early stages. Consequently, my data do not show clear, strong support for a radical interpretation of legal change.

On the contrary, there is ample evidence to suggest that a pluralist interpretation applies reasonably well to early efforts to enact federal strip mining legislation. During the 1970s those supporting strip mining regulation were described in the *Mining Congress Journal* as "impassioned crusaders," "environmental zealots," "small groups of elitists" and as a "vociferous and obstinate few." Their proposals were derided as "reckless folly" and "frenzied fretting." Efforts on behalf of environmental legislation were ridiculed as "arousing public passions" and "simplistic appeals." An examination of industry publications and congressional testimony suggests that the industry genuinely was concerned about the possible impact of environmental groups. Indeed, there seemed to be good reason for it to fear the efforts of these groups because they were successful in prompting Congress to examine the problems of strip mining and, eventually, to move toward new regulations. This clash between supporters of regulation and the coal industry is consistent, then, with a pluralist perspective on the process of legal change.

While a pluralist interpretation explains the early stages of the strip mining debate, this interpretation seems to break down when we examine later stages of the legislative process. In fact, limited support for the radical position can be found.

Is it possible that the coal industry, although it did not *originally* want federal regulation, eventually came to see the value of it or was successful in shaping proposed legislation to its own advantage? Evidence that it successfully employed such a strategy would tend to support a radical perspective—at least on the later stages and the outcome of the regulatory movement.

Friedman and Ladinsky's analysis (1967) of the emergence of workmen's compensation systems in the United States shows a comparable process at work—although it required Currie (1971) to point this out. Businesspersons initially were opposed to the enactment of workmen's compensation programs and effectively exercised a veto against them. Gradually, however, they came to see that such programs were not only inevitable but also desirable. Compensation systems would give businesses "a guaranteed, insurable cost—one which could be computed in advance on the basis of accident experience" and "would, in the long run, cost business less than the existing system" (Friedman and Ladinsky, 1967:68-69). Industry turned its attention to helping write the kind of legislation it wanted.

> [I]t was imperative that the new system be in fact as actuarially predictable as business demanded; it was important that the costs of the program be fair and equal in their impact upon particular industries, so that no competitive advantage or disadvantage flowed from the scheme. . . . In exchange for certainty of recovery by the worker, the companies were prepared to demand certainty and predictability of loss—that is, limitation of recovery. The jury's caprice had to be dispensed with. In short, when workmen's compensation became law, as a solution to the industrial accident problem, it did so on terms acceptable to industry [1967:69].

There is a lesson here: the clash of multiple groups in the early stages of a controversy does not mean necessarily that a resultant legal change equally reflects the interests of the various groups. It still can serve primarily the interests of the most powerful protagionists. As Carson (1974) wisely notes:

> [T]he emergence of criminal laws apparently antithetical to the interests of powerful groups is something which should be interpreted with considerable caution. While legislative compromises and a heterogeneity of elites must indeed be allowed for, this does not mean that the existence of overt attempts to regulate the activities of powerful interest groups automatically undermines the entire [radical] model of emergent criminal law [1974:75].

If some countervailing political forces are rendered impotent in the later stages of popular movements for legal reform, how does this process work? Gunningham's (1974) analysis of the passage of pollution laws in the United States and in England provides one answer. He notes that while the debate over pollution legislation appears to support the pluralist vision of the political process, this is misleading because the debate took place in a context in which serious questioning of prevailing political-economic structures and beliefs did not occur. Consequently, "any compromise solution to conflict is always resolved, not from within the full range of alternatives which represent the interests of the contending groups, but within a narrower span which favors the interests of capital" (1974:85). This process occurred repeatedly during debate over the strip mining statute. Throughout the debate, for instance, mining corporations continued to plan future mining ventures. During the later stages of the debate they used the alleged existence of these plans and investments as an argument for concessions from legislation supporters and from members of Congress. Their efforts were successful because the bill under consideration was modified to make it more "reasonable"—to protect their alleged investments.

Pluralistic processes also can be forestalled if there is a split within the ranks of an industry facing regulatory pressures. In such a situation, larger and more powerful elements of the industry covertly may support regulation—especially regulation requiring even moderate compliance costs—in order to control competition from smaller firms. Carson's examination of factory legislation in Britain led him to such a conclusion about the

> role of manufacturers, particularly some of the more substantial among them, in supporting and encouraging limited governmental interference in the affairs of industry through the applications of criminal law [1974:74].

I can only speculate about the occurrence of similar machinations by part of the coal industry during Congress's deliberations over the 1977 Act. As I noted earlier, the largest (that is, western) coal producers were not as opposed to federal regulation as the smaller, Appalachian firms. It can be argued that western coal producers and legislators used federal legislation to enhance the value of their coal by imposing high reclamation requirements/costs on Appalachian producers. By doing so, western coal could be made more attractive economically. It is possible also that the larger firms, recognizing that because of competition the industry could never police itself, supported federal reclamation legislation to force smaller producers to become more environmentally conscious in their mining operations. Finally, because larger firms must engage in longer-range planning, they may have been more concerned than smaller firms to attempt to stabilize and control potential sources of political uncertainty. Pressures from those opposed to strip mining was one source of political uncertainty. Consequently, larger coal companies may have cooled their resistance to or even supported federal regulation in order to curb the activities of environmentalists.

I have suggested that pluralist conceptions of the political process help us understand the origins and short-term consequences of efforts to regulate surface coal mining. I have suggested also that this view may not help us if we want to understand the fate of legislation after the point was reached when some type of bill seemed assured. While many people believe that the 1977 Act was a victory for environmental groups, I have shown that the coal industry's capitulation to some extent occurred at a propitious time, one of its own choosing. Moreover, analysis of the law shows that in nearly every case coal companies are permitted flexibility and variances. Sufficient administrative flexibility in the law resulted in a statute the mining operators could "live with."

## CONCLUSION

Max Weber argued that a system of rational law was an indispensable accompaniment of, if not a precondition for, the emergence of capitalism. "The capitalistic form of industrial organization, if it is to operate rationally, must be able to depend upon calculable adjudication and administration" (1961:208). Apparently, maximizing the rationality or predictability of law in action continues to be one of the principal objectives of capitalists, whether they are owners or managers. Perhaps sociologists' traditional concern with the *criminalization* of behavior per se has been misguided. The history of strip mining legislation indicates that businessmen do not object to the criminalization of their conduct so much as they object to the inclusion of irrational or incalculable elements in criminalizing legislation. When regulation seems inevitable or desirable, industry's strategies shift from trying to defeat or stall bills to assuring that whatever legislation is enacted is "realistic and workable"—in short, legislation that is predictable in its operation and that takes seriously its interpretations of problems and priorities. At the same time, industry endeavors to socialize costs while holding control over their operations, and maintaining if not increasing options and operating flexibility. Businessmen strive to eliminate sources of unpredictability in the law, or to convert them into *administrative* problems—which can be worked out later with regulators.

A close analysis of the Surface Mining Control and Reclamation Act shows that there are very few areas where operators are faced with inflexible provisions. In areas which impose financial burdens on the industry, such as the coal severance tax, the cost is fixed and, therefore, calculable. Finally, there are some provisions of the act which clearly are beneficial to the coal industry or, at least, to its largest producers. On balance, while the coal industry may not have wanted federal legislation, there is little or nothing in Public Law 95-87 which is overly harmful to it.

## REFERENCES

Annual Report 1978 (1979) Lexington, KY: Interstate Mining Compact Commission.

AYRES, R. F. (1977) Coal: New Markets/New Prices. A Battelle Columbus Laboratories Report. New York: McGraw-Hill.

BAGGE, C. E. (1973) "New day dawns for Great Plains coal." Pp. 196-203 in G. H. Gronhovd and W. R. Kube (eds.), Technology and Use of Lignite. Washington, DC: U.S. Dept. of Interior, Bureau of Mines.

CARSON, W. G. (1974) "The sociology of crime and the emergence of criminal laws." Pp. 67-90 in P. Rock and M. McIntosh (eds.), Deviance and Social Control. London: Tavistock.

CARTER, R. P. et al. (1974) Surface Mined Land in the Midwest: A Regional Perspective for Reclamation Planning. Argonne, IL: Argonne National Laboratory.

*Coal Facts* (1976) Washington, DC: National Coal Association.

*Coal Data* 1976 (1977) Washington, DC: National Coal Association.

CURRIE, E. (1971) "Sociology of law: the unasked questions." Yale Law Journal 81 (November):134-147.

FRIEDMAN, L. M. and J. LADINSKY (1967) "Social change and the law of industrial accidents." Columbia Law Review 67 (January):50-82.

GALLIHER, J. F. and H. E. PEPINSKY (1978) "A meta-study of social origins of substantive criminal law." Pp. 27-38 in M. D. Krohn and R. L. Akers (eds.), Crime, Law, and Sanctions. Beverly Hills, CA: Sage.

GUNNINGHAM, N. (1974) Pollution, Social Interest and the Law. London: Martin Robertson.

KATELL, S. and E. L. HEMINGWAY (1971) Basic Estimated Capital Investment and Operating Costs for Coal Strip Mines. Washington, DC: U.S. Dept. of Interior, Bureau of Mines.

KOLKO, G. (1965) Railroads and Regulation 1877-1916. New York: Norton.

MILIBAND, R. (1969) The State in Capitalist Society. New York: Basic Books.

SCHMECHEL, W. P. and R. L. HODDER (1973) "Operations of Western Energy Co." Pp. 11-19 in G. H. Gronhovd and W. R. Kube (eds.), Technology and Use of Lignite. Washington, DC: U.S. Dept. of Interior, Bureau of Mines.

STACKS, J. F. (1972) Stripping. San Francisco: Sierra Club.

Staff, U.S. Bureau of Mines (1971) Strippable Reserves of Bituminous Coal and Lignite in the United States. Washington, DC: U.S. Dept. of Interior, Bureau of Mines.

Untitled (n.d.) Lexington, KY: Interstate Mining Compact Commission.

U.S. Congress, House of Representatives (1972a) Regulation of Strip Mining. Hearings before the Subcommittee on Mines and Mining of the Committee on Interior and Insular Affairs. 92d Congress, 1st Session. Washington, DC: U.S. Government Printing Office.

——— (1972b) Providing for the Regulation of Strip Coal Mining, for the Conservation, Acquisition, and Reclamation of Strip Coal Mining Areas, and for Other Purposes. Report (Together with Separate View) from the Committee on Interior and Insular Affairs. 92d Congress. Washington, DC: U.S. Government Printing Office.

——— (1973) Regulation of Surface Mining. Hearings before the Subcommittee on the Environment and Subcommittee on Mines and Mining of the Committee on Interior and Insular Affairs. 93d Congress, 1st Session. Washington, DC: U.S. Government Printing Office.

——— (1975) Veto of the Surface Mining and Control Act of 1975. Message from the President of the United States. 94th Congress, 1st Session. Washington, DC: U.S. Government Printing Office.

——— (1977) Surface Mining and Control Act of 1977. Hearings before the Subcommittee on Energy and the Environment of the Committee on Interior and Insular Affairs. 95th Congress, 1st Session. Washington, DC: U.S. Government Printing Office.

U.S. Congress, Senate (1968) Surface Mining Reclamation. Hearings before the Committee on Interior and Insular Affairs. 90th Congress, 2d Session. Washington, DC: U.S. Government Printing Office.

——— (1971) Surface Mining. Hearings before the Subcommittee on Minerals, Materials, and Fuels of the Committee on Interior and Insular Affairs. 92d Congress, 1st Session. Washington, DC: U.S. Government Printing Office.

——— (1972) Surface Mining Reclamation Act of 1972. Report from the Committee on Interior and Insular Affairs. 92d Congress, 2d Session. Washington, DC: U.S. Government Printing Office.

——— (1973) Regulation of Surface Mining Operations. Hearings before the Committee on Interior and Insular Affairs, 93d Congress, 1st Session. Washington, DC: U.S. Government Printing Office.

——— (1974) Surface Mining Control and Reclamation Act of 1974. Conference Report to Accompany S.425 93d Congress, 2d Session. Washington, DC: U.S. Government Printing Office.

U.S. Department of Interior (1979) Permanent Regulatory Program Implementing Section 501(b) of the Surface Mining Control and Reclamation Act of 1977. Washington, DC: Office of Surface Mining Reclamation and Control.

WEBER, M. (1961) General Economic History (F. H. Knight, trans.). New York: Collier.

*Chapter 6*

# CORPORATE CRIME: A CROSS-NATIONAL ANALYSIS

CHARLES E. REASONS and
COLIN H. GOFF

"Order" approaches have been prevalent in the study of crime for some time (Horton, 1966; Bloom and Reasons, 1978); they have largely emphasized the study of the criminal. The law is a given factor which reflects "society's interests." In recent years, however, a competing perspective has emerged which views the law and its various manifestations as emanating from conflict rather than consensus (Reasons and Rich, 1978). This emphasis has produced a focus on power and conflict as essential for the understanding of crime and criminality.

Table 1 provides a contrast of order and conflict theories of crime. The order perspective views the criminal law as reflecting the common good and controlling the criminal. The conflict perspective identifies ruling class interests which are set into motion in order to maintain class dominance as the cause of criminal law. According to order theorists, criminal behavior is due to inadequate socialization and establishes moral boundaries, while a conflict perspective views such behavior as a consequence of class divisions and serving to reduce class strains. One radical economist has suggested that lower-class, organized, and corporate crime can be explained as rational reactions to circumstances (Gordon, 1973). Street crime represents a rational response to the oppressive conditions of low income life. Organized crime in areas of great public demand (drugs, gambling, prostitution) is also seen as a rational response to economic demands. Finally, corporate crime is perceived as an eminently rational way to earn profits in capitalist societies. Such crime offers high profits and holds little chance of detection, prosecution, or conviction. Therefore, given differences in power and subsequent economic alternatives, each form of criminal activity is a rational way to survive. This is quite contrary to the order perspective assumption that criminals are largely pathological and irrational in their behavior. While these differences in approach are presented in "ideal type" form, they nonetheless emphasize distinctions between order and conflict theories of crime.

*Table 1* Order and Conflict Theories of Crime*

| | *Criminal Law* | | *Criminal Behavior* | |
|---|---|---|---|---|
| | *Cause* | *Consequence* | *Cause* | *Consequence* |
| Conflict Paradigm | Ruling class interests | Provide state coercive force to repress the class struggle and to legitimize the use of this force | Class divisions which lead to class struggle | Crime serves the interests of the ruling class by reducing strains inherent in the capitalist mode of production |
| Order Paradigm | Customary beliefs that are codified in state law | To establish procedures for controlling those who do not comply with customs | Inadequate socialization | To establish the moral boundaries of the community |

*Adapted from Chambliss (1973).

## COMPETITION LEGISLATION

There is an increasing body of evidence supporting the conflict interpretation of the creation of laws, though much of this literature deals with "victimless crimes" and concerns the United States. In a recent empirical testing of the conflict and consensus theories, McDonald (1976) found general support for the conflict explanation. Using crime data from several nation-states, this author concluded that factors such as urbanism, GNP, police force size, extent of the school system, data collection apparatus, political representation, mass media, and unemployment explained much of the variance in crime rates. However, McDonald's analysis does not deal with the emergence of laws. Legislation controlling corporations provides an apparent contradiction to the conflict perspective's assumption that laws are specifically aimed at maintaining dominant class interests. Chambliss (1973) discusses this flaw in conflict analysis by noting that the view has not generally appreciated the extent to which laws will be passed in order to reduce the manifestation of conflict between social classes:

> An historical analysis of such laws would show that they emerge during times of open conflict between social classes and that the real extent to which the laws interfere with capitalists' interests through enforcement, subsequent legislation, and court decisions is negligible [Chambliss, 1973:22].

Furthermore, Chambliss suggests that traditional conflict analysis has failed to study the administration of laws and the extent to which such administration reflects elite interests. Finally, conflict theorists have tended to neglect the fact that there may be on occasion interelite conflict which is reflected in legislation.

This chapter provides a preliminary assessment of the usefulness of a conflict interpretation of the emergence and administration of major laws of economic competition in Canada, the United States, Australia, and the United Kingdom.[1] It will assess both the original competition legislation and its subsequent administration within the conflict perspective. The origin, enforcement, and administration of competition law becomes the major area of analysis, and the law is viewed as an instrument of the powerful rather than as serving the "public" interest.

The extent to which competition laws are *expressive* and *instrumental* also will be ascertained.[2] The expressive aspects of law refers to the values given expression by its enactment. Thus, competition legislation gives expression to the values of free enterprise and economic competition rather than to those of restricted and monopolistic market practices. The instrumental nature of a law is ascertained by looking at the magnitude of the sanctions and the extent of enforcement. By reviewing the laws' development historically, the expressive purpose will be discovered, while an analysis of studies concerning laws' impact will suggest instrumental effects.

## Origins of the Legislation

Legislation to foster competition emerged first in Canada in 1889, the United States in 1890, Australia in 1906, and Britain in 1948.

As both the United States and Canada became more industrialized, the appearance of corporations began to change the economic and social order in the latter part of the nineteenth century. Important factors contributing to the rise of state interference with the economy and with corporate dealings included (1) the movement from an agricultural to a commercial and industrial society; (2) increasing inequality in the distribution of property, and the amassing of wealth by a few; (3) a growing need to leave property in the hands of other persons; (4) the transformation of ownership of visible property into intangible powers and rights, such as corporate shares, including a system of social security in place of ownership of goods; and (5) the passage of property from private to corporate ownership (Geis and Meier, 1977:11).

In Canada, the Anti-Combine Act was passed in 1889, largely due to the efforts of small businessmen who were feeling the squeeze from emerging corporations and the combines/monopoly policy which ensued (Ball, 1934). As one commentator has noted:

> Legislation was only introduced and amended when class conflict threatened the ruling class; that is, when the petit bourgeoisie felt squeezed out of the competition, or when working class discontent, intensified during periods of economic depression, threatened severe disruption [Young, 1974:73].

Agricultural interests were also opposed to big businesses (Macmillan, 1972; Bliss, 1973). Furthermore, the conservative government in power at the time wanted to show that it was concerned about rising prices, while at the same time it desired to direct attention away from its national policy, which included a protectionist tariff to foster Canadianization of the business sector. Finally, there was an anti-U.S. economic imperialism argument based on the notion of keeping Canadian business in the hands of Canadians. Thus, as did the subsequent U.S. legislation, the Anti-Combine Act was enacted in Canada due in part to basic ideological and class conflicts.

In the United States, corporations were attacked for their oppressive and ruthless business practices; the fear of concentrated wealth and power; and policies of the government which favored big business at the expense of other groups (Dudden, 1957). Agrarian groups and other populist supporters felt that the foundation of U.S. economic ideology, such as free competition, free enterprise, and a relative diffusion of wealth and power, was being destroyed by large corporations and subsequent monopolies. Thus, it would appear that the passage of the 1890 Sherman Anti-Trust Act signaled a symbolic victory for the small farmer and other populists over the large corporation. The symbolic crusade (Gusfield, 1963) to control corporations was recognized by the state with the passage of this legislation, which supported the traditional values of the agrarian class rather than those of the emerging capitalist class.

The Australian Industries Preservation Act of 1906, prohibiting combines to the detriment of the public interest, appears largely to have been a response to concerns similar to those noted in the United States and Canada, although there was less vehement collective opposition (Lindgren et al. 1974). The act was aimed at foreign monopolies, particularly from the United States (Hopkins, 1979). Britain had no codified laws of competition until the 1948 Monopolies and Restrictive Practices Act. It may come as a surprise to learn that Britain, the "mother" country of the other three nation-states, was the last to pass equivalent legislation. However, before 1948 in

Britain the three legal doctrines of monopoly, conspiracy, and contracts in restraint of trade were believed to be sufficient to regulate the prevention and restriction of competition. While monopoly precedents date back to the Magna Carta, these proved to be too narrow, requiring exclusive control and willful and malicious intent. Furthermore, common law regarding conspiracy and restraint of trade proved largely ineffectual due to its vagueness and sociopolitical interpretation. As one authority on British competition policy notes:

> It is interesting to speculate why two potentially effective legal doctrines—conspiracy and restraint—had become so vitiated by the mid-twentieth century that completely new legislation was required to control restrictive practices. The development of the law offers no decisive logic or reason. . . . [T]he explanation of these apparently arbitrary swings in the public policy of the law on competition must be sought mainly in extra-legal considerations: the social and political environment and the personal evaluations of judges themselves [Hunter, 1966:72].

Furthermore, while populism was a contributor to American and (though to a lesser extent) Canadian legislation, the socialist movement in the late nineteenth century in Britain responded in a different way. British socialists had little faith in antitrust legislation and preferred to encourage consumer cooperatives, price control, and public ownership of industry.

The 1948 Act in Britain was largely due to the impetus of the White Paper on Employment Policy, published in 1944. Concern was expressed in the paper about the power of corporations to combine and the potential negative effects of such actions. Close association of business with government during the war gave officials an inside look at corporate practices, while work with U.S. corporations offered a contrasting perspective on business methods. Subsequently, U.S. and British comparative studies were undertaken which suggested the preference for competition rather than trade association regulations (Hunter, 1966). It was largely the civil service, rather than an outside pressure group, which pushed for such legislation in Britain.

**Enforcement of Competition Legislation**

While it would appear that the initial legislation in the countries under study primarily had symbolic significance, its instrumental impact may be discovered by looking at enforcement policies and practices.

The period immediately following a law's enactment is crucial for its effectiveness in behavior control. In the case of the Sherman Anti-Trust Act in the United States, no extra funds were provided by Congress for enforcement, nor was an antitrust division created in the Department of Justice until 1903 (Neale, 1960; Thorelli, 1955). In fact, until 1903 only one criminal and three civil suits were successfully prosecuted against corporate defendants. However, during this same period, six of seven suits against labor organizations were successfully pursued by the government. As McCormick observes:

> The significance of this early enforcement pattern should be apparent. Since the government was either unwilling or unable to execute the antitrust law, it could not be taken as a serious effort to regulate corporate behavior [1977:32].

Of the 1,551 antitrust prosecutions instituted in the United States from 1890-1969, only 45 percent were criminal cases, although the laws are essentially criminal violations. Of the 536 cases resulting in some type of criminal conviction, only 26 (4.9 percent) led to actual serving of a prison sentence. The first eleven imprisonments involved union and labor defendants, while it was not until 1961 (Electrical Conspiracy case) that businessmen were imprisoned for price-fixing and monopolization (McCormick, 1977). The use of nolo contendere pleas, fines, and orders of prohibition further indicated the "coddling" of corporate offenders (see also Clinard, 1952; Hartung, 1950; Sutherland, 1949; Posner, 1970). There appears to have been a consistent antilabor bias in the use of the Sherman Act, particularly in the imposition of penalties. This suggests the class nature of the enforcement.

Generally, enforcement in the United States has been token and the risk of getting caught, prosecuted, and penalized has been practically nonexistent compared with the potential benefits from such criminality. However, there has been increased attention to the anticompetition laws since the 1960s due to the following factors:

(1) the growth of the consumer movement, particularly the work of Ralph Nader;
(2) highly publicized corporate violations giving evidence of corporate irresponsibility;
(3) increased environmental concern;
(4) reaction to the overconcentration of concern with street crime and poverty problems;
(5) minority revolutions and crimes by government and corporations evidenced in Vietnam and Watergate;
(6) emergence of conflict analysis; and
(7) the increasing recognition of the power of large organizations over our lives [Clinard and Yeager, 1978].

The record of enforcement of combines legislation in Canada is even more appalling than in the United States. No permanent enforcement agency was established after passage of the 1890 law. It was not until 1899 that the legislation was changed to make it actually enforceable (Goff and Reasons, 1978).

In their analysis of combines enforcement from 1889-1972 Goff and Reasons (1976) used three indices:

(1) the actual enforcement record of combines laws;
(2) number of mergers and the prosecution of them by the government as well as the degree of economic concentration in various industrial sectors; and
(3) amount of financial assistance and the number of employees allowed to the Combines Branch by the federal government.

They argued:

> It is hard not to conclude that the federal Government has protected the growth of the largest Canadian corporations, not only through its lack of effective legislation and enforcement of combines laws, but also at whom it directs its policing power. The data collected suggest that the Combines Branch has centered its attention upon the investigation, prosecution and conviction of small and medium-sized companies and corporations, leaving the very largest corporations to freely engage in their monopolistic policies [Goff and Reasons, 1976:487].

Although the criminal law carries the threat of up to two years' imprisonment, no one was imprisoned under the combines laws in Canada until 1974! At that time, a small businessman was sentenced to two years for his second offense of misleading advertising concerning television sets (Snider, 1978). Many large corporations, such as Simpson-Sears and T. Eaton Company, have been frequent recidivists, but their representatives have not been jailed. Most penalties have been miniscule fines and orders of prohibition. Although mergers and concentration in Canada have rapidly increased since World War II, little attention has been paid to these areas. For example, between 1960-1972 there were 3,572 mergers in Canada, while 16 cases were prosecuted and 3 resulted in conviction under combines legislation. The penalties consisted of Orders of Prohibition for two defendants and a fine of $40,000 for the third. Since 1923, when mergers became possible offenses under law, only .003 percent of the total number of mergers have been charged as violating combines laws, and only .005 percent of the mergers have resulted in conviction (Goff and Reasons, 1978:103-104). Current proposed revisions include a legalization of monopolies through specialization agreements when they are felt to be beneficial to Canada in the international marketplace. The changes indicate that business interests are getting their wishes (Stanbury, 1977).

Although the Australian Industries Preservation Act of 1906 made it

> illegal to enter into a combination in relation to the trade and commerce among the states of the Commonwealth with intent to restrain trade or commerce to the detriment of the public or with intent to destroy or injure by means of unfair competition any Australian industry,

the meager evidence available suggests the act had no real impact. In fact, early judicial decisions so emasculated this provision that no cases were brought under the act from 1913 to 1964 (Pengilley, 1965). It appears that restrictive practices and the subsequent monopolistic or oligopolistic markets were viewed as being legitimate forms of business activity.

> Restrictive practices have a long history in Australia and have come to be regarded by businessmen and consumers alike as normal business behavior. Indeed, certainly until very recently the average businessman would have been rather hurt to hear his trade agreement described as restrictive [Karmel and Brunt, 1962].

Largely due to a 1958 Western Australian Royal Commission report on restrictive trade practices, and a 1959 constitutional committee recommendation that commonwealth powers be extended in the field of restrictive practices, the Trade Practices Act of 1965 was passed in Australia. Based on the British Act of 1956, it proved largely ineffectual. In debating on a new bill in 1974 the Australian attorney general concluded that the 1965 Act

> has proved to be one of the most ineffectual pieces of legislation ever passed by this Parliament. . . . Restrictive trade practices have long been rife in Australia. Most of them are undesirable and have served the interests of the parties engaged in them, irrespective of . . . interests of Australians generally. These practices cause prices to be maintained at artificially high levels. They enable particular enterprises to attain positions of economic dominance which are then susceptible to abuse—they interfere with the interplay of competitive forces which are the foundation of any market economy; they allow discriminatory action against small businesses, exploitation of consumers and feather-bedding of industries [Dale, 1976:227].

Subsequently, the Trade Practices Act 1974 was passed, modeled to some extent on the Sherman Act and Clayton Act of the United States. The 1974 Act prohibits anticompetitive activities, placing the burden of proof for exception on the company. Furthermore, it provides for financial penalties, rather than merely cease and desist orders. More specifically, it provides for up to a $50,000 fine for an individual and $250,000 fine for a body corporate if found guilty of restrictive trade practices provisions. Such proceedings are civil and not criminal; however, for violation of the consumer protection provisions a person can be fined $10,000 or imprisoned for six months (Proceedings, 1976).

Although modeled after U.S. legislation, the Australian Trade Practices Act of 1974 allows a business to obtain "authorization" exempting it from the act's control. It is required to show that the exemption does not harm competition and is beneficial to the public interest. In a recent review of the authorization practice, Pengilley (1978) notes that between October 1, 1974 and June 30, 1977 only 25 authorizations in restraint of trade were granted on merits, while 2,907 were denied on merits. However, the "other category" totaled 1,724, including an unspecified number of firms receiving "clearance," which amounted to an exemption to the law. Finally, it is noted that 1977 legislative changes occurred following a new coalition government's commissioned report. The public benefit test was changed because the committee believed it "too harsh upon applicants, particularly as regards the elements of 'substantiality' and 'not otherwise available' " (Pengilley, 1978:214). The committee was chaired by T. B. Swanson, formerly Deputy Chairman of Imperial Chemical Industries of Australia and New Zealand. The revisions portend a lessening of controls. The remarks of a magistrate and barrister-at-law seem appropriate:

> I now submit that neither these sections, nor all the provisions of the Companies Act, nor all the "relevant" Acts, comprise a code, in the sense of a complete system of rules, as to corporate offenders. Nor is such a code made complete by reference to the common law offense of conspiracy to cheat and defraud. I suggest we delude ourselves by seeking shelter under a detailed prescription of offenses and penalties. We have inspected and catalogued the trees; we have to look at the wood. . . . The Courts, at all levels, will continue to function and to play their parts as best they can. *I conclude, however, by suggesting that our society has hardly begun to comprehend the nature and extent of corporate crime let alone reach the point of realizing that our attempts to combat it are at a very primitive level* [Goldrick, 1976:61-62; italics added].

Nonetheless, judicial interpretation will be crucial in making the new provisions viable and instrumental. The history of the Australian judiciary suggests this law may end up like previous legislation.

The 1948 British Monopolies and Restrictive Practices Act set the stage for subsequent legislation. Based on a public interest criterion, the act was found lacking in effect and thus Parliament in 1956 passed the Restrictive Trade Practices Act. This act was based on the presumption that agreements restrictive of competition were contrary to the public interest, although it allowed for exemptions based on public benefit. It appears that this legislation brought about a dismantling of restraints of trade which had been so widespread in Britain (Cairns, 1976). An initial survey covering 262 agreements given up between November 1956 and mid-1957 found that prices were lower in 32 percent of the cases subsequent to termination, 5 percent were higher, and 63 percent were about the same. If the restrictive agreements had continued, 32 percent of the respondents felt there would have been less competition, 66 percent the same amount, and 2 percent believed there would have been more competition (Heath, 1961). Hunter (1966) concludes that the 1956 Act had considerable success: He notes that most restrictive agreements which have been prohibited have not been contested before the Restrictive Practices Court. At the end of 1964, there were only nine successfully exempted agreements of a total of 1,850 agreements voluntarily canceled.

While the 1956 Act appears to have reduced open and flagrant restraints of trade, other forms of anticompetitive practices emerged. Hunter (1966:161-190), in his chapter entitled "Results of the 1956 Act," states that "information agreements" arose to restrict competition. In such agreements, parties typically notify a trade association about data regarding price, discounts, rebates, and other market facts which are "shared" by others. Such price information allows for price uniformity and stability which leads to price leadership and price fixing, particularly where oligopolies exist. Thus, price leadership appears to have been one way of getting around the 1956 Act. Furthermore, Cairns (1976:343-357) suggests that the increased number of mergers giving rise to the 1965 Mergers Act was related to the "success" of the 1956 legislation. It seems that business responded to the 1956 Act with other methods which would restrict competition. The Merger Act of 1965 was passed in an attempt to control their growth. Nonetheless, only 3 percent of potentially reviewable mergers came before the Monopolies and Mergers Commission between 1965 and 1974, and only nine (less than 1 percent) were found contrary to the public interest and prohibited (Cairns, 1976:348). Although the 1973 Fair Trading Act somewhat widened the basic criteria for merger and monopoly decisions (one-third to one-fourth of market share), problems with proportion of assessed cases, legalese, criteria, investigation and enforcement resources—among others—suggest difficulty in pursuing cases in this most significant area. Finally, the political context of decision-making is all-important. Thus, the secretary of state, rather than a relatively independent official, has the power to refer mergers.

## THE STATE AND COMPETITION

In this analysis of competition legislation in four capitalist countries, it appears that such legislation is largely expressive and symbolic, rather than instrumental and effective. While the extent of "open class conflict" and severity of penalties varies from one nation-state to another, it appears that in both the emergence and administration of competition legislation the conflict perspective is more applicable than the consensus view. The role of the state in the creation, maintenance, and change of laws needs more careful consideration.

The concept of the state stands for various specific interconnected institutions. The state system includes the following elements: the government, the administration, the military and the police, the judiciary, and the units of subcentral government (Milibrand, 1969). In capitalist nations, such as those under investigation, the dominant economic class largely controls the state. The significance of discussing the role of the state in the study of crime is the realization that state interests represent dominant interests, and in terms of capitalist society, this means economic elites.

> The state is . . . a political organization created out of force and coercion. The state is established by those who desire their material basis and who have the power (because of material means) to maintain the state. The law in capitalist society gives political recognition to powerful private interests [Quinney, 1974:52].

While our contemporary system of laws arose with the establishment of the state (Tiger and Levy, 1977), the instrumentalist approach emphasizing that law is a direct response to elites of the capitalist class appears oversimplified (Panitch, 1977; Balbus, 1977).[3] The law, in general, and competition law specifically, must be analyzed within the context of the social, political, and economic realities of the nation-state. Competition legislation largely reflects the general interests of capitalism rather than necessarily the specific interests of particular capitalists. It provides the appearance of widespread control while its substance does not greatly inhibit increasing concentration and monopolization.

## DISCUSSION

While the order and conflict theories of crime provide ideal types for analyzing both criminal law and criminal behavior, they must be put to further scrutiny with specific analysis of particular types of laws and criminality. This analysis of the emergence and administration of competition legislation suggests the laws are largely symbolic and expressive, with both their enactment and periods of enforcement corresponding with specific social, political, and economic crises and conflict within the respective nation-states. With increasing inflation, unemployment, and growing movements for more consumer and local power, the state and its agents may be called upon increasingly to regulate or otherwise control the economy. Given the states' close relationship and reliance on business in these capitalist societies, commissions, inquiries, laws, prosecutions, or other remedies may go against the interests of specific capitalists, but will likely be supportive of the capitalist system.[4]

We must not only analyze the state in our study of crime, but also the influence one state, or its agents, has on other states. Thus, we should begin to provide international comparisons of crime generally, and upperworld/corporate crime more specifically.[5] The influence of the multinational corporation on the political economy of various nation-states must be addressed. The global corporation negates the assumptions of classical and neoclassical economic theory and transcends the boundaries of the nation-state in its values, interests, and concerns (Muller, 1976). Given the preliminary evidence presented here, we would concur with Block (1977:359) that

> the capacity and willingness of corporate leaders to reform society has been exaggerated by the theory of corporate liberalism. The strongest corporations have an aversion to the interference in their internal affairs which an extension of government power would entail.

Until recently, students of crime largely neglected power as an important factor in understanding the nature and scope of crime in society. Likewise, classical and neoclassical economists nearly excluded consideration of economic power in their analyses. ("Economic power exists when a person is able to get an economic advantage to the disadvantage of others who don't know anything of it or, if they knew it, are too weak to protect themselves" [Arndt,

1976:33].[6]) The power of the state and business interests in creating, shaping, and administering legislation in the best interests of capitalism is evident in this analysis. The notion that organizational and system needs are important in studying corporate crime transcends the individualistic orientation found in the study of crime generally and white-collar crime specifically. More attention needs to be directed to organizational crime, given the tremendous impact organizations have on our daily lives (Ermann and Lundman, 1978). A recent article defines the concept of organizational crime:

> Organizational crimes are illegal acts of omission or commission of an individual or a group of individuals in a legitimate formal organization in accordance with the operative goals of the organization, which have a serious physical or economic impact on employees, consumers or the general public [Schrager and Short, 1978:412].

The traditional approach toward white-collar crime, including establishing criminal intent, individual responsibility, and applying civil-criminal distinctions, fails to address adequately organizational behavior. Therefore, new methods of researching and controlling such behavior are needed (Lehmann and Young, 1974; Young, 1975; Lundman and McFarlane, 1976; Christie, 1976).

## NOTES

1. These countries were selected due to available information and their similar British common law background.

2. The general objective of legislation to control monopoly and restrictive practices is to maintain and, in some cases, restore competition in the relevant private sector of the economy (Hunter, 1966:15).

3. In noncapitalist nation-states the state explicitly represents working-class interests through the institutions of the state, including the law (Reasons and Rich, 1978). As Chambliss and Seidman (1971:4) note, a state's legal order is a self-serving system to maintain power and privilege and this is inevitable.

4. Adams (1976:24) suggests that of the three basic determinants of industrial structure—technology, basic institutions, or particular institutions—"particular laws and customs are probably the determinants of industrial structure most susceptible to alteration via public policy."

5. Clinard (1978) provides an interesting analysis of crime in Switzerland, showing how relatively little street crime they have, while white-collar and organizational crime is quite prevalent.

6. Arndt (1976:34) states that once we free ourselves from such traditional notions, we discover that (1) some kinds of economic power are compatible with economic competition; (2) some kinds of economic power are restrictive or preventive of economic competition; (3) certain kinds of economic power change the quality and character of competition; (4) state laws, institutions, and public administration set and can change economic conditions and rules of competition; (5) we must address the

power of multinational corporations to evade state laws and plan international trade and; (6) we should recognize the power arising with the separation of property and its control.

## REFERENCES

ADAMS, W. J. (1976) "International comparisons in the study of industrial organization." Pp. 19-32 in A. P. Jacquemin and H. W. de Jong (eds.), Markets, Corporate Behavior and the State. The Hague: Martinis Nijhoff.

ARNDT, H. (1976) "Power and concentration." Pp. 33-52 in A. P. Jacquemin and H. W. de Jong (eds.), Markets, Corporate Behavior and the State. The Hague: Martinis Nijhoff.

BALBUS, I. D. (1977) "Commodity form and legal form: An essay on the 'relative autonomy' of the law." Law and Society Review 11 (Winter):571-588.

BALL, J. (1934) Canadian Anti-Trust Legislation. Baltimore, MD: Williams and Wilkins.

BERMAN, H. J. and W. R. GREINER (1966) The Nature and Functions of Law. Brooklyn, NY: The Foundation Press.

BLISS, M. (1973) "Another anti-trust tradition: Canadian anti-combines policy 1889-1960." Pp. 39-50 in G. Porter and R. D. Cluff (eds.), Enterprise and National Development. Toronto: Hakkert.

BLOCK, F. (1977) "Beyond corporate liberalism." Social Problems 24 (February): 352-361.

BLOOM, D. M. and C. E. REASONS (1978) "Ideology and crime: A study in the sociology of knowledge." International Journal of Criminology and Penology 6 (July):19-30.

BROZEN, Y. [ed.] (1975) The Competitive Economy. Morristown, NJ: General Learning Press.

CAIRNS, J. P. (1971) The Regulation of Restrictive Practices: Recent European Experience. Ottawa: Economic Council of Canada.

_____(1976) "United Kingdom competition policy and practices." Pp. 335-390 in T. D. McDonald et al., Studies of Foreign Competition Policy and Practice, Vol. 2. Ottawa: Consumer and Corporate Affairs, Supply and Services Canada.

CHAMBLISS, W. J. (1973) Functional and Conflict Theories of Crime. Module 17:1-23. New York: MSS Modular Publications.

_____and R. B. SEIDMAN (1971) Law, Order and Power. Reading, MA: Addison-Wesley.

CHRISTIE, R. M. (1976) "Comment on conflict methodology: A protagonist position." The Sociological Quarterly 17 (Autumn):282-294.

CLARK, J. D. (1931) The Federal Trust Policy. Baltimore, MD: Johns Hopkins Press.

CLINARD, M. B. (1952) The Black Market. New York: Holt, Rinehart & Winston.

_____(1978) Cities with Little Crime: The Case of Switzerland. Cambridge, England: Cambridge University Press.

DALE, R. G. (1976) "Australian competition policy 1976 and practices." Pp. 219-259 in T. D. McDonald et al., Studies of Foreign Competition Policy and Practice, Vol. 2. Ottawa: Consumer and Corporate Affairs', Supply and Service Canada.

DUDDEN, A. P. (1957) "Men against monopoly: The prelude to trustbusting." Journal of the History of Ideas 18 (Fall):587-593.

EDWARDS, C. D. (1967) Control of Cartels and Monopolies, an International Comparison. Dobbs Ferry, NY: Oceana Publications.

(1969) "The world of antitrust." Columbia Journal of World Business (July-August):11-25.

______(1975) "Policy toward big business: What lessons after forty years?" Journal of Economic Issues 9 (June):343.

______(1976) Studies of Foreign Competition Policy and Practice, Vol. 1. Ottawa: Consumer and Corporate Affairs, Supply and Services Canada.

ERMANN, M. D. and R. J. LUNDMAN (1978) Corporate and Governmental Deviance. New York: Oxford University Press.

GEIS, G. (1968) White Collar Criminal: The Offender in Business and the Professions. New York: Atherton Press.

______and R. F. MEIER (1977) White Collar Crime. New York: Free Press.

GOFF, C. and C. E. REASONS (1976) "Corporate crime in Canada: A study in crime and punishment." Criminal Law Quarterly 18 (August):468-498.

______(1978) Corporate Crime in Canada: A Critical Analysis of Anti-Combines Legislation. Scarborough, Ontario: Prentice-Hall.

GOLDRICK, J. B. (1976) "Treatment of persons offending against the provisions of the relevant legislation: The role of the courts in regard to corporate offenders." Corporate Crime. Proceedings of the Institute of Criminology No. 19. Sydney: University of Sydney.

GORDON, D. M. (1973) "Capitalism, class and crime in America." Crime and Delinquency 19 (April):163-186.

GUSFIELD, J. (1963) Symbolic Crusade. Urbana: University of Illinois Press.

HART, P. E. et al. (1973) Mergers and Concentration in British Industry. Cambridge, England: Cambridge University Press.

HARTUNG, F. (1950) "White collar offenses in the wholesale meat industry." American Journal of Sociology 56 (July):25-32.

HEATH, J. B. (1961) "Restrictive practices and after." Manchester School, 29 (May).

HOPKINS, A. (1975) "On the sociology of criminal law." Social Problems 22 (June):608-619.

HORTON, J. (1966) "Order and conflict theories of social problems." American Journal of Sociology 72 (May):701-713.

______(1979) "Pressure groups and the law." Contemporary Crisis 3:69-81.

HUNTER, A. (1966) Competition and the Law. London: George Allen & Unwin.

JONES, F. D. (1926) "Historical development of the law of business competition." Yale Law Journal 35 :42-55, 207-234, 905-938.

KARMEL, P. H. and M. BRUNT (1962) The Structure of the Australian Economy. Melbourne: F. W. Cheshire.

LEHMANN, T. and T. R. YOUNG (1974) "From conflict theory to conflict methodology: An emerging paradigm for sociology." Sociological Inquiry 44 :15-28.

LINDGREN, K. E., H. H. MASON, and B. L. J. GORDON [eds.] (1974) The Corporation and Australian Society. Sydney: Law Book Company.

LUNDMAN, R. J. and P. T. McFARLANE (1976) "Conflict methodology: An introduction and preliminary assessment." Sociological Quarterly 17 (Autumn):503-512.

McCORMICK, A. E., Jr. (1977) "Rule enforcement and moral indignation: some observations on the effects of criminal antitrust convictions upon societal reaction processes." Social Problems 25 (October):30-39.

MACHLUP, F. (1952) The Political Economy of Monopoly. Baltimore, MD: Johns Hopkins Press.

McDONALD, L. (1976) The Sociology of Law and Order. Montreal: Book Center, Inc.

McDONALD, T. D. et al. (1976) Studies of Foreign Competition Policy and Practice, Vol. 2. Ottawa: Consumer and Corporate Affairs, Supply and Services Canada.

MACMILLAN, D. [ed.] (1972) Canadian Business History. Toronto: McClelland and Stewart.

MILIBRAND, R. (1969) The State in Capitalist Society. London: Camelot Press.

MORAN, L. [ed.] (1972) Monopolies, Mergers and Restrictive Trade Practices: An Examination of Federal Legislation. Sydney: Australian National University.

MULLER, R. E. (1976) "Systematic instability and the global corporation at home: The role of power in economic analysis." Pp. 239-263 in A. P. Jacquemin and H. W. de Jong (eds.), Markets, Corporate Behavior and the State. The Hague: Martinis Nijhoff.

NEALE, A. D. (1960) The Anti-Trust Laws of the United States of America. New York: Cambridge University Press.

NONET, P. (1976) "For jurisprudential sociology." Law and Society Review 10 (Summer):525-545.

PENGILLEY, W. (1965) "The prospective restrictive practices act of Australia." Antitrust Bulletin 10:155-173.

_____(1973) "Australian experience of antitrust regulation—A vindication of the per se approach." Antitrust Bulletin 18 (Summer):355-374.

_____(1978) "Public benefit in anticompetitive arrangements? Australian experience since 1974." Antitrust Bulletin (Spring):187-225.

POLANYI, G. (1973) Which Way Monopoly Policy. London: Institute of Economic Affairs.

PANITCH, L. (1977) The Canadian State: Political Economy and Political Power. Toronto: University of Toronto Press.

POSNER, R. A. (1970) "A statistical study of antitrust enforcement." Journal of Law and Economics 13 (October):365-419.

Proceedings of the Institute of Criminology (1976) Corporate Crime, No. 28. Sydney: University of Sydney Law School.

QUINNEY, R. (1974) Critique of the Legal Order: Crime Control in Capitalist Society. Boston: Little, Brown.

REASONS, C. E. (1975) "Social thought and social structure: Competing paradigms in criminology." Criminology (November):332-365.

_____and R. M. RICH (1978) The Sociology of Law: A Conflict Perspective. Toronto: Butterworth.

SCHRAGER, L. S. and J. F. SHORT (1978) "Toward a sociology of organizational crime." Social Problems 26 (June):411-412.

SICHEL, W. [ed.] (1970) Antitrust Policy and Economic Welfare. Ann Arbor: University of Michigan Press.

SNIDER, L. D. (1978) "Corporate crime in Canada: A preliminary report." Canadian Journal of Criminology 20 (April):142-168.

STANBURY, W. T. (1977) Business Interests and the Reform of Competition Policy, 1971-75. Toronto: Carswell/Methuen.

SUTHERLAND, E. H. (1949) White Collar Crime. New York: Dryden.

SWANN, D. et al. (1974) Competition in British Industry. London: George Allen & Unwin.

THORELLI, H. B. (1955) The Federal Antitrust Policy. Baltimore: Johns Hopkins Press.

TIGER, M. and M. R. LEVY (1977) Laws and the Rise of Capitalism. New York: Monthly Review Press.

TURK, A. T. (1976) "Law, conflict and order: From theorizing toward theories." Canadian Review of Sociology and Anthropology 13 (August):282-294.

WINKLER, J. T. (1975) "Law state and economy: The Industry Act of 1975 in context." British Journal of Law and Society 2 (Winter):103-128.

YOUNG, B. (1974) "Corporate interests and the state." Our Generation 10 (Winter/Spring):70-83.

YOUNG, T. R. (1975) "Some theoretical foundations for conflict methodology." Sociological Inquiry 46 (Winter):23-29.

*Chapter 7*

# THE INSTITUTIONALIZATION OF AMBIGUITY: EARLY BRITISH FACTORY ACTS

W. G. CARSON

At the beginning of his recent book, *Marxism and Literature,* Raymond Williams (1977:11) observes that the basic concept, culture, "embodies not only the issues but the contradictions through which it has developed." It both "fuses and confuses the radically different experiences and tendencies of its formation," he explains, and thereby it obliges any serious cultural analysis to reach toward a historical consciousness of the concept itself. Aware that he is hesitating before the richness of more immediate issues, Williams goes on to offer an eloquent and cogent justification for such hesitancy in general:

> When the most basic concepts—the concepts, as it is said, from which we begin—are suddenly seen to be not concepts but problems, not analytic problems either but historical movements that are still unresolved, there is no sense in listening to their sonorous summons or their resounding clashes. We have only, if we can, to recover the substance from which their forms were cast [Williams, 1977:11].

Among criminological concepts there can be few that match the degree to which white-collar crime manifests the contradictory tendencies of its own development. Proscribed by law, it is often substantially tolerated in practice, although commentators never tire of pointing to the extremely high social price which it exacts. While it is statutorily defined as crime, moreover, it is frequently dealt with through administrative agencies that are discontinuous in origin and far from the normal machinery of criminal justice. Similarly, many observers have noted that offenders and the public alike rarely view the relevant conduct as being "really" criminal (Fuller, 1942). Significantly too, white-collar crime is one of those areas where the doctrine of strict liability is often deployed for purposes of establishing criminal responsibility, a practice which has long been seen—at least by some—as a radical departure from the requirements of *mens rea* lying at the very heart of real crime (Hall, 1960). Just as some judges have held that offenses proved under such a rule can be only "quasi-criminal" in nature (Sweet v. Parsley, 1969), so some criminological theorists have seen the existence of this doctrine as a barrier to the formulation of general theoretical explanations within criminology (Cressey, 1961).

So deeply is contradiction embedded in the whole notion of white-collar crime that one of the most salient features of the concept's early history was a protracted debate among scholars as to the appropriateness of its inclusion in the criminological repertoire. It was this debate, this same sense of contradiction, that led Vilhelm Aubert (1952) to suggest that instead of attempting to resolve the crime/not crime controversy, theoretical analysis should preserve and focus on the ambiguous nature of the phenomenon. This ambiguity, he maintained, was the most interesting feature of white-collar crime, since it provided clues to normative conflicts, clashing group interests, and maybe even "incipient social change." In so doing, he demonstrated how this kind of crime was particularly sensitive to, and highly symptomatic of, "more pervasive and generalizable features of the social structure."

In the period which has elapsed since Aubert's incisive intervention in what he rightly saw as a "futile terminological dispute," it has become commonplace to acknowledge rather than to argue over or discount the ambiguity surrounding white-collar crime. With reference to the substance from which this ambiguous form is cast, however, comparatively little progress has been made. On one level, few if any of the theorists who recognize this as an issue have successfully retained the centrality of ambiguity while, at the same time, breaking free of the pluralism which so clearly dominated the work of Aubert and, indeed, of Sutherland (1949) before him. Equally, there has been little sign of hesitation before what Williams (1977:11) would call the seeming "richness of developed theory and the fullness of achieved practice" in order to attempt the recovery of a historical consciousness in connection with the concept of white-collar crime and its ambiguity. Least of all, perhaps, has there been any significant progress toward location of this ambiguous concept, as a historical movement, within analysis of the totality of the social order within which it emerges, survives, and remains unresolved (but see Pearce, 1976).

In this chapter, I shall attempt to recover the substance from which the ambiguous form of one kind of white-collar crime was cast within one particular period of British history. More specifically, I shall examine the conflicting forces, contradictory tendencies, and dynamic processes which, together, generated the aura of ambiguity that came to surround violation of the British Factory Acts during the first half of the nineteenth century. Despite such historical specificity, however, I would maintain that such an undertaking holds more than antiquarian interest. As one recent observer (Sumner, 1976) has noted, the "social censures" of the present—we may add, even ambiguous ones—can be seen as "historical monuments" to a society's past conflicts and to its social divisions of power, wealth, and consciousness. No less important is the realization that a history of the developments to be discussed here, a "ruptured history" which retrospectively smooths out the struggles of the past into the "consoling myth of the civilizing advance of the law" (Hall et al., 1978), continues to inform and facilitate the ambivalent attitudes of policy makers toward the factory crime of the present. Moreover, and despite the massive changes which have overtaken British society since the 1850s, I would suggest that there is a thread of continuity between the social order of the present and that of the early nineteenth century to justify a link, however tenuous, between our treatment of factory offenses today and their treatment during the period with which this study is concerned.

In undertaking this task of recovery, I shall also attempt to couch my analysis in terms of the social totality within which these crucial developments occurred. Moreover, I shall explicitly adopt an ontological position which, instead of conceiving "totality" as simply an aggregate of parts, stresses the patterned constellation of relationships whereby it is constituted, sustained, and changed. Thus, my approach to the early legislation will emphasize how it served to reproduce the totality of the social order which was taking shape during the first half of the nineteenth century, and how it was itself shaped by that totality, not least in the ambiguous mode of its operation. Similarly, my analysis of violation in this period will rest heavily on the assumption that within and between the elements which constitute the totality there is the possibility of contradiction, a contradiction which in this instance was, once again, ameliorated by the development of ambiguity. It is my hope that by such relational analysis the substance from which the ambiguous form of this white-collar crime was cast can be rendered more substantial.

## EARLY FACTORY LEGISLATION AND THE REPRODUCTION OF SOCIAL ORDER

British factory legislation dates from 1802 when an enactment known as the Health and Morals of Apprentices Act (42 Geo. III, c. 73) was passed. This statute purported to curtail some of the worst abuses practiced against the large numbers of pauper children who, during the closing decades of the preceding century, had been shipped from major centers of population to become apprenticed to cotton masters whose early, water-powered mills had been erected in remote locations where water, unlike labor, was in plentiful supply. Although space precludes description of the privations endured by these "pauper-apprentices," some idea of their plight can be gained from the terms of the enactment itself: for example, it banned their employment for more than 12 hours per day; provided for the eventual cessation of all night work by this class of employee; and insisted on the provision of separate sleeping accommodations for males and females, not more than two apprentices being allowed to share one bed. Some rudimentary provision was also made for their physical and intellectual well-being by requirements covering such matters as clothing, ventilation, cleanliness, and educational instruction.

The limited measure of protection afforded—at least on paper—to the parish apprentices in the textile industry was little enough reward for the part which they played in the early stages of industrialization. Their plight, however, was soon superceded by other developments stemming from further technological change. With the introduction of steam for the generation of rotary power, it became possible for manufacturers to abandon their remote locations and establish themselves in the towns where increasing economic pressure was rendering the laboring classes more amenable to factory employment, both for themselves and for their children. Although the transition to steam was a gradual one and much less rapid in branches of the industry other than cotton, the pattern of child-employment had radically altered by 1819 when, as a result of enthusiastic efforts of Robert Owen and the rather less fervent parliamentary sponsorship of Robert Peel, further legislative intervention took place. According to the latter, there were by then ten times as many "free" children employed in the cotton industry as there had formerly been apprentices (Hansard, 1818:342), and, accordingly, it was to this class of labor that the Act of 1819 offered some measure of protection. Restricted to cotton factories, this enactment fixed the minimum age for employment at nine years and prohibited the employment of those under sixteen for more than 12 hours per day (excluding meal times) or after 9:00 p.m. Subsequent measures, in 1825 and 1831, extended these provisions as to night working and, in the case of the second, enlarged the age group limited to 12 hours daily work to include all under the age of eighteen.

The next major step in the development of this body of legislation was taken in 1833 when, after two protracted and contentious official enquiries, a further enactment was passed (3 & 4 Will. IV, c. 103). Applying to a range of textile industries where steam, water, or other mechanical power was in use, this statute prohibited the employment of children under nine years of age, limited the labor of those between nine and thirteen to 9 hours per day, and restricted the employment of young people between thirteen and eighteen to 12 hours daily. For all under the age of eighteen, a ban was imposed—with some special exceptions—on their employment between 8:30 p.m. and 5:30 a.m. Children in the younger age group were to receive some elementary education, vouchers to that effect being made a prerequisite of their employment each week. A complex system of age certificates was also established in order to facilitate enforcement of the various provisions, and most important of all, four full-time inspectors of factories were to be appointed.

The history of factory legislation during the ten years following 1833 is largely dominated by the difficulties which the latter officials encountered when, after initial and substantial recalcitrance in the matter, they set out to enforce the law. A select committee which reported in 1840 examined these problems in some detail and, despite a further delay occasioned largely by controversy over the question of education, a further measure (7 & 8 Vict., c. 15) was placed on the statute book in 1844. Apart from going some way toward removing a number of the more obvious practical obstacles confronting the inspectors (a matter to which we shall return at a subsequent point), this enactment was notable for its restriction of women to the same working hours as young persons, and for introducing requirements as to the fencing of dangerous machinery. As far as child employees were concerned, while the minimum age for employment was reduced to eight, it became illegal to employ them for more than 6½ hours per day or during both the morning and afternoon work periods. The working hours of both children and young persons were also to be reckoned from the time when any child or young person commenced labor in the morning, the time to be regulated by a public clock.

From the early 1830s onward, however, another and more drastic form of regulation had been canvassed by the Ten Hours Movement, a loose-knit organization comprising both humanitarian reformers and many operatives who had formed themselves into Short-time Committees (Ward, 1962). As its title suggests, this body favored a limitation of restricted labor to 10 hours per day, even though—and, indeed, largely because—the interdependence of different classes of labor within a mill would mean that such a step would necessarily curtail the hours worked by all. A proposal of this kind was defeated in 1844, but pressure for such a measure continued to mount in the years immediately following. In 1847, just one year after the repeal of the Corn Laws, this pressure finally achieved some measure of success through an enactment which restricted women and all under the age of eighteen to a maximum of 10 hours work per day and 58 per week (10 & 11 Vict., c. 70). But the "normal working day," as it came to be known, was not quite so easily secured. Many manufacturers, availing themselves of statutory complexity combined with a legal decision (Ryder v. Mills, Parliamentary Papers, 1850:XLII)[1] to the effect that "reckoning" time did not have to mean that it was reckoned continuously from the time of first starting work, successfully contrived to continue working their factories for more than 10 hours by employing women and young persons in staggered relays (Thomas, 1948: chap. 18). When this loophole was removed by an amending act in 1850, it was only at the cost of accepting a 60-hour week (10½ per weekday and 7½ on Saturday) in return for a provision that women and young persons should not be employed outside the fixed hours of 6:00 a.m. and 6:00 p.m. during the week, nor after 2:00 p.m. on Saturdays, including a weekly total of 8 hours allowed for meals (13 & 14 Vict., c. 54). Even then the matter was not closed, for the government at that time had declined to include the children in the fixed time restrictions which were imposed in 1850. As a result, the last abuse with which the struggle for a standard working day had to contend was the unseemly one of mills continuing to work beyond 6:00 p.m. using relays of children to take the place of women and young persons. It was not until 1853 that a further enactment put an end to this practice (16 & 17 Vict., c. 104).

Such is the bare outline of the legislative enactments which are central to this chapter. But the salient question here is how analytical flesh can be added to the bare bones of this chronological history. Within the traditional approach to white-collar crime, of course, the answer would be to tease out the way in which competing interest groups battled for dominance in the legislative process, leaving the indelible mark of their uneven successes, compromises, and defeats on the form and content of the legislation in question. Following Newman (1977), the process might be portrayed as yet another "stormy legislative history" which resulted in a compromise "to lessen the dissatisfaction of multiple interest groups." In a similar vein, we might adopt Aubert's (1952) approach and, setting the legislative record against that of enforcement, seek to establish whether this body of law gave symbolic satisfaction to some powerful groups by the very fact of its enactment, while others were effectively placated by the slowness and inefficiency of its implementation. More sophisticatedly, Lemert's (1976) complex and perhaps convoluted notion of "neo-technic pluralism" might be called into play to account for the emergence of a set of criminal laws which, far from reflecting traditional and "sacred" values, represented the "specialized values of associations" within a newly emergent form of social integration.

It would not be difficult to marshall a considerable array of detail as illustrative support for any or all of these substantially similar approaches. Elsewhere, for example, I (Carson, 1974) have charted the ferocious battles surrounding the passage of the crucial Act of 1833, and have suggested that the issue of regulation did indeed assume momentous symbolic significance for powerful competing groups with radically divergent conceptions of social order. Equally, the entire period is littered with compromises: among different interests within the manufacturing class[2]; between ardent reformers and reluctant governments; between enforcers and violators; and, not least—though more in the nature of bargains imposed rather than struck—between legislatures and an emergent working class which had to fight hard for the concessions that it won. Nor, as we shall see, would it be a travesty of the historical facts to suggest that a substantial gap did indeed exist between the factory legislation in the books of this era and its implementation in practice, a gap which, at first sight, might seem to be the very epitome of how pluralist politics are replicated at the level of enforcement.

However, as a critic (Paulus, 1974) of one recent attempt to deploy a pluralist approach to legislation of a similar kind has said, this perspective produces a mass of interesting and even fascinating detail, but leaves one with the feeling that there must be something more. In keeping with the ontological position stated earlier in this study, I wish to suggest that the "something more" which such an approach would neglect in the present instance is the extent to which early British factory legislation had an important part to play in creating and recreating the conditions under which industrialization and, paradoxically, laissez-faire capitalism could thrive. Indeed, I shall argue that this period witnessed the realization of a kind of internal dynamic or logic within the emergent order of industrialization, a logic that generated an impetus toward rather than away from effective regulation. In subsequent sections I will suggest that this mounting impetus not only clashed with the prevailing organization and ideology of the productive process in this period, but also, thereby, created specific and substantial problems of enforcement. It was in the partial resolution of these problems, difficulties stemming from a basic contradiction rather than from the vagaries of pluralist politics alone, that factory crime assumed its ambiguous form.

At one level, perhaps the most obvious, it has been argued that whether one takes it as giving some firms—particularly the larger town-based ones—a competitive edge over others which depended much more substantially on the maintenance of long hours, or simply as tending toward a general equalization of conditions of competition, factory legislation was seen in this period as having potentially important effects on the competitive structure of the British textile industry. In the debates and enquiries which preceded the statutes of 1819 and 1833, for example, much was made of this issue (Great Britain, 1833), and, certainly, some such consideration seems to have occupied the minds of those "eminent manufacturers" who themselves proposed the creation of an inspectorate in the latter year. As the Royal Commission of that year put it, "the necessity of the appointment of inspectors has been most urgently stated by those manufacturers who have had chiefly in view the restriction of the hours of labor in other factories to the level of their own." To one Scottish employer, a measure which "would place the selfish and the generous, the unfeeling and the compassionate, the considerate and the inconsiderate, among the masters, on an equal footing was to be welcomed" (P.P., 1833:XX, 60); indeed, the subsequent period is strewn with reports of manufacturers who professed to obey the law, but objected strenuously to the unfair advantages gained by those who did not. According to *The Times* on May 18, 1838, protection from illegal competition at home was a matter of greater urgency than any action to deal with foreign competition:

> The fair trader MUST be protected. . . . It is not the bugbear of foreign competition which the enlightened and far-seeing manufacturers fear. . . . What the humane and honorable masters have chiefly to apprehend is a competition at home, not of skill and industry, and prudence, and capital, but of overreaching avarice.

What Marx (1936:537) was later to call "the cry of the capitalist for equality in conditions of competition" is not, however, the only evidence to suggest that a factory law which was more than hollow legislative phrases was seen to be of importance in the context of the industrial order taking shape in nineteenth-century Britain. In addition (and although we can only touch on it here), there is a strong case to suggest that effective regulation of factory labor in this period could play an important part in solving what was arguably the biggest problem of the age: namely, the creation and maintenance of a suitable workforce. On one level, of course, the issue here was what effects protracted toil under arduous conditions might have on the health and robustness of future labor, a consideration which was recognized as early as 1796 when the group of Manchester doctors who first drew attention to mill conditions noted, among other things, the deleterious effects on the fitness "of our species for the employments and duties of manhood (P.P., 1816:III, 139)." Such considerations were to become a recurrent theme in subsequent debates, often allied with concern over the moral profligacy engendered by factory labor, and often conflated with the no less important question of the predicted quality of military recruitment. When Peel could buttress his case in 1818 by pointing out that Manchester no longer furnished recruits to the army; when, nearly 20 years later, Sir John Elley (Hansard, 1836:XXIII, 765) could say that he "would never go to a manufacturing district to select grenadiers"; it lent a certain macabre quality to the humor of one Member of Parliament who, sharing a literary curiosity as to the whereabouts of the "Goddess Health," opined that "it would certainly have been an extraordinary solution of the perplexity of the poet, if when he enquired,

> In what dim and dark retreat
> the coy nymph fix'd her favorite seat?

it had been answered that it was in the cotton mill of Messrs. Finlay & Co. at Glasgow" (Hansard, 1818:XXXVIII, 358). The point was put bluntly to Lord Althorp, a leading member of the government, in 1833:

> [I]t was not by a race of squalid, rickety, half-starved paupers that your Lordship's patrimony and honors were defended from age to age, as long as danger lowered upon them; . . . but by brawny limbs, enlarged in the bone, through the agency of air, out-door exercise, and solid feeding. Merry England! what has become of thy name and attributes! [Crabtree, 1833:20].

Of even greater urgency, if not importance, within the context of industrialization was the need to create a workforce which would adapt itself satisfactorily to the unaccustomed discipline of factory labor. As historians like Pollard (1963), Thompson (1967), and McKendrick (1961) have pointed out, the production of a disciplined workforce was a sine qua non of the industrial revolution and involved the transformation of an entire culture. Many different forces were, of course, at work in this respect from the eighteenth century onward—ranging from the imposition of internal codes of conduct within the factory itself to the development of powerful, disciplining ideologies in religion and education—but once again, it is suggested, factory legislation had a substantial contribution to make. Its early sensitivity to the issue is evident, for example, in an inspection report which, having been compiled after one of the rare visitations carried out by justices of the peace who were initially responsible for enforcement, concluded with a remarkable tribute to the effect that the rules and ordinances of the mill in question "are highly calculated to inspire the lower orders with a spirit of industry and subordination" (P.P., 1816:III, 459). Similarly, one of the passing objections to the idea of introducing inspectors, in 1816, was that such a system might distract the children from their duty and weaken the authority of the master over them.

When a system of inspection was finally instituted in 1833, however, the disciplinary potential of factory legislation became more readily apparent. Indeed, with its emphasis on regularity and uniformity, on records of machinery operation and employees, on times of entry and departure from the mill, and so on, it is by no means fanciful to see the legislation of this era as contributing substantially to the broader processes so eloquently described by E. P. Thompson (1967) in his book, *Time, Work-discipline and Industrial Capitalism.* Equally, although the first inspectors may not have been notably successful in implementing the law's educational provisions, there is ample evidence to show that their efforts in this direction did help to disseminate an awareness of the advantages which might accrue to labor discipline from education of the factory children. Thus when, in 1838, they canvassed the views of employers who had established schools on their premises, a significant proportion responded positively with regard to changes which they had observed in "habits of subordination" (P.P., 1839:XLII, 355). As one respondent put it, "our conviction is that schooling the youngest hands is attended with great advantage to them, whilst it tends to make them more governable and orderly in the mill" (P.P., 1839:XLII, 394). Similar benefits also induced a significant degree of ambivalence in Henry Ashworth, a wealthy cotton manufacturer and vociferous critic of the law's operation.

> We have found so much advantage from our people being able to read and write that although opposed in feeling to the compulsory education forced upon us by the present Factory Law, we are anxious to see a law of the nation, a general law, enforcing education on all trades, by making it unlawful for any child, unable to read and write, to be found working out of its parents' house [Senior, 1837:44].

Even Ashley (Taylor, 1842:247), the champion of reform, received a back-handed compliment for "having wrought good which he never contemplated" by forcing attention to education on the mill owners, in keeping with the maxim that "if education is, as it ought to be, a system of training for the duties in which men are to be engaged in active life, then those who are to live by labor should early be trained to labor."

Against such a background, it is not surprising that when Alexander Redgrave, newly promoted from a clerical post to replace a deceased inspector, came to survey the general scene in 1853, he was able to report that both workers and employers "are equally sensible that that which was intended as a protection for the one has operated advantageously for the other" (P.P., 1852-1853:XL, 53). Such reciprocity and its role in the creation of a disciplined workforce did not, however, exhaust the significance of early factory legislation in the context of the reproduction of social order. In addition, this body of law had important implications for the broader ideological issue of how the social relations of the workplace could be represented, understood, and assented to in nineteenth-century Britain. Increasingly, as the period progressed, issues such as the duration and conditions of employment became matters of legal relationship, enforceable, if not always enforced, at the hands of government agents. No longer could they be quite so manifestly the product of personal whim, of an arbitrary relationship between employer and employee (benign or otherwise), or of the unalloyed play of market forces. Nor, as the following newspaper extract shows, was the ideological significance of factory legislation in this respect totally lost on contemporaries:

> We warn legislators of the infallible result of their not carrying out the protective character of Government. They may think there is danger in restricting labor; but there is certainly more danger in telling labor to shift for itself. Tell the British laborer that he must fight all his battles and make all his own conditions without help from the State, and what sort of feeling he is likely to have towards that State, towards its head and towards its aristocracy [*The Times* (London), May 9, 1844].

While discussion of implications such as these belongs more properly to consideration of the longer-term part played by factory legislation in legitimizing and masking the emergent class relations of the nineteenth century, such is not the case with regard to one last factor, again ideological in character, which assumed growing importance as the century wore on. As Thompson (1975:263) has remarked in connection with the function of law as ideology, one essential precondition of its success in this respect is that "it shall display an independence from gross manipulation and shall seem to be just." While this was precisely the precondition which factory legislation, in its earliest stages, singularly failed to fulfill, it was one that could only continue to be neglected at considerable ideological peril to the social order as a whole.

Most authorities on the initial phase in the history of factory legislation (Thomas, 1948) are in agreement that the early laws were violated with impunity, largely because of inadequacies in the enforcement machinery provided. Whatever the explanation, however, it seems clear that the first enactments were contravened on a substantial scale. Thus, for example, the evidence given before a select committee in 1816 (P.P., 1816:III) left little doubt that the Apprentices Act of 1802 had long been a dead letter. Visitors had rarely been appointed from among the local justices and, according to one Lancashire witness, it was the general understanding in that county that the enactment was neglected. Several others had never even heard of its existence. "In this inquiry," the *Westminster Review* (Editorial, 1836:179) later recalled, "it came out . . . that the provisions of the Apprentices Act were evaded and set at nought."

Nor do things seem to have improved substantially in this respect after passage of the 1819 act. Indeed, it was largely the extent to which the terms of that statute were violated that provided the immediate rationale for further legislative effort in 1825. According to Sir John Cam Hobhouse, parliamentary sponsor of the bill which was passed in that year, his proposal for further regulation rested squarely on a desire "to carry into effect that excellent statute which had long been shamefully evaded" (Hansard, 1825:XIII, 644). But his efforts then and some six years later do not appear to have produced the desired effect. Setting aside the hotly contested evidence given before the allegedly partisan committee of 1832 (P.P., 1831-1832:XV), the more sanguine proceedings of the Royal Commission established in the following year left little doubt that violation of the law was both widespread and unchecked. In country districts, according to the report, even attempts to enforce the law were seldom or never made; in several of the principal manufacturing towns it was openly disregarded; in others its operation was extremely partial and incomplete. "On the whole," concluded the commissioners, "we find the present law has been almost entirely inoperative with respect to the legitimate objects contemplated by it" (P.P., 1833:XX, 36).

Even after the appointment of four inspectors and a number of superintendents to work under them, in 1833, there was no immediate change. Acting under instructions to be "in communication exclusively with the employers, with a view to making the law acceptable to them" (P.P., 1849:XXII, 230), the new officials were extremely loath to prosecute and, indeed, even joined with some of the more influential manufacturers in calling on the government to repeal the final stages of the act's implementation. It was only when this plea was rejected, in 1836, that they were unequivocally instructed to put the law into effect. That the ideological implications of such dilatoriness in enforcing factory legislation did not pass unnoticed at the time is apparent in the following extract from the Memorial which the Manchester Short-Time Committee sent to the Home Office in February 1837:

> Your memorialists deeply regret that the due fulfillment of the intentions of the Legislature has hitherto, by one expedient or another, been delayed and postponed, causing extreme dissatisfaction to prevail among the operative classes in the manufacturing districts, and an impression (dangerous and alarming at any time, but especially so in a case like the present, where the evidence on which the feeling is founded is not obscure, and accessible to few, but clear and palpable, and within the reach of all) that justice, where the poor are concerned is no longer even handed, and that, in deference to the understood wishes of more opulent and therefore more influential parties, the law is in very numerous instances perverted and abused, and its more benevolent provisions trampled under foot [P.P., 1837:L, 203].

From evidence such as this, it is clear that factory legislation which continued to be a complete sham could have had highly detrimental effects on the capacity of the new industrial order to maintain its legitimacy. Thus, to the other forces that have been advanced as generating an impetus toward, rather than away from, regulation in this period must be added the growing pressure of another logic which necessitated not only legislation, but enforcement. The role of factory legislation in reproducing the totality of the social order within which it was located could not be played entirely with the rhetoric of empty phrases. As we shall see, however, the assiduous efforts which, from 1836 onward, did indeed go into the attempt to make regulation a reality, collided head-on with other intransigent forces embedded in the social organization of factory production in this period, a collision which culminated in ambiguity becoming the salient feature of factory crime.

## FACTORY PRODUCTION AND EARLY FACTORY CRIME

In the preceding section it was argued that in addition to the specific social movements pressing for factory legislation during the first half of the nineteenth century, there was an underlying impetus toward regulation within the system itself. Moreover, from the nature of the evidence adduced, it seems plausible to suggest that this argument need not simply be couched in terms of ex post facto theorization, which posits some unseen hand inexorably guiding law toward the fulfillment of its role in reproducing social order; effective factory legislation was frequently seen, albeit unevenly and sometimes only dimly, as having a potentially important part to play in this process. Because such underlying forces were at work, however, does not mean that the realization of their potential was automatic, as if a relationship of mechanistic equivalence prevailed between the different elements which conjoined to produce the totality of nineteenth-century society. For one thing, such an argument would be difficult to sustain in light of the very real and substantial resistance offered to most legislative proposals in this period; for another, it would drastically underestimate the extent to which violation, particularly with regard to overworking, was functionally integrated with the structure, organization, and ideology of the productive process during these years. In this section, I wish to focus primarily on the latter point as a prelude to discussion of attempts to enforce the law.

The attractiveness of juvenile and female labor to the textile manufacturers of this period is well known. Not only were such workers seen to be more tractable and therefore more easily disciplined to factory routine, but also, of course, their labor came cheaper than that of adult males (Bendix, 1956:34). Moreover, by depressing the wage levels of the male adult and, indeed, by diminishing his chances of factory employment just when exigency was driving him to it, the extensive employment of women and, particularly, juveniles formed part of a vicious circle which maintained pressure on the workforce as a whole (Thompson, 1968:341). According to some commentators (Bendix, 1956:39), it was precisely this adverse effect which the hiring of juveniles had on adult unemployment that provoked working-class demands for legislative restrictions on child labor.

Whatever the accuracy of this assessment, however, there is no doubt as to the pattern of the employment structure which characterized the textile industry during the first half of the nineteenth century. By 1819, as we have already seen, it was claimed that there were ten times as many "free" children employed in cotton factories as there had formerly been "pauper apprentices." In the early 1830s, one estimate (Thompson, 1968) put the proportion of employees in cotton mills who were under twenty-one at between one-third and one-half, while women were calculated to constitute well over half of all workers in the entire textile industry. When the then-recently appointed factory inspectors compiled figures on employment in 1839, the results showed that there were still more than 33,000 children between nine and thirteen (about 8 percent of the entire labor force) and nearly 161,000 young persons between thirteen and eighteen (approximately 38 percent) employed in textile factories coming within the provisions of the 1833 act (P.P., 1840:X, 154ff.). According to the statistics extrapolated by Professor Blaug (1961) from Chapman's (1904) earlier work on the cotton industry, about one-quarter of the workers in English cotton mills between 1834 and 1847 were adult men; more than half were women and girls; and the remainder, boys below the age of eighteen. As Blaug (1961) remarks, "the tendency to replace dear adult labor by cheap juvenile labor resisted the efforts of factory reformers until the last decades of the nineteenth century."

Straightaway then, it is apparent that the factory legislation which emerged during the first half of that century purported to impinge, not on some insignificant and coincidental aspect of the productive process, but on one of its most crucial features. However, it was not just by sheer force of numbers that juvenile labor—which, it will be recalled, was the sole focus of regulation up until 1844—was an integral factor in production. Additionally, because the tasks performed by children were regarded as vital to the working of the machinery by adults, their labor was taken to be inextricably linked with the very operation of the mill itself. Thus, for example, when a wealthy cotton manufacturer named Robert Greg (1837) came to write a spirited attack on the progress of factory legislation up to 1837, he could find only one important defect in the factory system as such: the "necessary union of the labor of adults and children." Only a year earlier Gaskell (1836:168) had inveighed in similar terms against the absurdity of the restrictions which the Act of 1833 had imposed on child labor. The statute had been founded on "a singular ignorance of the interior economy of mills," he asserted, and had in consequence failed to appreciate that the child performed an essential part of their operation. "There is a mutual dependence of the entire laborers one upon the other; and if the children who are employed principally by the spinner are dismissed, his work ceases and the mill is at a stand still."

What such mutual dependence of labor within the internal economy of the factory meant, of course, was that any particular class of worker was exposed to the employer's views as to the role of labor, as a whole, in the productive process. And here, the arithmetic was sanguinary indeed. Obsessed with the extent of their capital investment in fixed plant and machinery, most entrepreneurs assumed both that output varied commensurate with the length of time worked and that the cost of their investment fell as output was extended.[3] Hence, the "interdependency" of labor all too easily became fused with a broader calculus which led ineluctably to overworking. The convergence was put cogently by one manufacturer when he was asked whether his desire to restrict even "absolutely necessary" legislation to certain trades was grounded on a belief that these involved harder physical work:

> No; it arises from the tendency which I conceive to exist in businesses where much capital is sunk in buildings and machinery for production to be pushed (for the sake of diminishing cost) to an extent inconsistent with the permanent welfare of the operatives. In such establishments the subdivision of labor causes the different classes of workpeople to be dependent upon the aid of each other. The greater proportion must act simultaneously and work the same number of hours; hence the weak and the strong, the old and the young, must of necessity conform to the established duration of labor, which, in the absence of legislative restriction, would be regulated most probably more by the physical capability of the vigorous and robust than by the necessities of the far greater proportion of operatives of comparatively weaker powers of endurance [P.P., 1833:XX, 852].

In the context of the present discussion, the significance of such thinking lies not so much in the resistance that it generated to each successive proposal for further regulation as in the motivation which it provided for violation of the law. Whatever the advantages of effective restriction in the long term, in the short run the most obvious solution to problems of increased competition or declining profitability seemed to involve an extension of the hours of work; and because of the way in which the "internal economy" of the typical mill was organized, such a strategy entailed a constant temptation to overwork the restricted classes of labor. As Hobsbawn (1964) and others have pointed out, low productivity and inefficient labor management were not generally seen as the key to such problems until well into the 1840s or even later, employers in the earlier period preferring to exhaust the possibilities of cutting costs by increasing hours and reducing money wage rates. In consequence, there was a recurrent incentive to law-breaking, particularly when—as in the case of the cotton industry during the 1830s and '40s—fluctuations in trade concealed a progressively downward trend in rates of profitability (Foster, 1977:20-21). When times were bad, some employers with stocks in hand would try to survive by going for long hours and increased output, thereby adding to the pressure on their competitors (P.P., 1841:XX, 36). More commonly, when trade thrived, attempts would be made to meet the demand of relatively full order books on the basis of existing plant and machinery, necessitating, once again, extended hours.

Throughout this entire period there is ample evidence to show that violation of the law relating to hours of labor was a calculated response to the perceived exigencies of the trade. In the earliest days, employers seem to have increased working hours at will and, indeed, by 1833 it could still be claimed that the law had any semblance of efficiency only in "circumstances under which *it* conformed to the state of things already in existence" (P.P., 1833:XX, 36; italics added). In the more fully documented years following 1833, the newly appointed inspectors greeted every downward trend in violation with diffident disclaimers of credit, almost invariably pointing out that it was the slackness of trade rather than their effort that was responsible (P.P., 1847-1848:XXVI, 28). Conversely, when things picked up, they would note the increased incentive to violation and counsel themselves to greater vigilance (P.P., 1850:XXIII, 37). Even though manufacturers may have begun to turn toward other strategies during the 1840s—partly as a result of the slump at the beginning of that decade, partly as a consequence of the passage of the Ten Hours Act in 1847, and partly because they were gradually learning that reduced hours did not necessarily entail proportionately reduced output—the inspectors remained convinced that violation of these provisions was largely a function of the state of trade. As surviving records of prosecuted offenses involving overwork show, moreover, the pattern of their enforcement activity was substantially in keeping with such an interpretation. Dropping fairly sharply with the recession which followed the boom of 1836,[4] such prosecutions reached their lowest point with the depression that became most acute in 1842, picked up again with the slow recovery which produced prosperity in the greater part of 1845, only to decline with the subsequent recession that lasted until 1848 (see Table 1).

A plausible case can be made out, then, for suggesting that violation of the law's pivotal provisions with regard to hours of labor

*Table 1* Prosecutions for Overworking 1836-1849*

| *Year* | *No.* | *Year* | *No.* |
|---|---|---|---|
| 1836 | 356 | 1843 | 89 |
| 1837 | 253 | 1844 | 86 |
| 1838 | 246 | 1845 | 520 |
| 1839 | 105 | 1846 | 150 |
| 1840 | 65 | 1847 | 63 |
| 1841 | 101 | 1848 | 204 |
| 1842 | 36 | 1849 | 258 |

*Compiled from annual returns submitted by inspectors.

in this period was a calculated response to economic exigency, a response which reflected perfectly rational, if illegal, choices from within a range of possibilities ordained by the industry's employment structure, organization, and economic reasoning. Indeed, "calculational" was precisely the term that was used in protracted evidence to the Select Committee of 1840 in relation to both overworking and many other kinds of offenses against the act (P.P., 1840:X, 135). According to Superintendent Trimmer (P.P., 1841:IX, 191), for example, some mill occupiers had even told him that it answered their purpose better to pay the occasional fine rather than to obey the law. It is important, moreover, to realize that the competitive and other pressures that could generate such responses were not restricted to a minority of so-called "less respectable" employers. Even some of the most ardent of reforming masters, such as John Feilden (1969 [1836]), could feel compelled to increase their hours in order to match their trade rivals. Similarly, from 1833 onward, there was a constant stream of protests from law-abiding employers in which they not only complained about the illegal activities of competitors, but also stated their own intention of following suit if the offenders were not restrained. As Messrs. Sidgwick (P.P., 1849:XXII, 14), employers of more than 1,000 workers at Skipton, explained in 1849, the use of illegal relays in their area left them little choice but to engage in the same practice "in defense of our own interests (as regards the competition of parties who have increased their time of working) . . . to enable us to offer our goods on the same terms as they do."

The factory crime of this period was calculational and, as occasion demanded, pervasive. As Leonard Horner (P.P., 1849:XXII, 6), one of the first and arguably the most important inspector in this period, ruefully reflected after more than fifteen years' experience, "we unfortunately know too well that all mill-owners are not to be trusted; that many of them have a very loose kind of morality in regard to evasions of the factory law." Despite open admission of the grounds on which they might violate, however, employers were frequently none too willing to assume personal responsibility for the law having been broken. More often than not, juvenile labor was hired directly by the skilled adult operatives, the industry's employment structure again intruding, this time to lend superficial credibility to claims that the master was not the really culpable party. Moreover, as the law (3 & 4 Will. IV, c. 103, 30) was framed at the point when inspectors were first appointed and some measure of real control became a possibility for the first time, it was legally permissible to shift responsibility from the mill occupier to the employee, where the magistrates were satisfied that the offense had been committed without the personal consent, concurrence, or knowledge of the master.

By all accounts, this loophole was frequently not far from the minds of offending employers in the years following 1833. In some areas, for example, many masters put up notices saying that the law was to be obeyed and all penalties borne by the spinners, overlookers, and others who hired employees in the restricted classes (P.P., 1837-1838:XXVIII, 109-110). Not infrequently, there would be active collusion in the matter, the servant agreeing to admit the offense and the master agreeing to reimburse the minimal fine which, in view of the offender's professed or genuine poverty, the court would be likely to inflict (P.P., 1840:X, 121). While the inspectors may have attempted to follow the maxim *qui facit per alium facit per se* (a man who does a thing through another does it himself) (P.P., 1840:X, 10), their efforts were frequently of little avail:

> It not infrequently happens that the workman is paid by the piece and not by the day; and in this case the workman hires the children. . . . The tendency of this opening for shifting the responsibility from the master to the workman is to induce the former, the man of education, character and station, to represent himself, in case of prosecution, as having no knowledge of the proceedings of his work-people . . . so that he may escape from legal responsibility himself, although he is the person who ultimately profits by the evasion of the law, who can hardly be really ignorant of the acts of his work-people, and who ought to be responsible that the business of his factory is conducted according to the law [P.P., 1841:IX, 578].

What was at issue here was more than a legal nicety; it was a case of the carryover of traditional relationships into factory production—an overlap which Bendix (1956) and others have rightly interpreted as facilitating labor management in the early stages of industrialization—being used to surround violation of the law with structurally embedded patterns of rationalization. On such grounds could superficially plausible excuses of ignorance be advanced even though, as Inspector Howell complained (P.P., 1852:XXI, 15), the employer could hardly fail to know "how much material was worked up in an extra half-hour, or could fail to note to a nicety the extra profit accruing from even a few minutes extra work."

Displacement of responsibility onto others was not, however, the only strategy used by employers in this period to deny any real criminal guilt on their own part while continuing to profit from factory crime. Some, of course, deemed it sufficient to follow the letter of the law even though its spirit was grossly abused—Ashworth

(P.P., 1841:IX, 312), for example, maintained that even if a child was actually and patently under the permitted age, once an employer had paid sixpence for a certificate of age, however false, he had a license to work the child. Others contended that although they might indeed be in breach of the law, their delinquencies were merely formal or even technical offenses involving no substance of moral responsibility commensurate with conviction on a criminal charge. Reluctant to accept the obligation to oversee the detailed operation of the law's provisions with respect to their premises, some conceded that offenses might occur without their knowledge (P.P., 1852:XXI, 15). The mill owner, as it was archly explained to Nassau W. Senior (1837), for example, had other things on his mind than the prevention of 80 urchins from truancy. Still others maintained that they were liable to prosecution simply because one out of a number of children remained on the premises for a few extra minutes, perhaps to escape the cold, or because one child on one day started work at a time different from that shown in the time-book. For such violations, they insisted, they should hardly be held responsible in any real sense. Even less should they be criminally accountable for mere irregularities in the maintenance of the various records and registers required by the inspectors under their power to promulgate administrative regulations. On such plausible grounds it could even be conceded (Senior, 1837:21) that the "forms of the Act" were systematically disregarded in some areas; "the master, relying on his general high character, and not fearing to be suspected of having intentionally violated its substance."

Once again, however, there is reason to suggest that there was more to the matter than mere inadvertence, understandable pre-occupation, or clerical oversight. For one thing, the inspectors were convinced that so-called "formal offenses" often betokened the commission of substantive contraventions as well; that, as Inspector Saunders (P.P., 1837-1838:XXVII, 124) put it, in 1838, "neglect upon this head almost invariably proves that some other provisions of the Act have also been neglected or willfully violated." Equally, it must be remembered that employers' protests in this context very much reflected as yet untransformed patterns of control, organization, and authority in industry. If control over workers could be left largely in the hands of the subcontracted employee, why not responsibility for their illegal mistreatment? Similarly, the Factories Acts and, in particular, their administrative machinery necessitated an unprecedented degree of internal bureaucratization within the factory and as such were resisted on the grounds of unfamiliarity, inconvenience, and expense. Moreover, since the administrative regulations tended toward the separation of ownership from control over the means of administration within a firm, they were seen (Greg, 1837) as an expropriation of ultimate entrepreneurial authority and power. In this, as in other aspects of early factory crime, there was a strong element of resistance to interference in established entrepreneurial practice:

> The Inspectors' regulations are founded upon the principle of the master being a tyrant and a cheat; and that the operatives must look to the Inspector rather than to him for justice and protection. . . . Regulations, framed in such a spirit, necessarily throw the master into a false position . . . and throw power into the hands of the work-people, of which, it is too much to suppose, they will not sometimes avail themselves [Greg, 1837:127].

## ENFORCEMENT AND THE INSTITUTIONALIZATION OF AMBIGUITY

Thus far I have argued two things: that there was an internal dynamic or logic within the emergent order of industrialization pointing firmly toward, rather than away from, effective factory legislation; and that, this impetus notwithstanding, the most significant forms of factory crime in this period were firmly embedded in the structure, organization, and ideology of the relevant productive processes. In this last empirical section, I wish to show how the response to this contradiction at the level of enforcement invested factory crime with some of its most ambiguous characteristics. More specifically, I shall chart how, in the more active phase of control which followed 1836, attempts to pursue the logic of regulation through use of criminal law ran into difficulties stemming from the way in which factory crime was integrated with factory production in this period.

When R. W. Cooke-Taylor (1842) made some notes during a tour of Lancashire in 1842, he was pleased to be able to record that factory inspection seemed to be working well. His only residual fear was that the inspectors might fall into the error of "exacting literal obedience to arbitrary rules." As we have seen, however, many manufacturers were of the view that such errors had already been made, rendering them liable to prosecution on mere formalities arising out of administrative oversights or out of nothing more than technical violation of the law's more substantive provisions. Thus, the first problem confronting the inspectors after 1836 was the not uncommon one of demonstrating to those whom they supervised that their enforcement policy was not arbitrary or essentially unjust.

In order to accomplish this, they seem to have toyed, at times, with the idea of recognizing a class of "formal" or "accidental" offenses which might suitably be dealt with by some means other than the full rigors of the criminal law. But their other and more consistent strategy, one that was ultimately to become an institutionalized feature of factory inspection (Carson, 1970), was to insist that they would only have recourse to the criminal courts when they were satisfied that the offense stemmed from some concrete element of intention on the part of the occupier. As early as 1837, for example, Leonard Horner (Senior, 1837:39) felt able to challenge complainants to produce a single instance of prosecution for a "frivolous cause," and to insist that however technical the offenses charged in court might seem, they had only reached there because of systematic and protracted violation. His critics might have been more convinced, moreover, had they been privy to the instructions which he issued to his four superintendents in August of the same year:

> Where irregularities are met with, it is but justice to be slow in imputing them to willful or gross negligence; . . . make it evident that the punishments of the law will be employed only against willful and obstinate offenders. When you discover offenses which appear to you to deserve the penalties of the law, represent them to the mill-owner in person . . . in order that you may hear what can be said in mitigation [P.P., 1840:X, 155].

In instructions such as these, we can observe something important taking place very early in the history of serious factory inspection—namely, the incorporation of some notion of *mens rea* into the routine *decision-making* processes of the inspectorate with regard to prosecution. However, while adherence to this central principle of criminal law may have gone some way toward confounding the criticism of prosecution on mere formality, at the level of the legal process itself *mens rea* could all too readily be turned into an obstacle to effective enforcement. Under the 1833 Act, not only had a scale of minimal fines ranging from £20 down to £1 been imposed, but the justices had been given power to mitigate the penalty even further or, indeed, to discharge the offender altogether if they were satisfied that the offense was neither willful nor grossly negligent. Moreover, as we have already noted, this enactment empowered them to transfer liability from the employer to the servant where the offense had been committed without the personal consent, concurrence, or knowledge of the master.

Given the plausibility with which the internal organization of the factory system enabled employers to represent themselves as not really responsible for factory crime, not to mention the fact that the bench in this period often included other millowners, it is not surprising that these provisions were freely used. Between 1836 and 1842, for example, calculations from the inspectors' annual returns show that 68 percent of all fines imposed under the act amounted to £1 or less—the "sovereign remedy" as it was called—and the inspectors' reports for the same period are replete with instances in which liability was transferred to the servant. Thus, for the inspectors, who fully appreciated the calculational nature of violation as well as the fact that, in most instances, the employer was ultimately responsible for the offense, the way in which rules of *mens rea* (and its alleged absence) were operated by the courts rapidly became a barrier to effective implementation. Not only did it in many cases prevent the imposition of meaningful penalties; it often exonerated "the party ultimately profiting," the party who should "in this particular, as for his own interest he doubtless does in all the other details of his factory, use due diligence to see that his orders are attended to" (P.P., 1837-1838:XXVIII, 110).

Whereas the inspectors sought to solve the problem of their relationship with employers by insisting that something approaching *mens rea* was an integral consideration in their *own* decision-making, their solution to this second problem pointed firmly in the opposite direction. That is, they opted to dispense substantially with the issue of intention at the public level of court proceedings, rather than to secure its realistic incorporation into the decision-making processes of the court. Thus, early on, they were asking the crown lawyers whether it is necessary for them to aver willfulness in connection with legal proceedings; and, by 1840, they were pressing for the "unavoidable responsibility of the master" (P.P., 1841:IX, 576). Similarly, starting in 1837, they prepared a series of draft bills which would, among other things, have abolished the power to mitigate penalties for offenses which were not willful and established the principle that the employer should always be deemed guilty in the first instance.

The Act of 1844 (7 & 8 Vict. c. 15) went a considerable way toward meeting these demands. Thus, it stipulated that the employer should indeed be held guilty in the first instance, even though it also provided that where *he* could prove his own due diligence and that a third party had acted without his knowledge, consent, or connivance, a valid defense would be available. Equally, all reference to willfulness was removed from the sections relating to illegal employment, even though terms such as "knowing," "willfully," and "willful default" were retained in connection with those offenses to which people like parents, operatives, and schoolteachers were most prone. In short, the Act of 1844 took a substantial step toward the elision of *mens rea* and moral culpability from the public adjudication of the routine crimes of factory employers, a step toward institutionalization of the ambiguity, which is one of the distinctive features of such crimes even today.

Just how rapidly this process advanced in subsequent years can be judged from the fact that by 1853, in one of those exceptions which proves the rule, the inspectors were bringing *exceptional* evidence of intention to buttress appeals to the magistrates for the imposition of *maximum* penalties (P.P., 1852-1853:XL, 8). More commonly, however, and in keeping with the speed at which they came to accept the economic categories of the employers themselves, they predicated the need for punishment on the competitive rules of the market rather than on criminal intent. Indeed, by then the inspectors were even prepared to countenance the possibility of a "natural" disconnection between factory crime and "crime" itself, while still using the competitive argument to justify calls for support from the magistrates:

> It is not unnatural that magistrates should have some difficulty in associating the idea of CRIME [sic] with working young persons and women 11 hours a day instead of 10½; . . .but there is no part of the Factories Regulations Acts that I am so often called upon by mill-owners themselves to enforce with rigor. . . . They say, and most justly, that it is of the first importance that all who sell in the same market should be upon one footing as to time, and that those who strictly obey the law should be protected against the unfair competition of those who transgress it [P.P., 1851:XXIII, 5 ff].

Writing in 1836, Philip Gaskell observed that it was "an approximation to absurdity to believe that any man will accuse himself or family of flagrant or even of minor crime" (p. vii). Nor, in his opinion, was it much further from absurdity "to believe that any class, accustomed to a particular social and domestic condition, can be brought to acknowledge that it is essentially evil." What Gaskell was touching on here was something that had already been a bone of contention in the factory debate for some time. During the legislative struggle which had preceded the 1833 Act, the reformers had both campaigned for an unequivocally criminal status to be ascribed to offending employers and had rested their case for legislative interference, in substantial part, on the allegation that the manufacturing system and its entrepreneurs exhibited certain generically evil qualities (Carson, 1974).

These efforts were not entirely successful, even at the legislative level. As we have already seen, the act which was eventually passed left plenty of loopholes whereby occupiers could evade criminal responsibility and subjected those who could not to fairly minimal pecuniary punishments. Moreover, the Royal Commission of 1833, which provided the "legislative knowledge" that justified further intervention, firmly rebutted the charge of generic evil. Instead, it asserted, the system as a whole could be exonerated, legislation only being required because abuses were practiced by a few mill owners, mostly those who occupied smaller premises. Thus, the Act of 1833 received its justification from what has now come to be known as "the rotten apple thesis" in relation to white-collar crime (Taylor et al., 1962:30).

In a previous section, however, it was pointed out that the factory crime of this period—and particularly overworking—was not only a calculated response to economic exigency, but one which rested on acceptance of orthodox assumptions about the necessary interdependence of labor and about the relationship between hours of work, capital investment, and costs. Significantly too, we saw that the competitive and other economic pressures which could generate such responses were not restricted to some minority of less respectable manufacturers. Thus, when the inspectors moved into their more active phase of regulation, from 1836 onward, they immediately encountered a further problem arising from the fact that violation was often not a concentrated evil, but a pervasive one. Indeed, as early as June of that year, Leonard Horner (P.P., 1837:XXL, 56) was reporting "numerous instances of flagrant violations" from Manchester. Nor was he alluding only to small mills in "thinly peopled" districts; his criticism also extended to "some of the largest establishments in towns and populous places" where "in utter disregard of those parts of the law which have never been thought of being altered, children under twelve, nay even of eleven, ten, and sometimes as young as nine years were working twelve hours per day." By 1840, the same inspector (P.P., 1840:X, 25) could indeed be begging a select committee not to construe his evidence as a denial that "there is a very large proportion of the mill-owners who are perfectly incapable . . . of violating the law;" but one of his reports in the preceding year carried quite a different message:

> I can assure those honorable and benevolent mill-owners who, judging others by themselves, deny the necessity of this law, . . . that men of station and property are to be found, and often occupying very large factories, who will at least shut their eyes, and silently acquiesce in the oppressive treatment of children within their own premises [P.P., 1839:XIX, 440].

Throughout this period, the inspectors encountered recurrent difficulty in sustaining a consoling distinction between a large body of respectable employers who would never break the law and that corps of less reputable, mostly smaller mill owners who had previously been held out as the rotten apples in an otherwise wholesome barrel. On one level, of course, the problem here for effective regulation by means of criminal law was that such a course would have entailed collective criminalization which, extending far beyond some morally opprobrious minority, could have embraced many employers of considerable status, social respectability, and, in the wake of the 1832 franchise reform, growing political influence. As Troy Duster (1970:247) has observed, no social order can easily sustain deviant designations in relation to acts of which the predominant perpetrators are seen to come from its "moral center." At a more immediate level, however, the recurrent pervasiveness of factory crime in this period raised further problems with regard to the inspectors' interaction with employers. The law may not have been "passed for such mills as Greg's, Ashworth's or Ashton's" (Senior, 1837:33), but experience showed that these could require close scrutiny just as much as the premises of their less respectable neighbors.

Against this background, it is not surprising that the inspectors fairly rapidly evolved routine modes of inspection which, without abdicating from the attempt to regulate, acknowledged the power differentials permeating their relationships with employers. Thus, right from the start, superintendents were urged to be conciliatory. "Your best chance of success," Inspector Rickards (P.P., 1835:XI, 698) told his subordinates, "will be by courteous and conciliatory demeanor towards the mill-owners; by impressing on their minds that the object of your visits is rather to assist them in conforming to the Act . . . rather than to fish out grounds for complaints." Even in the changed atmosphere of 1836, a similar approach was counseled by Horner (P.P., 1840:X, 155). "Show by close examination," he told his superintendents, "that obedience to the Act . . . will be required; but endeavor, as much as possible, to effect this by explanation, respectful admonition and warning: make it evident that when you find things wrong you do so with regret."

Surviving evidence of the enforcement strategies employed by the superintendents and by the inspectors themselves leaves little doubt that such instructions accurately capture the ethos of factory inspection in this period. Warnings, for example, seem to have become rapidly institutionalized as a routine response to law-breaking. When, in 1853, Alexander Redgrave (P.P., 1852-1853: XL, 44) explained that he was "always unwilling to take legal proceedings unless persuasion and warning [proved] unavailing," he was only adding to a long catalogue of similar statements which had been made by the other inspectors over the course of the previous 20 years. Similarly, it was common to reach an accommodation with the employer whereby, provided he agreed to dismiss the child to whom the inspector objected during one of his intermittent visits, he would not be prosecuted for illegal employment in the intervening period. Horner (P.P., 1838:XXVIII, 136), for example, dealt with some 200 cases of illegal employment in this way during the first three months of 1838 alone, and in 1847 (P.P., 1847:XV, 5) he was still insisting that "this gentle punishment," as he called it, had been found to be effective in connection with violation of the law's educational provisions. In Ireland and Scotland, similar arrangements seem to have been an integral feature of enforcement; in the case of the latter, superintendents were even told that they should only report with a view to prosecution if, *"on leaving the mill,"* they were unable to certify that the law was substantially enforced, irrespective of what they might have found on entering (P.P., 1841:IX, 265). By 1876, Redgrave was able to look back over more than 30 years of involvement with factory inspection and state:

> In the inspection of factories it has been my view always that we are not acting as policemen, . . . that in enforcing this Factory Act, we do not enforce it as a policeman would check an offense which he is told to detect. We have endeavored not to enforce the law, if I may use such an expression, but it has been my endeavor . . .that we should simply be the advisers of all classes, that we should explain the law, and that we should do everything we possibly could to induce them to observe the law, and that a prosecution should be the very last thing we should take up [Thomas, 1948:41].

In the institutionalization of such strategies of control, we can see the beginnings of the process whereby modern factory inspection, despite its operation under criminal law, came to accept violation of that law as a customary and conventional feature of industrial production. Equally, we can see the genesis of that ambivalence to prosecution which is characteristic of so much white-collar crime and which, according to some (Becker, 1971), plays no small part in generating the aura of ambiguity surrounding it. Not least, in comments such as Redgraves', we can sense something of the diffidence with which these officials approached even the possibility of erecting a substantially criminal relationship between the state and the "normal" operation of capital in this period.

In this, of course, the inspectors were not alone. The legislature itself was often at great pains to accommodate orthodox thinking about the relationship between capital costs and hours of labor—the

1833 Act, for example, was framed in such a way as to facilitate the use of relays of children to support the more protracted labor of adults.[5] Similarly, as we have seen, the magistrates were scarcely enthusiastic about applying the full rigors of criminal law to those who were merely pursuing the logic of entrepreneurial calculations about investment, costs, and profits. Even the judiciary was diffident to the seemingly immutable laws of capital as occasion demanded. When a "false" relay system reappeared in the wake of the trade-revival of 1848, for example, its legality was upheld in the Court of Exchequer by Lord Parke in the case of Ryder v. Mills. It was no part of the court's task, he maintained, to ascertain whether enactments were dictated by sound policy; that was for Parliament. In the present case, the 1844 Act imposed penalties and must therefore be construed strictly, its looseness of phraseology thus permitting the use of discontinuous relays to work factories for more than ten hours. But a rather different version of the "legal" reasoning which would be deployed in this important case had been related to Lord Ashley, only a week earlier, by none other than the attorney general:

> They will give judgment, not according to law, but on policy. Judge Parke observed to me "I have no doubt that the framers of the Act intended that the labor should be continuous, but as it is a law to restrain the exercise of capital and property, it must be construed stringently" [Ryder v. Mills, in Thomas, 1948:311].

By the time this decision was made, the laws of capital which encouraged such ingenious strategies for overworking were, of course, beginning to change. Increasingly, and in some measure as a result of the inspectors' exhortatory efforts,[6] manufacturers were starting to appreciate that reduced hours did not necessarily entail diminished production or profit. Within three years, Lord Parke's loophole had been closed (16 & 17 Vict. c. 104), the normal working day had become a reality, and factory legislation could begin to move toward its more familiar, contemporary preoccupation with other issues. By this point, however, more had been achieved than the regulation of hours of labor. The pattern of factory law enforcement had been set, and the ambiguity of factory crime established.

## CONCLUSION

In this chapter, I have attempted to recover the substance from which the ambiguity of factory crime was cast during the first half of the nineteenth century. I have argued that, in terms of the totality of the social order which was emerging in this period, there was an internal dynamic which produced an impetus toward rather than away from effective regulation, and that this broader logic collided at a number of points with the prevailing organization and ideology of factory production. Finally, I have suggested that in dealing with the problems generated by this contradiction, the enforcers of early factory legislation fairly rapidly evolved strategies and perspectives which, while not entailing abdication from the task of regulation, led to the ambiguity of factory crime becoming institutionalized. It now only remains to comment briefly on the relevance of this type of analysis for the contemporary study of white-collar crime.

In this connection, I would claim, first of all, that work of the kind reported here is useful because it attempts to preserve rather than to annihilate the ambiguity inherent in white-collar crime. As important today as it was when first enjoined on us by Vilhelm Aubert, this approach deserves more attention than most students of white-collar crime, despite ritualistic obeisance to Aubert's insight, have been prepared to give it. Nor, indeed, have the proponents of broader sociological perspectives on crime and deviance fully appreciated the rich vein to be mined in studying this particular aspect of white-collar crime. Despite its sensitivity to the nuances of social reaction, for example, labeling theory never really escaped from its preoccupation with those areas of deviance which are clearly marked out and stigmatized. Just occasionally, and even then usually only in passing, did it comment on the complex, unclear, and extremely ambivalent reactions provoked by the white-collar criminal (Rock, 1973:142). While the resurgence of more structurally robust perspectives such as conflict theory and Marxist criminology have generated renewed interest in white-collar crime, the proponents of these approaches have signally failed, I would argue, to retain its essential ambiguity. Taylor et al. (1962:146), for example, rightly castigate labeling theory for its failure to appreciate that "most deviant and especially criminal, acts are physical acts which have quite clear social meanings." But they do not go on to develop the implications of white-collar crime as one of the main exceptions.

Even if we do preserve the vital theme of ambiguity, however, there still remains the question of the level at which its analysis should be pitched. I have explicitly stated my own view that the study of white-collar crime must be couched in terms of the totality within which it is proscribed, committed, sometimes controlled, and frequently tolerated. More specifically, I would suggest that the field would benefit substantially from an approach which starts by asking what part laws relating to white-collar crime may play in reproducing the social order that witnesses their creation and maintenance. Thereafter, by prying open the dynamic interrelationship among different elements within the totality, we may be able to uncover the forces which determine both the degree to which and the equivocation with which such criminal laws are enforced. To be sure, the fluctuating fortunes of interest groups and the clash of normative conflicts may be fascinating and relevant features of the interactional sequences through which ambiguity emerges and is sustained in this context; but its basic substance, I believe, is rooted deeper in the social order as a totality.

This chapter has attempted such an analysis in relation to the emerging totality of one specific historical conjuncture. But its value, I would hope, need not hinge solely on the extent to which it may or may not provide a better understanding of the past, or indeed, of the historical antecedents of current ambiguity. As with factory crime (so too with other kinds of white-collar crime), work of this kind can possibly help us to grasp the essence of ambiguity, not just as a historical movement, but as one which remains unresolved. Despite threads of continuity, totalities change and so too do the relationships among their constituent elements. Through history we can recapture an essential dimension of the sociological imagination and reconnect white-collar crime, even in the present, with the process of historical transformation. In so doing, students of this subject might come to a better appreciation, not only of the connection between this type of crime and the "big ups and downs" of the societies in which they live, but also of what "this connection means for the kinds of history-making in which they might take part" (Mills, 1970).

## NOTES

1. The Parliamentary Papers hereafter will be abbreviated as P.P.

2. The question of "making up lost time," for example, was of great importance for mills powered by water rather than by steam, and much of the legislation of the period reflects compromises on this score.

3. Such assumptions were, for example, central to Senior's (1837) famous calculation that the entire net profit made by a mill working 11½ hours daily was earned in the last hour, any reduction to 10 hours therefore being disastrous.

4. The figure for 1836 would almost certainly have been even higher had it not been for the fact that, in anticipation of the law being changed, the inspectors suspended their visits for much of the first half of that year (P.P., 1837:XXXI, 55).

5. This was the suggestion put forward by the Royal Commission which reported in that year. The plan of working "double sets" of children, it explained, was the only alternative to creating "an evil greater than that which it is sought to be remedied," namely, "a limitation of the labor of adults" (P.P., 1833:XX, 53).

6. In 1849, for example, Horner (P.P., 1850:XXIII, 4) reported that more and more employers were coming around to the view that by increasing machinery speed, "but mainly as a result of the greater activity and attention of workers during shortened hours," the reduction in output had been much less than expected.

## REFERENCES


AUBERT, V. (1952) "White-collar crime and social structure." American Journal of Sociology 58 (November):263-271.

BECKER, H. S. (1977) "Conventional crime." Chapter 22 in H. S. Becker, Sociological Work: Method and substance. New Brunswick, NJ: Transaction.

BENDIX, R. (1956) Work and Authority in Industry. New York: John Wiley.

BLAUG, M. (1961) "The productivity of capital in the Lancashire cotton industry during the nineteenth century." Economic History Review 13 (March):358-381.

CARSON, W. C. (1970) "Some sociological aspects of strict liability and enforcement of factory legislation." Modern Law Review 33 (July):396-412.

——— (1974) "Symbolic and instrumental dimensions of early factory legislation." Pp. 107-138 in R. Hood (ed.), Crime, Criminology and Public Policy. London: Heinemann.

CHAPMAN, S. J. (1904) The Lancashire Cotton Industry. Manchester, England:

COOKE-TAYLOR, R. W. (1842) Notes of a Tour in the Manufacturing Districts of Lancashire.

CRABTREE, G. (1833) Factory Commission: The Legality of its Appointment Questioned and the Legality of its Proceedings Proved. London: Seeley & Sons.

CRESSEY, D. R. (1961) "Foreword." Pp. ix-xii in E. H. Sutherland, White Collar Crime. New York: Holt, Rinehart & Winston.

DUSTER, T. (1970) The Legislation of Morality. New York: Free Press.

FIELDEN, J. (1969) The Curse of the Factory System (1836) (J. Ward, ed.). London: Frank Cass.

FOSTER, J. (1977) Class Struggle and the Industrial Revolution. London: Methuen.

FULLER, R. C. (1942) "Morals and the criminal law." Journal of Criminal Law and Criminology 32 (March-April):624-630.

GASKELL, P. (1836) Artisans and Machinery. London: John W. Parker.

Great Britain (1833) Report of the Factories Inquiry Commission. London: Her Majesty's Stationery Office.

GREG, R. H. (1837) The Factory Question. London: J. Ridgway.

HALL, J. (1960) General Principles of Criminal Law. Indianapolis: Bobbs-Merrill.

HALL, S. et al. (1978) Policing the Crisis. London: Macmillan.

HOBSBAWN, E. J. (1964) Labouring Man. London: Weidenfeld & Nicholson.

LEMERT, E. M. (1967) Human Deviance, Social Problems and Social Control. Englewood Cliffs, NJ: Prentice-Hall.

McKENDRICK, N. (1961) "Josiah Wedgwood and factory discipline." Historical Journal 4 (January):30-55.

MARX, K. (1936) Capital. New York: Modern Library.

MILLS, C. W. (1970) "The promise of the sociological imagination." Pp. 4-14 in J. Douglas (ed.), The Relevance of Sociology. New York: Appleton-Century-Crofts.

NEWMAN, D. J. (1977) "White-collar crime: An overview and analysis." Pp. 50-64 in G. Geis and R. F. Meier (eds.), White-Collar Crime. New York: Free Press.

PAULUS, I. (1974) The Search for Pure Food. London: Martin Robertson.

PEARCE, F. (1976) Crimes of the Powerful. London: Pluto Press.

POLLARD, S. (1963) "Factory discipline in the industrial revolution." Economic History Review 16 (February):254-271.

ROCK, P. (1973) Deviant Behaviour. London: Hutchinson.

SENIOR, N. W. (1837) Letters on the Factory Act. London: B. Fellowes.

SUMNER, C. (1976) "Marxism and deviance theory." Pp. 159-174 in P. Wiles (ed.), Crime and Delinquency in Britain, Vol. 2. London: Martin Robertson.

SUTHERLAND, E. H. (1949) White Collar Crime. New York: Dryden.
SWEET V. PARSLEY (1969) 1 All England Reports 347.
TAYLOR, I., P. WALTON, and J. YOUNG [eds.] (1962) Critical Criminology. London: Routledge & Kegan Paul.
TAYLOR, W. C. (1842) Notes of a Tour in the Manufacturing Districts of Lancashire. London: Duncan and Malcolm.
THOMAS, M. W. (1948) The Early Factory Legislation. London: Thames Bank.
THOMPSON, E. P. (1967) "Time, work-discipline and industrial capitalism." Past and Present 38 (December):56-97.
(1968) The Making of the English Working Class. London: Pelican.
(1975) Whigs and Hunters. London: Allen Lane.
WARD, J. T. (1962) The Factory Movement, 1830-1855. London: Macmillan.
WILLIAMS, R. (1977) Marxism and Literature. Oxford: Oxford University Press.

*Chapter 8*

# ANALYZING SUSPECTED COLLUSION AMONG BIDDERS

MICHAEL D. MALTZ and
STEPHEN M. POLLOCK

No one likes to be overcharged, not even a governmental agency. It is all the more galling when the overcharging is apparently blatant; when the agency requests closed bids from prospective suppliers and it finds (or suspects) that the suppliers are illegally conspiring in their bid submissions to keep their prices high.

This chapter describes a set of techniques for analyzing bids in which collusion is suspected. It is based on analytic work performed in conjunction with an investigation by a county prosecutor. We are constrained by pending litigation from describing the particulars of the situation,[1] the products purchased by the county agencies, the names of the vendors (which we still do not know), or the states and counties involved. The nature of the suspected collusion involved and the suitability of the techniques, however, are not specific to this particular situation and can be described without jeopardizing the case.

## COMPETITIVE BIDDING AND COLLUSION

Certain procedures have evolved over the past decades in an attempt to ensure that purchasers of goods and services deal fairly and honestly with vendors. The most widely used procedure is the closed competitive bid. The specifications and quantities of the desired goods and services needed are sent to all prospective vendors and are published in local newspapers or other periodicals. Vendors are given until a specified date to submit their bids, and all bids are opened and read immediately thereafter. With few exceptions, the lowest bidder wins the contract.

An immediate selection based on a closed competitive bid is possible only when purchasing goods and services that can be described completely using, for example, government or industry-wide standards. Janitorial services, crushed rock, milk, or pencils can be specified using commonly accepted standards, and the purchaser normally need not worry about adequate quality of the goods if the winning bid meets the standards. When dealing with goods and services that cannot be specified completely (for example, construction of a building or a ship, or research in a new area), bids are usually submitted in the form of proposals and are evaluated on the basis of the work plan as well as price.

In both cases the bidding procedure is designed to ensure that every bidder is given the same information and has the same opportunity to respond. It is meant to prevent friendship (or enmity) between a vendor and a purchasing agent from entering into the decision process. Of course, no procedure can entirely eliminate favoritism in bid selection. Cases abound where one bidder feels that his competitor has been "wired in," and that the bidding is just a *pro forma* exercise to lend the appearance of impartiality to the process. For example, a contract for radio equipment might specify a receiver sensitivity of 0.5 microvolts (achieved by one vendor) when 1 microvolt (achieved by others) will do.[2]

In contrast to rigged competitions are those cases in which nonspecified or nonspecifiable conditions are met by one vendor but not others. For example, one vendor may be much more amenable to delivering goods directly to the site where they are needed and in the necessary quantities, even though this is not part of the contract. In other words, there are drawbacks as well as benefits in attempting to limit the ability of a purchasing agent to "steer" a contract to one vendor.

Closed bidding procedures are designed primarily to ensure that there is no collusion between the purchasing agent and *vendors.* However, they do not prevent bidders from getting together to conspire with *each other* about who should win which bid and for what price. In most cases it is not a set of procedures but a set of laws that is used to deter such collusion: laws regarding restraint of trade, antitrust, and conspiracy to defraud, as well as those laws specifically directed against collusion on bids for government contracts. Despite these laws, the way most bids are evaluated—especially those for supplying goods and services to governmental agencies—makes it difficult for agencies to deter collusion among bidders.

Public agencies can take steps, other than procedural ones, to reduce the possibility of bidders colluding. Information from each bid is useful in determining whether there was collusion; however, very often the information about each bid is scrutinized alone, without anyone attempting to see if a pattern of collusion exists over time or across jurisdictions. Suspicious authorities in one jurisdiction do not ordinarily obtain information from other jurisdictions which have let similar bids, nor do they ordinarily look for suspicious patterns in bids from year to year. Yet, it is obvious that there are advantages to the vendors if they engage in collusion. The economics of such collusion has been discussed elsewhere (Comanor and Schankerman, 1976; Fellner, 1949; Kuhlman, 1978; Telser, 1972).

## Varieties of Collusive Bidding

Before discussing techniques useful in analyzing collusion, we will briefly describe the nature and varieties of collusive behavior that can occur. There are four general types of collusive bidding[3] that can be identified: predation, identical bidding, geographical market-sharing, and rotational bidding.

## Predation

In this case large firms agree among themselves to bid below prevailing market prices (and even below costs, if necessary) for a long enough period of time to drive out weaker firms. This serves to reduce competition and permits the remaining firms eventually to raise their prices with relative impunity.

Predatory behavior is difficult to detect. Although a victimized firm may "blow the whistle," the transient nature of predation makes it extremely hard to disentangle from normal competition. If the product has undergone technological innovation, predatory behavior is even more difficult to detect, but is not impossible: Kodak and Xerox have been challenged, with mixed success, for using high technological turnover (creating a "patent thicket") to stifle competition in their respective markets.

## Identical Bidding

All vendors agree to submit identical bids for every contract, although they may collectively vary the bid from contract to contract. The bid price is usually well above that which would be expected in a competitive market. Purchasing agents are often amenable to this type of bidding, since it gives them the freedom to select any or all bidders: they can split the award and keep all vendors happy; they can make their selection on the basis of unspecified but relevant criteria (for example, a vendor located in the jurisdiction, or one who has previously given a high level of service); or they can play favorites. Regardless of the selection procedure, a higher-than-competitive price is normally paid.

Smaller firms tend to favor this scheme (Comanor and Schankerman, 1976), since—if the purchasing agent is neutral—they are usually assured of getting a fairly stable share of the market without having to cut into their profit margin. This tactic is also used when a large number of vendors is involved, since coordination among the vendors is minimal. In addition, deviations from the agreed-upon price are easy to detect (particularly in public bids, where every vendor's bid price is available to all after the bids are opened).

Detecting identical bids, of course, is trivial; proving in court that they resulted from collusion is another matter. Although one is inclined to regard an instance where many vendors submit exactly the same bid as *prima facie* evidence of collusion, many industries employ standard bidding and pricing methods and "suggested price" lists, the use of which may not be illegal per se.

### Geographical Market-Sharing

The potential market is divided up in advance into "territories" within which only one member of the colluding group is permitted to submit a low bid (at a price higher than would be otherwise obtained in a competitive market). The remaining bidders, who are given other territories, either do not participate in that territory or submit artificially high ("complimentary") bids to give the illusion of competition.[4] Since the need for coordination among bidders is minimal, this scheme is probably favored when a large number of firms is involved.

Detection of this type of collusion is of course impossible without pooling information on bids submitted to agencies in the relevant geographical area. Colluders rely on the lack of coordination among the agencies as a means of maintaining the scheme.

### Rotational Bidding

This market-sharing scheme is more complicated than one based on fixed territories. The vendor who will submit the low bid is agreed upon in advance. Each vendor is given the opportunity to win contracts so that over a period of time he ends up with a predetermined allocation of market share. The difference between this scheme and geographical market-sharing is that the pattern of low bids is not fixed by territory. Again, the low bid is set to a higher value than that which would arise under competition. Close coordination among the bidders is essential, since the schemes can be quite complicated; therefore, these schemes probably involve fewer firms than do other bid-rigging schemes (Comanor and Schankerman, 1976).

Detection of a complicated rotational bidding scheme is difficult, even if jurisdictions pool their data. Distinguishing it from competitive bidding is not a simple task, especially since the scheme's complexity in all likelihood might be designed specifically to make it appear competitive. This was true of the rotational scheme used in the heavy electrical equipment conspiracy of the 1960s (Geis, 1968).

In the case described below, two of the four collusion methods, identical and rotational bidding, were suspected. In the sections that follow, we present the methods used to verify the suspicious bidding patterns and identify specific vendors whose bidding behavior warranted further investigation.

## THE INVESTIGATION

### Background

A county official became suspicious when bids were opened for a particular contract. All of the bids submitted were identical, except for one which was a few dollars lower (the bids were in the $50,000 range). This coincidence suggested collusion to the official, and was brought to the attention of the county prosecuting attorney.

A grand jury was empaneled and subpoenas were issued to suppliers. Other counties were contacted and asked to send information about bid prices on the same commodity for the past few years. As a result of the subpoenas and requests, a great deal of bid information was collected. The data were put on coding sheets by an investigator in the prosecutor's office, but the analysis went no further. The grand jury's term eventually ended; it had already been extended twice, and it was likely that there would be some turnover in the jury due to illness and other factors. Because bringing in new jurors after so much evidence had been presented would be difficult (and subject to legal challenge) in so complex a case as this, the prosecutor decided not to press for a continuation of the grand jury investigation.

The authors were apprised of the situation and began to work with the prosecutor on an informal basis. After a preliminary analysis demonstrated that further analytic work would be fruitful, work was continued on a more formal basis.

The data consisted of bids submitted in response to yearly county solicitations from about 30 suppliers. Bid information was requested from all counties in the state from 1972 to 1977. Had every supplier bid in every county in each of the five years, there would have been over 10,000 bids. Although this was not the case, we still had over 1,200 bids to work with. Forty-six counties (over half of the counties in the state) are represented. Data are missing (or sparse) for the rest of the counties, most of which are relatively unpopulated.[5] Thirteen of the suppliers were active enough during the entire period of interest to allow detailed analysis of their behaviors.

## Nature of the Product

The material involved in our study was a standard off-the-shelf manufactured product.[6] The product and its associated market had all of the characteristics that have been found to be associated with collusion (Rothrock et al., 1978; Hay and Kelley, 1974; Kuhlman, 1977; Erickson, 1969; Funderburk, 1974): (1) The product is relatively simple, and there is little or no technological innovation. (2) The predominant method of vendor selection is to take the lowest bid from among the qualified bidders, in a sealed-bid tender auction. (3) The demand for the product is relatively inelastic. (4) The number of vendors is relatively small, and they are organized in a trade association. (5) Purchasing standards and specifications set by the purchasers are essentially uniform throughout the industry. (6) The market is predictable; that is, the purchasers are the same from year to year and the annual demand for the product can readily be estimated.

## Sources of Bid Variation

### EFFECT OF TIME AND INFLATION

Figure 1 shows all of the bids for size 1 that were included in the data.[7] A number of patterns are clearly discernible. First, there are annual bidding "seasons," from late fall to early spring. Second, there appear to be "standard" bid prices in each bidding season, although a number of bids are below this standard bid price and a few are above it. Third, this "standard" price increased considerably from 1971 to 1976. In all years the standard price was taken to be the modal price.

These three patterns are of use in the data analysis. The seasonal nature of the data permits us to identify the bidding "seasons" and to aggregate the data by season to look for additional patterns. The existence of a "standard" price for each season permits us to normalize each season's bids (by dividing by the standard) in order to compare different seasons more readily. The inflationary nature of the standard price increase is seen by a comparison with the cost of the raw material (indicated by Xs in Figure 1) over the period of interest. Thus, normalization effectively serves as an appropriate "deflator."

## Effect of Discounts

The prices in Figure 1 are the actual prices bid to the jurisdiction. This industry has traditionally offered bids in terms of a gross unit price (the "standard" price), from which various discounts are

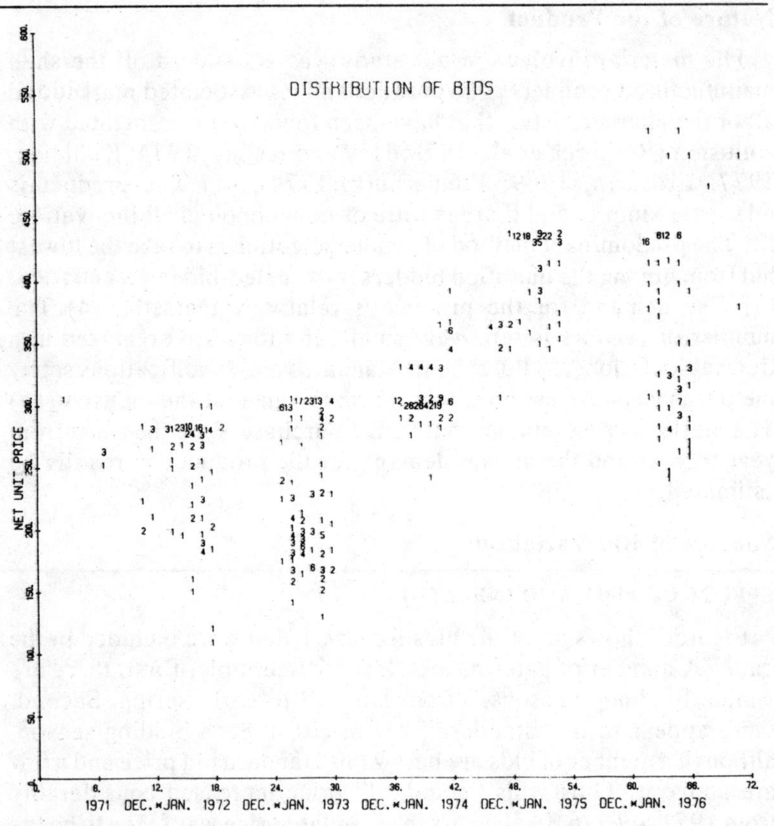


FIGURE 1 Bid Net Unit Versus Time for All Suppliers

offered. Thus, this figure portrays the bids after all discounts were taken into account. Four types of discounts were observed:

*Trade discounts:* flat discounts, offered as a percentage off the accompanying "List" or "Gross" unit price;

*level discounts:* applied to a necessary minimum order (these were actually offered on fewer than two percent of the bids);

*pick-up discounts:* applied to counties willing to pick up the product at the vendor's supply point; and

*financial discounts:* inducements to quick payment (usually a small percentage if paid within 10 days). There were a wide variety of these.

A net unit price (NUP) was calculated taking into account all possible discounts, and was treated as the actual bid price. The normalized net unit price (NNUP) is simply the net unit price divided by the standard price that year for all bidders. If one bid a gross unit price of $2.40 (the "standard" price that year), with a 20 percent discount, the NUP would be $1.92 and the NNUP would be 0.8.

### Effect of Distance

We also wished to determine whether the bid prices were affected by distance. The product is heavy and bulky, so transportation is a significant cost. We knew the county in which each supplier was located, so we calculated a "pseudo-distance"[8] between each supplier's county and the county letting the bid to see if transportation costs accounted for differences in bid prices. Had this been the case, we would see a trend of higher bid prices at greater distances. No relation between bid price and distance was found for any suppliers for any season—the suppliers were not using shipping discounts as a means of competing.

## THE ANALYSIS

### Cumulative Distribution of Bids

We next aggregated all bids submitted during each bidding season to see if there were season-to-season variations in their distribution. Figures 2-6[9] depict the cumulative distributions for all bids, and for low bids for the same contracts, for each of the five bidding seasons. Thus, for example, we see from Figure 2 that during the winter 1972 season about 10 percent of *all* bids were below a NUP of $2.20/unit, but that about 20 percent of the *low* bids were below this NUP.

The general shape of the curves indicates qualitative market behavior. A steep curve is the result of many bids at the same NUP (in 1974 about 80 percent of all bids had the same NUP—about $3.00/unit) and a less steep curve indicates a "spread" of bids (as in 1973). These curves show that 1973 and 1976 were more competitive seasons than 1972, 1974, and 1975. Furthermore, we see that the median bid (the bid exceeded by half of the other bids) actually decreased between 1975 and 1976!

Two factors confirm the striking visual impact of Figures 2-6. First, we were informed (after our analysis was completed) that the 1973 bidding season was known in the industry as the time of the big "price war." Second, the reappearance of competition in the 1976 bidding season was probably not unrelated to the initiation of an investigation and the issuance of subpoenas late in the 1975 season. This constitutes evidence of the deterrent effect of the investigation, a noteworthy finding. This issue has been considered previously

*(text continued on p. 187)*

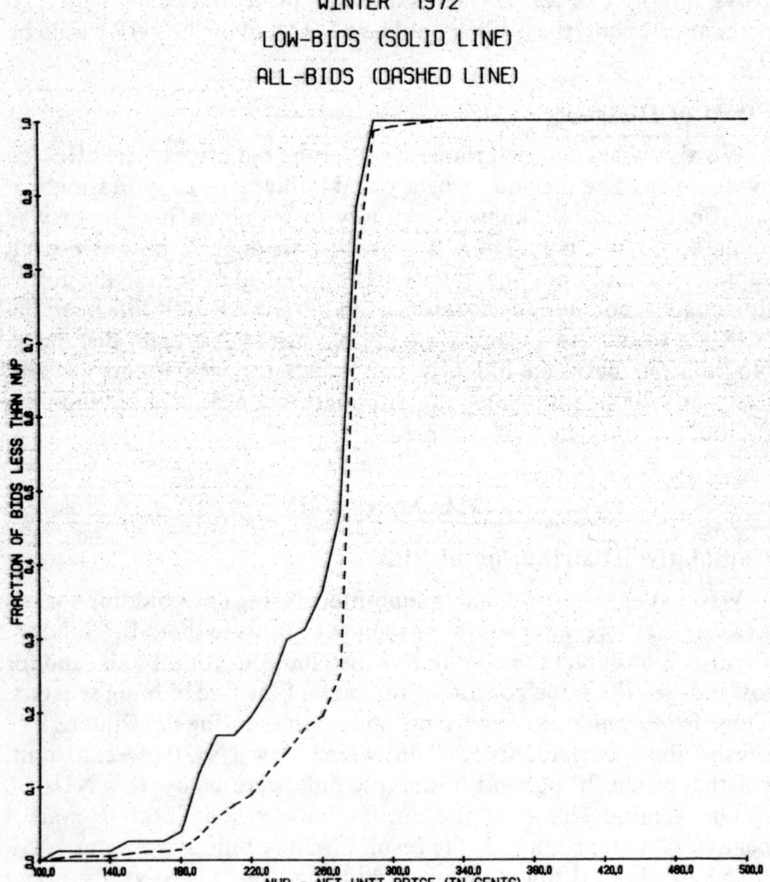


FIGURE 2 Comulative Distribution of All Bids and Low Bids, Winter 1972 Bidding Season

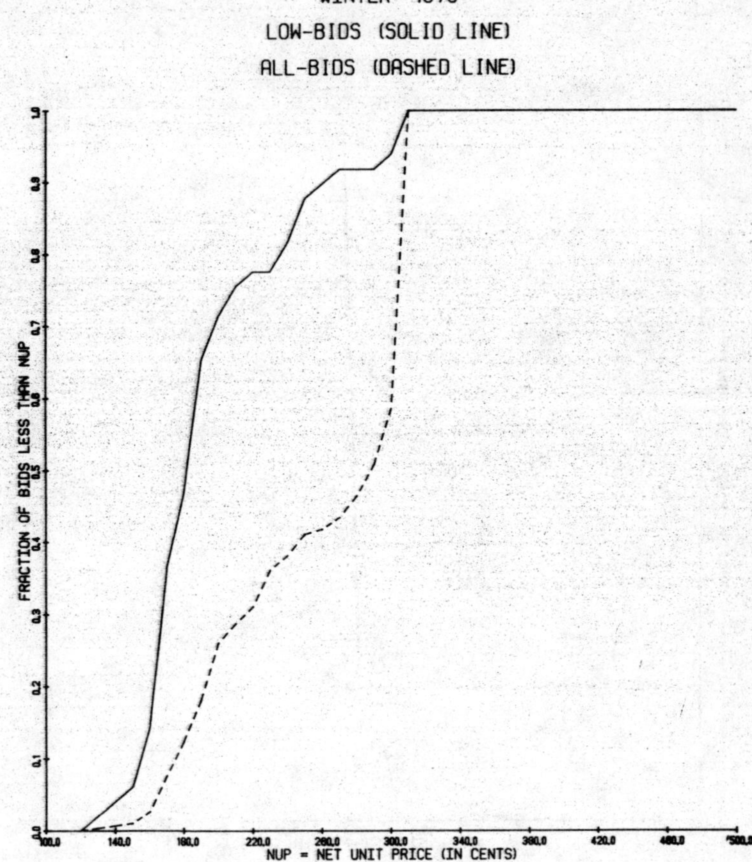


FIGURE 3 Cumulative Distribution of All Bids and Low Bids, Winter 1973 Bidding Season

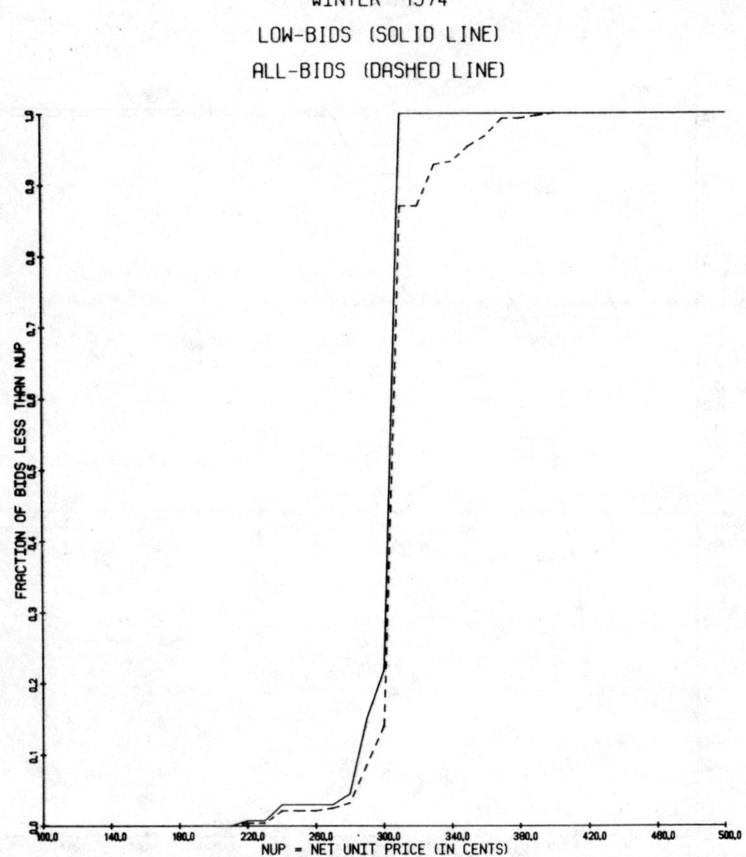


FIGURE 4 Cumulative Distribution of All Bids and Low Bids, Winter 1974 Bidding Season

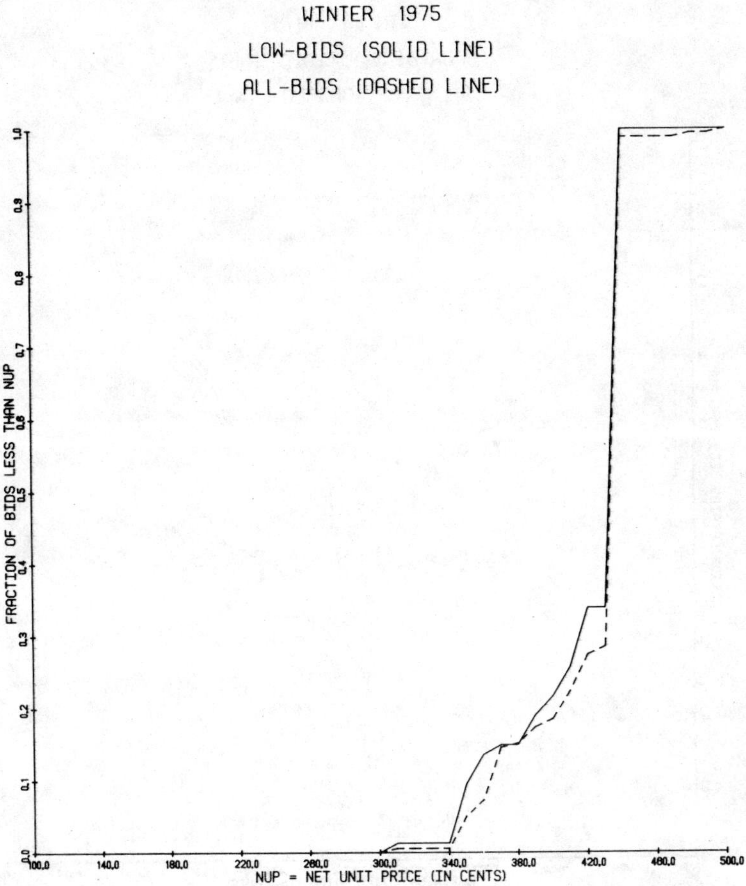

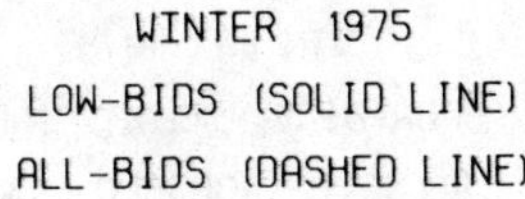


FIGURE 5 Cumulative Distribution of All Bids and Low Bids, Winter 1975 Bidding Season

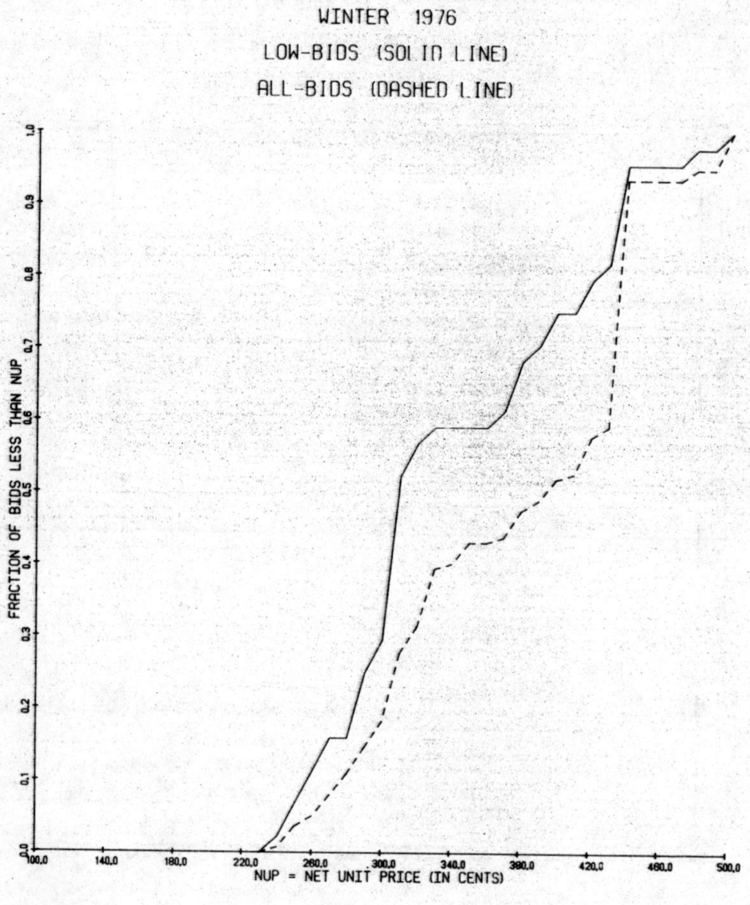

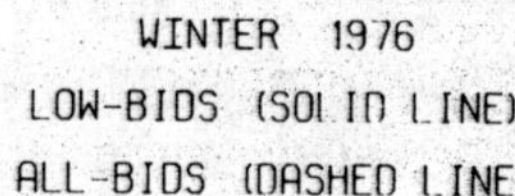


FIGURE 6 Cumulative Distribution of All Bids and Low Bids, Winter 1976 Bidding Season

from both ethical (Allen, 1978) and analytic (Block et al., 1978) standpoints.

One indication of the degree of competition from year to year is the standard deviation (SD) of bids,[10] year by year. In 1972 the SD was 29; in 1973 (the year of the "price war") it rose to 53, indicating a greater degree of competition; in 1974 it was 21; in 1975 it was 30; and in 1976 (after the investigation had begun), the SD was 73.

Another approach indicates the degree of competition within contracts. In general, in a competitive market, the relation between two cumulative distributions—that for *all* bids and that for *low* bids—would be similar to that shown in Figure 3. Specifically, if the cumulative distribution of all bids is given by F(x), and if there were n competitors acting (statistically) independently of each other, then the cumulative distribution of the low bid, G(x), is given by (Bury, 1975:71)

$$G(x) = 1 - [1 - F(x)]^n.$$

Since we have data for G(x) and F(x) for each season, it is possible to obtain a value of n which provides a "good" fit between the left- and righthand sides of this equation. We can choose for this "estimator" $\hat{n}$, the value of n that minimizes the conventional Kolmogorov-Smirnov measure

$$\max_x \left| [1 - F(x)]^n - [1 - G(x)] \right| .$$

This gives an "equivalent number" of bidders consistent with both the data and the hypothesis of independence (competitiveness). The value of $\hat{n}$ can be compared with the *actual* number of bidders in each contract (or, in the case we have of data aggregated over season, with the average number, $\bar{n}$, of bidders per contract). Table 1 shows $\hat{n}$ and $\bar{n}$ for each season. The smaller the ratio of $\bar{n}/\hat{n}$, the more evidence there is for bid independence.[11] We see that 1973 is still the most competitive year using this measure, but that now 1976 seems to be the least competitive. Thus, this new measure points out the possibility that in the postsubpoena period the high bid variation may

*Table 1* Equivalent Number of Independent Bidders ($\hat{N}$) and Mean Number of Bidders ($\bar{N}$) per Contract, 1972 through 1976

| | *1972* | *1973* | *1974* | *1975* | *1976* |
|---|---|---|---|---|---|
| No. Contracts | 41 | 40 | 46 | 30 | 28 |
| No. Bids | 346 | 277 | 272 | 154 | 128 |
| $\bar{N}$ | 8.4 | 6.9 | 5.9 | 5.1 | 4.6 |
| $\hat{N}$ | 5.5 | 6.5 | 4.5 | 3.5 | 2.5 |
| $\bar{N}/\hat{N}$ | 1.5 | 1.1 | 1.3 | 1.5 | 1.8 |

be masking within-contract dependence (and therefore reduced competition).

## Comparisons of Pairs of Suppliers' Bids

The above analysis led us to the conclusion that noncompetitive activity occurred during the 1974 and 1975, and possibly 1976, seasons.[12] However, we still had to explore the individual behavior of the suppliers in order to establish evidence as to the *kind* of collusion scheme being used, and thus the kind of supportive evidence to be sought by other means. To do this, we compared each pair of suppliers' bids by plotting one against the other. (Again, in order to remove the effect of inflation-caused price increases we used the normalized net unit price [NNUP] rather than the net unit price ) The results, for selected pairs of suppliers, are shown in Figures 7 through 10. In these figures, a point is produced for each contract in which *both* suppliers of a given pair submitted a bid. The NNUP for one supplier is plotted along the vertical axis; the NNUP for the other supplier is plotted on the horizontal axis. The number written on the graph at a specific point[13] indicates the number of times that pair of normalized bids was observed. For example, in Figure 7, the "40" at the point (1.00, 1.00) indicates that there were 40 separate contracts during the five-year period on which both supplier 8401 and supplier 2306 each bid a NNUP of 1.00.

The resulting pattern indicates the behavior of pairs of suppliers on those contracts when they were bidding against each other. Four general types of patterns may appear.

(1) One supplier always bids close to the "standard gross unit price" regardless of the bid of the other supplier, and the second supplier submits bids over a range of values. This behavior is seen in Figure 7: Supplier 2306 bid fairly close to the standard gross unit price while supplier 8401 bid a range of values. Thus, not only does 2306 rarely offer a discount, those times when he does are not coordinated with the bids of 8401.

(2) Both suppliers offer occasional discounts from the standard gross unit price, but act independently of each other. For example, Figure 8 shows that (a) 10 out of the 28 pairs of bids are at (1.00, 1.00): (b) there are nearly an equal number of bids when supplier 2902 bid near 1.00 while supplier 6416 bid lower, as when supplier 6416 bid at 1.00 while supplier 2902 bid lower; (c) five of the 28 pairs of bids are those when both suppliers came down from 1.00 (i.e., offered discounts) simultaneously.

Neither of these patterns offers overt evidence of collusion (nor do they necessarily rule out collusion).

*(text continued on p. 192)*

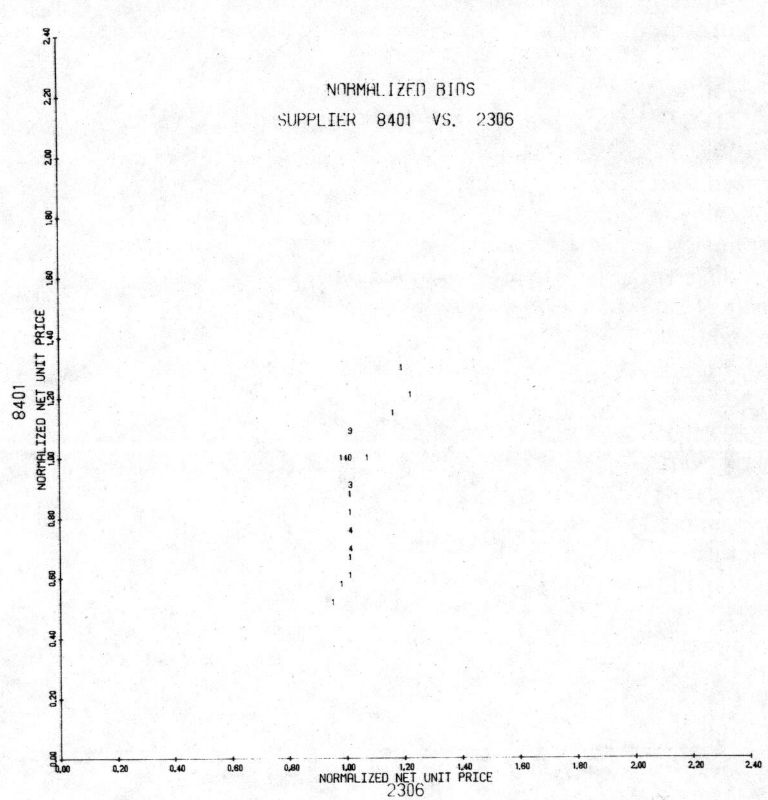


FIGURE 7 Normalized Bids Submitted by Suppliers 8401 and 2306

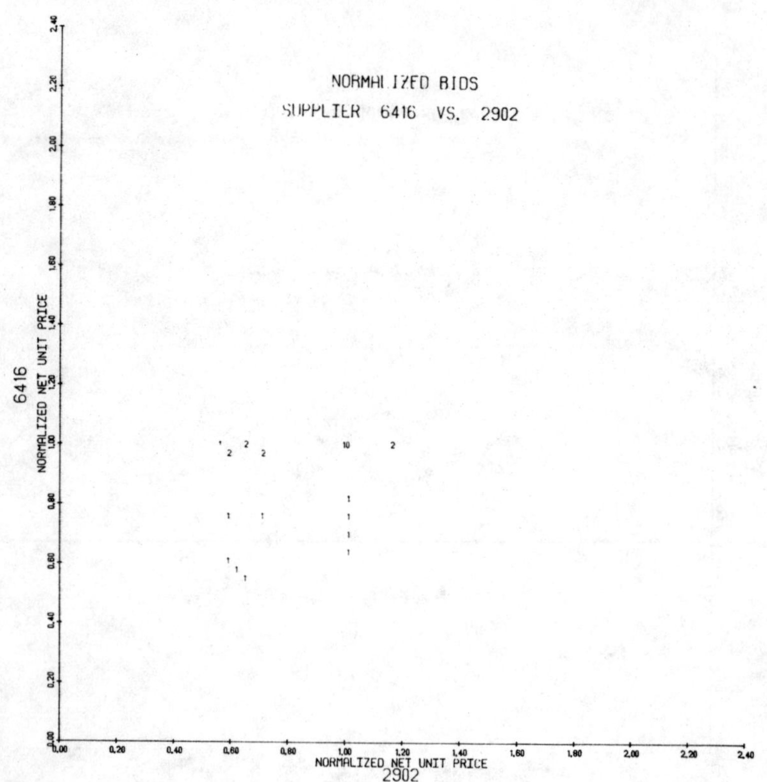


FIGURE 8 Normalized Bids Submitted by Suppliers 6416 and 2902

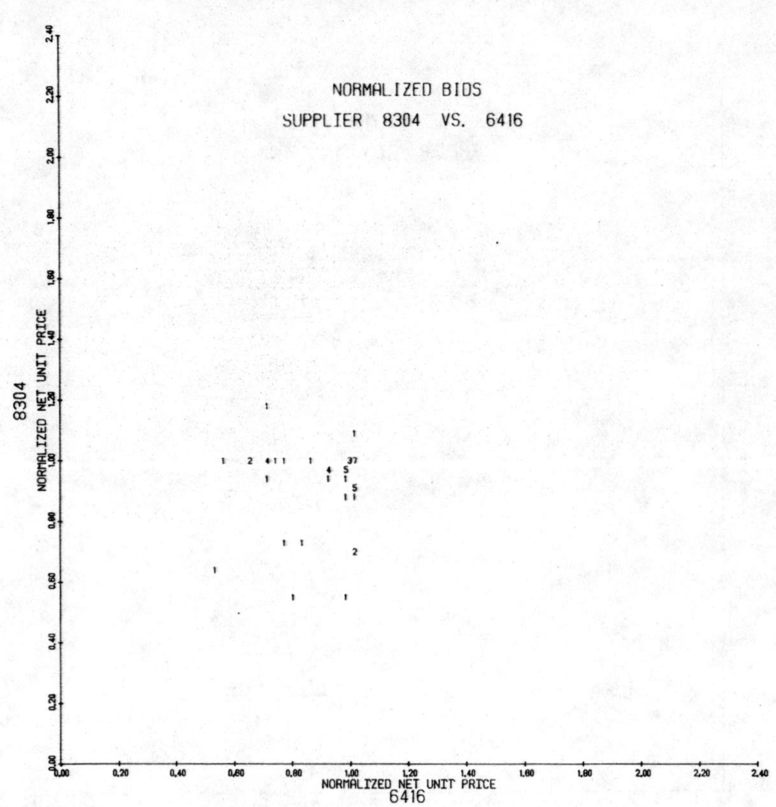


FIGURE 9 Normalized Bids Submitted by Suppliers 8304 and 6416

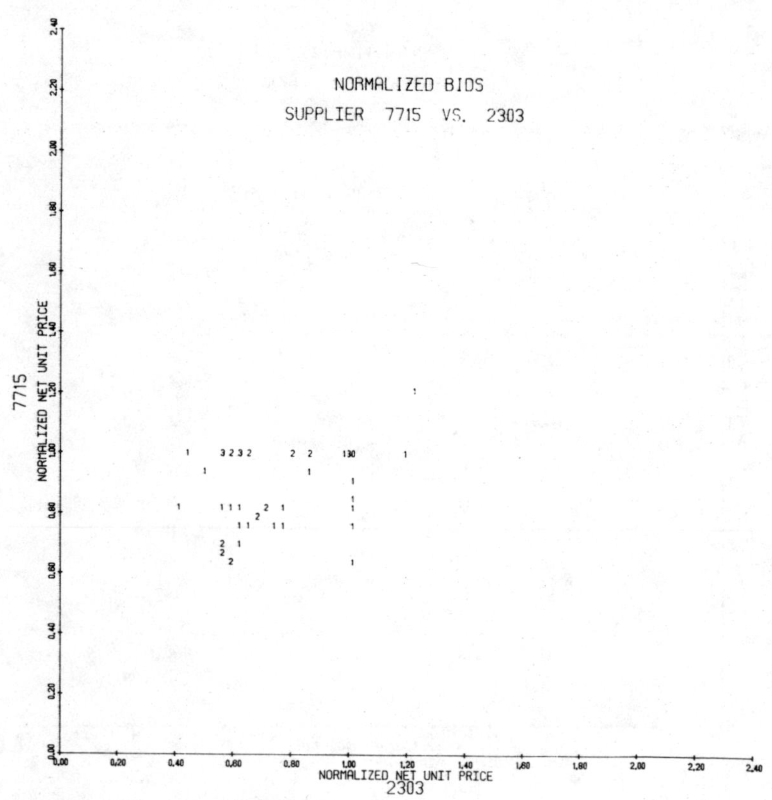


FIGURE 10 Normalized Bids Submitted by Suppliers 7715 and 2303

(3) A relative absence of points corresponding to the two suppliers simultaneously offering discounts, and the presence of a large number of occurrences when one of the two suppliers bids low and the other stays at 1.00. Such a pattern, suggested by Figure 9, is consistent with a rotation type of scheme.

(4) Two suppliers almost always submit bids of nearly the same value. This is the most easily recognizable pattern: Most of the points are clustered around the 45-degree line going from the origin to the point (1.00, 1.00). Figure 10 exhibits this behavior. Note that the pattern reveals the presence of many nearly identical joint bids, suggestive (but not by itself evidence) of collusion.

## Statistical Tests of Dependence

By characterizing such plots, for all pairs of suppliers, as falling into one of the four patterns, it is possible to establish which pairs are acting relatively independently of each other—even though they may be taking advantage of legally shared market information—and which ones exhibit (at least statistical) dependence.

This can be accomplished by forming 2x2 contingency tables for all pairs of suppliers during selected periods of concern. The cutting points in these tables were .98 of NNUP, and the cell entries were the number of bids in each category for the two suppliers. For example, in Figure 10 suppliers 7715 and 2303 both bid NNUPs of 0.98 or greater 33 times; in five cases supplier 2303 bid more than 0.98 and supplier 7715 did not; in sixteen cases supplier 7715 bid more than 0.98 and supplier 2303 did not; and both bid NNUPs below 0.98 in 23 cases. The chi-square statistic was used to test for independence of bidding behavior. For this pair of suppliers a value of 15.5 is obtained ($p. < .001$), strongly suggestive of information-sharing between them. The results of analyzing the joint bids of every pair of suppliers (using $p. < .01$ for significance) are summarized in Figure 11. This led us to recommend to the prosecutor to search for other overt evidence of collusion among the six firms linked together.

We see, then, that bidding irregularities can be detected from this analysis. (It is possible to go beyond consideration of supplier pairs to triplets of suppliers, but it is difficult to analyze them graphically, since data may be sparse for these cases.)

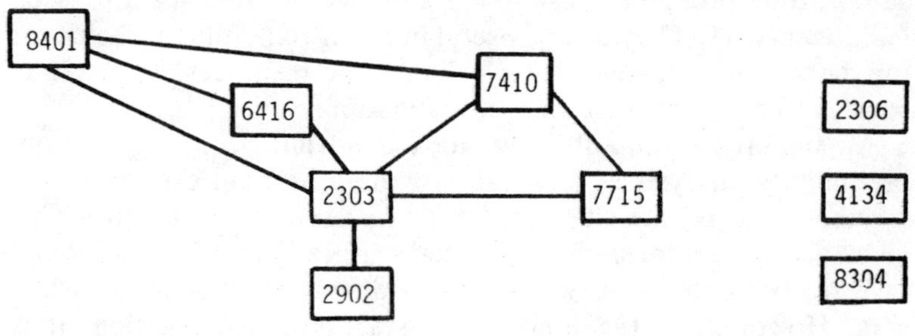


FIGURE 11 Bid Dependencies Among the Nine Major Suppliers

# OBSERVATIONS

## Use of Statistical and Computer Methodology

*No single bid-rigging "package."* We feel quite strongly that there will *never* be a computer package that can be installed in every prosecutor's office and used whenever collusion on bids is suspected. Each case is *sui generis* and must be analyzed differently, in much the same way that writing a brief on the admissibility of evidence depends on the particulars of the case. Although some general packages have been proposed (Gallo, 1977), they can be used only in fortuitous circumstances when the collusion is of a particular type and the available bid information is unambiguous.

*Limited role of analytic techniques.* Both descriptive and inferential statistics can be used to analyze bid data. Descriptive statistics summarize the data in a convenient form. Inferential statistics use the data to draw inferences about hypotheses[14] or parameter estimates. However, neither technique can be relied on to substitute for a "smoking gun" or the "hot document," concrete evidence necessary to link the actors to the collusive acts (Funderburk, 1974).

*Simplicity of most collusive schemes.* Analysts should be aware that the most likely collusive behavior is a simple one. Complicated schemes and codes are likely to be discarded, or at least not trusted, because of the possibility of error, lost communication, or defection on the part of one or more of the colluders.

*Uses of analytic techniques.* Finally, there are strong and compelling reasons to use the analytic techniques reported here: (1) They can provide investigators with leads, by generating hypothetical scenarios of what happened, when it happened, which firms were involved, and the nature of the collusive activity. (2) They can be used to convince a judge to issue warrants and subpoenas, and to demonstrate probable cause to a grand jury to cause them to issue indictments. (3) They can be useful in ruling *out* collusive behavior (or detectable collusive behavior) in some instances, forestalling what is likely to be a fruitless investigation.

An important and often overlooked advantage is that a brief preliminary analysis of bids can provide a first-cut estimate as to whether collusive activity appears to be present in an industry. This gives the prosecutor a chance to make a preliminary "pro-active" investigation of his own, rather than waiting for a complaint before he acts. However, in the preliminary stages of investigation, it is important for local prosecutors to recognize the potential problem of selecting a few bids or vendors for a "pilot" study. Often, the existence of collusion is only apparent by examining the *entire* history of bids. A subset, no matter how judiciously and statistically properly selected, may provide little relevant information.

Even though statutes of limitations may preclude collusive bids from earlier years from being prosecuted, they are useful in the analysis to demonstrate a pattern of continuing collusive activity.

In many cases the collusive bidders rely on the lack of coordination among different jurisdictions (particularly smaller ones) to perpetrate their schemes; these analytic techniques provide the framework within which bid data from different jurisdictions can be coordinated.

Collusion between suppliers and purchasing agents can also be investigated using these methods. For example, if one county never receives bids below the "standard" price while the surrounding counties are obtaining discounts, it may be that the purchasing agent is receiving a "discount" personally.

There have been instances of judges not admitting computer-based data as evidence, on the grounds that it is hearsay evidence (Katz, 1975). Thus, special pains must be taken by the expert witness presenting the analysis to personally review and validate all of the data and the procedures used to analyze them, should it be necessary to use the actual data in court. Indeed, the expert should have, by himself, performed each step of every calculation or data manipulation for at least a number of bids, set of vendors, or purchasers. If there are *any* errors in the data, the defense will undoubtedly seize them to discredit all of the data and the ensuing analysis. By the same token, basing an analysis on a theoretical model of the firm or of industry behavior is not advisable unless there is strong evidence to support its use. Models and other assumptions (for example, that bids are normally or exponentially distributed) can be torn apart in a courtroom (LoCascio, 1978). Even such fundamental statistical concepts as independence must be carefully approached if they are to be used in testimony.

When data are to be used as evidence, a number of precautions must be taken. An analyst will normally make obvious changes without recording them, but if a court case is involved all such changes should be documented. Preparing and presenting data in a case also takes a good deal of care. In most cases, it is best if the data are presented in figures and pictorial exhibits rather than (or as a complement to) tabular form. Other useful tactics are discussed in Fellmeth and Papageorge (1978).

## CONCLUSION

We have shown how computer and statistical techniques can be used to organize large amounts of quantitative information for use as evidence in a bid-rigging investigation. In the case at hand, we were able to find patterns of joint bidding that suggested collusive activity among suppliers: to show when and in which jurisdictions the patterns occurred; and to determine which suppliers appeared to be sharing information and which were bidding independently. The methods we have presented will not discover all collusive behavior, nor will all inferences based on these methods necessarily imply illegal activity: additional supporting evidence must be employed to "make a case." Since each bidding situation has its own peculiarities, analysts, investigators, and attorneys must work together to learn the limitations and constraints of the others' methods. A number of problems exist in using statistical evidence in a courtroom, but none are insurmountable if adequate preparations are made. For assistance in cases of this kind, see Tribe (1971a, 1971b), Attanasi and Johnson (1976), Attanasi et al. (1976), Edwards (1974), Elzinga and Hogarty (1972), Federal Trade Commission (1967), Fellmeth and Papageorge (1978), Gallo (1970), Ramsey (1978), Sigal (1969), Van Matre and Clark (1976), and Weinstein and Stelnik (1971).

As combating economic crime rises in the priorities of the criminal justice system, cases will become more complex and will involve the handling and analysis of more and more data. Old techniques will have to be modified and new ones developed. This chapter has demonstrated how well-known statistical concepts and techniques can be tailored to assist in the investigation and prosecution of economic crime.

## NOTES

1. The data described herein have been disguised.

2. Since the specifications are published, the purchasing agent can be called upon to justify them. This can help to overcome the problem of writing overly exclusive specifications.

3. A related illegal activity—price fixing—in which list prices are agreed upon, is not discussed here.

4. Often such complimentary bids are justified in terms of keeping the firm's name on future bidders' lists even if they do not intend to satisfy the contract at hand.

5. Data from the most populous county were not available. However, the contracting arrangements in this county are sufficiently different from the others to justify its exclusion.

6. The product was supplied in a number of different sizes; four sizes accounted for the preponderance of the purchases and one size (size 1) accounted for the greatest volume. An examination of the bids showed that, with relatively few exceptions, for all the vendors the bid prices submitted for sizes 2, 3, and 4 were simple fixed multiples of the bid price for size 1. Thus, little information about relative bid patterns was lost by consideration of bids for size 1 alone. In fact, the existence of this simple relationship is further evidence of collusion, although of a price-fixing (rather than bid-rigging) nature.

7. In this and subsequent figures the little numbers on the graph represent numbers of bids. Thus, in December 1971 eight bids were made: six were at $3.10, two at $2.50, and one each was at $2.80 and $2.40.

8. The "pseudo-distance" is proportional to the distance between the midpoint of the supplier's county and the midpoint of the bidding county. Thus, it is a rough indicator of delivery distance.

9. Although statisticians are accustomed to seeing cumulative distributions as depicted in Figures 2-6, the attorneys involved in the case felt that they were more understandable with the axes reversed, with the horizontal axis denoting the net unit price (NUP).

10. Economists have yet to develop a model of a noncompetitive market, but simulations (Attanasi, 1975) and analyses (Geiss and Kuhlman, 1978) have demonstrated that as markets share information—legally or illegally—the variation in the submitted bids decreases.

11. One cannot use this ratio as a means of testing to see if there is "significant" evidence of collusion. However, it provides a quantitative measure of the bid behavior apparent from Figures 2-6.

12. This conclusion is not based on the explicit use of inferential statistics, but it can easily be shown that the probability is infinitesimally small that the 1973 bids were generated by the same process that generated the bids in other years.

13. For the purpose of interpretation of these plots, the normalized bids shown have been rounded off to the nearest .03, an insignificant difference for the purposes of discerning patterns of collusion.

14. Inferential statistics were not used as direct evidence in this analysis because of the lack of appropriate—and court-acceptable—hypotheses. For example, the condition of statistical independence is inappropriate in a market with a considerable amount of legally shared information, providing a common causal event.

## REFERENCES


ALLEN, F. A. (1978) "Regulation by indictment: The criminal law as an instrument of economic control." Thirteenth Annual William K. McInally Memorial Lecture, Graduate School of Business Administration, University of Michigan.

ATTANASI, E. D. (1975) "Expectations, market structure and sequential bid pricing." Southern Economics Journal 42 (July):18-32.

——— and S. R. JOHNSON (1976) "Norms for bid distributions in sealed tended markets: An approach through simulation." Simulation and Games 7 (December): 439-464.

——— and D. R. KAMERSCHEN (1976) "A numerical analysis of bid distributions in sealed tender markets." In R. T. Masson and P. D. Oualls (eds.) Essays on Industrial Organizations: In Honor of Joe S. Bain. Cambridge, MA: Ballinger.

BLOCK, M. L., F. C. NOLD, and J. G. SIDAK (1978) "The deterrent effect of antitrust enforcement: A theoretical and empirical analysis." Center for Econometric Studies of the Justice System, Stanford University. (unpublished)

BURY, K. V. (1975) Statistical Models in Applied Science. New York: John Wiley.

CASTRO, B. and K. WEINGARTEN (1970) "Toward experimental economics." Journal of Political Economy 78 (May/June):593-607.

COMANOR, W. S. and M. S. SCHANKERMAN (1976) "Identical bids and cartel behavior." The Bell Journal of Economics 7 (Spring):281-286.

EDWARDS, C. D. (1974) "Economic concepts and antitrust litigation: Evolving complexities." Antitrust Bulletin 19 (Summer):295-319.

ELZINGA, K. G. and T. E. HOGARTY (1972) "The problems of geographic market delineation in antimerger suits." Antitrust Bulletin 18 (Spring):45-81.

ERICKSON, W. B. (1969) "Economies of price fixing." Antitrust Law and Economics Review 2 (Spring):83-122.

Federal Trade Commission (1967) "Economic report on the baking industry." Report of the Federal Trade Commission (November).

FELLMETH, R. C. and T. A. PAPAGEORGE (1978) "A treatise on state antitrust law and enforcement: With models and forms." Washington, DC: Bureau of National Affairs, Inc.

FELLNER, W. (1949) Competition Among the Few. New York: Alfred A. Knopf.

FUNDERBURK, D. R. (1974) "Price-fixing in the liquid asphalt industry: Economic analysis vs. the 'hot document'." Antitrust Law and Economics Review 7:61-74.

GALLO, J. C. (1970) "Oligopoly and price fixing: Some analytical models." Antitrust Law and Economics Review 4 (Fall):101-118.

_____(1977) "A computerized approach to detect collusion in the sealed-bid market." The Antitrust Bulletin 22 (Fall):593-619.

GEIS, G. [ed.] (1968) White-Collar Criminal: The Offender in Business and the Professions. New York: Atherton.

GEISS, C. G., and J. M. KUHLMAN (1978) "Estimating price lists, list changes, and market shares from sealed bids." Journal of Political Economy 86 (April): 193-290.

HAY, G. A. and D. KELLEY (1974) "An empirical survey of price fixing conspiracies." The Journal of Law and Economics 17 (April):13-38.

KATZ, C. P. (1975) "Presentation of a confidence interval estimate as evidence in a legal proceeding." The American Statistician 29 (November):138-142.

KUHLMAN, J. M. (1977) "Inferring conduct from performance: An analysis of a price fixing case." (unpublished)

_____(1978) "Nature and significance of price-fixing rings." Antitrust Law and Economics Review 2 (Spring):69-82.

LOCASCIO, V. R. (1978) "An example of management science techniques in antitrust cases." Presented at the Joint National Meeting of the Institute of Management Sciences and the Operations Research Society of America, New York City.

RAMSEY, J. B. (1978) "Competitive or discriminatory bidding: Who Prefers which?" Presented at the OBSA/TIMS Joint National Meeting, November.

ROTHROCK, T. P., J. McCLAVE, and J. ALLSTOCK (1978) "A computerized economic and statistical investigation of the Florida school bread market." Antitrust Unit, Attorney General's Office, State of Florida.

SIGAL, P. (1969) "Judicial use, misuse and abuse of statistical evidence." Journal of Urban Law 47:165-190.

TELSER, L. (1972) Competition, Collusion and Game Theory. Chicago: AVC.

TRIBE, L. H. (1971a) "Trial by mathematics: Precision and ritual in the legal process." Harvard Law Review 84 (April):1329-1393.

_____(1971b) "A further critique of mathematical proof." Harvard Law Review 84:1810-1820.

VAN MATRE, J. and W. N. CLARK (1976) "The statistician as an expert witness." The American Statistician 30 (February):

WEINSTEIN, R. and M. E. STELNIK (1971) "A broad view of collusion." Antitrust Bulletin 16 (Fall):543-568.

*Chapter 9*

# COMPUTER-RELATED WHITE-COLLAR CRIME

DONN B. PARKER

There are no explicit criminal laws that define white-collar crime, but it has become useful in the study and prevention of crime to identify this particular form. It is sufficiently different from physical and overt crime to require different methods of deterrence, prevention, detection, and recovery. Perpetrators, modi operandi, environments of acts, forms of assets subject to loss, timing, and geographic range of acts are generally different. Computer-related crime is resulting in even more profound variations in forms of crime.

There are few reliable statistics of incidence, loss, or other characteristics of white-collar crime. Whether it is increasing or decreasing is not known, and it is surmised that most white-collar crime is not reported at all or not reported in ways amenable to collection of data. The lower bound of what little data there is indicates that losses are large enough to justify identification of white-collar crime as a significant social problem. The leverage for causing larger losses achieved by using computers for white-collar crime is adding a significant but equally unknown increase in the social problem of crime.

Edelhertz et al. (1977) have defined white-collar crime adequately for present purposes as

> an illegal act or series of illegal acts committed by nonphysical means and by concealment or guile, to obtain money or property, to avoid the payment or loss of money or property, or to obtain business or personal advantage.

In addition, Edelhertz and his colleagues identified five principal elements of white collar crime: (1) Intent to commit a wrongful act or to achieve a purpose inconsistent with the law or public policy; (2) disguise (of purpose); (3) reliance by the offender on ignorance or carelessness of the victim; (4) voluntary victim action to assist the offender; and (5) concealment of the violation. They further list four classifications of white-collar crime as personal crimes, abuses of trust, business crimes, and con games. This definition and its extensions apply equally when computers are involved.

However, the increasing use of computer and data communications technology has resulted in a new dimension of crime that is as different from white-collar crime as white-collar crime is different from street crime. In fact it is sufficiently different and represents such a danger to society that, unlike the lack of legislation identifying white-collar crime, legislators are enacting explicit criminal laws against it. Senator Abraham Ribicoff has introduced a specific bill (S240 at this writing) into the U.S. Congress; five states have adopted specific laws and at least 12 others have pending legislation.

## DIFFERENCES IN CRIME CAUSED BY USE OF COMPUTERS

Computer-related crime can be identified by using the general names of crimes: fraud, theft, larceny, robbery, embezzlement, arson, conspiracy, extortion, murder, sabotage, and espionage. In addition, much computer-related crime can be identified as a new form of white-collar crime, though it still fits within the Edelhertz et al. definitions above. Therefore, it is not mutually exclusive of other crime, but is a new dimension in all types of crime; new in terms of perpetrators, environments, modi operandi, forms of assets subject to loss, timing, and geographic conditions.

The perpetrators use new skills, knowledge, and means of access to assets. Many of the offenders are in new occupations, with titles such as computer programmer, computer or terminal operator, computer engineer, tape librarian, job setup clerk, EDP auditor, and data entry clerk. In fact, white-collar crime offenders in traditional occupations are often in collusion with these technologists when computers are involved in criminal acts.

The environments of this new crime include computer facilities with raised floors, dropped ceilings, many-colored boxes, and fan motor and air conditioning noise. Some of the crime takes place inside computers and communication circuits that are removed from any direct human observation.

The modi operandi include manual methods that have been automated and adapted to electronic computer environments and entirely new methods, such as "salami" techniques that would not be productive crimes in manual environments. These methods and others are described in a later section. There are no practical ways of detecting or preventing some of them.

The forms of assets subject to crime involving computers include all those found in other crime, including money. In addition, secret information, records of physical assets in electronic and magnetic form, and computer services, computers, and computer programs represent new forms and kinds of assets. A person need only discover that his most current checking account balance in the bank is known only in electronic form in a computer to understand that money in electronic and magnetic form is a reality.

Computers are rapidly becoming the vaults for our assets, and digitized telephonic data communications are the means for moving assets. More than 60 percent of all U.S. banks with over 90 percent of the nation's negotiable assets are automated. The Fedwire, one of three data communications networks connecting bank computers for transfer of funds, transmits an amount equivalent to the national debt every four days. One of the largest banks transmits 30 to 60 billion dollars every day from one minicomputer to another over a telephone line. Acts of crime focus on where the assets are located. The assets are being rapidly shifted from physical environments and forms into computer and data communication systems in electronic forms. Obviously, the focus of crime will shift there also.

Some incidents of white-collar crime, including erasure of the evidence, are now occurring in a few thousandths of one second. Computer-related crime must be anticipated in a new time scale of milliseconds, microseconds, and nanoseconds. The concepts of real time and nonreal time enter the picture and must also be understood to determine how crimes happen. Most manual white-collar crime occurs in real time. The criminal acts occur in such a way that the perpetrators are simultaneously engaged in the acts and influence the outcome as they occur.

However, most sophisticated computer-related crimes occur in at least two stages. The first consists of the manual or physical acts of the perpetrator that will cause one or more electronic actions to take place at future times. The electronic actions then occur in a computer independent from any further action by the perpetrator that could influence the outcome. This may or may not directly result in conversion to gain for the perpetrator and loss to the victim. When it does not, a later physical act by the perpetrator may be required to convert the electronic acts to actual gain. The perpetrator's fraudulent acts were performed in nonreal time relative to the actual events that resulted in his gain. His acts occurred well before and possibly after the loss event. In addition, in an automated crime the actions resulting in the perpetrator's gain may be automatically repeated periodically over weeks, months, and years.

For example, it is suspected that a perpetrator secretly inserted several computer instructions in among 5 million instructions in a bank's computer (the Trojan horse technique). Every night when the checking account balances were updated, his instructions caused a transfer of a few cents from each of several hundred randomly selected accounts from among the 300,000 accounts into his own account (the salami technique). No controls were violated and the system of accounts balanced because no money was removed from the system; it was only rearranged by small amounts that would be a minor annoyance to a small number of account holders who bothered to notice a few cents missing in their bank statements. Presumably, the perpetrator periodically and legitimately withdraws the accumulation as it builds up. He acted and probably continues to act in nonreal time relative to the automatic acts that actually produce the losses to victims and the gain to himself.

Finally, different geographic conditions add to the difference between computer-related crime and other kinds of crime. Crime generally requires the presence of the criminal at the site of his crime. Many kinds of computer-related crime generally do not. In fact, it is not physically possible for any person to be at the site of an electronically perpetrated crime that takes place in a computer or even to observe it in real time (while it is occurring). Thus, the battles between those who perpetrate automated, electronic crimes and those who would detect, prevent, or investigate them must be waged by remote control, unseen and in nonreal time.

Even greater geographic distance of the perpetrator from the site of his crime is afforded by computer systems that are on-line to data communication services. This can make the location of any telephone in the world the site from which a crime might be conducted in any other part of the world where an on-line computer is located.

For example, in Ward v. California (Parker, 1976) the perpetrator took a copy of a computer program protected as a trade secret from the computer belonging to his employer's competitor. He transferred the copy in electronic pulses over a telephone circuit to his computer terminal where it was printed on paper. The judge in the preliminary criminal hearing stated that the transfer through the telephone circuit did not constitute asportation under grand theft law. However, when the perpetrator carried the listing from his terminal to his desk 12 feet away, this was asportation, and the judge declared that he probably violated the law. This made the terminal the site of the alleged crime, and the criminal act was carrying the listing the 12 feet from the site of the crime to the desk. If he had merely looked at the program printout or had displayed the program on a cathode ray terminal to observe its contents (which was his declared only purpose), there would likely have been no crime committed. This and many other similar cases involving on-line computers demonstrate different geographic conditions in computer-related crime.

The differences cited above show that while computer-related crimes may satisfy the basic definitions of crime—and in particular the Edelhertz et al. definition—they represent a significant new dimension to crime and produce new problems for the criminal justice community and society.

## COMPUTER-RELATED CRIME MODI OPERANDI

As computer-related crime methods become more widely known in the computer field, jargon terms are assigned to them: Trojan horse, salami, superzapping, logic bombs, data leakage, data diddling, piggybacking, and scavenging. These methods have become fascinating to computer technologists because they generally require great skill and detailed knowledge of the system to be attacked. In addition, if they are used with sufficient care, they usually are neither preventable nor detectable even when their use is suspected.

Each of the known technical methods is described below briefly in nontechnical terms.

*Data diddling.* The unauthorized modification, replacement, insertion, or deletion of data before or during its input to a computer system is called data diddling. This can be done by altering input data forms, punch cards, magnetic tapes or disks, or by direct keying at a terminal or computer console. It is the simplest and usually the safest method of perpetrating a fraud in a computer. All of the data input validation controls in the computer must be known and subverted.

*Superzapping.* This is the unauthorized use of utility computer programs to modify, destroy, disclose, or use data or computer programs in a computer system. Utility computer programs are for general use. Computers that contain access controls require a means of gaining access that successfully violates all safeguards in case of control and authorization failure. In most IBM computer installations a utility program called "Superzap" is used for this purpose and is the source of the criminal method term.

*Impersonation.* Taking and using the identity of an authorized computer user to use the computer in his stead is called impersonation. Computer systems usually have authorized user identification data files that are employed automatically to verify the identity and access authorization of computer users. If an individual can obtain the necessary identification of another person he can impersonate that person to the computer.

*Piggybacking.* Piggybacking is the unauthorized interdiction of a communication circuit to covertly replace an authorized user. This could be done by electrically inserting a computer terminal on the same communication circuit to a computer as an authorized terminal and interacting with the computer when the authorized user is momentarily not using his activated terminal. This is another form of impersonation.

*Wire tapping.* This is the commonly understood method of covertly tapping into a communication circuit, but the circuit carries digitized data instead of voice data.

*Trojan horse.* As its name implies, this is a method of covertly inserting computer instructions into a computer program that is authorized for use in a computer. The secretly altered program will perform properly but the inserted instructions are also executed to perform an unauthorized act in conjunction with the correct functions of the program. A few instructions can be hidden in a typical computer program with 10,000 or 200,000 instructions in ways that defy detection (Parker, 1976).

*Asyncronous attack.* This is a method of compromising a computer system by taking advantage of weaknesses in its asyncronous functions. A computer system asyncronously processes tasks to be performed by queuing them up and performing them out of sequence as sufficient resources become available. It is sometimes possible to change some of the conditions after the system starts, taking action based on those conditions. Further description of this method would require an understanding of computer technology beyond the scope of this material.

*Trap door.* A trap door is a weakness or error introduced into or left in a computer program that can be exploited at a later time to compromise a computer system. Occasionally, a computer programmer will inadvertently weaken a program while developing, maintaining, or changing it. The programmer may also place functions in the program that are not needed for its ultimate purposes but aid in testing or maintenance. These weaknesses, functions, or errors that have been introduced may be used later by persons intent on unauthorized acts.

*Salami methods.* Salami methods are based on transferring small amounts of assets (slices of salami) from a large number of accounts into a favored account which then can be converted to a fraudulent gain. The possibility of discovery is minimized, because no single victim or account custodian has lost enough to notice or complain about it. It may also be successful because assets are not removed from the system of accounts but only transferred within the system; therefore, the total sum of assets is not changed. The classical salami is the "round down" fraud, in which fractions of pennies remaining from interest calculations for savings accounts are collected in one account rather than being distributed among all accounts. The salami methods require placing changes or additional instructions into the computer program that performs the processing of accounts (Trojan horse method) or developing a program that can be run in a computer with access to a large file of accounts (Parker, 1976).

*Logic bomb.* A logic bomb is a computer program or part of a program that is automatically repeatedly executed to test the state and contents of a computer system. When all prescribed conditions are met, the program triggers an unauthorized act in the computer system. A logic bomb could examine the day of year and time of day clock in a computer (a time bomb) to select an optimum time for a fraud to take place providing the greatest safety to the perpetrator (Parker, 1976).

*Data leakage.* A method for covertly obtaining data from a computer system by leaking it out in small amounts is called data leakage. This might be done by coding the data in a computer in the form of different lengths of printed lines on the output printer. The resulting printed output listing would contain innocuous information, but the length of each printed line could represent a letter of the alphabet or digit. Many other methods could be devised.

*Simulation.* Simulation of processes or systems is a common computer application that can be used to simulate a fraud for planning purposes or as an aid in regulating, monitoring, or accounting in the perpetration of an ongoing complex fraud. Any one or combination of these technical methods represent only one part of a crime. Other actions could include studying the computer system and application, computer programming, entering the computer system, neutralizing or avoiding controls, suppressing evidence, and converting results of acts to removable gain.

## FRAUD IN TRANSACTIONS CHANGED BY USE OF COMPUTERS

Business transactions of all types have been an attraction for white-collar crime: Transactions involving the exchange of assets, goods, and services are conducted for illegal purposes; legitimate transactions are the targets of illegal acts; privileged knowledge of legal or illegal transactions can play a role in various frauds; and real or fictitious transactions can be represented in illegal deception or intimidation.

Computers are being used increasingly in transactions. They replace the real time functions of human agents; for example, as in use of automated teller machines by banks and other financial institutions. They are used in payment, reconciliation, and collection systems that automatically create and cancel negotiable instruments. They complete the transfer of funds in point-of-sale transactions. Finally, they store, process, and communicate data after the fact, in nonreal time in manual transactions.

When computers participate either actively or passively in transactions, they change the nature of transactions. This, in turn, changes the nature of white-collar crime and of protection from crime in transactions in a number of positive and negative ways.

*Participant identification verification.* Automatic methods of verification of personal identity by computer replace handwritten signatures with the use of magnetic strip plastic cards, encrypted identification data, and personal identification numbers. The advantage of this form of identification is that more effective verification is based on multiple, independent factors. Unfortunately, it becomes easier to transfer identity for impersonation.

*Determination of participant authorization, good faith, and obligation capacity.* Authorization, good faith, and capacity to obligate parties to a transaction can be determined from computerized searches of authorization and credit files. Credit ratings, negative reports, and retrieval determination of possession of sufficient resources to engage in a transaction are possible from computerized information retrieval from large files over great distances. This is the escrow function that computer technology makes instantaneous or shortens. On the positive side, more relevant facts available from reliable sources reduce the exposure of all parties to fraud, poor decisions, and error. However, instantaneous or quick decisions may be too rapid for sufficient human thought processes and good judgment to occur. Trust in the completeness and integrity of computer output can be more easily accepted without question than may be justified.

*Forced adherence to and sustainability and inflexibility of explicitly determined rules and protocol.* Computers tend to be programmed to allow little deviation from proscribed transaction rules and protocol. (However, flexibility can be built in but at significant cost and effort.). Rules and protocol that are under real time control of people tend to deteriorate over time. This is one of the most common vulnerabilities used in fraud. In contrast, computer functions do not deteriorate over time. In addition, modifications can be controlled more effectively than real-time behavior of people. Thus, the possibilities for real-time fraud are considerably reduced by preventing deviation from well-developed and explicitly implemented rules and protocol. However, inflexibility under a set of rules reduces the likelihood of full benefit from transactions where human emotions, empathy, and generosity could otherwise prevail, assuming good faith in all parties. In addition, the computerized rules and protocol may be flawed.

*Reduced number of participants.* Automation reduces the total number of participants and among the remainder reduces the number of those who have the skills, knowledge, and access to make changes in the system for illegal purposes. Fewer participants in transactions with capabilities to engage in unauthorized acts reduces the exposure of the transactions to crime. Unfortunately, each of the reduced number of participants must share a larger portion of responsibility and trust.

*Detection of deviations from expected events.* A computer is the most ideal, cost-effective device for detection of deviations at the most detailed level. In addition, a computer is an effective rapid data reduction and analysis device. Thus, not only can all deviations imaginable be identified in the greatest detail, but the high volume of data produced can be analyzed and reduced to reasonable amounts of meaningful information for human consumption in a timely manner.

This represents the most powerful capability introduced by use of computer technology to reduce white-collar crime among nontechnically qualified people. Their every action is susceptible to timely analysis, and the likelihood they have not anticipated or learned of all detection controls is high. However, this capability results in the escalation of white-collar crime in the sense of reducing incidence but increasing average loss per case. A few people, the technologists who know and can compromise the detection controls, become immune to detection, while human detectors of crime become ineffective because of misplaced reliance on untrustworthy controls. The result is fewer but more successful white-collar criminals.

*Personal privacy.* Use of computers is being blamed for increasing loss of personal privacy. Business transaction data are among the most sensitive personal information. As such transactions become automated, however, fewer people possess the information and fewer still have access to it under potentially highly secure, absolutely enforced rules of confidentiality as a result of storing the data in computers.

White-collar crime almost always results in the exposure of personal information. In addition, those who would detect white-collar crime in manual environments possess much personal information about many people, most of whom never engage in white-collar crime. In automated transaction systems, most of the personal data is never exposed outside of the computer system except to the owner and those he designates (implicitly more often than explicitly). Since detection of fraud is automated also, personal data is exposed only when there is suspicion of criminal acts, and it is exposed to fewer and probably more responsible people.

The escalation effect can also be used to the detriment of security. While fewer people receive personal information, they can possess much more of it and process it more effectively. These fewer people are put in higher trust positions and could cause more harm to more people by violating their privacy.

*Robinhood syndrome.* White-collar criminals frequently differentiate doing harm to people, which is highly immoral, and doing harm to organizations, which they can justify to themselves. According to Cressey (1974), this justification is made by white-collar criminals who do not see themselves as criminals. In computer-related crime, an extension of these verbalizations is possible: even organizations are not harmed, but only inanimate computer systems that cannot react to abuse in ways that produce remorse or guilt in the criminal.

*Object of blame.* The computer is an ideal target for blame when suspected fraud, errors, or omissions occur in automated transactions. The victims, the perpetrators, and persons acting as the catalysts in the loss can all safely blame the computer and avoid direct antagonistic confrontation with other people. The public media encourage this thinking by reporting sensationalized stories of "computer errors." This blame-the-computer syndrome can be effectively used by white-collar criminals to delay or even prevent the discovery of their crimes by blaming losses on "computer errors." This effect will be used by con artists until potential victims overcome their lack of familiarity and their misunderstanding of the nature of computers and of the causes and expected rates of errors and omissions.

*Law, regulation, and insurance.* The inadequacy of criminal law in dealing with computer-related crime has been well documented (Nycum, 1976). U.S. attorneys generally indicate that they have been able to prosecute computer-related crime successfully, but they have used laws not developed for this purpose, which makes prosecution circuitous and more difficult. In Pennsylvania, two computer programmers stole $144,000 of computer services from their employer to engage in a business of automatically rescoring sheet music and were convicted of mail fraud. Over a telephone circuit from a terminal at his home in Virginia, a programmer stole a copy of a computer program out of the storage of his former employer's computer in Maryland (Nycum 1978). He was convicted of wire fraud. A prosecutor in Maryland indicated that if he had lived in Maryland there would have been no applicable law to convict him. Laws are needed to clearly identify as crimes malicious acts involving computers for purposes of deterrence and in fairness to both perpetrators and victims. U.S. Senator Abraham Ribicoff has taken significant steps in this direction with his computer fraud and abuse legislation, and, as noted above, state legislative action is increasing. Regulation is also lagging behind the advancement of the technology, and data processing insurance premiums are high in the absence of sufficient actuarial data for policies that are not changed rapidly enough to anticipate technology changes. The most serious problem is that even with the present level of action, the rapid advancement of technology is likely to continue to outstrip law, regulation, and insurance.

The changes wrought in business transactions by the increasing roles of computers can be summarized as a displacement and change in the nature of trust. Business transactions are based on trust. The trust relationships among transaction participants are changed when computers are used. The number and types of people in differing positions of trust; the degree, timing, and methods of determining the sufficiency of enough trust; and the rules and protocol by which it is accomplished are all changed.

## COMPUTER-RELATED CRIME INCIDENCE AND LOSSES

Experience indicates the significance of computer-related crime and the change in white-collar and other types of crime. An ongoing study at SRI International since 1971, funded in part by the U.S. National Science Foundation, has produced at least a lower bound of data on computer abuse. Computer abuse has been defined in the study as intentional acts involving computers where a perpetrator made or could have made a gain; and victims suffered a loss or could have suffered loss. This broad definition fits the purposes of the study which are to learn empirically from experience about vulnerabilities in the use of computers and how to protect against losses.

If the purposes of the study had been different, the definition would be different. For example, a new project at SRI International to produce a Manual for the Investigation and Prosecution of Computer-Related Crime for the U.S. Department of Justice, Law Enforcement Assistance Administration, used the definition of the subject as any illegal acts where the knowledge of computer technology is essential to successful prosecution. Again, the definition is broad but serves its purpose, since the limits of crime associated with computers is still unknown. New types and circumstances of such crime continue to appear. The definition makes computer-related crime a subset of computer abuse.

The only comprehensive data from experience concern computer abuse. The data base consists of documents describing 632 cases that occurred from 1958 through June 1979. The documentation for each case ranges from a short paragraph in a newspaper article to several thousands of pages of documents, including newspaper and magazine articles; victim, perpetrator, and prosecutor interview notes; police and auditor investigation reports; and legal documents including arrest warrants, search warrants, charges, depositions, convictions, opinions, and court transcripts. The data were gathered from scanning news media, using a news clipping service, copying from legal and private files, and engaging in conversations and interviews with case participants. Approximately 20 cases have been investigated in depth by field interviews of victims, perpetrators, witnesses, investigators, and prosecutors. Authorizations to interview prisoners in state and federal penal institutions were obtained, and three perpetrators were interviewed while incarcerated.

Field investigations were concentrated in the New York City, Philadelphia, San Francisco Bay, and Los Angeles regions. Several brief investigations were made in European cities. Cases were chosen for field investigation in which the opportunity to gather detailed information seemed most promising to investigators and the information to be gained had the greatest potential for application to the development of safe use of computer technology and insights on applicable legal issues.

Seventy-one cases were reported in the form of returned questionnaires filled out by recipients of a report, *Computer Abuse* (Parker et al., 1973), documenting the first year of the research. Information gathered in several cases is private because victims and perpetrators agreed to provide the information only if they would not be identified. Other content of the data base is in the public domain and available for inspection.

The data base is believed to represent a nearly exhaustive collection of all computer abuse that has been reported in the public media since 1965. Table 1 shows the distribution of 518 cases by source to October 1977. The large number reported in *Computerworld* is the result of this trade newspaper's practice of searching for cases, primarily from newspapers through clipping services. A number of cases found in newspapers and newsletters were subsequently reported in *Computerworld,* but are attributed to newspapers and newsletters as the first source in which they were found.

It is conjectural as to what proportion of the total known cases this sample represents. Several certified public accountants have indicated that they know of many confidential cases among their clients that have never been revealed to police agencies or the public and are not included in the computer-abuse data base. Most universities and colleges record cases perpetrated by students, but only 64 were included in the computer-abuse data base. Many more cases can be

*Table 1* Computer Abuse Case Sources
(September 1977)

| | |
|---|---|
| Questionnaires | 72 |
| Computerworld | 90 |
| Newspapers | 162 |
| Private sources | 102 |
| Magazines, journals | 53 |
| Books | 22 |
| Oral presentations | 13 |
| Unpublished documents | 4 |
| Total | 518 |

SOURCE: SRI International, Menlo Park, CA.

found and included if resources to locate them become available. Also, many more cases could be found by seeking case histories of white-collar crime where related data could have been stored or produced in computers. For now, the computer-abuse data base must be treated only as a small collection of known cases in which the computer has played a significant role. Business disputes over computer products and services where the types of products and services would make no substantial difference to the issues of the dispute are not included in the study. Possible biases of the collection are identified below.

Numbers of cases by year are shown in Figure 1. The data base is suspected of being biased in some ways: The incidence of reported cases of computer abuse in Figure 1 appears to show an exponential growth through 1975, but the growth rate may be inaccurate because of a sample bias caused by changing news-reporting practices of publicizing cases, changing amounts of resources available to search for and to record cases, changing willingness of victims to reveal their experiences publicly, or an increasing population of computers in environments where white-collar crime and malicious mischief is so commonplace that it is seldom reported.

There might also be a "skyjack" syndrome effect causing an actual increased incidence where publicity of attractive and exciting types of crime encourages more of the same. This was evident in a series of computer-abuse incidents where blank deposit slips printed with perpetrators' MICR account codes were left on counters in banks resulting in crediting the perpetrators' accounts with deposits of other customers who used the blanks when computer processing was based on the MICR code alone. Many applicable cases may be overlooked because the involvement of a computer was not perceived and recorded. The apparent downturn of incidence of computer abuse in 1976 and 1978, as shown in Figure 1, is caused by a time lag between occurrence and reporting of cases. Cases continue to be discovered that occurred in the 1960s and early 1970s.

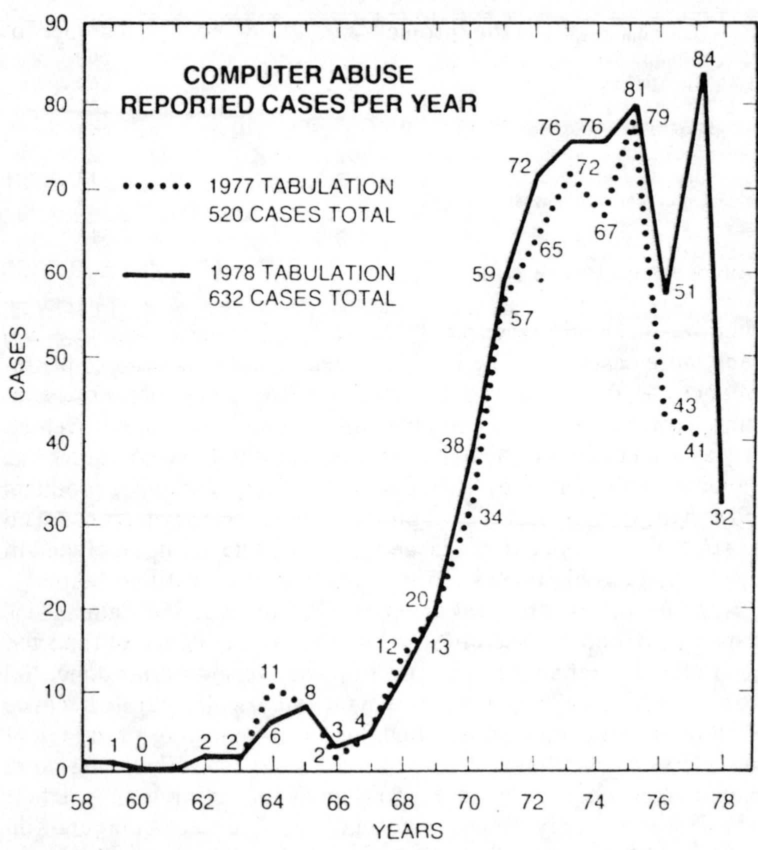


SOURCE: SRI International, Menlo Park, CA (January 1979).

FIGURE 1 Computer Abuse Case File History

The fact that reported computer abuses indicates only the minimal possible seriousness of the problem might be seen by considering cases relative to the number of computers in use. The assumption that there were 100,000 computers in 1965 and 200,000 in 1975 (worldwide) indicates that there was one reported case per 10,000 computers in 1965 and possibly five cases per 10,000 computers in 1975 (assuming 100 cases will ultimately be reported for 1975). A rate of one per year for each 2,000 computers seems unreasonably low, possibly indicating that only a small number of known cases are reported, or only a small number of computers are in environments of potential risk.

Resources devoted to searching for and recording cases have been uniformly applied since 1970 to the present. Howcver, growing public awareness of the project has increased the number of unsolicited contributions of information about cases and has increased the number of cases privately reported. At the very least, the existence of the problem is demonstrated by the data presented in Figure 1 with a documented lower bound of incidence.

Losses have averaged about $5 million per year over the past 11 years and about $10 million over the past 4 years (not counting the Equity Funding Insurance fraud in Los Angeles in 1973 where the loss was $2 billion [Loeffler, 1974]). This is insignificant compared with estimates of losses from white-collar crime of all types. The U.S. National Chamber of Commerce estimated current annual white-collar crime losses to be not less than $40 billion (Chamber of Commerce, 1974). This estimate includes $100 million from computer-related crime (only 1/400th of all white-collar crime).

Losses per incident of computer abuse provide further insight. The average loss per case of missing funds in financial institutions as reported by the FBI was about $7,000 in the late 1960s and increased to $19,000 per case in the 1970s. In another study from the computer abuse file of 42 computer-related bank frauds and embezzlements in the period 1962 to 1975, the average loss per case was $430,000 (total $18 million, range $200 to $6.8 million). The average loss over all reported computer abuse cases (not including the Equity Funding Insurance case) where dollar losses are stated (144 cases) is $450,000 per case.

The large losses in computer-related cases can be explained in several ways. There might be bias in the sample because cases with larger losses might be reported in the public media more than those with smaller losses. White-collar crime losses may be larger when they involve computers because the assets are more concentrated. Once a system is compromised, it is as easy to steal large amounts as small amounts (the automation of theft), and the danger of detection and greater efforts needed forces the perpetrators to look for a larger return on their investment in crime.

There was concern that geographical bias might be present in the collection of cases. Figure 2 shows the geographical distribution of cases, indicating a generally good correlation with population centers that likewise represent concentrations of computers. A particularly heavy concentration in California could demonstrate a small bias caused by location of the research project in the San Francisco region.

Distribution of cases in other countries is shown in Table 2. It is consistent with the number of computers in each country with three

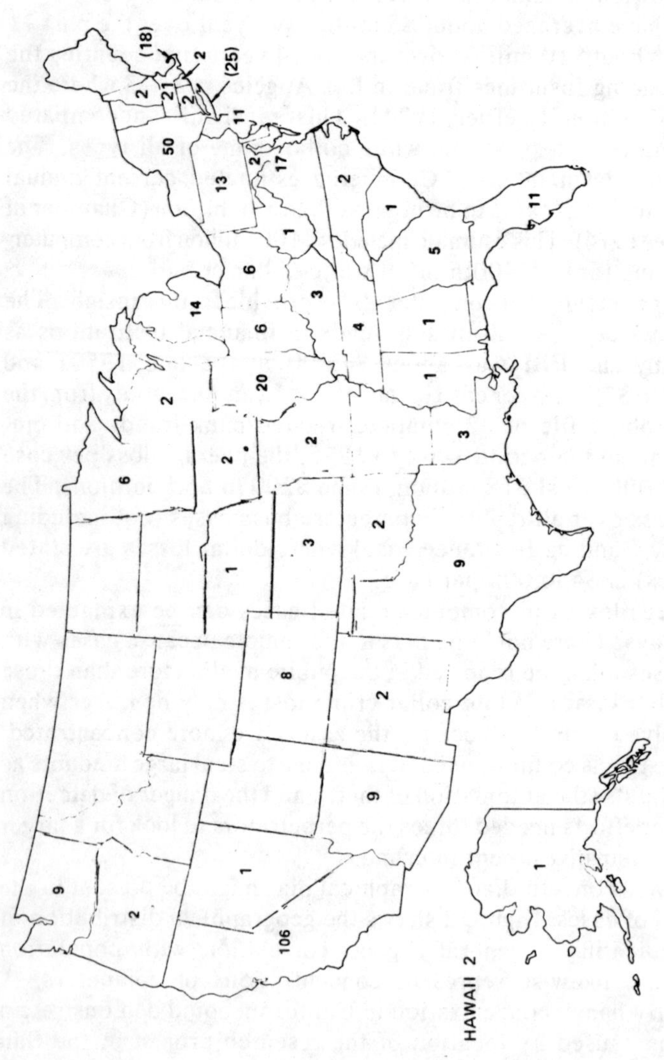


FIGURE 2 Geographic Distribution of Computer Abuse in the U.S.A. (September 1977)

exceptions: (1) The unexpected large number of cases in the United Kingdom is explained, in part, by more contacts among people of the United States and the United Kingdom who are interested in the subject. (2) The English language media make the search for published cases easier and, therefore, more complete. (3) The large number in Sweden is a result of Swedish police identifying computer-related crime among all crime and reporting it to the author.

The third discontinuity is the small number of cases in Japan. Discussions with several Japanese banking electronic data-processing (EDP) professionals indicate that Japan has had practically no white-collar crime. Further inquiry reveals that the more likely explanation is that white-collar crime flourishes but is hardly ever reported outside of victim organizations. Perpetrators are punished and rehabilitated by their employers. This is attributed to social values including paternalistic, lifelong relationships between employees and employers. However, this is changing; employee mobility is increasing and along with it, white-collar crime.

There seems to be no difference in types of computer abuse among countries. Computers, computer operations, and computer applications are similar throughout the world—leaving little possibility for variations in computer-abuse methods and concentrating what differences there are in the areas of motives and social values.

A distribution of cases by type of business of the victims in Figure 3 presents no surprises. Expectation of incidence is high among financially oriented victims, such as banking and government, where there is significant monetary liquidity; this is supported by the data. The large number of reported banking cases is also high because of the legal requirements of banks to report fraud and embezzlement. The large number of cases in education is a result partly of the willingness to report cases publicly and partly of the inability to

*Table 2* Computer Abuse in the World
(January 1979—633 cases)

| | | | |
|---|---|---|---|
| United States | 472 | Japan | 3 |
| Sweden | 35 | South Africa | 3 |
| United Kingdom | 23 | Korea | 3 |
| Germany | 21 | Netherlands | 2 |
| Italy | 19 | Philippines | 2 |
| France | 9 | Belgium | 1 |
| Norway | 7 | European | 1 |
| Canada | 5 | Yugoslavia | 1 |
| Australia | 4 | Mexico | 1 |
| Denmark | 4 | New Zealand | 1 |
| | | Not Specified | 16 |

SOURCE: SRI International, Menlo Park, CA.

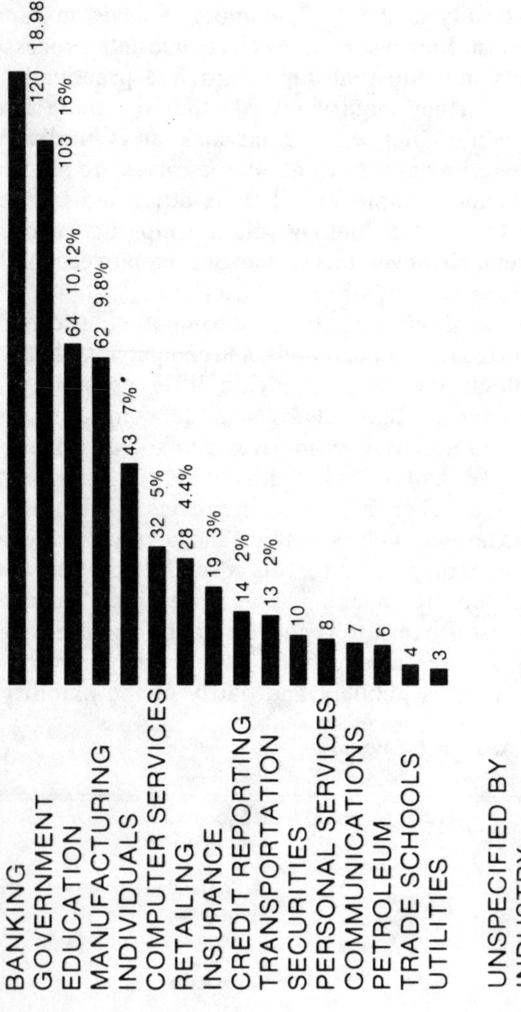


FIGURE 3 Computer Abuse Incidence by Industry (632 cases)

control public exposure. Also, students represent a large population of potential perpetrators because of their access to computers; in many instances they are encouraged by faculties to attack computers as a game.

Computer abuse has also been identified by types of losses shown in Table 3 in the following four categories.

*(1) Loss from vandalism.* This consists of destruction or damage of equipment, programs, data, facilities, or supplies. Losses are measured in estimates or actual costs of repair, replacement, and interruption or termination of computer services. Intentional acts causing such losses are called vandalism, sabotage, or malicious mischief. The acts originate in almost equal numbers between external sources (people not employed in computing facilities such as those involved in riots) or internal sources (employees in positions of trust within computing facilities, most often motivated by disgruntlement). When collusion involving both internal and external people is found, the case is identified as internal vandalism.

*(2) Loss from information or property fraud or theft.* The perpetrator's gain may be financial but requires the additional step of

*Table 3* Reported Cases of Computer Abuse (by year and type)

| *Year* | *Vandalism* | *Information or Property Theft* | *Financial Fraud or Theft* | *Unauthorized Use or Sale of Services* | *Total* |
|---|---|---|---|---|---|
| 1958 | — | — | 1 | — | 1 |
| 1959 | — | — | — | — | — |
| 1960 | — | — | — | — | — |
| 1961 | — | — | — | — | — |
| 1962 | 2 | — | — | — | 2 |
| 1963 | 1 | — | — | — | 1 |
| 1964 | 1 | 2 | 3 | — | 6 |
| 1965 | — | 1 | 4 | 3 | 8 |
| 1966 | 1 | — | 1 | — | 2 |
| 1967 | 2 | — | — | 2 | 4 |
| 1968 | 2 | 3 | 6 | 2 | 13 |
| 1969 | 4 | 8 | 4 | 4 | 20 |
| 1970 | 8 | 6 | 13 | 11 | 38 |
| 1971 | 7 | 20 | 24 | 8 | 59 |
| 1972 | 17 | 18 | 19 | 18 | 72 |
| 1973 | 10 | 25 | 30 | 11 | 76 |
| 1974 | 7 | 19 | 35 | 13 | 74 |
| 1975 | 5 | 21 | 46 | 9 | 81 |
| 1976 | 5 | 18 | 30 | 4 | 57 |
| 1977 | 13 | 15 | 44 | 13 | 85 |
| 1978 | 9 | 8 | 12 | 2 | 31 |
| Total | 94 | 164 | 272 | 100 | 630 |

SOURCE: SRI International, Menlo Park, CA.

converting the results of the act to financial gain, if that is the purpose. An example is copying and selling computerized mailing lists.

*(3) Loss from financial fraud or theft.* This results from the modification, disclosure, or denial of use of data that are or represent financial assets stored in computer systems or stored in forms meant for processing in computer systems. The loss is directly financial rather than one requiring conversion as in type 2.

*(4) Loss from unauthorized use or sale of services.* Many computer-abuse cases involve the theft of services, such as those provided by commercial time-sharing companies. Others involve EDP employees engaged in personal business ventures performing EDP services for their own customers, unknown to their employer. Several cases have also occurred in which non-EDP employees obtain EDP services for unauthorized personal gain.

The four types are generically different in terms of direct losses, and the evidence that a loss has occurred is often in different forms. However, many cases of computer abuse include combinations of the four types of losses. Precedence ordering by type solved this problem. Thus, a case of unauthorized use of a computer to manipulate both financial and nonfinancial data followed by destruction of the computer would be a case of type 1 vandalism. If the computer had not been destroyed, it would have been a type 2 data fraud. If the computer had not been destroyed and nonfinancial data had not been objects of the acts, it would have been a type 3 financial fraud or theft. Finally, if none of the foregoing had occurred, it would have been an unauthorized use.

It can be seen that type 3 financial fraud or theft is gradually dominating the data. The increased vandalism in recent years is the result of adding 18 cases in the last three years that consist of computer centers that were blown up and burned by the Red Brigade's international terrorists in Italy.

Evidence of acts can also be identified in the four classifications. Damaged or destroyed equipment, facilities, programs and data, or supplies can be visually or functionally identified after the act or when use is attempted. There is no experience of more subtle forms of damage, such as causing computer logic circuit failures over a period of time, resulting in undetected but irreversible processing errors. Information theft is often difficult to detect because computer-stored data are not directly visible, and copies of the data can be made so easily without disturbing the data and without leaving a trail of records of access or copying. Financial fraud or theft detection is heavily dependent on programmed controls and journaling within computer systems. However, in many cases the controls and journaling are usually subverted by the perpetrator. These cases are more often detected by irregularities in the negotiable instruments, printed financial records, or in handling records after removing them from the EDP environment. In such cases, detection requires close cooperation of the EDP organization and external organizations and individuals. Evidence of unauthorized use of services requires observation and analysis of service usage records. Again, as in financial fraud, the perpetrator usually destroys or changes the records (making the act a type 2 case), poses as a legitimate service user, or makes the theft obvious but avoids being identified by other means not related to his computer usage.

## CONCLUSIONS

Computer abuse is a recent phenomenon unanticipated by most computer users, computer service suppliers, and computer manufacturers. Computers have been designed and used on the assumption of benign environments. Computer abuse as crime is still categorized as fraud, embezzlement, theft, larceny, extortion, espionage, sabotage, and conspiracy. However, beyond naming the crime, automation has significantly changed its nature. The occupations of perpetrators, the environments of acts, the modi operandi, and forms of assets attacked are all new, making the problem a new challenge to society. In addition, computers are changing the nature of trust in business transactions that, in turn, changes the nature of fraud.

Evidence indicates an emerging problem of computer abuse that could assume the magnitude of current levels of white-collar crime. However, relative to white-collar crime incidence and losses today, the problem still seems minimal. The true size of the problem, however, is not thoroughly known, but the lower bound of incidence and loss based on the 632 reported cases demonstrates its existence and indicates significant growth. This is made more serious by the growing reliance on computers, proliferation of computer use into sensitive business and other societal functions, increasing storage of negotiable assets in computer systems, and concomitant increasing positions of trust required in the relatively new EDP occupations.

The nature of the problem so far revealed leads to a belief that computer-related crime generally is of low incidence but results in large loss per incident. Computer-related crime focuses on negotiable assets stored in computer media, on computer-stored data convertible to unauthorized gain, on sabotage, and on unauthorized use of services. It is perpetrated by the limited number of people who have computer-related skills, knowledge, access, and resources. Computer-related crime is a universal and uniform threat wherever computers are used.

## REFERENCES


Chamber of Commerce (1974) A Handbook on White Collar Crime. Washington, DC: National Chamber of Commerce.

CRESSEY, D. R. (1974) Other People's Money. Belmont, CA: Wadsworth.

EDELHERTZ, H., E. STOTLAND, M. WALSH, and M. WEINBERG (1977) The Investigation of White-Collar Crime: A Manual for Law Enforcement Agencies. Office of Regional Operations, Law Enforcement Assistance Administration, U.S. Department of Justice, Washington, DC: U.S. Government Printing Office.

LOEFFLER, R. M. (1974) "Report of the trustee of Equity Funding Corporation of America." October 31. Los Angeles, CA: U.S. District Judge.

NYCUM, S. H. (1976) The Criminal Law Aspects of Computer Abuse. Menlo Park, CA: SRI International.

——— (1978) "Anatomy of a computer crime." American Federation of Information Processing Societies Conference Proceedings 47:1151-1155.

PARKER, D. B. (1976) Crime by Computer. New York: Scribner's.

PARKER, D. B., S. NYCUM, and S. OURA (1973) Computer Abuse. Menlo Park, CA: SRI International.

*Chapter 10*

# DETECTING MANAGEMENT FRAUD: THE ROLE OF THE INDEPENDENT AUDITOR

JAMES E. SORENSEN,
HUGH D. GROVE,
and THOMAS L. SORENSEN

What is management fraud? Is the independent auditor responsible for detecting management fraud? What auditing tools and techniques are available for detecting management frauds? Can they be improved? Are new tools needed? How should the independent audit firm be organized to be most effective in discovering management frauds? This chapter seeks to identify *why* the auditor role in detecting management frauds is increasing and *how* independent auditors can sharpen their approach to unearth such frauds.

## Perspective

Deceit and serious abuse of management's position and trust coupled with unwary and sometimes inadequate auditing methods have led auditors to a current (and sometimes unwelcomed) public visibility. As an outgrowth of management frauds leading to audit failures and losses in the millions, auditors' standards of care for fraud detection have received renewed interest in the 1970s. The call for new auditing standards results from deliberate violations by management, the profession's reluctance to accept expanded responsibility for detecting management fraud, only a recent emergence of systematic audit review practices by outside peers, and the acknowledged weaknesses of existing audit methods to reveal deliberate management frauds. At stake is the future of the profession of auditing. The need for dependable financial statements is widely recognized but no one profession or group *unilaterally* can fulfill that need. New mechanisms are needed by which auditors, the Securities and Exchange Commission (SEC), and concerned in-

AUTHORS' NOTE: *Portions of this article have been adapted with permission from James E. Sorensen and Thomas L. Sorensen,* Detecting Management Fraud: Some Organizational Strategies for the Independent Auditor, *Interdisciplinary Symposium on Management Fraud (New York: Peat, Marwick, Mitchell and Co., 1978).*

vestors and citizens can work together to enhance the authenticity of financial reports.

### Approach

In tracing the career of management fraud as a social problem, the first step will be to propose a revised definition of management fraud, followed by a discussion of the auditor's concern for fraud. Next, a typology will be developed by examining the motivations, benefits, organizational locus, conditions, and practices surrounding management frauds. The typology identifies early warnings or "red flags" alerting the auditor that management fraud may exist. Then the typology will be illustrated with recent audit failures. The study will then apply a sociological perspective to the claims-making process generated by management fraud and will identify the current stage of the career development of management fraud; finally, it will outline future stages which could be harmful to the auditor and to the SEC. Recently developed auditing approaches to detect management fraud will be examined from a behavioral perspective.

## THE CAREER OF MANAGEMENT FRAUD AS A SOCIAL PROBLEM: AN OVERVIEW

Fraud is an ever-present threat to any organization. Almost any management could circumvent the accounting system controls to misappropriate or misuse financial information or mislead financial statement users. The independent auditor's role in the detection of fraud has been spotlighted because of a number of audit failures precipitated by undetected management frauds. The current public visibility of audit failures accompanied by management fraud (Allen, 1977; Hershman, 1974; *Wall Street Journal,* 1972, 1973, 1974) highlights the fuzzy responsibility of the independent auditor for fraud detection.

> Independent auditors have always acknowledged some responsibility to consider the existence of fraud in conducting an audit. Nevertheless the nature and extent of that responsibility have been unclear. Court decisions, criticisms by the financial press, actions by regulatory bodies, and surveys of users indicate dissatisfaction with the responsibility for fraud detection acknowledged by auditors [Commission, 1978:31].

### Clarifying the Definition of Management Fraud

Management fraud is a subset of acts which is more generally defined as "white-collar" crime (Turner and Uretsky, 1978:23). A widely accepted definition of white collar crime is

> an illegal act or series of illegal acts committed by nonphysical means and by concealment or guile, to obtain money or property, to avoid the payment or loss of money or property, or to obtain business or personal advantage [Edelhertz, 1970:3].

White-collar crime invariably displays certain characteristics which may be useful in developing a working definition of management fraud as well as guiding the actions of auditors in their pursuit of management fraud. Five principal elements characterize white-collar crime [Edelhertz et al., 1977:21]:

(1) *Intent* to commit a wrongful act or to achieve a purpose inconsistent with law or public policy.
(2) *Disguise* (of purpose): Falsities and misrepresentations employed to accomplish the scheme.
(3) *Reliance* by the offender on ignorance or carelessness of the victim(s).
(4) *Voluntary victim action* to assist the offender.
(5) *Concealment* of the violation.

## Discussion of the Elements

For fraud to exist, management must have *intended* to commit wrongful acts and will have misrepresented facts and disguised their true purpose to deceive potential victims. A management intending to defraud relies on the carelessness or ignorance of the victim and voluntary victim action or acquiescence to assist or cooperate with the perpetrators. Concealment seeks to keep the victim in perpetual ignorance.

## Narrowing the Definition

"Any intentional act designed to deceive or mislead other is fraud" (Commission, 1978:32). An analysis of our daily interactions provides hundreds of examples of conversation or behavior undertaken with the intent to deceive. The kind of fraud envisioned is committed by a narrow group occupying high managerial positions, charged with the responsibility for achieving organizational objectives, and possessing the authority to fashion policies and direct organizational behavior.

Several definitions of management fraud have been offered within the accounting literature (Commission, 1978:32; Kapnick, 1975:21; Turner and Uretsky, 1978:21), but they do not contain three of the five suggested elements of white collar crime: (1) reliance on the ignorance or carelessness of the victim, (2) voluntary victim action, and (3) concealment of the violation.

A management fraud does rely on ignorance or carelessness of an investor or auditor, and only if the victim acts voluntarily is the fraud effective (for example, the auditor provides an unqualified opinion or the investors rely on the opinion believing the company's financials are fairly presented). Finally, for the fraud to be successful, it must be concealed. For our purposes, management fraud consists of (1) management's intent to commit wrongful acts (2) through falsities, misrepresentations, and concealment (3) and of reliance on the ignorance or carelessness of the victim, (4) to induce voluntary victim action.

The independent auditor's interest in management fraud is linked to the material impact such management frauds have on the fair presentation of financial statements.

## Evolution of the Auditor's Concern for Fraud

Beginning around the turn of the century, determination of fairness of reported financial position as a major audit objective began to overshadow fraud detection, which disappeared around 1940, undoubtedly influenced by the effects of the McKesson-Robbins case (SEC, 1940) on the profession. In 1939, *Extensions of Auditing Procedure* stated: "The ordinary examination incident to the issuance of an opinion respecting financial statements is not designed and cannot be relied upon to disclose defalcations and other similar irregularities" (Commission, 1978:35). For over 20 years the pronouncement stood and to many was a disavowal of concern for fraud detection. In 1960, the negative and defensive tone was modified (AICPA, 1960:100.05). Nonetheless, the extent of the auditor's responsibility in detecting management fraud was still unclear.

Most of the auditing literature generally complemented the American Institute of Certified Public Accountants (AICPA) posture of *not* construing an unqualified opinion on the financial statements as a representation that no undetected material fraud exists. As one seasoned auditor reflected: "There is no more justification for an auditor to be a guarantor than there would be for . . . a doctor to guarantee that an operation will be successful" (Catlett, 1975:16). If, however, the doctor fails to make a complete diagnosis or misclassifies the symptoms of a major disease, the client is likely to have just cause against the doctor. When a doctor certifies to normal health and the client has a dreaded, contagious disease, those relying on the health certificate are justifiably indignant. Similarly, if the auditor states that the amounts in the accounts can be relied on, "it is absurd to say that they are all right subject to the possibility that undetected fraud may make them all wrong" (Morrison, 1971:122).

The expectations of nonauditors are clear. The SEC in Accounting Series Release (ASR; SEC, 1940) in 1940 noted:

> [A]ccountants can be expected to detect gross overstatements of assets and profits whether resulting from collusive fraud or otherwise. . . . [T]he discovery of gross overstatements in the accounts is a major purpose of . . . an audit [Touche Ross, 1974].
>
> Perhaps the discussion of the auditor's responsibility for the detection of fraud has not yet diminished because it was . . . removed as an objective by the profession rather than by a change in demand of clients of accounting firms. A solicitous consuming public could reinstate it [Willingham, 1974:59].

Since 1960, and most notably in 1977, the profession of independent auditing has moved to increase its responsibility for the detection of deceptive financial practices (AICPA, 1975d), errors, irregularities (AICPA, 1977d), and illegal acts (AICPA, 1977c); to better document the management representations relied on by the auditor (AICPA, 1977b); and to require communication of material weaknesses in internal accounting controls (AICPA, 1977a).

## Proposed Typology

Management fraud can be viewed from many different dimensions. Fraud can be for or against the welfare of the organization, while the perpetrator's benefits may be received either directly or indirectly. Similarly, fraud can be located either inside or outside the organization. Finally, varying situational conditions conducive to management fraud, as well as numerous facilitating practices, combine with these dimensions to form a complex pattern. Patterns such as these often can be better understood through a typology such as the following: (1) For those who are receiving direct or indirect *benefits,* is the fraud motivated for or against the *welfare* of the organization? (2) Is the organizational locus of the fraud *internal* or *external* to the organization? (3) What are surrounding *conditions* conducive to management fraud? (4) What accounting and auditing *practices* have facilitated recent management frauds?

## Benefits

Benefits can be classified as direct where the criminal receives immediate or readily convertible advantages:

(1) Converting company assets for personal benefit; (2) receiving increases in compensation (such as raises, promotions, bonuses, profit sharing); (3) enhancing personal holdings of company stock; (4) retaining present position within company; and (5) receiving

benefits from outside parties (for example, money, vacations, social recognition) (Turner and Uretsky, 1978:23).

Benefits can also be classified as an indirect advantage which will eventually be converted into a direct benefit:

(1) Surviving a temporarily bad situation (for example, inadequate cash flow, meeting terms of existing loan agreements); (2) retaining control of company; (3) maintaining prestige of company; (4) supporting presently unprofitable ventures; (5) obtaining credit, financing, or additional capital investment for the company; and (6) increasing net profits as a result of fraudulent acts (Turner and Uretsky, 1978:24).

These various classifications are summarized in Figure 1 and generate the typology used to classify major management frauds.

Elaboration of these four types of fraud follow in the development of specific management fraud cases. Improper corporate political contributions or payments to foreign government officials illustrate type I acts. Examples of consumer fraud include misrepresented real estate developments and sales of counterfeit securities. Under type II acts, improper transfer pricing refers to misvalued goods exchanged between related parties, such as the parent corporation and a subsidiary where the former has significant influence over the latter. Prohibited business activities refer to those forbidden by government regulation or by contractual agreement. Examples include maximum loan limits by banks to any one customer or requirements against secret negotiations with a person under contract to another entity.

Under type III acts, bribes or kickbacks could include the obtaining of proprietary information or special discounts. Under type IV acts, theft differs from embezzlement because it involves stealing physical assets from a company, while embezzlement involves cash or cash-equivalent assets, such as negotiable securities.

The model in Figure 1 can be used to classify any management fraud. Auditors have traditionally focused on internal fraud (types II and IV) through an adequate system of safeguarding assets and proper financial statement disclosure. Two major categories of external management fraud have been deemphasized historically (types I and III). Also, the motivations for committing type II fraud (for the organization) may be quite different from type IV fraud (against the organization).

## Conditions and Practices

To understand management fraud fully, the typology must be expanded by four general conditions and four general practices surrounding recent instances of management fraud. Conditions are:

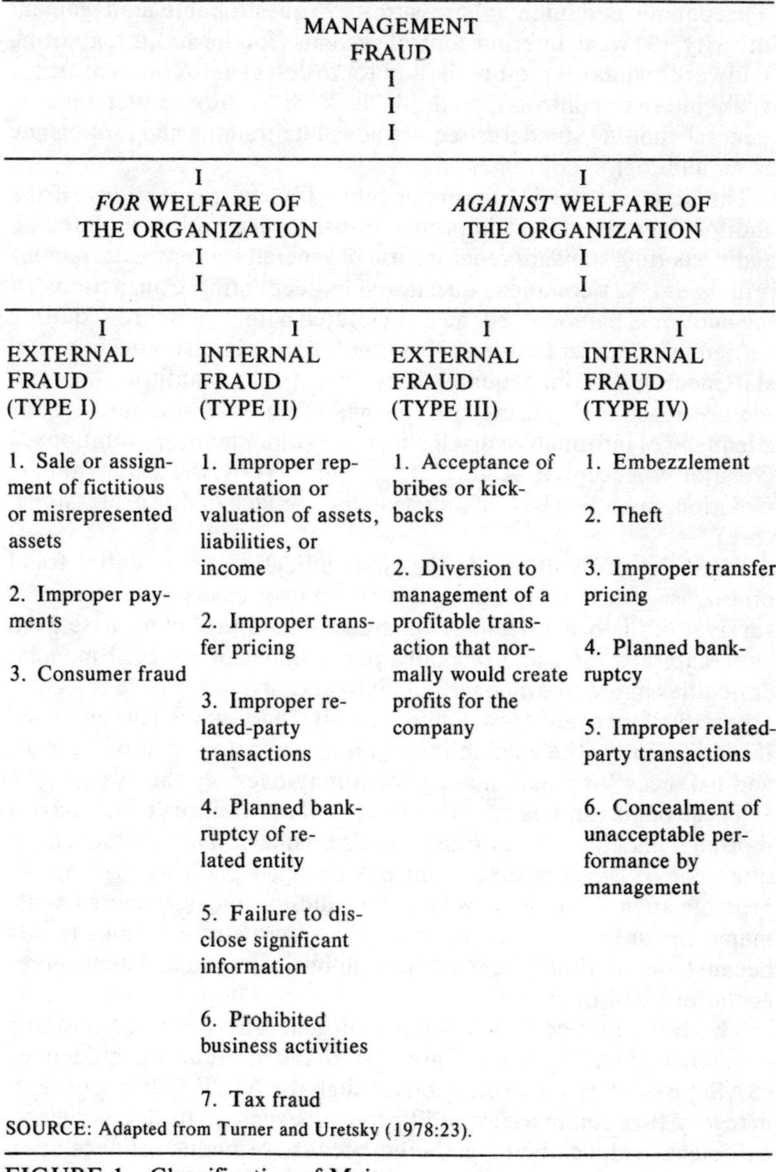

MANAGEMENT FRAUD

| *FOR* WELFARE OF THE ORGANIZATION | | *AGAINST* WELFARE OF THE ORGANIZATION | |
|---|---|---|---|
| EXTERNAL FRAUD (TYPE I) | INTERNAL FRAUD (TYPE II) | EXTERNAL FRAUD (TYPE III) | INTERNAL FRAUD (TYPE IV) |
| 1. Sale or assignment of fictitious or misrepresented assets | 1. Improper representation or valuation of assets, liabilities, or income | 1. Acceptance of bribes or kickbacks | 1. Embezzlement |
| 2. Improper payments | 2. Improper transfer pricing | 2. Diversion to management of a profitable transaction that normally would create profits for the company | 2. Theft |
| 3. Consumer fraud | 3. Improper related-party transactions | | 3. Improper transfer pricing |
| | 4. Planned bankruptcy of related entity | | 4. Planned bankruptcy |
| | 5. Failure to disclose significant information | | 5. Improper related-party transactions |
| | 6. Prohibited business activities | | 6. Concealment of unacceptable performance by management |
| | 7. Tax fraud | | |

SOURCE: Adapted from Turner and Uretsky (1978:23).

FIGURE 1 Classification of Major Management Frauds

(1) economic and financial pressures; (2) questionable management integrity; (3) weak internal control systems (for the auditor, auditing fieldwork standards require the auditor to detect or to compensate for weak internal controls); and (4) lack of auditor understanding (general auditing standards require adequate training and proficiency as an auditor).

The practices are (1) improper related-party transactions (if the auditor does not detect improper transactions, he has violated an audit-reporting standard requiring use of generally accepted accounting principles); (2) complex, questionable accounting transactions (if the auditor is bamboozled, he has violated a field standard requiring sufficient competent evidential matter for an opinion on the financial statements); (3) inadequate disclosure (if the auditor does not require reasonable disclosure, he has violated a standard on the adequacy of informative disclosures); (4) other auditor violations of Generally Accepted Auditing Standards (GAAS; for example, violations such as a lack of independence or lack of due professional care).

Financial difficulties are the first indication of potential fraud problems. When working capital (primarily cash) is lacking, the survival of the organization is at stake. These problems arise from undercapitalization and/or poor operating performance. Financial difficulties may force management into acts of questionable integrity, especially if there are a few dominant individuals running the business. If, additionally, the accounting internal control system of "checks and balances" is weak, management may override the system.

These opportunities are more inviting if the auditors do not have a thorough understanding of the client's business. This problem most often occurs when management has changed auditors, perhaps to promote such a problem! When little auditor understanding exists, management increases its opportunity to perpetrate various frauds because the auditor places undue emphasis on management representations and opinions.

The last practice is a violation of generally accepted auditing standards (GAAS) which are the detailed auditing guidelines (SASs) issued by the profession through the AICPA. It is a general category that summarizes audit problems such as little competent, sufficient evidence being gathered because of undue reliance upon management representations. It is a miscellaneous category to accommodate other audit problems not previously categorized.

Table 1 provides illustrative situations of the conditions and practices set forth above.

*Table 1* Conditions and Practices Surrounding Management Fraud*

| *Conditions/Practices* | *Illustrative Situation* |
|---|---|
| 1. Economic and Financial Pressures | • Lack of sufficient working capital and/or credit<br>• High demands for new capital in a developing industry with intense competition for the capital<br>• Pressure to finance expansion via current earnings rather than through equity or debt<br>• Profit squeeze because sales are not keeping pace with increasing costs<br>• Need to show continued favorable earnings record to support the price of the company's stock<br>• Need for additional collateral to support existing obligations<br>• Dependence on single or relatively few products or clients for ongoing success<br>• Industry is declining or is characterized by a large number of failures<br>• Rapid expansion of business or product lines<br>• Reduction in sales order backlog heralding future sales decline<br>• Difficulties in collection of certain classes of customers (e.g., energy-related businesses)<br>• Sizable increases in inventory without comparable increases in sales<br>• High obsolescence danger because the company is in a rapid technology industry<br>• Competition from low-priced imports<br>• Manufacturing cycle is long<br>• Excess capacity has befallen the firm<br>• Extensive litigation (e.g., stockholders and management)<br>• Extensive diversification through acquisitions |
| 2. Questionable Management Integrity | • Executives with records of malfeasance<br>• Management's reluctance to provide additional information to improve the clarity and comprehensiveness of the company's financial statement<br>• Progressive deterioration in quality of earnings; e.g., switching from an accelerated depreciation method to straight-line without good reason<br>• Management's tendency to exert extreme pressure on executives to meet budgets<br>• Overly optimistic earnings forecast |

*(continued on next page)*

*Table 1* Continued

| *Conditions/Practices* | *Illustrative Situation* |
|---|---|
| 3. Weak Internal Control System | • Accounting and financial functions appear understaffed, thus resulting in crisis conditions<br>• The company seems to need but lacks an adequate internal audit staff<br>• Key financial positions do not seem to stay filled very long<br>• Management is dominated by a few individuals<br>• General legal counsel is not used or is switched frequently |
| 4. Lack of Auditor Understanding | • Auditor is not familiar with the industry and its practices<br>• Audit of inventories requiring evaluation of physical qualities not within the expertise of the auditor<br>• The company uses different auditors for major segments of the business |
| 5. Improper or Related-Party Transactions | • Material transactions (perhaps deceptive) occur between related parties<br>• Material transactions occur near year-end and may have been backdated<br>• Absence of a written conflict of interests policy |
| 6. Complex and Questionable Accounting Practices | • The company is highly diversified with numerous businesses and accounting systems<br>• Business locations are widely dispersed, key documents are created at outlying locations with evidence of major transactions in more than one location<br>• Audit closing requires numerous substantive adjusting entries |
| 7. Inadequate Disclosure | • Bogus assets not identified<br>• Deceptive transactions between related parties not fully disclosed |
| 8. Other Violations of GAAS | • Lack of independence by auditor<br>• Lack of due audit care<br>• Lack of sufficient and competent evidence for opinion |

*Illustrations partially developed with materials from Touche Ross (1976), Coopers and Lybrand (1978), and SEC (1975, 1974, 1940).

## Use of a "Red Flag" Approach

A comprehensive analysis of management fraud demands multiple determinants such as the opportunity to commit fraud (for example, poor or inadequate internal controls), the environmental predisposers (such as outside factors bringing financial pressure to bear on the enterprise), and supporting normative structures (for example, survival at any cost). Management fraud is likely, therefore, to be the result of major economic and sociocultural pressures, and no single factor alone yields a sufficient explanation. Probably a similar conceptualization could offer an explanation of the *single* individual who engages in management fraud. An opportunity coupled with personal pressure and a personal belief and control structure supportive of deviant behavior converge to involve the single individual in a fraud. If the individual is highly placed, then it becomes a management fraud. Single-person frauds perpetrated by circumventing the internal control system should be detected by study and evaluation of the internal controls (Willingham, 1974:58). In any event, single-person management frauds and multiple-person management frauds are interactive products of economic, sociocultural, and personal determinants, and systematic research at several levels could offer a convincing theoretical and empirical synthesis. What an auditor needs is an early-warning system to spot the "red flags" associated with management fraud.

A first step would be a careful retrospective review of the red flags related to known fraud cases to sharpen the general approach. The red flags are tied to conducive economic conditions, conducive business structures, lack of auditor understanding, and presence of facilitating practices. The red flag approach is proposed as one cost-effective approach for the auditor. Drastic new measures to prevent management fraud can be both expensive and incapable of preventing or detecting every malfeasance. Hanson (1975:18) implies that devising practical measures such as a rational and reasonable early-warning system will serve in the great majority of cases, so that when fraud does strike, the auditor can explore its sources, prosecute the guilty, and learn from the experience.

# A SAGA OF MAJOR MANAGEMENT FRAUDS

The detected management frauds are probably only an infinitesimal portion of similar acts involving some of the thousands of companies offering public securities valued at $825 billion and owned by over 32 million stockholders (Hanson, 1975:31). Each of the ten illustrative cases of management fraud is abstracted in Table 2 using the

*Table 2* Ten Known Cases of Management Fraud by Type

| *Type of Fraud* | *Example* | *Known Case* | *Presence of Fraud-Associated "Red Flag" Condition or Practice* | | | | | | | |
|---|---|---|---|---|---|---|---|---|---|---|
| | | | *Economic Pressure & Financial Difficulty* | *Questionable Management Integrity* | *Weak Internal Control System* | *Lack of Auditor Understanding* | *Related-Party Transactions* | *Complex Questionable Accounting* | *Inadequate Disclosure* | *Violation of GAAS* |
| I | For Welfare of Organization: External | | | | | | | | | |
| | • Sale of fictitious assets | 1. Equity Funding | Yes | Yes | Yes | No | Yes | Yes | Yes | Yes |
| | • Sale of overvalued securities | 2. National Student Marketing | Yes | Yes | Yes | Yes | Yes | Yes | Yes | Yes |
| | | 3. Bar Chris | Yes | Yes | Yes | Yes | Yes | Yes | Yes | Yes |
| | • Sale of overvalued corporation | 4. Talley Industries | Yes | Yes | Yes | Yes | No | Yes | Yes | Yes |
| | • Improper loan received | 5. Ultramares | Yes | Yes | Yes | Yes | No | Yes | Yes | Yes |
| II | For Welfare of Organization: Internal | | | | | | | | | |
| | • Improper representation of assets, liabilities, and income | 6. McKesson & Robbins | Maybe | Yes | Yes | Yes | No | No | Yes | Yes |
| | | 7. Penn Central | Yes | Yes | Yes | Yes | Yes | Yes | Yes | Yes |
| III | Against Welfare of Organization: External | | | | | | | | | |
| | • Diversion of a profitable transaction to management | 8. Vesco | Yes | Yes | Yes | Yes | Yes | Yes | Yes | Yes |
| IV | Against Welfare of Organization: Internal | | | | | | | | | |
| | • Embezzlement | 9. Hochfelder | Yes | Yes | Yes | Yes | No | No | Yes | Yes |
| | | 10. Continental Vending | Yes | Yes | Yes | No | Yes | Yes | Yes | Yes |

suggested typology. Table 2 identifies the types of fraud and the presence or absence of the eight fraud-associated conditions or practices.

## External Fraud for Welfare of Company (Type I)

The following discussion does not emphasize the implications of technical legal liability; rather, it stresses the methods of the fraud and related auditing problems.

### SALE OF FICTITIOUS ASSETS: EQUITY FUNDING (SEIDLER ET AL., 1977)

Equity Funding was possibly the most spectacular and massive fraud in recent years. Many management and auditing personnel were convicted of fraudulent activity. While both external and internal fraud for the welfare of the company occurred, the focus here is primarily on the massive external (type I) fraud, since $2 billion of the total $3 billion in life insurance policies were phony. Once the frauds were exposed, the company went into receivership and various lenders and investors sued the company and its auditors.

Problems began because of a perpetual lack of working capital. The company would make loans to employees and customers for the purchase of life insurance policies. To generate cash, the company would then sell policies to other life insurance companies, receiving $1.80 for each dollar of life insurance sold in the first year. All subsequent life insurance premiums collected on the policies sold to other companies would go to those companies. These reinsurance transactions, therefore, became only a temporary solution to the cash flow problems of the company.

As a "permanent" solution, the company, with direction from the top management, created phony life insurance policies to sell as reinsurance. To keep a positive cash inflow each year, more policies would have to be created and sold, since the purchaser of the reinsurance policies received all cash premiums in subsequent years.

The fraud was perpetrated by massive collusion on the part of perhaps 30 employees, including top management. Such massive collusion can override almost any internal control accounting system of checks and balances, and is generally accepted as an inherent limitation of any internal control system.

The fraud was compounded by the acquiescence of the top-level auditors who were convicted of "aiding and abetting" the client scheme. There appeared to be complete auditor understanding. The independence of the audit partner who had helped design the reinsurance scheme (which is legal if *real* insurance policies are sold) was challenged during the trial. Generally, accepted auditing standards require that auditors be independent.

The entire bogus insurance policy creation occurred through a subsidiary of the parent corporation. The parent management would give the subsidiary management the earnings desired for a particular period and the subsidiary management would work backward through the accounting system to create such earnings with the bogus policies (that is, improper related parties). The complex accounting for loans to purchase the policies and for the reinsurance sales did not acknowledge possibilities of cancellations or contingent liabilities, nor was the magnitude of these transactions fully disclosed in the financial statements. GAAS were violated by the auditors because of (1) lack of independence in auditing the client and (2) lack of due audit care. In fact, the auditor's working papers and plans were left unguarded. Management took advantage to make a copy of the audit plans and thus anticipate each audit procedure. In addition, there was (3) lack of evidence in missing the bogus insurance policies and in relying upon a false confirmation which represented bond securities or 70 percent of the subsidiary's assets.

### SALE OF OVERVALUED SECURITIES: NATIONAL STUDENT MARKETING CORPORATION [NSMC] (SEC, 1975:25-29)

Sales and, therefore, income were recorded prematurely (or fictitously) to inflate earnings and the auditors were easily misled because of their lack of understanding of how the business operated. These inflated earnings and corresponding inflated assets were used in a proxy financial statement to attract investors to buy more common shares of NSMC. NSMC then merged with another company. When the inflated earnings were eventually uncovered and disclosed by the auditors, the auditors were sued by the United States government for violation of the Securities Exchange Act of 1934. The audit partner was convicted of providing false and misleading statements in the proxy (registration) statement.

The major business of NSMC was the provision of a college-based marketing distribution system for various products. The unique business was started by college students and, as NSMC grew, it needed new capital. Various proxy statements were issued to raise capital. To attract investors, performance had to be strong and business had to grow.

To maintain such positive performance, management turned to questionable and occasionally erroneous sale (and income) recognition procedures. The crux of the case was an exception to the GAAP of only recognizing a sale when performance is completed and goods or services delivered. The exception is the "percentage of completion revenue recognition" and is acceptable only when all of the following criteria are met: (1) the ultimate realization of the revenue (cash collection) is reasonably assured; (2) the completion of the contract requires a relatively long time; (3) the partial performance of the contract is a reasonable measure of business activity; and (4) the cost of completion can be reasonably estimated (SEC, 1974:28; AICPA, 1955).

Percentage of completion is generally used in the construction industry where projects may take several years. To avoid the distortion in financial statements of showing no sales and income until the final year, sales and income are recognized on a percentage basis.

The method generally is *not* used in industries other than construction because the four factors cannot be met, especially the one concerning completion of a contract over a relatively long time. The SEC ruled that none of the four factors was met in the NSMC case, which involved a marketing service, not a construction company. NSMC management had used the percentage-of-completion method to inflate earnings in the two annual reports and the proxy statement prior to the merger. The corrected proxy statement would have decreased the $700,000 earnings to an $80,000 loss. Also, $750,000, or 15 percent, of the 1968 sales in the annual report were fictitious. Why was NSMC allowed to perform this type of creative accounting? Two conditions and four practices prevailed:

*(1) Weak internal control system.* Records were in very poor condition (little documentation or "audit trail") and were a couple of months behind; in fact, financial statements were prepared from audit workpapers, not client records, which raises the issue of audit independence—that is, the financials must be "fairly presented" because we helped prepare them.

*(2) Auditors had little understanding of how this new industry worked.* Marketing agreements thus became the basis of revenue recognition rather than the performance of a marketing service.

*(3) Related party transactions.* Subsidiaries with operating losses were sold to employees to eliminate the unfavorable impact on earnings.

*(4) Complex, questionable accounting.* Sales and corresponding unbilled accounts receivable were recognized prematurely or falsely in some situations. For example, NSMC would frequently "discover" current period income after the year was over but before financials were issued.

*(5) Inadequate disclosure.* The questionable (erroneous) use of percentage of completion accounting for sales was not fully disclosed,

nor was the magnitude of the problem. For example, in 1969 over 75 percent ($1.3 million) of the 1968 revenue recognized on this questionable basis was written off but not disclosed in the 1969 report.

*(6) Violation of GAAS.* (a) Lack of adequate training and due audit care in failing to understand the nature of the client's business and in failing to investigate fully the reasons behind the switch in auditors (the previous auditors would not accept the client's revenue recognition methods); (b) lack of evidence in relying upon management representations (the weakest possible form of evidence); and (c) violation of GAAP in agreeing to unacceptable application of percentage of completion revenue recognition.

**SALE OF OVERVALUED SECURITIES: BAR CHRIS (LARSEN, 1971; ESCOTT V. BAR CHRIS, 1968)**

Bar Chris filed a registration (proxy) statement to sell convertible bonds in early 1961 and went bankrupt 17 months later. The auditors had given an unqualified opinion on the 1960 annual report and were sued by the investors and eventually found guilty of negligence.

The heart of this case is the sale-leaseback transaction used to inflate earnings and assets, to deflate liabilities, and to raise or conserve working capital. Bar Chris would take its own bowling alleys and sell them mainly to affiliated companies. Working capital was generated by the down payments of the "sales" or at least conserved because the new owner would have to pay all the property maintenance costs. The affiliated companies would lease back the bowling alleys to Bar Chris at "reasonable" annual rental fees. Sales, earnings, and receivables would be inflated by these transactions. Any possible contingent liabilities for Bar Chris, such as for property maintenance, would not be recognized.

Management integrity was questionable, since these sale-leaseback transactions were mainly to management-controlled affiliated companies, which is the definition of a related party. The sale-leasebacks were sham related-party transactions to inflate sales and earnings. The internal control system was overridden by management in recording such transactions.

The auditors, primarily the senior person in charge of the day-to-day audit operation, had little understanding of sale-leaseback transactions or of the bowling industry. This lack of understanding again led to an undue reliance on management representations and problems in accounting and disclosing the sale-leaseback transactions.

Violation of GAAS is a convenient way to summarize this case from the actual court decision.

Lack of training and proficiency:

> The auditor was then about thirty years old. He was not yet a CPA. He had no previous experience with the bowling industry. This was his first job as a senior accountant. He could hardly have been given a more difficult assignment [Escott v. Bar Chris, 1968:698, as summarized by Larsen, 1971:2].

Lack of planning and supervision:

> [Instead of daily, only] toward the close of the senior accountant's work, the audit manager reviewed it and made various comments and suggestions to the senior [Escott v. Bar Chris, 1968:698; Larsen, 1971:2].

Lack of independence, due audit care, and evidence:

> In substance, what the senior did in the subsequent events review is that he asked questions, he got answers which he considered satisfactory, and he did nothing to verify them. . . . He was too easily satisfied with glib answers to his inquiries. . . . GAAS require further investigation under these circumstances. It is not always sufficient merely to ask questions. . . . As far as results were concerned, the senior accountant's subsequent events review was useless [Escott v. Bar Chris, 1968:702-703; Larsen, 1971:2-3].

## SALE OF OVERVALUED CORPORATION: TALLEY INDUSTRIES (SEC, 1975:41-49)

This case arose from a merger of Talley Industries with General Time Corporation. A private investigation by the SEC determined that the most recent annual report prior to the merger and the nine-month financial statements included in the merger proxy statement were materially false and misleading (SEC, 1975:41). Talley had shown as an asset excess costs or cost overruns on current projects for the U.S. Armed Forces, which Talley hoped to recover on new government contracts. If these costs were not shown as assets, but as expenses to reduce income, the earning per share in the annual report would have been reduced 43 percent from $1.71 per common share to $.74 per common share.

The crux of this case is the application of accounting theory for an asset or a resource. If an expenditure has future service benefits, such as potential conversion to cash or potential generation of cash through manufacture of goods, then it should be shown as an asset on the statement of financial position; if not, it should be expensed in the statement of operations. Do cost overruns, which are not billable on current defense contracts, represent future cash inflows to the company by billing the U.S. Armed Forces or by generating cost savings on future defense contracts? Most accountants would say no, since future cash inflows are too uncertain. The SEC concurred in this treatment in ruling against the audit firm.

How were the auditors convinced to take a stand which generally differs from GAAP for assets? They relied too heavily on management representations in assessing the fairness of accounting for "excess costs." The auditors apparently were not sufficiently knowledgeable about the defense industry generally and their client's operation specifically to ascertain that the excess costs would not be recovered from billings or production cost savings on future contracts. The auditors did not fully consider the financial difficulties of less cash inflow from these cost overruns and corresponding pressure on management's integrity in covering up this poor performance problem by showing the cost overruns as assets. Management's justification was to forecast future contracts to be awarded Talley and corresponding future cost savings. However reasonable the justification, it was negated by the failure to achieve such projects (that is, the 1970 projections were only 24 percent fulfilled). Talley's accounting system could not provide details on the cost overruns except on an annual basis.

Unfortunately, the auditors did not fully acknowledge this weak accounting system and did not require the write-off or expensing of the excess costs until after the merger was completed. Complex, questionable accounting and inadequate disclosure covered up the excess costs.

## IMPROPER LOAN RECEIVED: ULTRAMARES (CAUSEY, 1976)

This 1931 landmark case limited auditor liability for negligence to only specific (foreseeable) third parties, but the legal question continues to be litigated. However, the focus here is on the major audit problems in detecting management fraud, not just the legal implications. Ultramares relied on audited financial statements to make loans to Stern and Company, a rubber importer. Stern subsequently went bankrupt and court evidence indicated the auditors had failed to investigate unusual (penciled in at bottom of sales journal) entries which turned out to be fictitious. Ultramares could not collect from the auditor, who was not liable to unidentified third parties for negligence (as opposed to fraud). The auditor did not know that the audited financial statements were to be used to procure a loan (Causey, 1976:319-26).

The client's import business continually generated need for working capital which was procured by borrowing. This continual financing need generated pressures for favorable earnings and asset reports which led management to falsify information; that is, assets were overstated 28 percent by phony receivables of $700,000. The unscrupulous client management also attempted to overstate inventories by $300,000, which was caught and adjusted by the auditors.

The accounting records were eight months behind and management was able to override any internal controls easily. Even with all the problems mentioned, the auditors did not extend procedures in other fraud-prone areas, primarily in receivables and sales. The lackadaisical attitude indicates an absence of auditor understanding of potential problem areas. Questionable accounting for "penciled-in" receivables was not investigated and resulted in inadequate disclosures. Accordingly, the GAASs of due audit care and evidence were violated.

## For Welfare of Company: Internal Fraud (Type II)

The analysis now focuses on internal, as opposed to external, fraud for the welfare of the company. Type II fraud differs from type I fraud because it does not involve direct sale of misrepresented assets or overvalued stock to outsiders or improper procurement of a loan from outsiders. It does involve misstated or erroneous financial statements—primarily assets, income, and liabilities—but these financial statements are not being directly used to sell assets or securities or to obtain loans. Outsiders, especially the common stockholders, are only indirectly affected when the fraud is discovered, and only if the common stock prices decrease or become worthless. Type II fraud is designated as internal fraud because outsiders are only indirectly affected.

### IMPROPER REPRESENTATION OF ASSETS AND INCOME: MCKESSON AND ROBBINS

This 1938 fraud was the first case that caused the revision of audit procedures. Before, auditors did not physically observe inventories or confirm accounts receivable by writing to customers to verify the legitimacy of their accounts with the client. McKesson and Robbins showed $87 million assets but had created $10 million fictitious inventories and $9 million fictitious accounts receivable by false book entries for purchases and sales. The auditors agreed without litigation to pay the bankruptcy trustee $500,000, the previous five years' audit fees. In analyzing the case, the SEC made the following ruling:

> Even though the auditors are not guarantors and should not be responsible for detecting all fraud, the discovery of gross

> overstatements in the accounts is a major purpose in an audit even though every minor defalcation might not be disclosed [SEC, 1940].

The development of general, fieldwork, and reporting standards of GAAS were also motivated by the SEC analysis and rulings in this case.

Financial difficulties were not specifically discussed in the case but possibly were a motivation for the majority owner to create the phony assets. The questionable integrity of management was key to this fraud. The majority owner had two previous convictions for similar management fraud and had spent three years in jail. He also had been involved in an alcohol bootlegging operation during Prohibition before taking over control of the McKesson and Robbins company. Yet, the auditors were not sufficiently alert to these possible problems to take additional precautions. They relied exclusively on the management's representations that the inventories and receivables existed, rather than independently verifying their existence through observation and confirmation procedures. The fraud occurred through a weak internal control system which allowed management to falsify purchase and sale documents.

### IMPROPER REPRESENTATION OF ASSETS, LIABILITIES, AND INCOME: PENN CENTRAL

In February 1968, the Pennsylvania and New York Central railroads merged and became Penn Central. The auditors issued reports for the 1968 and 1969 financial statements. These reports had only minor qualifications for the failure to recognize deferred federal income taxes. In June 1970, Penn Central filed a petition for reorganization under federal bankruptcy laws.

The severe financial difficulties were evidenced by the resultant bankruptcy proceedings. The SEC summarized the questionable management integrity:

> Penn Central management had engaged in a program of concealing the deterioration of the company. . . . Management's efforts involved misrepresentations as to affairs, prospects, financial results, and value of assets of the Penn Central complex. The misrepresentations were made in many forms of communications to the investing public and shareholders [SEC, 1975:61].

The modus operandi for management was the questionable or false related-party transaction. At least six related companies, subsidiaries, or significantly influenced investee companies were involved. The details are too numerous to review, but a summary of related party transactions and financial statements impacts is provided in Table 3 (SEC, 1975).

These related party transactions thus created the misleading financial statements which showed a solvent Penn Central up to the moment that bankruptcy occurred. The auditors' lack of understanding led them to acquiesce in such "fairly presented" financial statements. They failed to assess the economic substance of these related-party or "sham" transactions; instead, they accepted the

*Table 3* Analysis of the Penn Central Case

| *Related Party* | *Transaction* | *Financial Statement Impact* |
|---|---|---|
| 1. Lehigh Valley Railroad Company | Failed to include (consolidate) Lehigh's financial statements with Penn Central which owned 97% of Lehigh's stock; | Income before taxes was overstated about $63 million in both 1968 and 1969 due to Lehigh's income statement losses |
| 2. New York-New Haven and Hartford Railroad Company | Failed to include current maintenance expenses as charges against income but set up as assets instead | Expenses and liabilities understated and income overstated by about $35 million in 1969 |
| 3. Great Southwest Corp. (GSC) | In three major deals, sold real estate to limited partnerships created by Penn Central; however GSC maintained control, risk of loss and opportunity for gain; in substance no exchange occurred | Assets and income were overstated $13.4 million in 1968 and $18.4 million in 1969 |
| 4. Madison Square Garden Corp. (MSGC) | Penn Central exchanged stock with MSGC but no change in economic interests occurred; in substance no exchange occurred | Assets and income were overstated $21 million in 1968 |
| 5. Washington Terminal Company (WTC) | Stock of WTC was given to Penn Central but in substance position of consolidated Penn Central was unchanged concerning possession, operation, and maintenance of WTC (a subsidiary) property; thus, no exchange occurred | Assets and income were overstated $11.7 million in 1968 |
| 6. Executive Jet Aviation (EJA) | Investment was illegal per aeronautics laws prohibiting railroads from air transport-cargo fields; EJA had sustained losses in all five years of operation (1965-69) | $21 million investment was sold at "substantial loss" in 1970 but no prior write-downs were made in 1968 or 1969 |

technical form of such transactions. Perhaps the auditors were not familiar enough with the railroad industry. The auditors were so preoccupied with detailed procedures that they failed to assess the overall solvency of the company. They accordingly violated GAAS as follows:

(1) lack of training in not adequately understanding the substance, rather than the form, of the complex related-party transactions in the railroad industry;
(2) lack of due audit care in relying too heavily on management representations of such transactions and in failing to assess the overall solvency of Penn Central;
(3) lack of internal control analysis in not expanding audit work due to continual management override of accounting system;
(4) lack of evidence for conclusion that related-party transactions and thus financial statements were fairly presented;
(5) violation of GAAP which in spirit attempts to reflect the economic substance, not form, of business transactions; and
(6) lack of disclosure of magnitude and details concerning related-party transactions.

**External Fraud: Against Welfare of Company (Type III)**

Vesco can easily be classified as type I, type III, and type IV frauds. Vesco used a related-party transaction to inflate income $3.6 million in his controlled company, International Controls (ICC); he then lent money to Investors Overseas Services (IOS) and received a promissory note and warrants to purchase IOS common stock through which he acquired control of IOS (type I fraud). He then looted IOS in a scheme called "Vesco's $224 Million Syphon" (Briloff, 1975:187). IOS still had hundreds of millions of dollars in liquid assets, primarily securities in major U.S. corporations, which had the potential to generate dividend and interest income and capital gains for IOS and thus ICC. However, Vesco diverted these transactions to his own newly created, thinly capitalized foreign companies in Luxembourg and the Bahamas (type III fraud). The end result was a massive embezzlement of securities owned by IOS (type IV fraud).

The accounting controls were virtually nonexistent, as Vesco was easily able to create related-party transactions to syphon off $200 million. The auditors did not sufficiently understand the complex mutual fund structure of IOS to prohibit or disclose the Vesco embezzlement scheme. Vesco also created his own foreign companies (or related parties) to transfer (embezzle) the $200 million securities. These "transfers" were shrouded in the veil of legal technicalities. This questionable, complex accounting portrayed the form, not the economic substance, of the (embezzlement) transactions. Also, disclosure of such transactions was inadequate or nonexistent.

Numerous examples of type III fraud are found in the public sector. Recent examples of accepting bribes or kickbacks, another form of type III fraud, include the Korean payoffs to members of Congress and the overpayments made by the Government Services Agency to various related parties.

## Internal Fraud: Against Welfare of Company (Type IV)

The case analysis of management fraud concludes with the study of internal fraud against the welfare of the company (type IV). The major example is embezzlement.

### EMBEZZLEMENT: HOCHFELDER

Nay, president of the First Securities brokerage firm, owned 92 percent of its stock. Hochfelder et al. were customers of First Securities. Nay persuaded them to invest funds in escrow accounts purported to yield a high return. Nay subsequently committed suicide, leaving a note that First Securities was bankrupt and the escrow accounts nonexistent. Hochfelder et al. then sued the auditors under the SEC Acts (Hampson, 1976:69-74).

The embezzlement was based on Nay's "mail rule" stipulating that all mail addressed to him was to be opened only by him. In his absence, the mail was placed on his desk and opened only on his return, regardless of how long he was gone. Nay diverted all such "escrow account" investments to his personal use. The transactions were never recorded on First Securities' books. The customers made out their checks to Nay or to his designated bank account and never received records or receipts of these transactions.

The auditors won the lawsuit in the United States Supreme Court. The court ruled that negligence is insufficient to make auditors liable to third parties under the 1934 Securities Exchange Act (which primarily deals with regular financial statements as opposed to proxy statements for the sale of securities under the 1933 Act). Auditors are liable to third parties under the 1934 Act only on a showing of intentional or willful conduct according to the court in this 1976 case.

Brokerage firms by nature have very little capital from shareholders, using mostly lending sources to raise money. Since very little stockholder capital is available to absorb losses, bankruptcy is more probable. First Securities indeed was bankrupt at the time of its president's suicide. Management integrity was critical, since customers' money was embezzled through illegal behavior of the president of the firm. A weak internal control system allowed the embezzlement to occur. Nay's "mail rule" would never be permitted in a reasonable system of internal control.

The auditors evidenced lack of understanding in two major ways. First, they were not sensitive to the potential bankruptcy threat in a brokerage firm; the financial statements did not disclose any such possibilities. Second, the auditors were not sensitive to the embezzlement possibilities through various investment schemes. Why wasn't Nay's "mail rule" discovered and fully investigated?

**EMBEZZLEMENT: CONTINENTAL VENDING (LARSEN, 1971, SUMMARIZING UNITED STATES VS. SIMON, 1969)**

Continental Vending resulted in the first criminal conviction of auditors, who were then given a full presidential pardon by President Nixon. The embezzlement involved the looting of a company, Continental Vending, through related party transactions with Valley Corporation by the company's president, Roth. The embezzlement reached $3.5 million by the end of 1962 before it was disclosed publicly.

Roth controlled Continental Vending through owning 22 percent of its stock and controlled Valley Corporation through 25 percent ownership of its stock. Roth would have Continental advance or lend cash to Valley, who would then lend the cash to Roth for his personal use—questionable management behavior.

The financial difficulties were extreme in this case. The trend can be observed in the account balances in Table 4. Continental borrowed money through the "payable to Valley" in an attempt to overcome its financial problems. Continental would issue notes to Valley, which would borrow money from banks with the notes and advance this money to Continental. Observe that the legitimate borrowing stayed almost constant over the three-year period. However, note also that the "receivable from Valley" (the embezzlement or looting account) increased approximately 1,000 percent in this same time period. Speculating on these trends, Roth may have been motivated to increase his embezzlements as the financial difficulties of Continental continued unabated by looting a "sinking ship." This type of analysis emphasizes again how financial difficulties can pressure management into questionable or even illegal acts. In fact, the cash audit for the September 30, 1962, balance showed $286,000 which resulted only from 30-day loans of $1.5 million from two banks (United States vs. Simon, 1969:802-803).

No internal controls over related-party transactions existed or were viable, as Roth overrode all such attempts with his 20-25 percent control of both Continental and Valley. The auditors were criminally convicted of aiding this fraud by not sufficiently dis-

*Table 4* Details of the Continental Vending Case

| *Fiscal Year September 30* | *Receivable from Valley (President's looting)* | *Payable to Valley (company's financial difficulty)* | *Net (inadequate disclosure)* |
|---|---|---|---|
| 1960 | $ 398,000 | $ 950,000 | $ 552,000 |
| 1961 | 848,000 | 780,000 | 68,000 |
| 1962 | 3,543,000 | 1,029,000 | 2,514,000 |

closing all the facts known to them during the audit. As previously described, the related-party accounting transactions were critical in the embezzlement; they were justified with the collateral of Roth's personal common stock holdings in Continental. Since Continental's stock price nosedived when the embezzlement became public, the collateral eventually went from dubious to almost worthless value.

Inadequate disclosure eventually led to the auditors' conviction of aiding this embezzlement. Briefly, the auditors allowed the "receivable from Valley" to be offset and netted out against the "Payable to Valley" in the footnote, which is also a violation of GAAP. These net figures obscured the magnitude of the embezzlement, the "receivable from Valley" account. Details of the terms and collateral were also obscured in the nebulous footnote. The court summed up this point well:

> The jury could reasonably have wondered how accountants who were really seeking to tell the truth could have constructed a footnote so well designed to conceal the shocking facts [United States vs. Simon, 1969:807].

## FRAUD AS A SOCIAL PROBLEM

With the historical and developmental background sketched, the focus now turns to the analysis of management fraud as a growing social problem. One sociological approach to the study of social problems contends that social problems emerge when some organized group asserts the need to eradicate or change some condition thought to be harmful or undesirable (Hartjen, 1977). Social problems such as traditional criminal offenses have alarmed the nation during the past decade and have created much concern over "law and order." The public's preoccupation with "street crime" has tended to obscure the consequences of "profitable deviance" engaged in by respectable middle- and upper-class offenders in the course of their occupations. Johnson and Douglas (1978:151) point out that the recent exposure of managerial fraud in Equity Funding was "one of the largest securities and investment frauds ever perpetrated on the American public, eventually involving losses somewhere between two and three billion dollars, more than the total losses of *all* street crime in the United States for one year." The U.S. Chamber of Commerce estimates that even the short-term, direct cost of white-collar crime is at least $40 billion annually (Chamber of Commerce of the United States, 1974:5).

Wheeler (1975) notes that sociologists have largely neglected the study of corporate crime, fraud, embezzlement, stock manipulations, and the like. He points out that in the two-volume *Criminology Index* (Wolfgang et al., 1975), which contains theoretical and empirical work in criminology from 1945 to 1972 listing some 3,700 books or articles, only 2.5 percent deal with white-collar or corporate criminality. Even the monumental study by the President's Commission on Law Enforcement and Administration of Justice—*The Challenge of Crime in a Free Society*—devoted only *two* pages to the entire subject of "white-collar offenders and business crimes," with a mere seven-page discussion buried in one of the nine lengthy task-force reports (Hills, 1971).

## MANAGEMENT FRAUD: AN EMERGING SOCIAL ISSUE

Spector and Kitsuse (1977:75) define a social problem as "the activities of individuals or groups making assertions of grievances and claims with respect to some putative conditions." Activities such as filing lawsuits, calling press conferences, and supporting or opposing some governmental practice or policy are everyday examples of claims-making. Viewing social problems as processes, Spector and Kitsuse (1977:142) propose a four-stage model of the emergence, maintenance, history of claim-making, and responding activities:

*Stage 1:* Group(s) attempt to assert the existence of some condition; define it as offensive, harmful, or otherwise undesirable; publicize these assertions; stimulate controversy; and create a public or political issue over the matter.

*Stage 2:* Recognition of the legitimacy of these group(s) by some official organization, agency, or institution. This may lead to an official investigation, proposals for reform, and the establishment of an agency to respond to those claims and demands.

*Stage 3:* Reemergence of claims and demands by the original group(s) or by others, expressing dissatisfaction with the established procedures for dealing with the imputed conditions, the bureaucratic handling of complaints, the failure to generate a condition of trust and confidence in the procedures, and lack of sympathy for the complaints.

*Stage 4:* Rejection by complainant group(s) of the agency's or institution's response, or lack of response to their claims and demands; and the development of activities to create alternative, parallel, or counterinstitutions as responses to the established procedures.

Spector and Kitsuse (1973:147) contend that the development of a social problem may proceed through these distinct stages with each stage "described by different processes, casts of characters and kinds of activities." This model of claims-making suggests that "management fraud" has elements of an emerging social problem, not just a set of technical disagreements among professionals over the proper selection of auditing standards.

Applying the model to the subject of management fraud permits one to trace the various activities of complaining groups (Stage 1) regarding auditing practices that have allegedly failed to reflect accurately the economic substance of corporate business activities. Many of these complaints focus on corporate fraud and the auditor's responsibility for its detection. As Turner and Uretsky (1978) point out, the most common complaint against auditors prior to 1940 was a breach of contract based on their alleged failure to detect embezzlement. The 1960s and 1970s have seen an increase in pending lawsuits from 100 cases in 1966 to 1,000 cases in 1974.

Adding substantially to the chorus of controversy over auditor performance have been the actions of the SEC. Hershman (1974:53) contends that the "SEC is the most aggressive force in the battle to make accountants take more responsibility for detecting fraud." As a consequence of recent audit failures to detect management fraud, the SEC itself has initiated legal actions against auditors. Finally, there have been congressional inquiries into accounting practices. Representative John E. Moss's Subcommittee of Oversight and Investigations of the House Committee on Interstate and Foreign Commerce and the Metcalf subcommittee hearing and report in 1977 have emphasized the importance of restoring public confidence in the usefulness and integrity of corporate financial reports certified by independent auditors.

The complaints over audit failures to detect fraud have generated official responses (Stage 2) by the accounting profession. New auditing standards on the detection of errors and irregularities (AICPA, 1977d) and illegal acts by clients (AICPA, 1977c) issued by the AICPA, as well as the formation of the Cohen Commission, indicate the profession's concern over the increasing number of lawsuits, the activities of the SEC, and the growing attention of Congress. The Cohen Commission (1978:31) explicitly recognizes that "[n]o other major aspect of the independent auditor's role has caused more difficulty for the auditor than questions about his responsibility for the detection of fraud." The overall effectiveness of these recommendations, plus whatever additional steps auditors take to improve their efforts at fraud detection, will determine if the "social problem" of management fraud is satisfactorily resolved. If it is not, we may expect the reemergence of claims and demands (Stage 3) by the original groups or by others. In this third stage even more aggressive action by the SEC may be anticipated.

The possibility of future events in Stage 3 that might result in the SEC or a new agency taking over the determination of auditing standards and the overall management of firms rendering audits on SEC clients has prompted debate within the accounting profession. Burton (1978), for example, advocates the creation of a self-regulatory body to oversee the profession. Sommer (1978) disagrees with Burton on how best to alter the institutional structure of the accounting profession to meet the demands for changes pushed for in Stage 1. Sommer (1978:71) rejects the idea of cooperative regulation, "when every decision, every rule-making endeavor, every disciplinary proceeding is subject to reversal or modification by the SEC." For most auditors, reliance on gradual changes and self-regulation probably is preferable to outside control through new layers of federal regulation. The Stage 3 outcome will likely have a profound effect on the nature of the accounting profession.

The final stage of the Spector-Kitsuse (1973:156) model is somewhat of a residual category in which "groups organize their activities on the contention that it is no longer possible to 'work within the system'." Should matters reach this stage, all efforts to solve the problem appear to have failed. In this final stage even the legitimacy of established institutions (such as the SEC) is challenged. We do not foresee the likelihood of the career of management fraud as a social problem proceeding into the events that characterize Stage 4.

Viewing management fraud as a social problem focuses attention on the multiple activities of a number of groups as they seek to generate and sustain claims and demand institutional responses to them. The complexity of the issue of fraud detection and the persistent claims-making activities of many groups appear to have manifold consequences for the accounting profession and the independent auditor. The success with which accountants can close the gap between public expectations and auditor performance will ultimately determine the amount and intensity of future claims-making activities.

## REFERENCES

ALLEN, B. (1977) "The biggest computer frauds: Lessons for CPAs." Journal of Accountancy 143 (May):52-62.

AICPA [American Institute of Certified Public Accountants] (1955) Accounting Research Bulletin Number 45. Long Term Construction-Type Contracts. New York: American Institute of Certified Public Accountants.

——— (1960) "Codification of statements on auditing standards." Statement on Auditing Standards Number 1 (November).

——— (1975a) "Communications between predecessor and successor auditors." Statement on Auditing Standards Number 7 (October).

——— (1975b) "Related party transactions." Statement on Auditing Standards Number 6 (July).

——— (1977a) "Required communication of material weaknesses in internal accounting control." Statement of Auditing Standards Number 20 (August).

——— (1977b) "Client representations." Statement on Auditing Standards Number 19 (June).

——— (1977c) "Illegal acts." Statement on Auditing Standards Number 17 (January).

——— (1977d) "The independent auditor's responsibility for the detection of errors or irregularities." Statement on Auditing Standards Number 16 (January).

BLUNDELL, W. (1976) Swindled! Princeton: Dow Jones Books.

BRILOFF, A. (1975) "We often paint fakes." Vanderbilt Law Review 28 (January): 165-200.

BURTON, J. (1978) "The profession's institutional structure in the 1980's." Journal of Accountancy 145 (April):63-69.

CATLETT, G. (1975) "Relationship of auditing standards to detection of fraud." CPA Journal 45 (December):13-21.

CAUSEY, D. Y. (1976) Duties of Liabilities of the CPA. Bureau of Business Research, University of Texas.

Chamber of Commerce of the United States (1974) White Collar Crime, Everyone's Problem, Everyone's Loss. Washington, DC: U.S. Government Printing Office.

Commission [Manuel F. Cohen et al.] (1978) Report, Conclusions, and Recommendation. The Commission of Auditors' Responsibilities. American Institute of Certified Public Accountants.

COOPERS & LYBRAND. (1978) Newsletter (March-April):1-12.

EDELHERTZ, H. (1970) The Nature, Impact, and Prosecution of White-Collar Crime. U.S. Dept. of Justice, LEAA. Washington, DC: U.S. Government Printing Office.

——— E. STOTLAND, M. WALSH, and M. WEINBERG (1977) The Investigation of White-Collar Crime: A Manual for Law Enforcement Agencies. U.S. Dept. of Justice, LEAA. Washington, DC: U.S. Government Printing Office.

ESCOTT v. BAR CHRIS CONSTRUCTION CORPORATION (1968) F. Supp. 643.

HAMPSON, J. J. (1976) "Accountants' liability—The significance of Hochfelder." Journal of Accountancy 142 (June):69-74.

HANSON, W. F. (1975) "Focus on fraud." Financial Executive 43 (March):14-19.

HARTJEN, C. A. (1977) Possible Trouble: An Analysis of Social Problems. New York: Praeger.

HERSHMAN, A. (1974) "The war over corporate fraud." Dun's Review 104 (November):51-55.

HILLS, S. (1971) Crime, Power, and Morality: The Criminal-Law Process in the United States. San Francisco: Chandler.

JOHNSON, J. M. and J. D. DOUGLAS [eds.] (1978) Crime at the Top: Deviance in Business and the Professions. Philadelphia: J. B. Lippincott.

KAPNICK, H. (1975) "Management fraud and the independent auditor." Journal of Commercial Bank Lending 58 (December):20-30.

LARSEN, J. (1971) "Bar Chris, Continental Vending, and Generally Accepted Auditing Standards." University of Southern California. (unpublished)

MORRISON, A.M.C. (1971) "The role of the reporting accountant today-II." Journal of Accountancy 82 (March):120-130.

PEAT, MARWICK, MITCHELL & CO. (1975) Accounting Series Release and Other Details of Settlement with SEC. New York.

Securities and Exchange Commission (1940) Accounting Series Release No. 19: In the Matter of McKesson and Robbins, Inc. Washington, DC: U.S. Government Printing Office.

——— (1974) Accounting Series Release No. 153: In the Matter of Touche Ross and Co. Washington, DC: U.S. Government Printing Office.

——— (1975) Accounting Series Release No. 173: In the Matter of Peat, Marwick, Mitchell & Co., 21-116. Washington, DC: U.S. Government Printing Office.

SEIDLER, L. J., F. ANDREWS, and M. J. EPSTEIN (1977) The Equity Funding Papers: The Anatomy of a Fraud. New York: John Wiley.

SOMMER, A. A. (1978) "The lion and the lamb: Can the profession live with 'cooperative regulation'?" Journal of Accountancy 145 (April):70-75.

SORENSEN, J. E. and T. L. SORENSEN (1978) Detecting Management Fraud: Some Organizational Strategies for the Independent Auditor. Interdisciplinary Symposium on Management Fraud. New York: Peat, Marwick, Mitchell & Co.

SPECTOR, M. and J. I. KITSUSE (1973) "Social problems: A re-formulation." Social Problems 21 (Fall):145-149.

——— (1977) Constructing Social Problems. Menlo Park, CA: Cummings.

SYKES, G. M. (1978) Criminology. New York: Harcourt Brace Jovanovich.

TOUCHE ROSS (1976) Management Involvement in Material Transactions. Audit Technical Letter 149. Revised Edition, February 1.

TURNER, J. L. and M. URETSKY (1978) "Management fraud—a framework for discussion." (unpublished)

UNITED STATES vs. SIMON (1969) 425 F. 2d 796.

*Wall Street Journal.* (1972) "Eight are cited in Four Seasons fraud indictment." December 5:8.

——— (1973) "Some assets missing, insurance called bogus at equity funding life." April 2:1, 10.

——— (1974) "U.S. Financial Inc. accused of fraud to create profit." February 26:4.

WHEELER, S. (1976) "Trends and problems in the sociological study of crime." Social Problems 23 (June):525-534.

WILLINGHAM, J. J. (1974) "Discussant's response to relationship of auditing standards to detection of fraud." Contemporary Auditing Problems: Proceedings of Arthur Andersen/University of Kansas Symposium on Auditing Problems. (May 9-10):57-62.

WOLFGANG, M. E., R. M. FIGLIO, and T. THORNBERRY (1975) Criminology Index 1945-72. New York: Elsevier.

*Chapter 11*

# DO CONVICTIONS DETER HOME REPAIR FRAUD?

EZRA STOTLAND,
MICHAEL BRINTNALL,
ANDRÉ L'HEUREUX,
and EVA ASHMORE

The controversy about the effect of sanctions on crime rate has been extensive and inconclusive; sociologists generally interpret the findings as not indicating the widespread occurrence of general deterrence. Economists, on the other hand, have argued that there is evidence that, for at least some types of crimes, sanctions generally do deter. Despite this controversy, there has been a recent and increasingly widespread belief that the certainty of punishment does deter, while the severity of punishment does not. In 1977, the National Academy of Sciences asked a team of scholars to review and analyze the data on deterrence to draw more systematic conclusions. The group first examined research in which the data on crime rate and sanctions were based on the same period of time—that is, more or less simultaneous relationships. Although these data tended to be consistent with a general deterrence hypotheses, the possibility of causation going in the reverse direction was underscored by Blumstein et al. (1978). They argue that in many parts of the criminal justice system, high crime rates could generate low sanctions and low crime rates could generate high sanctions. For example, if the incidence of crime is sufficiently heavy, the likelihood of apprehension might drop if the number of police remains stable.

Blumstein et al. point out that the best way to settle this chicken-and-egg problem is to do quasi-experimental studies in which a change in sanctioning policy and/or practice is examined to see if there are consequent changes in crime rates in the same geographical

AUTHORS' NOTE: *The authors wish to express sincere appreciation to Gene Anderson, Director of the Fraud Division, King County (Washintgon) Prosecutor's Office; Charles Elhert, Former Director, Seattle Department of Licenses and Consumer Affairs; June Appal, Department of Licenses and Consumer Affairs; Sheila Gouch, and the staff of the King County Attorney General's Consumer Protection Division. Their assistance and cooperation helped to make possible the gathering of the data for this research.*

area but not in other, comparable areas. Although it is obviously not possible to conduct scientifically pure experiments in the everyday world, such quasi-experimental studies do partake of some of the qualities of an experimental design and thus have earned their name. As part of this overall effort by the National Academy of Sciences team, Zimring (1978) examined four such quasi-experiments, dealing with changes in the type of police patrol, number of arrests for drunk driving, toughness of the drug laws, and total funding available for the Criminal Justice System in a limited locality. He concludes that most studies have been badly flawed by things such as a lack of adequate monitoring of what policy/practice changes actually occurred, by a lack of certain knowledge of what the crime rates actually were, by the great "natural" variation in the crime rates. Thus, there is ample room for improvement in these quasi-experiments (see also Zimring and Hawkins, 1973).

It has long been believed that if convictions for crime have any general deterrent effect, that effect would be on white-collar criminals. Such offenders are assumed to be deterrable because they are believed to cooly calculate the material costs and benefits of commiting a crime, which includes the stigma of a criminal conviction. Although this assumption of rational calculation as the sole motivation of white-collar criminals has been called into question by one of the authors (Stotland, 1977), he nevertheless did not reject the hypothesis that avoidance of stigma is an important motivation and may be particularly salient for a given group of criminals. Nevertheless, to date there have been no studies that demonstrate general deterrence of white-collar crime.

## METHOD

The present study is an attempt to provide some systematic data consistent with the hypothesis that deterrence works with respect to a particular type of white-collar crime: home repair fraud. This crime was selected for reasons of availability of indices and of a change in policy and practice by a prosecutor in a given jurisdiction. The researchers were able to take advantage, after the fact, of a change in the Prosecutor's Office in King County, Washington (Seattle and environs), in which the number of prosecutions of unlicensed contractors (which was a convenient legal technique for dealing with such cases) increased markedly over a period of three to four years in order to allow a quasi-experiment study.

The general hypothesis of this study is that as the number of convictions and the severity of the punishment increase from one time period to the next, the amount of home repair fraud will decline significantly. The indices for the occurrence of home repair frauds were derived from two agencies which were administratively independent of the county prosecutor—the City of Seattle's Department of Consumer Protection and the King County Branch of the Washington Attorney General's Consumer Protection Division. Both of these offices were appropriate places to which citizens could and did submit their complaints. The independence of these two offices from the prosecutor's office minimizes the possibility that the decisions to prosecute were a simple function of any variation in the magnitude of the intake of complaints about home repair fraud—that is, that crime complaint rates determined the level of sanctions. In fact, the attorney general of the State of Washington at the time, like most others in similar positions in the United States, had a policy of using civil rather than criminal sanctions, so that the prosecutor's increased efforts over time are very unlikely to have been a direct result of the magnitude of complaints to that office. In fact, neither of the consumer offices appear to have had a systematic policy of comparing changes over time in the magnitude of complaints about home repair fraud. Another advantage of this separation of prosecutor from consumer complaint offices is that there would be no temptation to distort the complaint data in order to justify prosecutorial policy.

The reason that the number of prosecutions began abruptly and increased over time was that a new prosecuting attorney had been elected, partly on a platform of increasing the consumer fraud and general white-collar crime prosecution, but most probably because of the corruption that had been uncovered involving his predecessor. Shortly after taking office in 1970, the new man established a special unit with an acting director to work on consumer and related problems. After a national search, a permanent director, Gene Anderson, was appointed from another jurisdiction in August 1972, and the Fraud Division was established. Anderson expanded his division, upgraded its quality, and developed new areas of prosecution. A period of 17 months elapsed from the election of the new prosecutor and the first conviction for home repair fraud. Thus, the increase in the prosecution of home repair defrauders was a result of a policy and administrative change in the prosecutor's office, not obviously a result of a sudden rise in home repair defrauding.[1]

The unlicensed contractor violation was used as the vehicle of prosecution because the great bulk of the perpetrators did not have licenses from the State of Washington, a misdemeanor violation. A recent study by the prosecutor's office shows that contractors who commit offenses are by and large the unlicensed ones (personal communication). Another reason for the use of this law is that the prosecutions are much easier to consummate, since the proof of actual fraud is considerably more difficult. Data on prosecutions were collected from October 1973 to December 1976, the beginning date being selected because that was the time when more systematic recording of white-collar crime cases in the prosecutor's office began. The data were derived from the log books of the prosecutor's office.

As can be seen from Figure 1, the number of convictions increased as this period progressed. This increase can be seen in the correlation between time, counted as the number of the month starting with October 1973 as 1 and ending with December 1976 as 39, and a dummy variable indicating whether or not there was a conviction during a given month. The correlation between these two variables is .31 ($p < .05$). This increase in frequency is confounded with an increase in the severity of the punishment—a variable we termed "sevcon." For each month this variable consisted of the sum of the number of convictions, plus the number of jail sentences, fines, restitutions, and sentences actually served. Sevcon correlated .53 ($p < .01$) with time. On the basis of these relationships, we expected to see a decline in complaints over time attributable to these increased sanctions. We could not expect, however, to distinguish unambiguously between the effects of increased frequency and increased severity of sanctions. During this total period there were only six cases in which a conviction was not attained. Two cases involved persons whose charges had been dismissed, three of the accused fled, and one case was settled out of court. Since there were 33 cases filed during this period, the sanctioning rate was very high.

The Consumer Protection Office of the City of Seattle is located on the ground floor of the Municipal Building (City Hall) in downtown Seattle. This office receives complaints from the public regarding the whole range of consumer issues. Citizens register their complaints over the telephone, in person, or by mail; most of the complaints come in by telephone. If the complaints over the telephone seemed to agency personnel more serious than an inquiry for information, then the caller was sent a form to fill out and return regarding the complaint. The forms were then acted on and classified by the complaint handler as to type. Home repair fraud was one of the categories. These data were tabulated each month; the tabulations provided data for the present study.

The Consumer Affairs Division did not change its basic intake procedures during this period of time. However, it did benefit from an increase in personnel through CETA funding—primarily during the middle of the study—and a decline in the latter part. However, the activity of the office still appears to have been maintained at a high

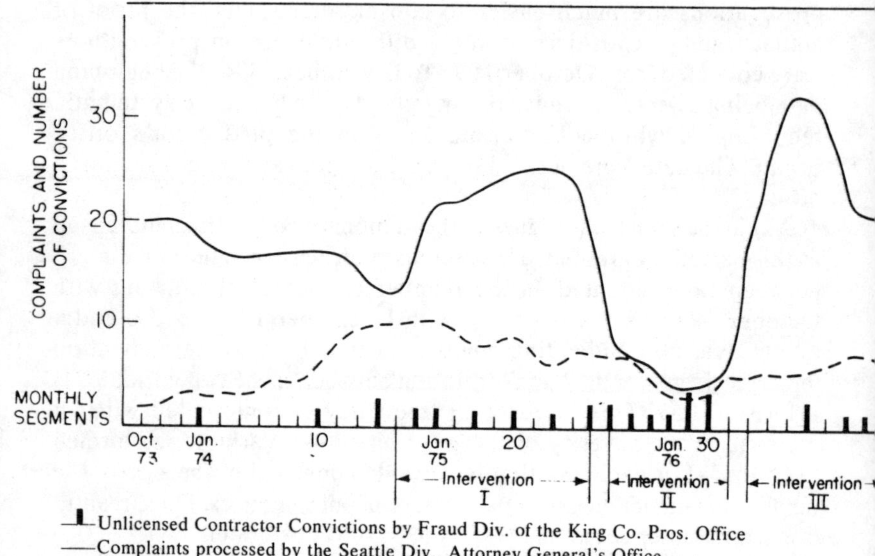


FIGURE 1 Home Improvement Complaints and Convictions, October 1973 to December 1976 (smoothed curves based on running medians taken from groups of three ovservations. [Turkey, 1977])

level, and even increased throughout this period. The number of public contacts was 20,556 in 1974; 24,272 in 1975; and 25,609 in 1976. This office developed investigations into activities which its personnel thought might be criminal, and referred such cases to the county prosecutor if this was warranted (Annual Reports of the Consumer Protection Division).

On the other hand, the Attorney General's Office did not refer cases to the county prosecutor, since it dealt only in civil law approaches and the latter was oriented to criminal prosecutions. During the period in question it brought only one civil case related to home repair fraud. It received complaints from the public by phone and mail almost exclusively, since it did not have a storefront office. Furthermore, it received telephone complaints only in the afternoons, because of personnel shortages. Calls were received from the whole of King County, including Seattle but encompassing a much wider geographical and population base. The number of public contacts was 6,316 in 1973; 5,144 in 1974; 4,663 in 1975; and 5,118 in 1976. Thus, its activity tended to fluctuate during this period (personal communication, Attorney General's Office), although there were no basic changes in personnel or procedures. Complaints were classified by agency personnel, among the categories being home repair fraud. These figures were tabulated by the agency each month on report forms, providing the source of data for the study.

Obviously, there are many instances of home repair fraud in the community which are not reported to these agencies. This failure to report may stem from the victims' ignorance of being defrauded; from the victims' rationalizing away their losses; from ignorance of the governmental resources available; from a decision to use other, non-criminal-justice-oriented remedies; and from an unwillingness to report the victimization for any other possible reasons. Certainly, the absolute number of home repair frauds reported to the agencies should not be interpreted as a direct indicator of the absolute number of home repair frauds committed. However, the hypothesis of this study refers to changes in the level of crime, not to the absolute levels. Thus, the number of home repair frauds reported to the agency is taken only as an index of the amount of fraud occurring; and the analysis focuses on changes in the level of this index. There is no reason to believe that the degree of unreliability of the index is greater in one year than in another within the three to four years of the study.

The basic statistical tool for the analysis is an interrupted time series analysis. The particular version of this tool employed here is a form of multiple regression analysis: It is a technique for evaluating the impact of a discrete or continuing intervention on an outcome variable which has a discrete quantity for each unit in the time series.[2] This technique has several advantages, one being that the effects of factors other than the intervention can be introduced into the analysis so that their influence can be controlled for or removed. This is a great advantage in a time series, since it enables us to eliminate the effects of many of the extraneous factors which might also influence the outcome variable in question. In the present study, many other factors besides the intervention can have an influence on the number of home repair fraud complaints, the outcome variable.

There are two ways to treat both extraneous variables or interventions. The first is simply to treat them as another continuous variable, like time, and enter them into the equation. If the variables are not continuous, we can treat them as dummy variables—that is, having two magnitudes, one and zero. For example, one could be legislature in session that month; zero could be legislature not in session, though some would argue that in this case the numbers should be interchanged. If the dummy variable is an intervention, the pre-and postintervention periods can be designated zero and one: The first period is the baseline, the second is the postintervention. In either case, the dummy variable is entered into the multiple regression equation and its power determined by seeing if the level of the outcome variable differed between periods.

The dummy variable technique can be used to test the impact of an intervention by looking at changes in slope as well as level. For example, this technique can show whether the slope of the regression line during the months 10 to 15 was significantly different from the slope from month 1 to 30. A change in slope might be attributed to an intervention.[3] One major advantage of the analysis of change of slope is that it takes into consideration any longer-term trends in the occurrence of the crime; that is, it tests for an effect in the form of a change of rate of commission of the crime.

Our approach, in summary, has been to treat prosecutive activity as an intervention expected to reduce the number of home improvement frauds over time, as measured by numbers of home improvement fraud complaints in two offices. As discussed in the following section, we have identified a baseline period of low prosecutive activity and three subsequent periods in which we expect a relative decline in complaints due to the intervention of the prosecutive program. These periods are measured by dummy variables introduced as interaction effects with time. Simultaneously, we have controlled for external effects attributed to changes in demand for home repairs and short-term publicity effects on complaining through the use of continuous and dummy variables in a regression equation.

## RESULTS

We will first present the results directly bearing on the hypothesis, which were obtained after the effects of some extraneous variables were statistically controlled. Concurrently, we will present the results of the statistical controls for one of these extraneous variables, thereby clarifying the apparent discrepancy between some of our results and the slope of the curve in Figure 1. We will report the rest of the results dealing with these extraneous variables after the direct tests of the hypotheses have been described.

The home repair fraud data for the Seattle Department of Consumer Affairs (DCA) and the Attorney General's Office (AG) were analyzed separately. The regression analysis in Table 1 shows that the complaints of reports of home repair fraud in AG tended to drop over the total time period, as expected, although the drop was significant only at the .06 level. The DCA complaint level shows a marginally significant rise ($p < .06$) over the same time period, but a relative decline during the intervention periods we identified. On the other hand, the AG data shows an insignificant rise in complaints over these periods.

*Table 1* Multiple Regression Analysis of Home Repair Fraud Complaints (N = 39 months)

| A. Attorney General Data ($R^2$ = .65; F = 4.6**) | | |
|---|---|---|
| *Variable* | *Beta* | *t* |
| Time | −1.6 | −1.5 |
| Winter | .6 | .1 |
| Special Alert | 21.1 | 2.3** |
| Caseload | − .1 | −1.7* |
| Number Homes | 1.0 | .0 |
| Number Permits | .2 | .2 |
| Press Releases | 6.8 | 1.4 |
| Convictions | − .4 | − .1 |
| Intervention 1 | .7 | .9 |
| Intervention 2 | .4 | .4 |
| Intervention 3 | 1.2 | 1.3 |
| Constant | 49.8 | |

| B. Seattle Department of Consumer Affairs ($R^2$ = .37; F = 1.9) | | |
|---|---|---|
| *Variable* | *Beta* | *t* |
| Time | .5 | 1.7 |
| Winter | 2.5 | 2.2* |
| Number Homes | 8.4 | .1 |
| Number Permits | .0 | .5 |
| Press Releases | − .3 | − .3 |
| Convictions | 1.5 | 1.5 |
| Intervention 1 | − .3 | −1.2 |
| Intervention 2 | − .4 | −1.8* |
| Intervention 3 | − .4 | −1.7 |
| Constant | −100.9 | |

* $p < .05$
** $p < .01$

The analysis based on changes in the slope of the regression line needs some explanation. During the first 13 months (from October 1973 through October 1974) there were only four convictions, as can be seen in Figure 1. That figure also shows that for the next 11 months, the rate of prosecutorial activity went up to seven convictions. This period of 11 months was therefore identified as the first intervention period. The rate of conviction increased even more markedly to 11 convictions during the next seven-month period. This seven-month segment constitutes the second intervention period.

The cutoff is made at that point because during that month the Attorney General's Office mounted a large-scale effort to warn the public, especially elderly people, about a highly organized gang of home repair defrauders, the Williamsons, which was believed to have entered the area. Among other things, the Attorney General's Office issued press releases, informed 23 local agencies dealing with the elderly, contacted all the telephone answering services in the area (since they were "used" by the gang), and notified local law enforcement agencies. This massive effort, far greater than any effort by the previous attorney general, generated a great many telephone calls related to possible home repair fraud, as can be seen in Figure 1. Since it is unlikely that the rise reflects only an actual rise in home repair fraud but probably includes a mixture of actual rise and simple reactions to the AG's communications, we felt it appropriate to treat the segment of time after this AG effort had begun as a distinct segment in the analysis of both the DCA office and the AG.

As a further way of dealing with the AG effort, we treated the specific months that the alert was in effect as a separate dummy variable, called Special Alert, to control for its influence. As Table 1 shows, its influence was statistically significant at the .01 level for the AG data. On the other hand, the DCA data do not show any particular effect of the Special Alert, supporting the interpretation that the rise in calls during this period was a reflection mainly of the communication from the AG's office, which in turn generated calls back to the AG's office.

To return to the analysis of the change of the slope during the three segments of time, the AG office data do not show any influence (see Table 1). However, the DCA data show that during the second intervention there was a significant downward change in the slope of the regression line ($p < .05$). This change was almost significant in the third intervention period as well ($p < .06$). These downward shifts in the slope are consistent with the hypothesis, since they declined as the conviction frequency rose.

In sum, the overall, although marginally significant, trend in the DCA data was for a general upswing in the amount of home repair fraud over the total period. However, the steepness of the upswing was significantly reduced at the time that the sanctions became more frequent and more severe, as we expected. In the AG office, no parallel results were found. Reasons for the difference between the two offices will be discussed below.

The results just reported were predicated on controlling statistically the effects of some of the extraneous variables which might influence the amount of home repair fraud. The first possible extraneous variable effect is the season of the year, since some outdoor repair work might be inhibited by winter weather. A dummy variable for the winter season (October through April) showed no effect on the AG data, but the DCA did show a significant drop in home repair fraud in the winter, as shown in Table 1. It is unclear why the two offices should differ on this score.

A second possible extraneous variable is a change in the number of homes in the area. Clearly, the greater the number of homes, the greater the number of possible home repair frauds. The total number of single-family residences increased markedly in King County, from 283,567 in 1973 to 300,209 in 1976 (Puget Sound Inter-Governmental Council). Since King County is part of the jurisdiction of the AG, the number of homes was introduced into the regression equation by dividing the total number each year by 12, so that the average per month could be estimated and the results introduced into the regression equation. However, it can be seen in Table 2 that the number of houses did not have a significant effect on home repair fraud. The number of houses in Seattle tended to decline during this period, from 133,366 in 1973 to 132,777 in 1976 (Seattle Office of Policy Planning). However, Table 1 shows that there was no significant relationship to the number of home repair frauds reported. This is not surprising, since the drop in homes in Seattle was less than one-half a percentage point during this period.

A third extraneous variable is changes in the amount of home repair work going on, which were described above. Changes in the amount of home repairing can be guaged by the number of home repair permits issued. Table 2 shows that the total number of permits increased over time for Seattle, for Bellevue (the second largest city in the county), and for the unincorporated areas of the county.[4] (Obtaining the data from the 23 remaining municipalities was not deemed worthwhile in view of the consistency of the trends from the major areas.) The total for each year was divided by 12; the number of home repair permits was introduced into the regression equation for both the offices, and not found significant in either. In any case, since home repairs were on the rise, a decrement in home repair fraud cannot easily be explained by changes in the amount of repairing.

A fourth extraneous variable is the level of activity in the two offices with respect to all complaints from the public. One index of this level of activity in the AG office was the total caseload minus the home repair caseload. This was computed by taking the yearly total, dividing by 12, and then introducing this into the regression analysis.

*Table 2* Permits for Home Improvements—Additions

| *Year* | *King County Unincorporated Areas**** | *Seattle** | *Bellevue*** |
|---|---|---|---|
| 1973 | 743 | 1,658 | 154 |
| 1974 | 819 | 1,974 | 176 |
| 1975 | 903 | 1,982 | 202 |
| 1976 | 1,060 | 1,950 | 245 |

*Source: Seattle Housing Department
**Source: Bellevue Housing Permit Office
***Source: King County Building Permit Office

As can be seen in Table 1, there is a significant negative relationship between total (non-home-repair) caseload and home repair fraud caseload. This relationship may reflect a type of ceiling effect of capacity of the office: When home repair reports go up, there is less time for the other types of cases, and vice versa. For the DCA, the number of contacts with the public rose dramatically, but the rise was almost perfectly negatively correlated with the decline in the number of homes in Seattle. Thus, this collinearity made it statistically difficult to make inference separate from the effects of the increased number of homes. Accordingly, no analysis was performed, especially since neither variable was found to be related to the number of home repair fraud cases.

A fifth extraneous variable is the issuance of a press release by the prosecutor warning the public of the danger. (This variable covers periods of time different from the Special Alert.) Such press releases could stimulate a short-term increase in responses from the public. The effect was tested by creating a dummy variable of all months in which there was a press release. As Table 1 shows, press releases led to an increase in the number of complaints from the public to the AG, but this variable was not significant. There was no effect in the DCA.

A sixth parallel extraneous effect is the expected short-term increase in complaints following a conviction, caused by the attendant publicity. A dummy variable analysis paralleling the one for press releases was computed. Table 1 shows that there was a slight rise in the number of complaints to the DCA office, but it was not significant.

## SUMMARY AND DISCUSSION

The hypothesis of the study was supported from the data from the DCA in that a tendency toward an upward rise of home repair fraud was reduced by convictions. This shift appears to be independent of the effects of such extraneous factors as season, number of homes, number of permits, press releases, and number of convictions. However, the increased sanctions did not appear to have completely reversed the upward movement of home repair fraud. It may be that the increase in home repair fraud was due to other factors which limited the possible deterrent effect of prosecutions. One such factor might be the overall increase in home repair activity in Seattle on a stable or declining number of residences.

On the other hand, the negative relationship between the amount of home repair fraud and general complaint level in the AG's office suggests a ceiling of the total number of cases than can be received. Since the number of calls received by the AG's office tended to fluctuate somewhat irregularly over this period, there may have been changes in this ceiling over the years. Thus, the number of home repair fraud complaints is of uncertain meaning in the AG office. The Special Alert also had such a major impact that any deterrent effect as reflected in the complaint load might have been too greatly overshadowed. As mentioned above, the DCA data show a downward shift in the slope of the regression line in the second intervention segment. This downward shift can be seen in Figure 1 during 1975 and a few months into 1976. Figure 1 also shows that in the latter half of 1975 and for three months into 1976, the AG's office also showed a decline in home repair fraud. The fact that both lines changed in a parallel way during this period leads one to believe that at least some of the decline with AG data during that period was due to a deterrent effect.

In short, our data are consistent with a hypothesis of the deterrence of home repair fraud by convictions, even though one of our two sources of data appears to be excessively subject to extraneous influences. We hope our results will encourage increases in prosecution of home repair defrauders and increases in the severity of sanctions.

## NOTES

1. Such an abrupt policy initiative at the discretion of the prosecutor is not an unusual characteristic of white-collar crime politics (Brintnall, 1979).

2. Interrupted time series analysis has received a great deal of attention in the methodological literature in recent years, especially because of the increase in understanding the behavior of time series data. The major factor which distinguishes the analysis of time series data from unordered data is the problem of autocorrelated error terms. Measurements of the world always have built-in inaccuracies. This usually does not bias an analysis, because the inaccuracies in most data are randomly distributed between the observations—the amount or direction of inaccuracy in one measurement is independent of another measurement. With time series data, however, this independence is not at all likely. For instance, a bureau which fails to count all of its complaint load in one time period might "stash" the missed complaints for the next counting period.

Powerful techniques are being developed for using this autocorrelation in the analysis of the time series data itself, and much innovative work is being done in developing procedures by which this technique can be used in interrupted time series analysis. These techniques lack certain flexibility, such as the ability to introduce control variables—especially dummy-coded variables—which are available with more customary regression approaches. Much work is now being done to integrate Box-Jenkin time series approaches with regression, particularly by modeling the autocorrelation directly into the regression analysis through a process of generalized least squares. The approach adopted in this analysis follows this second tradition, although we have found it unnecessary after all to correct our analysis for problems of autocorrelation. Examination of residuals from our regression analysis indicates that the most likely pattern of autocorrelation in our data is a first-order process. The presence of first-order autocorrelation can be tested for by the Durbin-Watson statistic. This statistic indicates regions in which the null hypothesis of no serial correlation can be accepted and rejected and regions in which the test is indeterminant. In the time series regressions presented here the Durbin-Watson statistic is in the indeterminant region or supports the null hypothesis of no serial correlation. Thus, we have not attempted to correct the following analysis for serial correlation. The cost of failing to remove serial correlation when it is present is loss of efficiency of the estimators, but not bias in the estimators. The reader, therefore, should be alert to the fact that our tests of significance may appear slightly more precise than is actually the case (Blumstein et al., 1978; Campbell, 1969; Glass et al., 1975; Hibbs, 1974; Maki et al., 1978; Ostrom, 1978; Pindyck and Rubinfeld, 1976; Ross et al., 1970).

3. Coefficients (beta) for dummy variables representing discrete periods of time represent differences from the overall slope of the regression line for the entire period being examined if the dummy is introduced as an interaction effect with time. The coefficient is then not the actual slope during the period in question; the actual slope is based on the slope for the total time in the equation plus the dummy period.

4. It is conceivable that one reason for the rise in home repair permits is that the increasingly heavy sanction on repair frauds and prosecutor's use of the law regarding licensing of contractors may have frightened a number of previously unlicensed contractors enough that they obtained licenses. But we do not know how strong such an effect was.

## REFERENCES

BLUMSTEIN, A., J. COHEN, and D. NAGIN (1978) Deterrence and Incapacitation: Estimating the Effects of Criminal Sanctions on Crime Rates. Report of the Panel on Research on Deterrent and Incapacitative Effects, Assembly of Behavioral and Social Sciences. Washington, DC: National Academy of Sciences.

BRINTNALL, M. (1979) "Entrepreneurship and federal influence in the local prosecution of economic crime." Policy Studies Journal 7 (Spring):577-592.

CAMPBELL, D. (1969) "Reforms as experiments." American Psychologist 24 (April):409-429.

GLASS, G. V., V. L. WILLSON, and J. M. GOTTMAN (1975) Design and Analysis of Time Series Experiments. Boulder, CO: Associated University Press.

HIBBS, D. (1974) "Problems of statistical estimation and causal inference in time series regression models." In H. Costner (ed.), Sociological Methodology. San Francisco: Jossey-Bass.

MAKI, J. E., D. M. HOFFMAN, and R. A. BERK (1978) "A time series analysis of the impact of a water conservation campaign." Evaluation Quarterly 2 (February):107-118.

OSTROM, C. W. (1978) "Time series analysis: Regression techniques." Sage University Paper Series on Quantitative Applications in the Social Sciences, No. 07-009. Beverly Hills, CA: Sage.

PINDYCK, R. S. and D. L. RUBINFELD (1967) Econometric Models and Economic Forecasts. New York: McGraw-Hill.

ROSS, H. L., D. T. CAMPBELL, and G. V. GLASS (1970) "Determining the social effects of a legal reform: The British 'Breathalyzer' crackdown of 1967." American Behavioral Scientist 13 (March-April):493-509.

STOTLAND, E. (1977) "White collar criminals." Journal of Social Issues 33 (Fall):179-196.

TUKEY, J. (1977) Exploratory Data Analysis. Reading, MA: Addison-Wesley.

WONNACOTT, R. J. and T. H. WONNACOTT (1970) Econometrics. New York: John Wiley.

ZIMRING, F. E. (1978) "Policy experiments in general deterrence: 1970-75." In A. Blumstein, J. Cohen, and D. Nagin (eds.), Deterrence and Incapacitation: Estimating the Effects of Criminal Sanctions on Crime Rates. Report of the Panel on Research on Deterrent and Incapacitative Effects, Assembly of Behavioral and Social Sciences. Washington, DC: National Academy of Sciences.

and G. J. HAWKINS (1973) Deterrence: The Legal Threat in Crime Control. Chicago: University of Chicago Press.

*Chapter 12*

# CONSUMER ABUSE OF OLDER AMERICANS: VICTIMIZATION AND REMEDIAL ACTION IN TWO METROPOLITAN AREAS

MARY V. McGUIRE and HERBERT EDELHERTZ

The victim of white-collar crime by and large has been omitted from discussions of economic and white-collar crime (Walsh and Schram, this volume). This does not appear to be the result of an absence of concern for victims of consumer abuse; on the contrary, consumer protection organizations and consumer-oriented legislation manifest sincere concern for consumer victims. Nevertheless, while information is routinely gathered concerning victims and classes of victims of conventional street crimes (such as U.S. Department of Justice, 1978), little is known about the victims of consumer abuse. The information that is available on this subject is found in anecdotal accounts or case studies of victims of specific frauds, presented in terms of type of abuse rather than type or class of victim (see, for example, Carper, 1973). Likewise, consumer protection agencies and organizations are oriented toward victims generally and do not routinely gather or report information concerning classes or characteristics of victims.

The research described in this chapter attempts to expand understanding and knowledge of one class of victims of consumer abuse: older consumers. Accordingly, this research required overcoming some of the obstacles to researching victims of a crime problem that typically overlooks the type of victim. It was necessary, for example, to establish protocols in consumer protection offices to screen

AUTHORS' NOTE: *This research was supported by Grant #90-A-1019(02) from the Administration on Aging, U.S. Department of Health, Education and Welfare. Points of view or opinions stated in this document are those of the authors and do not necessarily represent the official position or policies of the Department of Health, Education and Welfare, or of Battelle. The authors are indebted to Marilyn E. Walsh for her extensive work on this research project and her comments and help with preparing this chapter; also, Michael Brintnall's assistance with data analysis as well as the support of the Battelle staff are greatly appreciated.*

complainants on the basis of age. It was also necessary to select particular aspects of the problem for inquiry, recognizing that the paucity of information concerning older victims of consumer fraud and abuse would mean that many questions would remain for further research.

This research was designed to explore the nature and extent of consumer frauds and abuses experienced by persons aged 55 years or older in two metropolitan areas, Flint-Genesee County, Michigan, and Seattle-King County, Washington. (This age cutoff was chosen because the typical retirement age for Flint automobile workers is 55.) It involved two separate studies. The first, an in-office study, examined the complaints filed in two local consumer protection offices by older consumers and by a sample of younger consumers during a six-month period. The in-office study was conducted in the Consumer Protection Division, Office of the Prosecuting Attorney of Genesee County, Michigan, and in the Seattle Office of the Washington State Attorney-General, Consumer Protection and Antitrust Division. The second study, a community survey, involved telephone interviews with older residents of the communities served by these two consumer protection offices.

This research demonstrated that complaints filed by older consumers in local consumer protection offices do not differ substantially from those filed by younger consumers. During the six-month period of study, however, the proportion of complaints filed by older consumers was lower than would be expected, given the proportion of the population comprised of older people. This research did not examine the levels of victimization among younger consumers and therefore did not preclude the possibility of differing levels of victimization among older and younger consumers. The surveys of older residents of the Flint and Seattle communities did suggest that older victims of consumer fraud tend to underreport their experiences of victimization. Even those abuses involving considerable losses or inconveniences were reported to a public agency, consumer protection office, newspaper, or Better Business Bureau far less frequently than were street crimes. As would be expected, a higher percentage of respondents who sought relief for a consumer abuse, either by reporting the incident to a public agency or by taking private remedial action, obtained remedies than did respondents who made no attempt to rectify their abuses. This research found, however, that a surprising proportion of respondents who sought relief said that their consumer abuses remained unrectified.

Research methods, procedures, and major findings of the in-office study and of the community survey are discussed below. The final section of this chapter draws conclusions based on both studies and discusses the implications of the research for consumer protection services.

## IN-OFFICE STUDY

### The Research Setting

The Flint in-office study was set in the Consumer Protection Division, Office of the Prosecuting Attorney of Genesee County. This division of the Prosecutor's Office is one of the oldest and largest local consumer protection agencies in a public prosecutive agency.[1] The office receives slightly over 400 consumer complaints each month. It maintains visibility with the Flint-Genesee community through a popular weekly radio program and ongoing contacts with community groups.

The Seattle in-office study was conducted in the Seattle office of the Washington State Attorney-General, Consumer Protection and Antitrust Division. This office serves residents of the Seattle-King County area, as well as a large portion of Western Washington.[2] The Seattle office estimates that it handles an average of 800 formal complaints each month.

It was anticipated that the visibility of these offices in their communities, their size, and the volume of complaints handled by each would attract a sizable number of older complainants and thus provide a sample large enough to support the purposes of this research project.

### Research Methods and Procedures

Prior to the study, the Flint and Seattle office procedures were reviewed and research protocols to meet the needs of the offices and the research effort were written. These protocols guided the research, minimized its intrusiveness in the offices, maximized the amount of data gathered, and protected the confidentiality of complainants.[3] The research was conducted between May 1977 and October 1977 in Flint, and between August 1977 and January 1978 in Seattle.

#### SELECTION PROCEDURES

During the period of study, all persons filing complaints in the two offices were screened to determine whether they were 55 years of age or older. Since consumers contact both the Flint and Seattle offices in person, by telephone, and by mail, several screening methods were used: In-person and telephone complainants were either asked if they were 55 or older and told the purpose of the question or screened by means of an attachment to the office complaint form filed by complainants. When complaints received by mail were reported on office complaint forms, screening was accomplished by means of the attachment to the complaint form. When mailed complaints were described in unsolicited letters, screening required assessment of the nature and content of the letter for an indication of the complainant's age. This last category of complaints presented the greatest problem for screening and undoubtedly resulted in some loss of cases, either by complainants' failure to indicate age or by the absence of any indicator of age in unsolicited letters.

As a result of these screening procedures, 195 complainants to the Flint office and 132 complainants to the Seattle office were identified as at least 55 years of age. Samples of younger complainants were then selected in both offices to compare abuses reported by older consumers with those reported by younger consumers. In Flint, each complaint involving an older consumer was given an office file number; the complaints having the next file numbers submitted by younger consumers formed the sample of 194 younger complainants. In Seattle, complaints are recorded in a log book as they are received; the complaints filed by younger consumers immediately after each older person's complaint comprised the sample of 131 younger complainants.

## RESEARCH METHODS

The following information was coded from the complaint files in Flint and Seattle: the nature of the complaint, the activities and parties of which consumers complained, steps taken by the office to assist the complainants, and the outcome.

Since office case files do not ordinarily contain demographic data or detailed descriptions of complainants and their experiences, additional information was sought concerning the older complainants. All were asked to complete an optional consumer questionnaire that was either self-administered (Flint and Seattle) or personally administered (Flint). This questionnaire solicited demographic information (age, sex, race, educational background, former and current occupation), personal data (handicaps, illness, living situation), and some additional complaint-related data (characteristics of the party complained of, how complainant heard of the party). Of the 195 identified older complainants in Flint, 99 (50.8 percent) completed the optional consumer questionnaire. In Seattle, 83 of the 132 older complainants (62.9 percent) completed the questionnaire.

Additionally, all older complainants were approached concerning their willingness to participate in personal interviews (Flint) and/or in telephone interviews (Flint and Seattle). Those who completed the interviews provided information not only relating to the experience about which they complained, but concerning other similar experiences, street crime victimization, usual buying practices, and their mobility and sociability. Forty-one interviews were conducted in Flint; 34 in Seattle.

## Findings

The in-office studies of older victims of consumer fraud and abuse amassed much information concerning the complaints filed by older consumers, complaints filed by the matched sample of younger consumers, characteristics of the older consumers, and details concerning the older consumers' victimization experiences, background, and lifestyles (Edelhertz et al., 1977, 1978a-1978e). The findings described here derive from data which permit comparisons of older and younger complainants and comparison of those persons studied in-office with those participating in the community survey.

The in-office studies revealed few striking differences between the complaints filed by older and younger complainants to consumer protection offices. Similarly, very few differences emerged between the complaints filed in Flint and those filed in Seattle. Even the demographic and background characteristics of older complainants in Flint were, for the most part, comparable with those in Seattle.

### THE OLDER COMPLAINANTS

*Demographic characteristics.* The sample of older complainants in Flint and Seattle differed substantially from what would be expected given the population of Flint and Seattle residents in one respect: both the Flint and Seattle older subgroups were dominated by males—almost 55 percent of the complainants in Flint and 62 percent in Seattle were men. However, according to the 1970 census statistics, only 45.6 percent of Flint-Genesee County residents 55 and over are males and 43.2 percent of the Seattle-area residents in that age bracket are males.[4] Other characteristics of the Flint and Seattle samples reflected the population characteristics of the communities.

The majority of complainants in both sites were white (80.6 percent in Flint; 97.5 percent in Seattle), and more of the Flint complainants were members of racial minorities (primarily blacks) than were the Seattle complainants. Almost 61 percent of the Flint complainants and 45 percent of the Seattle complainants were between 60 and 69 years of age, while younger and older age groups were less heavily represented in both offices.

Most complainants in Flint and Seattle were retired, though a larger proportion of Seattle complainants worked either part- or full-time (Flint: 89.9 percent were retired, 10.1 percent employed; Seattle: 63.8 percent retired, 21.7 percent employed). The most common occupational category (slightly over 20 percent) of complainants in both offices was "craftsmen, foremen, and skilled workers."

Almost two-thirds of complainants in Flint had completed at least a partial secondary school education, and about one-fourth of the complainants had at minimum graduated from high school. The educational attainment of complainants in Seattle was somewhat higher than Flint: about 90 percent had completed some secondary school training and over 70 percent had graduated from high school.

*Representation of older and younger consumers in the Flint and Seattle offices.* Perhaps the most interesting aspect of the sample of older complainants relates not to individual characteristics but to sample size. In both research sites, older consumers were underrepresented among the complainants.

During the six-month period of study, the Flint Consumer Protection Office received 2,507 complaints. The complaints filed by older consumers represented 7.7 percent of the total. This is a lower proportional representation than population figures would predict, since persons 55 and older comprise 13.6 percent of the Genesee County population. Likewise, the Seattle office received 4,816 formal, written complaints during the study period; older comsumers represented 2.7 percent of these complaints. This, too, is a lower representation for the aged than population figures would predict, since persons 55 and older comprise 16.9 percent of the Seattle-Everett Standard Metropolitan Statistical Area.

*Attitudes toward consumerism.* The optional telephone or personal interviews conducted in Flint and Seattle shed some light on the attitudes of complainants toward consumerism. The majority of those interviewed indicated believing that "It's a good idea to tell someone when you are not satisfied with an item or service" (92.7 percent of those interviewed in Flint, 83.3 percent of those interviewed in Seattle). Only one person in Flint and one in Seattle felt that it "never does any good to tell anyone, so why bother?" A small group felt that "it might be a good idea to report dissatisfaction, but it's usually too much trouble" (6.5 percent in Flint, 13.9 percent in Seattle).

When asked where they would go for help or advice if complainants were not satisfied with a product or service, most felt that they would go to the store or other source of the unsatisfactory product or service (34, or 82.9 percent, in Flint; 28, or 77.8 percent, in Seattle).

The remaining complainants indicated that they would seek the help or advice of family, neighbors, or some other person. As is seen below, this preference for private remedies is consistent with the reporting patterns of those consumers interviewed in the community surveys.

## NATURE OF COMPLAINTS

The consumer protection offices have received complaints concerning virtually all types of consumer abuse and occurring in a wide variety of settings. Most of the complaints studied, however, involved common marketplace activities occurring at the vendor's place of business. Reports of victimization at the consumer's home, through the mail, or by telephone were relatively rare (though slightly more prevalent among older complainants). Similarly, complaints of sophisticated schemes to defraud consumers and victimization by con artists were relatively uncommon among older and younger subgroups.

The subject matter of each complaint in the older and younger samples was classified along three dimensions: (1) the type of *product or service* that was the subject of complaint; (2) the type of *transaction* about which consumers complained (for example, contracts, rentals), and (3) the type of *activity or scheme* about which consumers complained (such as failure to provide goods or perform services).[5] For example, a typical complaint was that car repair work was inadequate. In this case, the product or service involved was automobiles, the transaction was repairs, and the activity or scheme was failure to perform services. This form, then, is representative of most complaints, focusing on normal, frequent areas of marketplace activity.

Of the 16 product/service categories, general merchandise (consumer goods including food, appliances, fuels, clothing) and automobiles (including motorcycles, trucks, parts, and accessories) were the products of which older and younger consumers most frequently complained in both Flint and Seattle. In Flint, 45.8 percent of all complaints, 43.1 percent of which were filed by older consumers and 48.5 percent by younger consumers, concerned general merchandise and automobiles. In Seattle, 40.7 percent of all complainants, 43.9 percent of which were filed by older consumers and 37.4 percent by younger consumers, involved these products.

The four types of transactions most often noted in complaints involved sales/purchases, contracts, repair/service, and rentals. In Flint, 73.8 percent of all complaints—74.3 percent of older consumers' complaints and 73.2 percent of younger consumers complaints—cited such transactions. In Seattle, 68.8 percent of all complaints, of which 72.0 percent were filed by older consumers and 65.6 percent by younger consumers, involved these transactions.

Eighteen types of activities were considered. Those most frequently involved in consumer complaints in both Flint and Seattle involved failure to provide promised goods or services, disputes over monies paid or owed by the consumer, and false claims or misrepresentations made to the consumer. The one activity about which consumers in Flint and Seattle most frequently complained was the failure to perform services (Flint: 28.5 percent; Seattle: 16.7 percent).

Although minor differences emerged between complaints filed by older and younger consumers and between complaints filed in Flint and in Seattle, the relative importance of different complaint categories discussed above was similar for all subgroups. The only clear difference between older and younger consumers' complaints involved three products or services: mobile homes, construction, and health care. While these were not major categories of complaint in either city, the finding that almost two-thirds of the complaints in these areas were filed by older consumers suggests that the products/services are more common areas of abuse for older consumers than for younger consumers. These product/services, however, typically attract older consumers: With increased age often comes increased need for health services; mobile homes provide an inexpensive and attractive lifestyle for many older persons and retirees; older persons are likely to use construction services for home repairs and improvements to their older homes. Thus, such increased reports of abuse among older consumers may not reflect an increased likelihood of victimization due to age, but an increased likelihood of victimization due to increased marketplace activity within these product/service areas.

## AMOUNT OF MONEY INVOLVED IN COMPLAINTS

Consumer complaints were also characterized in terms of the amount of money involved in each complaint. For a sizable proportion of complaints (54.5 percent in Flint, 26.6 percent in Seattle) it was either impossible to determine the amount of money involved, if any, or no money was involved in the complaint (for example, the complainant requested information only). Where some amount of money was in contention, the complaints of older consumers in Flint on the average involved larger amounts of money than those of younger Flint consumers, while in Seattle younger consumers' complaints on the average involved more money than older consumers' complaints. However, the median losses were the same for both subgroups.

Generally, complaints filed in Seattle involved more money than did complaints filed in Flint. These findings are reflected in Table 1.

**OUTCOME OF COMPLAINT**

Once formal complaints are filed in Flint and Seattle, the consumer protection offices act to resolve or dispose of them. The outcome, or resolution, of a consumer complaint was often difficult to assess. Some proportion of the complaints filed with the consumer protection offices was undoubtedly unwarranted, although the offices classified only 4.6 percent of the Flint complaints and 2.7 percent of the Seattle complaints as "unjustified." Additionally, at the close of the period of study, a number of complaints were still pending; data on complaint outcomes were therefore available for only 75.3 percent (293) of the complaints filed in Flint and 70.3 percent (185) of the complaints filed in Seattle.

In Flint, 49.5 percent of the complainants whose outcomes could be assessed received assistance from the office resulting in monetary recovery or savings, services performed, benefits received, or some other settlement. In Seattle, 37.3 percent of the consumers whose complaint outcomes could be assessed received such assistance and results from the consumer protection office. Therefore, a fairly sizable group of complainants received no palpable results from the offices. These complaints were inappropriate for office resolution; were outside the jurisdiction of the offices; were referred elsewhere; or were dropped because, among other reasons, the office could not reach the complainant, could not locate the party about which consumers complained, or the complaint appeared unjustified or unwarranted.

However, most complainants whose complaints had been rectified or settled with office help obtained some monetary recovery. Almost 28 percent of all complainants in Flint and 24 percent in Seattle obtained a monetary recovery. In Flint, a larger proportion of

*Table 1* Amount of Money Involved in Complaints

| | Flint | | | Seattle | | |
|---|---|---|---|---|---|---|
| | *Total Sample* | *Older Sub-group* | *Younger Sub-group* | *Total Sample* | *Older Sub-group* | *Younger Sub-group* |
| Mean Value of Complaint (in dollars) | 711 | 1000 | 355 | 914 | 823 | 982 |
| Median Value of Complaint (in dollars) | 100 | 100 | 100 | 175 | 175 | 175 |
| Sample Size (N)[a] | 177 | 81 | 96 | 193 | 87 | 106 |

[a]Number of complaints involving a specifiable amount of money.

younger consumers (32.0 percent) recovered monetarily than did older consumers (23.6 percent recovered). In Seattle, on the other hand, slightly more of the older consumers (25.8 percent) recovered monetarily than did their younger counterparts (22.1 percent of whom recovered). In both Flint and Seattle, the median recovery by older and younger complainants was between $50 and $100.

## COMMUNITY SURVEY

The community survey was designed to assess the incidence of consumer abuse and the extent of reporting such abuse among older residents of the Flint-Genesee County and Seattle communities.

### Research Methods and Procedures

Different selection procedures were employed in Flint and Seattle; the procedures are, therefore, discussed separately for the two research sites.

#### FLINT-GENESEE COUNTY: SELECTION AND INTERVIEW PROCEDURES

Telephone interviews were conducted with a randomly selected sample of 603 Flint-Genesee residents over the age of 55. The community survey was conducted by the Systems Development Institute between November 1, 1977, and December 31, 1977, shortly after that group conducted the Mott Foundation's Quality of Life Survey in Flint. Therefore, the selection of Flint-Genesee residents for participation in this survey involved two steps: (1) the selection of the large community sample participating in the Mott survey and (2) the selection from the Mott sample of a smaller group of residents 55 years or older for participation in the survey of consumer behavior.

First, using randomly generated telephone numbers, interviews were conducted with 6,917 Flint-Genesee residents as a part of the Mott Quality of Life Survey. Of those residents interviewed, 2,075 were identified as being 55 years or older. Second, 1,200 of these 2,075 older participants in the Mott survey were randomly selected to be potential respondents in the consumer survey. Experienced female interviewers who worked in their homes completed telephone interviews with 603 of the 1,200 potential respondents. If a potential respondent declined to participate in the consumer survey, or if an interviewer was unable to reach a respondent after three attempts to telephone, that name was dropped from the list. Additionally, 17 of the completed interviews were dropped from the total number of interviews, since these respondents were erroneously placed on the initial list of 1,200 potential respondents. Thus, the Flint community survey data is based on a total of 586 telephone interviews.

## SEATTLE-KING COUNTY: SELECTION AND INTERVIEW PROCEDURES

In Seattle, telephone interviews were conducted with a randomly selected sample of 467 Seattle-area residents 55 years of age or older. The survey, including sampling, screening, interviewing, and verifying data, was conducted by the Educational Assessment Center of the University of Washington between December 15, 1977, and January 25, 1978.

A sample of potential survey respondents was created by attaching random sets of four-digit numbers to each of the three-digit telephone exchange numbers in the city of Seattle.[6] For each telephone exchange, the number of four-digit numbers attached was directly proportional to the number of residential phones in the exchange area. A total of 6,000 telephone numbers was generated in this fashion, of which 4,951 numbers were used in the survey. Telephone interviewers then screened these numbers to determine (1) whether they were residential phones and (2) whether an eligible respondent—that is, a person 55 years or older—resided in the household. A total of 2,273 telephones was determined to be residential, and eligible respondents were located in 633 (27.8 percent) of these residences.[7] Twenty-six female interviewers were trained in interviewing techniques by the Educational Assessment Center. Interviewers then conducted the screening and interviewing from their home telephones. Interviews were completed with 467 (73.8 percent) of the eligible respondents.

## COMMUNITY SURVEY QUESTIONNAIRE

The questionnaire developed for use in the community surveys was designed to explore (1) respondents' recent experiences of consumer dissatisfaction and abuse; (2) actions taken by older consumers following a dissatisfying or abusive experience; and (3) a variety of demographic and personal data, including respondents' attitudes toward consumerism and recent experiences of street crime.

Two types of questions inquired into respondents' experiences of consumer abuse during the last two years. First, several questions explored specific areas of potential consumer abuse. Respondents were asked questions about recent experiences with four types of *repair* transactions (repairs of televisions or household appliances, of automobiles, of home, and of apartments). Similarly, they were asked questions about recent consumer problems resulting from two common activities or schemes: *overcharging* ("During the last two years, have you ever been quoted a price for a product or service and found out later that you were being charged a higher price?") and *bait-and-switch* tactics ("During the last two years, have you seen any advertisement for a product at a special price, but when you tried to buy it you were told that they were 'all sold out' or the 'offer has expired'?").

Second, two sets of nondirective questions were included in order to aid respondents in identifying and self-reporting instances of consumer abuse by which they were victimized. Respondents were asked if, in the last two years, they were involved in *any* situation in which they thought they were being cheated or swindled and if, for the same period, they were involved in any situation in which they were taken advantage of or misled in some way involving money or property. The nature of both these experiences was explored through additional questions.

Whenever respondents described an abusive consumer experience, they were queried as to their actions following the experience: Did respondents complain or report the abuse? To what agency, organization, or individual was the abuse reported? What was the result of reporting the abuse?

## Findings

The results of the community survey suggest that consumer abuse of older people is fairly widespread, though not necessarily serious, and that consumer abuses often go unreported and unrectified. A greater number of abuses were described by respondents in Seattle than by those in Flint, but the nature of these consumer abuses and the actions taken in response to the abuses were very similar in the two research sites.

### DESCRIPTION OF SURVEY RESPONDENTS

*Demographic characteristics.* As with the in-office study, the demographic and background characteristics of survey respondents in Flint were similar to those of the respondents in Seattle. The majority of survey respondents were women (75.1 percent in Flint; 68.6 percent in Seattle); therefore, men were overrepresented in the in-office study, but women were overrepresented in the community survey. (According to 1970 census statistics, 54.5 percent of Flint residents and 56.8 percent of Seattle residents, aged 55 and over, are females.)

Most survey respondents were white (87.5 percent in Flint; 93.2 percent in Seattle), several were black (Flint: 70, or 12.3 percent; Seattle: 20, or 4.4 percent), and a few were members of other racial/ethnic minorities (0.2 percent in Flint; 2.4 percent in Seattle).

In light of the recent census data, blacks appear somewhat overrepresented in both the Flint sample (where 7.8 percent of the residents are black) and in the Seattle sample (where 3.3 percent are black).

The age distribution of survey respondents was generally representative of the age distribution of older community residents. Sixty-six percent of the Flint respondents and 70 percent of the Seattle respondents were under 70 years of age, while 64.7 percent of Flint residents and 63.8 percent of Seattle residents were under 70.

Most respondents were retired at the time of the survey (77.6 percent in Flint; 60.8 percent in Seattle). The most frequently cited occupational affiliation among Flint respondents was "unskilled workers or laborers" (42.8 percent). The most common occupational affiliation among Seattle respondents was "professionals or managers" (32.5 percent); the second most common occupational affiliation in Seattle was "skilled workers" (22.1 percent).

As with the in-office study, educational attainment was higher in the Seattle sample than it was in the Flint sample. In Flint, 50.4 percent of respondents had at least a high school diploma and 55.8 percent had at least a partial secondary school education. In Seattle, however, 76.4 percent of respondents had at least a high school diploma, and 90.5 percent had at least a partial secondary school education.

*Attitudes toward consumerism.* The community survey questionnaire explored respondents' attitudes toward good or careful buying practices; their familiarity with community organizations designed to assist or protect consumers; and their evaluations of four hypothetical instances of consumer abuse.

Most respondents (Flint: 456, or 77.8 percent; Seattle: 400, or 87.1 percent) indicated that they agreed strongly with the statement, "When getting something repaired, it is *always* a good idea to get an estimate of the cost in writing." Most respondents (Flint: 388, or 66.2 percent; Seattle: 272, or 59.8 percent) indicated that they disagreed strongly with the statement, "A spoken promise from a store manager is just as good as a written guarantee."

In Flint and Seattle, nearly all respondents were familiar with at least one consumer-oriented organization in their community: 576 (98.6 percent) of the Flint respondents said they knew of at least one of the seven organizations about which they were queried, and 461 (98.7 percent) of the Seattle respondents knew of at least one of the 10 organizations about which they were queried. Furthermore, 278 Flint respondents (47.4 percent) and 357 Seattle respondents (76.4 percent) knew of more than half of the local consumer-oriented organizations about which they were queried.

Respondents were also asked to evaluate four hypothetical abusive consumer experiences. The first concerned false claims about an arthritic cream; the second concerned a guarantee on a new hearing aid; the third involved the receipt of unsolicited merchandise; and the fourth concerned overcharging for automobile repairs. Between 28 and 50 percent of the respondents in Flint and Seattle indicated that they would respond to the first three hypothetical experiences (if they would respond at all) in a manner that *precludes* redress or remedy for the situation—for example, by simply "walking out [of the hearing aid dealership]," or by "telling all my friends." Only in the case of the automobile repair hypothetical experience did the majority of respondents (Flint: 74.9 percent; Seattle: 62.5 percent) indicate an intention to respond actively to the abuse by, for example, refusing to pay or contesting the bill, reporting to a consumer protection agency, or seeking legal assistance.

When asked *who* should take action (rather than *what* they would do) following these abuses, between 40 and 65 percent of the respondents indicated that they (themselves) should take action. This leaves a sizable number of respondents unwilling to accept the responsibility to act themselves and placing that responsibility on someone else or denying the responsibility altogether.[8]

Survey respondents, therefore, appeared to be informed consumers who were aware of consumer-oriented organizations in their communities and who favored cautious buying practices. However, when faced with several hypothetical instances of consumer abuse, many respondents suggested that they would react in an ineffective manner—if at all—were they to experience such an abuse.

## FREQUENCY AND TYPE OF CONSUMER ABUSE

During the telephone interviews, respondents were given the opportunity to describe a maximum of eight instances of consumer abuse which they experienced within the last two years: four types of repair-related abuses (television or household appliance repairs; auto repairs; home repairs; apartment repairs); an overcharging abuse; bait-and-switch abuse; and two abuses of nearly any type (in response to the two nondirective questions).

In Flint, 205 respondents (35.0 percent) and 256 Seattle respondents (54.8 percent) indicated that they had been victims of at least one such instance of consumer abuse. Forty-seven of these Flint victims and 99 of the Seattle victims were victims of more than one consumer abuse. Table 2, which presents the number of abuses experienced by respondents in Flint and Seattle, shows that no respondent described more than four abusive experiences. This table also shows a substantial difference between the two research sites: a larger number of Seattle respondents reported instances of consumer abuse, including multiple abuses, than did Flint respondents.[9]

As illustrated in Table 3, the most commonly reported type of consumer abuse involved bait-and-switch tactics, with 123 Flint and 157 Seattle respondents indicating that they had, at some point in the last two years, been told that a product was unavailable at an advertised special price. The second most prevalent type involved repair transactions. The most frequently experienced type of repair-related abuse in both sites involved the repair of televisions or household appliances, followed by automobile repairs and home repairs, in that order. As can be seen in Table 3, respondents indicated experiencing relatively few instances of consumer abuse other than those involving repairs and bait-and-switch tactics.

*Table 2* Number of Consumer Abuses Experienced by Survey Respondents in Flint and Seattle

| *Number of Abusive Experiences* | *Number and Percentage of Respondents in Flint* | *Number and Percentage of Respondents in Seattle* |
|---|---|---|
| 0 | 381 (65.0%) | 211 (45.2%) |
| 1 | 158 (27.0%) | 157 (33.6%) |
| 2 | 33 (5.6%) | 68 (14.6%) |
| 3 | 12 (2.0%) | 28 (6.0%) |
| 4 | 2 (0.3%) | 3 (0.6%) |
| 5 or more | 0 (—) | 0 (—) |
| TOTAL | 586 | 467 |

*Table 3* Instances and Type of Consumer Abuses Reported by Flint and Seattle Survey Respondents

| *Type of Abuse* | *Instances of Abuse in Flint* | *Instances of Abuse in Seattle* |
|---|---|---|
| Bait-and-switch | 123 | 157 |
| Repair-related | 86 | 136 |
| "Cheated or swindled" | 31 | 47 |
| "Misled or taken advantage of" | 12 | 29 |
| Overcharging | 16 | 20 |
| TOTAL[a] | 268 | 389 |

[a]The number of *instances* of consumer abuse differs from the number of *individuals* who reported experiencing consumer abuse (205 in Flint and 256 in Seattle), since some individuals reported more than one such experience.

## EXTENT OF CONSUMER ABUSE

The majority of respondents (73.2 percent in Flint and 65.6 percent in Seattle) who indicated experiencing consumer abuses suffered neither a lengthy delay in the delivery of repair services nor a very large or unanticipated monetary loss. Only 55 respondents in Flint and 87 respondents in Seattle described consumer experiences as a result of which they (1) were required to wait at least one week longer than anticipated before their repair work was completed; (2) paid at least $25 more than the estimated repair costs; and/or (3) lost at least $25 due to bait-and-switch tactics, overcharges, being "cheated," or being "taken advantage of."

The examination of more serious abuses led to an interesting finding: eight of the respondents in Seattle and seven in Flint who described consumer experiences involving delays of at least one week or losses or increased costs of at least $25, did *not* portray themselves as victims of consumer abuse. All 15 were white women, who indicated no perception of dissatisfaction or abuse—yet, these women comprise 12.7 percent of the more seriously abused survey respondents in Flint and 9.2 percent in Seattle. These respondents serve as reminders of a significant problem confronting white-collar crime enforcement: the recognition by victims of white-collar crime and related abuses that they have been harmed.

## ACTIONS TAKEN IN RESPONSE TO CONSUMER ABUSES: REPORTING BEHAVIOR

Of the 205 respondents in Flint who described themselves as victims of at least one instance of consumer abuse, 61 (29.8 percent) took no action subsequent to any abuse. Sixty percent (123) of the respondents sought a private remedy for at least one of their experiences of abuse; that is, they said they reported to a friend, family member, or member or employee of the organization or business responsible for the abuse. Only 10.2 percent (21) of the respondents reported one or more experiences of abuse to a public agency, consumer protection office, newspaper, or Better Business Bureau. Likewise, in Seattle, of the 256 respondents who indicated experiencing at least one instance of consumer abuse, 59 (23.0 percent) took no action subsequent to any abuse. One hundred seventy-eight (69.5 percent) respondents sought a private remedy for at least one of their experiences of abuse; and 19 (7.4 percent) respondents reported one or more experiences of abuse to a public agency, consumer protection office, newspaper, or Better Business Bureau.

This tendency to favor private remedies was foreshadowed by in-office complainants who were interviewed regarding the people or organizations from whom complainants would seek help for problems with a product or service. Likewise, the responses to the four hypothetical abuses reflect a tendency to take somewhat passive responses and to favor private remedies when confronted with a consumer abuse. There was, however, some indication that survey respondents perceive themselves more likely to seek redress for consumer problems than they actually are: under six percent of the Flint survey respondents and five percent of the Seattle respondents described themselves as people who never report a problem with a product or service to someone in charge; yet, about 30 percent in Flint and 23 percent in Seattle took no action when they actually experienced such abuse.

## FACTORS AFFECTING REPORTING BEHAVIOR

*Type of abuse.* Table 4 presents the rate of reporting for each type of consumer abuse explored in the community survey. The reporting rates varied among the different types of abuses; the most frequently described type, bait-and-switch, was reported least often. Respondents frequently sought private remedies for bait-and-switch tactics, however: Respondents sought private remedies for 99 (80.5 percent) of the Flint and 126 (80.3 percent) of the Seattle bait-and-switch abuses.

Most frequently reported abuses involved overcharging schemes and the abuses described in response to the two nondirective questions: situations in which respondents felt "cheated or swindled" or "misled or taken advantage of." Repair-related abuses were infrequently reported by respondents, though they were reported more often than bait-and-switch abuses.

*Seriousness of abuse.* The 55 Flint and 87 Seattle respondents who were victims of more serious abuses (involving delays of at least one week or increased costs or losses of at least $25) reported the abuses to a public agency or organization more often than did victims of less serious abuse. While 7.0 percent in Flint and 4.5 percent in Seattle reported less serious abuses, 18.2 percent in Flint and 12.6 percent in Seattle reported the more serious abuses.

*Number of abusive experiences.* The number of abuses experienced by respondents does not appear related to their tendency to report such abuses. None of the respondents experiencing more than one instance of consumer abuse reported all such experiences to a public agency; no one having two abusive experiences reported both to a public agency; and nearly all respondents[10] reported only one of their abusive experiences to a public agency, if they reported at all.

*Table 4* Rate of Reporting Each Type of Abuse

| *Type of Abuse* | *Flint* | | *Seattle* | |
|---|---|---|---|---|
| | *Total Instances of Abuse*[a] | *Number & Percentage of Abuses Reported to Public Agency/Organization* | *Total Instances of Abuse* | *Number & Percentage of Abuses Reported to Public Agency/Organization* |
| Bait-and-Switch | 123 | 1 (0.8%) | 157 | 0 (—) |
| Repair-Related | 86 | 9 (10.5%) | 136 | 8 (5.9%) |
| Overcharging | 16 | 3 (18.8%) | 20 | 2 (10.0%) |
| "Cheated" | 31 | 7 (22.6%) | 47 | 6 (12.8%) |
| "Taken" | 12 | 2 (16.7%) | 29 | 4 (13.8%) |
| TOTAL | 268 | 22 (8.2%) | 389 | 20 (5.1%) |

[a]This table presents *instances* of abuse, which, it will be recalled, are greater than the number of individuals experiencing abuses due to the multiple abuses experienced by some respondents

*Knowledge of local consumer-oriented organizations.* Although it might be expected that familiarity with community organizations concerned with handling consumer problems would increase the likelihood of reporting consumer abuses, no relation between the number of organizations with which respondents were familiar and their postvictimization reporting behavior emerged. It appears, therefore, that knowledge of where to seek help in remedying a consumer abuse is unrelated to Flint and Seattle respondents' tendency to report consumer abuses.

*Respondent characteristics.* The examination of respondent characteristics offered virtually no insight as to who is the likely victim of consumer abuses; the level of victimization remained constant regardless of age, race, or most demographic and background characteristics. However, two subtle differences emerged between victims who reported their consumer abuses to public agencies or organizations and those who did not report.

First, in both Flint and Seattle, slightly more male respondents reported the more serious abuses, while women were more likely to report less serious abuses (see Table 5). Furthermore, as noted above, while all of the male respondents who were victims of more serious abuses recognized the abusive nature of their experiences, seven women in Flint and eight women in Seattle failed to do so. These findings suggest that older males may be better able to recognize the presence of an abuse—and to report more serious abuses—than are older females.

The second aspect of respondents' backgrounds that appeared to affect reporting rates concerned respondents' experiences with street crimes. Table 6 describes the reporting behavior of victims of consumer abuse in terms of their past experiences with street crime victimization. In both Flint and Seattle, the respondents who reported consumer abuses most frequently had been victims of street crime within the last two years.

This relationship between reporting of consumer abuses and street crime victimization could be due to several factors. While the level of street crime victimization during the last two years was fairly low in this sample (Flint: 51, or 8.7 percent; Seattle: 91, or 19.5 percent) respondents indicated that nearly all of these crimes were reported to the police (Flint: 78.8 percent, Seattle: 81.8 percent). These victims may be people who tend to report all abuses. It may be that experiences of street crime victimization generally sensitize victims and therefore increase the likelihood that they will report consumer abuses. Perhaps some people are concentrated in neighborhoods and environments where all forms of abusive behavior flourish and have experienced a host of abuses. Street crime victimization may not

*Table 5* Level of Victimization and Reporting Rates for Male and Female Victims of Consumer Abuse

| Sex of Respondent | Level of Consumer Victimization | Flint: Total Number of Victims of Consumer Abuse[a] | Flint: Reporting Victims of Consumer Abuse | Seattle: Total Number of Victims of Consumer Abuse | Seattle: Reporting Victims of Consumer Abuse |
|---|---|---|---|---|---|
| Male | Serious abuses | 12 | 3 (25.0%) | 28 | 4 (14.3%) |
| | Less serious abuses | 31 | 2 (6.4%) | 56 | 1 (1.8%) |
| Female | Serious abuses | 42 | 7 (16.7%) | 59 | 7 (11.9%) |
| | Less serious abuses | 122 | 8 (6.6%) | 121 | 7 (5.8%) |

[a]Data on respondents' sex was missing for five victims of consumer abuse, one of whom reported the abuse.

*Table 6* Street Crime Victimization and Reporting Rates for Victims of Consumer Abuse

| Street Crime Victimization | Flint: Total Sample | Flint: Victims of Consumer Abuse | Flint: Reporting Victims of Consumer Abuse | Seattle: Total Sample | Seattle: Victims of Consumer Abuse | Seattle: Reporting Victims of Consumer Abuse |
|---|---|---|---|---|---|---|
| Within 2 years | 55 | 32 | 7 (21.9%) | 91 | 62 | 6 (9.7%) |
| More than 2 years ago | 51 | 20 | 2 (10.0%) | 80 | 55 | 2 (3.6%) |
| No street crime victimization | 474 | 158 | 12 (7.6%) | 287 | 142 | 11 (7.7%) |

increase the likelihood of these people reporting; they may simply have more to report and therefore appear in the "victims of street and of consumer abuse" group more often. This research, however, did not address the nature or cause of the relationship found between reporting of consumer abuses and street crime victimization.

## OUTCOME, OR RESULT, OF REPORTING

The community survey questionnaire asked respondents to describe the resolution, if any, of their bait-and-switch abuses, overcharging abuses, experiences of feeling "cheated," and experiences of feeling "taken."

Respondents who described themselves as victims of bait-and-switch abuses were asked if they ever received the product at its special advertised price. Of the Flint respondents, 40 (34.8 percent) and 70 (46.1 percent) of the Seattle respondents indicated that they did eventually receive the product at the special price.

As expected, victims of bait-and-switch abuses who took action following the abuse were far more likely to receive the product at its special price than were victims who took no action following the abuse. In Flint, only 10 percent (2 of 22) of the respondents who took no action following the abuse received the product at its special price; but 41 percent (38 of 93) who sought a private remedy (complaining at the store) received the product at the special price. Similarly, only 13 percent (4 of 31) of the Seattle respondents who took no action following the abuse received the product at its special price; while 55 percent (66 of 121) of those who sought a private remedy received the product at its advertised price.

Table 7 describes the final outcome of abusive experiences for respondents who took no action and for those who either sought private remedies or reported to public agencies following their overcharging, "cheated," or "taken" experiences.[11] As with bait-and-switch abuses, comparison of the victims taking no action with those seeking either public or private remedies revealed that a higher percentage of respondents taking action following their abuses obtained remedies than did those taking no action.[12] Based on 30 cases in Flint, 42 percent of those who sought public or private remedies obtained some remedy, while only 18 percent of those taking no action obtained a remedy. Based on 43 cases in Seattle, 41 percent taking action obtained a remedy, and 14 percent taking no action obtained a remedy. It is of interest, however, that the magnitude of these differences is not greater than it is. The finding that less than 50 percent of those taking any action obtained a remedy for their abuses may suggest that the assistance offered victims of consumer abuse could be more effective than it is, but this

*Table 7* Outcome of Respondents' Overcharging, "Cheated," and "Taken" Abuses in Terms of Postvictimization Reporting Behavior (collapsing over type of abuse)

| | *Flint* | | | *Seattle* | | |
|---|---|---|---|---|---|---|
| | *Outcome* | | | *Outcome* | | |
| *Postvictimization Reporting Behavior* | *Total Number of Abuses for Which Outcome Is Known* | *Obtained Remedy* | *Obtained No Remedy* | *Total Number of Abuses for Which Outcome Is Known* | *Obtained Remedy* | *Obtained No Remedy* |
| Took no action | 11 | 2 | 9 | 14 | 2 | 12 |
| Sought private remedy | 10 | 4 | 6 | 20 | 7 | 13 |
| Sought public remedy (reported to public organization) | 9 | 4 | 5 | 9 | 5 | 4 |
| TOTAL | 30 | 10 | 20 | 43 | 14 | 29 |

research provided no basis for assessing the quality or validity of these complaints.

### Complainants to Public Agencies: A Comparison of Survey Respondents and In-Office Complaints

It should be noted that in both Flint and Seattle, the demographic backgrounds of survey respondents who reported consumer abuses to public agencies or organizations were similar to those of the older complainants participating in the in-office studies.

Most survey respondents who reported consumer abuses were women under 70 years of age. The majority were white, with a slightly greater number of blacks reporting in Flint. Most who reported were retired, and the most common occupational category in both sites was "unskilled workers." Educational levels were somewhat higher in Seattle than in Flint; 89 percent of those reporting in Seattle and 70 percent in Flint had, at minimum, some secondary-level education.

Thus, survey respondents who reported their abuses differed from in-office complainants only in that a higher proportion of reporting survey respondents were women, and the predominant occupational category for reporting survey respondents was "unskilled workers." The difference due to the predominance of women in the group of reporting survey respondents was not surprising, however, in that women far outnumbered men in the total survey sample. The difference in terms of occupational category may also be explained by the difference in terms of sex; the increased number of unskilled workers may simply reflect the increased number of women in the sample of reporting survey respondents.

## DISCUSSION

This research suggests that consumer abuse is not only widespread, but that its victims are often silent, notwithstanding the proliferation of consumer agencies, media publicity, and other consciousness-raising activities. While the research did not directly address problems and challenges of minimizing consumer abuse or maximizing the effectiveness of efforts to assist victims of consumer abuse, some of the findings resulting from this research pertain to these issues.

First, the key to prompting victims of consumer abuse to report their abuses (or to the prevention of consumer abuse) does not appear to be increasing "Consumer I.Q." The older persons participating in this research were generally well-educated, well-informed consumers who strongly favored defensive consumer practices. Yet, many were victims of consumer abuse, and only some of those victims chose to report their abuses—to seek assistance in remedying their problems by utilizing public resources which they knew were available.

Increasing consumers' awareness of good buying practices and of services available to rectify consumer abuses once they occur is not a fail-safe preventative. Two factors appear to form very real barriers between older victims of consumer abuse and agencies or programs which seek to assist the victims: the victim's unawareness of having been victimized, and the low rate of payoffs for victims who report their abuses.

Naturally, consumers who fail to perceive their marketplace experiences as illegal, unusual, or abusive will not report their victimization to a public agency. Such was the case with approximately 10 percent of the more seriously abused survey respondents in Flint and Seattle.[12] It appears, therefore, that programs designed to increase older consumers' sensitivity to the illegal or abusive character of their own consumer experiences could effectively increase the reporting rate of consumer abuses. This would not be an easy task—by definition, many consumer and economic crimes are difficult for anyone to detect—but reporting rates may well be increased by strengthening consumers' beliefs that, no matter how commonplace abusive consumer experiences may be, they should not occur, and they should be rectified once they do occur.

Hand in hand with this argument, however, goes the argument that in order to reasonably expect a victim of consumer abuse to go through the often time-consuming process of reporting an abuse, consumers must believe that public agencies *will* provide assistance in remedying the problems. This research found, however, that many reported consumer abuses remain unresolved. As Table 7 illustrated, 18 percent of the victims in Flint and 14 percent in Seattle who took no action following an abuse obtained some remedy for the abuse; 40 percent of those in Flint and 35 percent in Seattle who sought private remedies obtained a remedy; and 44 percent in Flint and 56 percent in Seattle who reported to public agencies obtained a remedy. Thus, as expected, taking action following abuses increased the likelihood of obtaining remedies, but the likelihood of obtaining a remedy did not appear to be strongly linked to particular postvictimization behavior.

There may be many reasons for the failure of consumer protection agencies to achieve remedies for a greater proportion of complainants; for example, many of the abuses that are reported may be very difficult to resolve, may be unfounded, may not warrant resolution to the consumer's benefit, or may be beyond the agency's jurisdiction. If, however, such agencies were to achieve remedies in a greater proportion of the cases processed, this may do much to encourage a higher level of reporting.

If consumers were better able to recognize the seriousness of abuses inflicted on them and to know that consumer-oriented agencies and organizations would, in fact, successfully remedy meritorious consumer complaints, reporting of legitimate consumer problems would undoubtedly rise among older consumers. Increased reporting would, in turn, make possible a better grasp of the problems of older consumers and hence assist the design of more effective and economical remedies.

## NOTES

1. It was formed in 1971 and is staffed by four attorneys (three of whom are part-time), four consumer specialists, one business specialist, five consumer investigators, and two secretaries.

2. The Seattle office of the Consumer Protection Division was established in 1961. It is staffed by four attorneys; six paralegals; five investigators; eight clerical staff; five CETA staff, administrative trainees, and claims representatives; one public information specialist; one education specialist; and four volunteers on a full-time basis. Also, approximately nine part-time staff members are employed by the office, of whom eight are university student interns who work as consumer complaint processors and law clerks and one part-time paralegal. During the six-month period of study (August 1, 1977, to January 31, 1978), the majority of formal complaints (69 percent) were filed by residents of the Seattle-King County area; 26.1 percent were filed by other residents of Washington; and 2.7 percent of the complaints were received from outside Washington State.

3. Copies of the research protocols and the instruments used in data collection are set forth in Edelhertz et al. (1978c). The following reports were prepared for the Administration on Aging, Office of Human Development, U.S. Department of Health, Education and Welfare: *Consumer Fraud and Abuse: Problems of the Elderly in the Marketplace, A Glossary of Terms and Annotated Bibliography* (Edelhertz, et al., 1977); *Communicating Consumer Protection and Anti-Fraud Information to the Elderly* (Edelhertz et al., 1978a); *Descriptive Report on the Elderly as Victims of Fraud and Consumer Abuse: The Flint and Seattle Experience* (Edelhertz et al., 1978c); *Final Report, Consumerism and the Aging: The Elderly as Victims of Fraud* (Edelhertz, et al., 1978e); *The Impact of Fraud and Consumer Abuse on the Elderly* (Edelhertz et al., 1978d); and *Providing Consumer Protection and Anti-Fraud Services to the Elderly* (Edelhertz, et al., 1978b).

4. For the Flint area, comparisons between research participants and the population are based on census statistics for Genesee County, the area served by the Flint Consumer Protection Office and surveyed in the community survey portion of this study. For the Seattle area, comparisons are based on census statistics for the Seattle-Everett Standard Metropolitan Statistical Area; 85.2 percent of the elderly complainants in Seattle resided in this area (though the Seattle Consumer Protection Office serves all of Western Washington) and the community survey was conducted in this area. Population figures reported here and below are found in U.S. Bureau of Census (1970).

5. This three-part classification scheme was developed by the Battelle Law and Justice Study Center (1975).

6. These exchanges reach residents beyond city limits at Seattle's south and southwest borders; it is estimated, therefore, that less than one percent of the potential respondents were not residents of the city of Seattle.

7. The percentage of eligible, elderly respondents located through screening calls closely reflects the proportion of elderly Seattle residents: 24.6 percent of Seattle residents are 55 years and over according to the 1970 census.

8. The following percentages of respondents indicated that, were they victims of such abuse, either someone other than the respondent/victim, or no one, should take action following the abusive experience: arthritic cream: Flint, 56.1 percent, Seattle, 60.8 percent; hearing aid: Flint, 44.2 percent, Seattle, 47.1 percent; unsolicited merchandise: Flint, 35.5 percent, Seattle, 49.7 percent; automobile repair: Flint, 37.7 percent, Seattle, 39.4 percent.

9. Although this difference may reflect a higher level of victimization in Seattle, these findings offer no conclusive evidence concerning victimization levels in Flint and Seattle. The difference may also be a function of any of a number of differences in interview procedures followed in the two sites. For example, Seattle interviews tended to last longer than did Flint interviews (40-45 minutes versus 15-20 minutes). Perhaps the slower-paced interviews conducted in Seattle served to jog respondents' memories, leading to more reports of abuse, whatever the relative incidence of abuse may have been in the two sites.

10. Two respondents, one in Flint and one in Seattle, who experienced more than two consumer abuses reported two of these abuses to a public agency; no other respondent reported more than one abuse.

11. *Remedies* include obtaining the product/service at its original price, partial or total adjustment or refund, receiving repairs or replacement item, an investigation of the problem, and prosecution of the party responsible for the problem.

12. The reader will recall that the 10 percent consisted entirely of older women, a fact which may be significant to those designing programs to protect older consumers.

## REFERENCES

Battelle Law and Justice Study Center (1975) Research and Evaluation Report on the Second Year of the Economic Crime Project, August 15, 1974, to August 14, 1975. Seattle: Battelle Human Affairs Research Centers.

CARPER, J. (1973) Not with a Gun. New York: Grossman.

EDELHERTZ, H., M. WALSH, and D. BERGER (1977) Consumer Fraud and Abuse: Problems of the Elderly in the Marketplace, A Glossary of Terms and Annotated Bibliography. Seattle: Battelle Human Affairs Research Centers.

EDELHERTZ H., D. BERGER, and B. H. HOFF (1978a) Communicating Consumer Protection and Anti-Fraud Information to the Elderly. Seattle: Battelle Human Affairs Research Centers.

EDELHERTZ, H., M. BRINTNALL, and B.H. HOFF (1978b) Providing Consumer Protection and Anti-Fraud Services to the Elderly. Seattle: Battelle Human Affairs Research Centers.

EDELHERTZ, H., M. WALSH, and M. V. McGUIRE (1978c) Descriptive Report on the Elderly as Victims of Fraud and Consumer Abuse: The Flint and Seattle Experience. Seattle: Battelle Human Affairs Research Centers.

______(1978d) The Impact of Fraud and Consumer Abuse on the Elderly. Seattle: Battelle Human Affairs Research Centers.

EDELHERTZ, H., M. WALSH, M. BRINTNALL, M. V. McGUIRE, B. H. HOFF, and D. BERGER (1978e) Final Report, Consumerism and the Aging:

The Elderly as Victims of Fraud. Seattle: Battelle Human Affairs Research Centers.

Law Enforcement Assistance Administration (1977) National Crime Panel Victimization Surveys. Washington, DC: U.S. Department of Justice, National Criminal Justice Information and Statistical Service.

U.S. Bureau of Census (1970) Census of Population: Vol. 1, Characteristics of Population, Part 29, Washington; Part 24, Michigan. Washington, DC: U.S. Government Printing Office.

U.S. Department of Justice, Federal Bureau of Investigation (1978) Uniform Crime Reports for the United States. Washington, DC: U.S. Government Printing Office.

*Chapter 13*

# INVESTIGATING COMPANY FRAUD: CASE STUDIES FROM AUSTRALIA

ADAM C. SUTTON and
RONALD WILD

This chapter has two objectives: to present case studies from recent investigations into Australian public companies, and to interpret this data in the light of ideas developed by Marx and Weber concerning corporate crime, law, and capitalism. Most of the material is derived from reports by special investigators appointed to inquire into the affairs of public companies and their subsidiaries in New South Wales (NSW). Under Australian law each of the six states and the Commonwealth enacts and enforces its own companies and securities legislation. Generally, each jurisdiction has taken United Kingdom law as its model, and government agencies have only limited powers to investigate the affairs of private corporations. Corporate Affairs inspectors can visit the registered offices of companies and inspect the books and records required to be kept under the Companies Act. However, they cannot seize or copy these records (Sutton, 1978; Santow, 1977).

Special investigators are in a different position. Nominated by the attorney general and with specific terms of reference, they can interview witnesses under oath and seize relevant books and records. They report directly to the minister. Special investigations, whether by nominated individuals or by the Corporate Affairs Commission (CAC) of the state concerned, usually are initiated when a major public company has gone into liquidation or receivership and it is suspected that criminal offenses may have been committed.

## MARX AND WEBER ON CORPORATE CRIME

Marx's comments on corporate crime form part of his discussion of the concentration and centralization of capital. For Marx, the concentration of production in larger firms at the expense of smaller ones occurred both as a response to periodic crises in capitalism and as the result of constant attempts by capitalists to undercut their rivals by economies of scale. Centralization refers to the institutions which emerged to facilitate the accumulation of capital required by large-scale enterprises. Most significant were the development of sophisticated banking and credit systems and the evolution of the joint stock corporation.

Marx argued that the centralization of capital would have ambivalent consequences. It would facilitate commodity production on a massive scale, but also transform relations of production within capitalism:

> The two characteristics immanent in the credit system are, on the one hand, to develop the incentive of capitalist production, enrichment through exploitation of the labor of others, to the purest and most colossal form of gambling and swindling, and to reduce more and more the number of the few who exploit the social wealth; on the other hand, to constitute the form of transition to a new mode of production. It is this ambiguous nature, which endows the principal spokesmen of credit from Law to Isaac Pereire with the pleasant character mixture of swindler and prophet [Marx, 1971:441].

Centralization of capital takes economic power from a myriad of small-scale owner entrepreneurs and concentrates it in the hands of an elite whose position in joint stock corporations or in the credit and banking system gives access to other people's money. This results in capitalism without the capitalist, consequently giving rise to a new range of potential conflicts between those who own capital and the new controllers. This elite is provided with unique opportunities to "gamble" with wealth they did not own and even to "swindle" the owners.

Marx saw the centralization of capital as transforming the relations of production but not bringing about anything resembling a socialist society. The new economic elite's power remained logically dependent on the existence of private property, on a market for labor and commodities, and on the separation of the public and private sectors. Moreover, as recent research has confirmed, an important qualification for admission to this elite is the ownership of property (Domhoff, 1967). This ensures an ideological commitment to the system and support for such statutes as companies and securities legislation, which are designed to protect the rights of small property owners. For this reason, corporate crime is of central relevance to Marxist analysis. Here is evidence of the growing inconsistencies between the dominant ideology of advanced capitalism, which stresses the rights of ownership and laissez-faire doctrine, and economic realities where ownership does not necessarily guarantee control.

In the 1890s Weber wrote a series of articles dealing with legal and economic aspects of stock and commodity exchanges. His major concerns were (1) to debate the widespread view that the stock exchange was a "league of conspirators" engaged in fraud and deception at the expense of honest working people and was best abolished, and (2) to examine possible methods for bringing stock exchange activities under control (Bendix, 1962:24).

Weber's studies confirm many of the points made by Marx. He found that stock and commodity exchanges were an efficient means for ensuring the expansion of trade and production and the predictability of economic transactions; however, they also increased the opportunities for "gambling and wild speculation" (Bendix, 1962:24, 29). The major point of departure from Marx was Weber's preoccupation with possible methods for controlling such abuses. He emphasized that law is often ineffectual, for example, in attempting to distinguish pure speculation from more sound business practice: "The German Supreme Court had discarded one criterion after another . . . even though the distinction was real enough" (Bendix, 1962:29). The problem was that the only difference often lay in the intentions of the participants, a matter difficult to establish under western law.

For more effective methods of controlling stock exchange activities, Weber turned to such countries as England and America. In the former, exchanges were

> exclusive private associations, which were governed autonomously in accordance with their own statutes. Admissions to the exchanges were similar in principle to admission to an exclusive club. . . . [T]he transactions themselves were in effect regulated by the rules of the association rather than by the civil jurisdiction of the national government, as, for example, in the London Stock Exchange [Bendix, 1962:25].

These autonomous exchanges could be much more flexible in their judgments, and apply a wider range of sanctions, than the ordinary courts. Weber points out, however, that for "courts of honor" such as these to be effective the individuals involved "would have to be roughly in the same social position, with similar personal and moral qualities" (Bendix, 1962:27). In other words, they would need to belong to the same status group.

The ineffectuality of state laws for controlling stock exchange abuse and the comparative effectiveness—in some countries, at least—of status-group-oriented controls establish two themes which assumed major significance in Weber's later writings. These are the ever-increasing possibilities for conflict between an emphasis on formal rationality and substantive concepts of justice in law and administration, and the relevance of noneconomic orientations for behavior in the business sphere.

To understand the first topic it is necessary briefly to review Weber's discussion of rationality in capitalist societies and the comparison he makes between rational-legal and other authority systems. Weber identified two types of rationality—formal and substantive—as of special relevance to capitalism. He defined formal rationality as the use of rules and procedures which ensure calculability and predictability in social behavior. Substantive rationality involved the selection of specific means to obtain desired ends or goals. For Weber, one of the central characteristics of capitalism is the ever-increasing emphasis on these two principles and the ever-increasing potentiality for conflict between them. The more judges and administrators, for example, acted in accordance with principles of formal rationality and applied preexisting rules inflexibly—taking into account only those factors which the legislators, judicial precedent, and administrative codes defined as relevant—the more it would be possible that their decisions would conflict with common-sense judgments based on all evidence at hand. This type of problem is, moreover, almost unique to societies characterized by rational-legal authority. In a patrimonial system, for example, judicial authorities and government officials are personal appointees of, and owe loyalty to, their ruler. Their authority is limited only by tradition, and "the master obviously has a major interest in keeping these limits vague . . . for once he adopts a formal regulation he may be forced to observe his own rules" (Bendix, 1962:332). Because the idea of applying rules impartially and with due regard for precedent is not highly developed, the possibilities for conflicts between this principle and the achievement of the administrator's substantive goals are not acute in the traditional authority system.

Weber saw the conflict between formal and substantive rationality as one of the major dilemmas of capitalist society, affecting not only senior judicial and administrative personnel but almost every individual. He argued that the increasing emphasis on formal rationality would result in the spread of bureaucracy; the ideal form of organization in an increasingly rational society. The more social existence was encompassed by bureaucratic organization, the more people would find themselves trapped in the "iron cage" of routine rules and regulations. More and more workers would find their sense of values evaporating, feel alienated from the means of administration, and lose sight of the objectives of their organization (Gouldner, 1955; Selznick, 1966). They would become organization men and women whose individual experience was segregated "into relatively limited areas of interaction and communication" (Taylor et al., 1973:120).

We argue that this idea of bureaucratic alienation is of central relevance to the interpretation of data on corporate crime. We are, of course, aware that Weber's theoretical constructs are ideal types and that actual societies consist of mixtures of types of authority and rationality. His allusion to the status group orientation of English exchanges is a case in point: Here authority conforms more to the traditional than to the rational-legal model, and would thus be less vulnerable to schemes designed to stay within the letter of the law but not its spirit.

After presenting our case studies, we will return to the ideas outlined above, and will attempt to emphasize the relevance of distinctive historic and economic aspects of Australian society—such as its position on the periphery of world capitalism—to our data.

## CASE STUDIES

### The Bartons

Alexander Buchalter arrived in Australia as a refugee in 1950, and by April 1954 owned a plumbing and draining business in Sydney which employed up to 12 people.

The business eventually failed, although a last-minute settlement with creditors avoided bankruptcy. In 1955, Buchalter changed his name to Alexander Barton. Thereafter, Barton formed several private companies to manufacture and install treatment units. Most of these companies failed.

In November 1961, he came into contact with Australian Factors Limited (AFL). This public company, whose board of directors included two members of the NSW Parliament and an eminent academic, was in the business of "factoring"; that is, purchasing the book debts of other businesses. Factoring had for some time been an established form of money-lending in the United States, but it was relatively new to Australia.

Although factoring is a sound concept, the system which Australian Factors used was faulty in several respects. First, it failed to check the credit worthiness of its prospective debtors. Second, it neglected to institute a system for verifying that purchased debts were bona fide. Third, the company failed to ensure that when it took over a debt it established a legal entitlement to the money owed. These organizational flaws made it easy prey for speculative businesses in need of capital. Eventually, the company collapsed, but until the final days AFL executives went to great lengths to conceal the problems from both directors and shareholders.

In its early stages the company had considerable funds. The directors' main preoccupation was with "getting this money out" in the form of loans. Barton was amazed and delighted to discover such an easy source of credit, and became one of AFLs most valued clients. The investigators estimate that factoring with him eventually cost the company over $100,000. Alexander Armstrong, a member of Parliament and one of AFL's directors, was so impressed with Barton's business acumen that he invited him to become manager of Palgrave Corporation Ltd. Barton accepted, but only after Palgrave acquired his company, Home Septics, for $50,000. During the takeover, the Australian Factors directors made some last-minute discoveries concerning the extent of Home Septics' factoring with AFL. This was the first of a number of disappointments for Armstrong in his business relationship with Barton. By January 1967, the situation had so deteriorated that Armstrong was prepared to sever all connections with Palgrave. However, in return for agreeing to sell his shares, Armstrong extracted a generous settlement which stripped Palgrave of its major assets and precipitated its liquidation. Barton subsequently attempted to renege, claiming the agreement had been signed under duress. After a series of court actions, culminating in a hearing by the Privy Council in England, the issue was decided in Barton's favor. Although Barton won the case, his own credibility, as well as Armstrong's, suffered greatly in the course of the hearings.

By the time the Privy Council's decision was handed down in 1973, Barton's career had seen further significant developments. The postwar growth in the Japanese economy had generated a strong demand for minerals. The discovery in 1966 of significant nickel deposits by the Western Mining Corporation and their subsequent exploitation triggered off a frenzy of exploration and prompted the appearance of innumerable new mining companies. Before the discoveries, Western Mining had been a weak company with a low share price. After, its share price shot up from $1.40 to $80.00. The possibility of such windfall gains attracted immense amounts of speculative capital. Attention focused on smaller companies, whose share prices would be expected to skyrocket if they made a discovery. Tax concessions for investment in oil exploration gave impetus to the boom which Barton was not slow to exploit. Between 1969 and 1972 he and his son Thomas had a hand in floating, or gained control of, more than 60 public and private companies, most of them in mineral and oil exploration.

Most of these companies are now defunct or in liquidation. Subsequent investigations indicate that the Bartons engineered a complex series of transactions which shuffled assets among various companies and that very little, if any, of the money raised for exploration was used for this purpose. In June 1972 the Bartons concluded a complex agreement with Bela Csidei which gave public and private companies dominated by Csidei control over the mineral and oil explorers. Investigators, who later unravelled this agreement, described it as a round robin series of check exchanges in which no money actually changed hands and where Barton kept control of the assets he wanted. Csidei's purchase of the Barton group was financed by an indirect loan of $3.3 million from Barton companies (Burke, 1976).

Between January 1970 and May 1973, following allegations received from businessmen and stockbrokers and a referral from the attorney general, commission officers investigated a number of possible offenses in Barton-controlled companies, but concluded that the available evidence did not justify prosecution. However, in April 1973, after an inspection of numerous company records and the review of progress in individual enquiries, the attorney general granted the commission's request that a special investigation be declared. Just ten days later, the Bartons and their wives left Australia.

The Bartons subsequently claimed their departure was prompted by incorrect advice from their legal adviser, whom they had retained on a salary of $70,000 per year, a man who was subsequently charged. The Australian government made several unsuccessful attempts to obtain extradition orders from Brazil and Paraguay, where Alexander Barton had made substantial investments. The Bartons returned voluntarily to Australia in 1977 and were immediately arrested and charged with several offenses.[1] One set of charges has been dismissed at the committal hearing stage but the defendants have been found to have a case to answer on other matters.

Five documents relating to the Bartons' affairs have been tabled in the NSW parliament. The summaries below of findings on two companies illustrate the activities which occupied the investigators' attention.

*Harbourside Oil Ltd.* Harbourside Oil was floated as a public company in 1969. The promoters took maximum advantage of tax concessions available to investors in oil companies, and when the float was announced, subscriptions already exceeded the number of shares available. Alexander Barton was one of the founding directors (Sykes, 1978:51).

Despite claims in its prospectus that Harbourside was formed to engage in oil exploration in Australia, CAC investigators found that of $4,096,359 subscribed to the company only $422,041 had been expended on exploration (Ryan, 1973:4). Instead, Harbourside advanced a considerable proportion of its capital to Brins Investments Pty Ltd., a private company controlled by the Bartons. Much of this money was used to support Jetair Australia Ltd., a public company which had some directors in common with Brins Investments. In most years Jetair incurred losses. Among the amounts loaned to Jetair were the proceeds of a ten-cent call on Harbourside shares. The call notice stated that the company intended that the money would be expended on oil exploration.

The Corporate Affairs Commissioner reported that his legal officers had advised against the prosecution of any Harbourside directors, even though Jetair received its loans on very favorable terms. There were two possible grounds for prosecution: that the directors had neglected the interests of their company in lending the money to Jetair, and that the call statement had contained a false and misleading statement about the way the money would be used. For prosecution on the first basis to succeed it would have to be shown that the loans to Jetair had no commercial justification. However, there was at least one reason—the speedy recoverability of the money—on which a loan to Jetair could be preferred to a loan to a financial institution. For prosecution on the second ground to succeed it would have to be shown that even when the call notice was issued, the directors had not intended to use the money for oil exploration. The directors could plausibly argue that they had simply changed their minds after the money was received.

*Brins Australia Ltd.* Brins Australia was incorporated in NSW to act as an investment house and to offer management consulting services in finance and investment. It sponsored the flotation of several mineral and oil exploration companies, and was converted to a public company in 1969. Brins became a holding company for several Barton-controlled concerns, including Jetair Australia Ltd.

In 1971, the Bartons reported to the Sydney Stock Exchange that during the six months ending December 31, 1970, Brins and its subsidiaries had recorded a consolidated net profit of $81,247. Shortly afterward, the Brins group auditors lodged a complaint with the CAC alleging that accounts which they had prepared, but which the Bartons had rejected, showed that the group had incurred a $1.3 million loss for the relevant period. Special investigators identified six areas—most of them relating to Jetair Ltd.—where the accounts which formed the basis of the published statement could have been misleading. The Bartons subsequently were charged with publishing a false statement with intent to deceive. At ensuing committal hearings, they were defended on the grounds that there are no hard and fast rules for financial reporting: The way particular items are valued and the way group accounts should be consolidated are matters of opinion.

The Brins hearings resulted in a significant victory for the Bartons. Not only did the presiding magistrate find that they had no case to answer, he also criticized the CAC for its preparation of the prosecution case, stating that they should have produced a true set of accounts to be compared to the Bartons' allegedly false figures.

### Mineral Securities of Australia Ltd. (MSAL)

MSAL was founded in 1965, with an issued capital of $300,000—more than half of it raised overseas (Rae, 1974; Sykes, 1978; Rath et al., 1977). By the end of 1979, the company and its subsidiaries had acquired assets worth more than $100 million. The company's stated objective was to make profits from share-trading and to divert them into long-term investments. At the height of its prosperity MSAL and its subsidiaries was one of the largest groups of public companies in Australia, controlling more than 20 percent of the world's rutile and ranking as the second largest producer of tin and wolfram in Australia.

MSAL was founded by Kenneth McMahon. He established Kenneth McMahon and Partners Pty. Ltd., a mining consulting business, in the early 1960s. This company managed MSALs affairs from its inception, and even at the height of its activities major decisions affecting the group were made by a handful of McMahon and Partners' staff. They were headed by Thomas Nestel.

MSAL's problems started early in 1970, when there was a downturn in the prices of mining shares, and it incurred serious losses. These were exacerbated when, anticipating a rally, the company reentered the market in June 1970. In July and August alone, MSAL lost more than $4.5 million. The directors then decided to intensify participation in long-term mining projects. Their plan involved making takeover offers for two groups of mining companies, Kathleen Investments and Thiess Holdings, and building up to 51 percent the group's holding in Robe River Ltd., a company which was beginning to exploit substantial iron ore deposits.

The takeovers were accomplished by exchanging MSAL shares for shares in the target companies, and involved no monetary outlays. To finance its program of share purchases, however, the group required cash, and it began to borrow heavily. Borrowing was preferred to issuing new shares, because the directors were afraid the latter would make the group vulnerable to takeover. Despite the group's size, financial institutions in Australia and overseas were wary about extending long-term loans to a company whose main source of income was sharemarket speculation, and it was forced to turn to the Australian "money-market" for its loans.[2]

MSAL was in difficulties. Share-trading was losing money and the company was borrowing heavily at high interest rates to finance a program of diversification into mining projects not likely to yield significant dividends for several years. However, the company concealed these problems to obtain loans. Until its sudden collapse in February 1971, therefore, the company continued to report reasonable profits, mostly through the adroit use of accounting techniques. The most controversial technique arose from a series of transactions labeled the Robe River Shuffle.

MSAL made its first major investment in Robe River in 1970, when it purchased a 40 percent interest. In June 1970, Robe River Ltd. floated publicly, and the price of its shares steadily appreciated. The Japanese demand for iron ore intensified throughout 1970, and even though Robe River was developing lower-grade deposits than were being exploited elsewhere, its prospects for long-term profits were good (Sykes, 1978:249-52). As long as Robe River's share price continued to appreciate, MSAL had the opportunity to record significant profits by selling some or all of the shares it had purchased when the iron ore miner was an unlisted company. However, MSAL's long-term policy was to increase, not to decrease, its holdings in Robe River. The "shuffle" enabled it to resolve the dilemma of needing to record "profits" from the sale of Robe River shares and at the same time increasing equity in that company.

Nestel negotiated an agreement with a firm of stockbrokers, whereby they would purchase Robe River shares from MSAL at current market prices, and MSAL would be able duly to record a "profit" from these sales. Nestel also arranged that Minsec Pty. Ltd., a subsidiary of MSAL, would continue to buy Robe River shares. The finance for these purchases was provided by MSAL in the form of interest free loans. As well as buying shares in the open market, Minsec Pty Ltd. would buy back the shares which the stockbrokers had bought from MSAL. Shares purchased by Minsec would be classified as long-term investments, and even though Minsec would pay Hattersley and Maxwell the same amount as the stockbrokers had originally paid to MSAL, this would not affect MSAL's "profits."

Such transactions are common and are employed by groups of companies owning shares which have declined in value in order to minimize taxation commitments. Sale and repurchase of the shares enables them to record a tax-deductible loss.

The unusual aspect of MSAL's transactions was that it was used to record a profit. Moreover, although Nestel had given the company auditors and directors a broad outline of what he intended to do, he had not explained the mechanics of the transaction. They were under the impression that the shares were being sold on the open share-market, and when they learned that the shares were being sold direct to a broker, without being registered with the stock exchange, they began to have doubts. The directors obtained legal advice that stated that the sales were not genuine. They decided that $6.7 million derived from sales of Robe River shares would have to be deducted from the results for the last half of 1970, and a profit of $3.5 million became a loss of $3.2 million, including lost cash in the form of stockbrokers' fees. As a result, MSAL and its subsidiaries experienced greater and greater problems in finding the money to repay loans. The only solution was to roll over these debts; that is, raise new loans to pay off the old ones.

Responsibility for finding this money fell on Kenneth Stringer, an employee of Kenneth McMahon and Partners who controlled the MSAL group's money-market operations.

The report alleges that as security for loans Stringer often pledged shares or bills of exchange which were the property of, or had been lodged with, Robe River or other subsidiaries or associates of MSAL. In doing so, he treated these companies as if they were identical to MSAL. The problem was particularly severe when Stringer used securities not even owned by subsidiaries or associates, but which outside companies had temporarily entrusted to them in return for loans.

Stringer also allegedly utilized his position as financial controller of the group and its associates to obtain substantial loans from Robe River Limited for the MSAL group. Robe River had a debenture trust deed which limited the amounts of money it could lend to associated companies. Stringer got around this problem by arranging for Robe River to lend to an independent merchant bank, which would then lend this money to MSAL or a subsidiary. It was suggested that about $5.5 million were obtained by this method (Rath et al., 1977:161-174). After the group collapsed, several merchant banks found themselves owing Robe River substantial amounts of money. Claims that they had only been acting as intermediaries meant nothing in law. When the investigators confronted Stringer with their evidence, he claimed he had been obeying orders from Nestel. MSAL made a last-ditch attempt to resolve its problems by redeeming its shares in two mutual funds it had established in 1970. A subsidiary was joint manager of the investment institutions, and three out of the five fund directors were on the board of MSAL. Both funds, moreover, had invested heavily in the MSAL group or in companies which the group was planning to control: By October 1970 they had committed more than 55 percent of their capital in this way.

MSAL redeemed its shares just one day before the directors released their $3.5 million profit to $3.2 million loss statement. The investigators found that the two fund directors who had approved the redemptions were on the MSAL board and that they had not used reasonable diligence.

The collapse of the MSAL group came close to setting off a domino reaction among other financial institutions. Nevertheless, the only parties so far to have incurred sanctions from an official body are the stockbrokers. The Sydney Stock Exchange fined each of the three partners in the firm $5,000 for their part in the Robe River Shuffle. The CAC brought charges against the five directors of MSAL, on the basis that the profit statement of January 25, 1971 was false and misleading. After a month-long trial the presiding judge directed the jury to acquit the defendants because "in his view the Crown had not established sufficient evidence, fit to go to a jury, which would indicate that the consolidated profit statement was false" (Booth, 1977:1). Nevertheless, the company was liquidated, mostly by selling off its assets to overseas investors.

Less than two years later, McMahon announced that he had become a consultant for Dr. Armand Hammer, Chairman of Occidental Petroleum.

**Cambridge Credit**

Cambridge Credit was incorporated in NSW in 1950. It took over enterprises previously carried on by R.E.M. Hutcheson and his father, R.E.B. Hutcheson. Throughout its history Cambridge and its subsidiaries was dominated by the Hutchesons. The special investigators point out that the Cambridge directors were employees of Hutcheson family companies, and argue that from 1962 onward considerable amounts of money had been channeled from the public companies into family concerns.

After 1956 the company concentrated on property investment and land development. In 1957 it was granted a stock exchange quotation and in 1958 issued its first debenture stock. The issue heralded a period of rapid growth, and by 1966 Cambridge had interests in many tracts of undeveloped land. As Cambridge grew, more of its investments tended to be long term and eventually they were not capable of generating sufficient cash to service the land projects and the loans obtained from the public. Like the MSAL group, Cambridge was forced to rely increasingly on borrowings to maintain liquidity.

If Cambridge's problems were similar to MSAL's, so were its solutions. By manipulating accounting rules, the company was able to continue to report profits. Indeed, in 1974, just 14 days before it announced that it would be unable to meet interest payments due to holders of debentures, Cambridge notified shareholders that profits were up by 33.2 percent on the preceding financial year. It was this announcement, followed by the sudden appointment of receivers to the company, that prompted the NSW attorney general to declare a special investigation.

Most projects of Cambridge had three stages. First, it would form a joint venture with a real estate developer who had detailed knowledge of the geographical area to be exploited. The joint venture would acquire a suitable tract of land, financed by Cambridge. On the basis of a specific development proposal, Cambridge was able to revalue the purchased property and negotiate a loan from some outside financier. The loan money would be made available to a second joint venture in which Cambridge retained an interest. The loan would enable this second-stage joint venture to purchase the land from the first-stage joint venture at a price determined when the land was revalued. These were termed "front-end sales," and generated "front-end profits" for Cambridge and other partners in the first-stage venture. The third stage occurred when a specific development or zoning proposal was submitted. The land was sold by the stage two to a third-stage venture in which an outside financier was a capital-contributing partner.

After 1970 a significant proportion of Cambridge's reported trading profits came from front-end sales, and here special investigators have many criticisms to make. They point out, for example, that in determining the profit from these sales, the directors usually paid no regard to any interest which the company might retain in the land through its holding in the stage-two purchaser.

A symptom of their flexible approach to accounting was that the Cambridge directors used at least two mutually incompatible methods of quantifying front-end profits. The first system, the accural method, involved including the total profit from a front-end sale—that is, the difference between the purchase price of the land and the price at which it was later sold—in the accounts for the period in which the contract for sale was completed. Under the second, the cash emergent system, only that portion of the price which actually had been paid was included in the profit for a relevant period. The directors had even used these inconsistent methods when determining profits from the same transaction over different accounting periods.

Fell and Starkey, an Australian firm of chartered accountants, were the auditors of Cambridge and its subsidiaries. The investigators discovered that there had been an "extensive debate between Cambridge and Fell and Starkey, and within Fell and Starkey in 1972 and 1973" (Wright et al., 1977:55) on the topic of front-end sales. The debate was inconclusive. Within the audit firm this type of profit had its strong opponents, but they were disinclined to take a stand on a matter of principle when they were outnumbered. Those in favor of front-end profits tended to criticize their opponents as conservatives who were more preoccupied with theory than with practical accounting matters. The directors' views of front-end profits prevailed.

According to the investigators, audits which Fell and Starkey carried out on the accounts prepared by Cambridge were characterized by the same lack of rigor that pervaded the front-end profits debate. The auditors failed to check out relevant details of transactions; hence the inclusion of several front-end profits which did not meet even the directors' own criteria. Second, the auditors often failed to notice changes in the basis of accounting in different periods. Third, the absence of a coordinating program made it difficult for the auditors to pick up last-minute changes made in subbranch figures from the subbranches into which it was divided when these were integrated into group accounts.

The winding-up of Cambridge's affairs proceeds slowly. In February 1978 receivers announced a first distribution to debenture holders of three cents on the dollar. They estimated that complete realization of Cambridge assets could take up to ten years and that unsecured noteholders, other shareholders, and creditors, with claims of $53 million, would receive no return. In May 1977 and January 1978 writs were issued against Fell and Starkey and some former Cambridge directors by the receivers and the trustee for Cambridge debenture holders. The outcome of these writs has yet to be decided (Robins, 1978).

## Gollin Holdings Ltd.

At the height of its activities, Gollin Holdings Ltd. was the largest international trading company based in Australia. Founded in the 1840s, its board included some of the country's most prominent businessmen. It had 80 subsidiaries, maintained operating divisions in ten nations, and conducted trading activities in more than 50 countries.

In June 1976, a liquidator was appointed to the Gollin empire: This followed the announcement of a $15 million loss for the 1974-1975 financial year and the failure of a proposed $10 million rescue operation by Australian banks. It was later disclosed that the group's deficit exceeded $50 million. The collapse prompted the NSW attorney general to appoint a special investigator.

In a 1975 report to the Sydney Stock Exchange, the directors of Gollin stated that the group had recorded a profit of $885,192 in the six months ending February 28, 1975. After reviewing the accounts, the investigator contended that the group should instead have reported a loss of almost $11 million. First, the directors deliberately inflated the value of steel stocks held by Gollin subsidiaries. The market value of the steel had declined since Gollin had purchased it, and it was the company's general accounting practice to include assets in their accounts at market value when this was lower than the purchase price. However, in the accounts which formed the basis of the April 28 report, the steel stocks were included at their original cost.

Second, the directors had not allowed for losses by a Californian company in which Gollin Holdings had a 50 percent shareholding and whose banking obligations the group would be obliged to meet if the American company failed. Third, they included extraordinary profit items—proceeds from a claim against former auditors and proceeds from the sale of shares by the group—in the half-yearly result, but without clearly describing them as extraordinary items. Finally, the group understated by $120,000 the amount of accured interest on loans due to be paid. The person allegedly responsible for this understatement was the group's chief accountant, whose job it had been to prepare consolidated figures for the directors. When the deduction was made he had already been under intense pressure from his managing director to find ways to inflate Gollin's figures.

Over a period of a month, he had boosted the group's profits to $716,000, only to be told that he would have to find an additional $120,000. In desperation "he went to the draft final accounts for the Group Administration Division and simply reduced by $120,000 the sum payable for accrued interest charges" (Spender, 1977c:50).

*The loans.* The investigation alleges that in the last few years of Gollin's existence, two directors, Gale and Glenister, had obtained loans totaling more than $1.2 million and $330,000, respectively. Gale still owed more than $900,000 and Glenister more than $220,000. Four different types of loans were distinguished. We will concentrate on the first of these, the "Interconsult" loans.

Gale and Glenister arranged for a group of wholly owned Gollin subsidiaries in Luxembourg to lend money to Interconsult Ltd., a company incorporated in Guernsey. This company then lent the money to the two directors. Interconsult, the pivotal company in these transactions, was formally independent of Gollin, but two of its directors were directors of the Luxembourg companies which made the money available. Other Gollin executives eventually brought the Interconsult loans to the attention of Willis, the Gollin chairman, who questioned Gale. Gale clouded the issue by attempting to introduce commissions for contracts as the reason for the loans to Interconsult. Apparently, Gale had earlier mentioned to Willis that a government official had been paid a commission (in other words, a bribe) for helping to secure, "at a very good price," a coal contract from France. No questions were asked concerning this payment. As Willis commented, "if it was a secret commission, which it could easily have been, I did not want to become involved in it" (Spender, 1977a:42).

In October and December 1977, Gale and Glenister were charged on 21 counts concerning their alleged loans from the Gollin group. Committal proceedings established that they had a prima facie case to answer. Trial is yet to be held.

## DISCUSSION

The case studies are consistent with, and help to develop, Marx and Weber's observations and provide some insights into specific aspects of Australian society.

The data underline the inconsistencies between the ideology and reality of advanced capitalist societies. It would be difficult to argue, for example, that the Bartons were outstanding businessmen. Their greatest abilities seem to have been to sell themselves to other businessmen, to sniff out readily available capital, to obtain good legal advice, and to engage determinedly in litigation. Most of the small businesses Alexander Barton launched in the 1950s soon folded, and when father and son left for Paraguay the majority of companies formed in the late 1960s also went into liquidation. Despite this they were able, in less than 25 years, to accomplish a remarkable rags to riches story. At the height of their careers the companies they controlled had assets valued at about $22 million, and despite their current legal entanglements they still seem to maintain a lavish lifestyle. There could be nothing more remote from the image of the prudent capitalist entrepreneur.

The MSAL, Cambridge, and Gollin reports present a more complex picture. Most of the directors mentioned showed considerable ability and helped their companies expand. Nonetheless, the reports indicate that major miscalculations by the directors went unpunished by the system for considerable periods, during which the companies were able not only to hang on but to report profits, attract loans, and take over other businesses. Considerable amounts of capital still are tied up as liquidators and receivers try to sort out the problems, and this, of course, does not take into account amounts which went to the directors. This situation must cast doubt on the efficiency of capitalism as an allocator of resources and expose what Marx called its "gambling" nature.

The case studies disclose major conflicts of interest between the directors of large public companies and the investors whose assets they control. In such instances the small investor always suffered. As Marx emphasized, these conflicts are evidence of the way centralization has transformed capitalism and should lead to a questioning of ideology and raise doubts about the legitimacy of such institutions as private property and the separation between the public and private spheres.

In Australia, however, periodic crashes by public companies and the ensuing reports on their operations have failed to generate such questions, either in the community or among researchers. The Marxist viewpoint has an easy answer. Australia lacks a sufficiently class-conscious proletariat, this being the only class capable of seizing on inconsistencies as part of its program of transforming capitalism by revolution. From our perspective this is an inadequate explanation.

The tabling of special investigations allows the veil of secrecy that surrounds public companies to be lifted, but the reports only concern companies that have crashed and the individuals responsible. The business community has been able to put considerable distance between the failed companies and their own viable operations and to argue that it must have been illegitimate and deviant practices that caused the failures. Liberal and radical criminologists, anxious to highlight the moral failings of the white-collar criminal and to condemn the lenient treatment received in comparison with other offenses, also tend to focus on individuals rather than social institutions and processes. Courtroom dramas which follow special investigations often accentuate the individualist approach. Even if alleged offenders are acquitted, the response is merely to blame the relevant CAC for an inadequate prosecution rather than to ask questions concerning the system.

From a Weberian point of view, the case studies underline the inconsistencies between an emphasis on principles of formal rationality and substantive considerations of justice in capitalist societies. Most of the directors mentioned had a hand in elaborate schemes to get around the spirit of the law, yet obey the letter. The Brins accounts prepared by the Bartons and the loans from Harbourside to Brins are examples. The Robe River Shuffle and the loans from Robe River to MSAL via merchant banks also were artificial devices, and Cambridge's front-end profits represented similar evasions. The memoranda on the Barton companies to the NSW attorney general was prompted by a recognition of the CAC's helplessness against such maneuvers and it suggests more flexible regulatory bodies, such as shareholders' tribunals.

Gollin's maneuvers to escape the ban on public company loans to directors by laundering the money through an independent company also indicated a recognition by company controllers that criminal laws regarding their behavior will be applied with a strong emphasis on principles of formal rationality. In other words, the courts will concern themselves with the letter of the law rather than the spirit. In an earlier article (Sutton and Wild, 1978) we argued that conflicts between principles of formal and substantive rationality in applying criminal law in capitalist societies are most significant in accounting for the white-collar offender's apparent immunity; more important than class- or status-oriented bias on the part of law enforcers or the judiciary (Sutherland, 1949), and more important than compromise clauses that may have been built into relevant legislation because of political influence (Aubert, 1952).[3]

As Weber pointed out, British law is less formally rational than law in other capitalist countries, and does indeed have a class bias: "A dual policy of formal adjudication of disputes within the upper class, combined with arbitrariness or *de facto* denegation of justice for the economically weak" (1954:120). We contend that even if this class bias were eliminated, white-collar defendants, because their positions within the occupational structure put more emphasis on rational and calculating behavior, would have greater chances of being acquitted or convicted only of technical breaches.

According to Albrow (1975), an increasing emphasis on formal rationality is closely tied to the capitalist ideology that law and business should be separate spheres. Weber made a similar assertion when he pointed out that one of the major forces for the emergence of legal rationality in western societies was demands by the bourgeoisie for "an unambiguous and clear legal system, that would be free from irrational administrative arbitrariness" (Weber, 1954:267). The case studies reaffirm this observation. The Australian judiciary is especially reluctant to interfere in business by making substantive judgments on the commercial wisdom of directors' decisions. This is evident in the Brins and MSAL cases, and heavily influences the CAC's discussion of the Barton maneuvers.

The case studies also highlight the roles played by employees or employee directors. Rarely did they offer resistance to corporate maneuvers, and in several instances they showed considerable initiative in ensuring that their directors' needs were met even if this involved questionable activities on their own part. Many of Bartons' employees were prepared to sign almost any document. The MSAL money-market man clearly put loyalty to the company above all else. Gollin executives also showed considerable reluctance to disobey orders. Finally, the attempts to dampen the company chairman's interest in the Interconsult loans by indicating that they may have been commissions—that is, illegal bribes—suggest that even the most reputable company heads may expect their executives to bend or break the rules to achieve company objectives (Geis, 1967).

Explaining why apparent pillars of their communities, with no record of criminal activity, are suddenly exposed as having systematically engaged in unethical or even illegal activities has become a major preoccupation for criminology. Gross (1978) has offered perhaps the most satisfactory resolution of this problem in approaching it from an organizational theory perspective rather than relying on traditional criminology. Part of the answer lies in the increasing bureaucratization of capitalist societies, particularly its effects on individual behavior. Most employees in question were organization men for whom adherence to social norms, even those codified into laws, came second to a commitment to the company. When individuals at the top of the corporate structure are faced with inconsistencies between corporate goals and the law, they are able to enlist expert assistance and devise maneuvers to resolve the difficulties.[4] Middle-level executives, charged with the day-to-day running of company affairs and harassed by their superiors to produce results, have fewer options and are more likely simply to ignore the law.

Organization men, however, will only need to break the law if the requirements of the company (that is, of their superiors) are inconsistent with legislative enactments. As we discussed above, it was Marx who indicated how inconsistencies between capitalist law and ideology and the real interests of corporate controllers can arise.

Earlier we referred to self-regulation in the business sphere. Citing the English stock exchange, Weber argued that sometimes voluntary associations, recruited from an appropriate status group, were most effective in imposing controls. The MSAL case may appear to support this view. Several participants were criticized in the report, yet only the stockbrokers incurred official sanctions. Their discipline was imposed by the Sydney Stock Exchange Ltd., a voluntary association. Compared with state law enforcers, the exchange was remarkably swift in its response: The three partners were fined just five weeks after MSAL went into liquidation.

Despite this evidence, we doubt the effectiveness of self-regulation. First, the Australian business sector does not consist primarily of traditional, broad based, and powerful status groups able to influence a significant proportion of company controllers. Australian business does not have the traditional constraints of the British system as indicated by the different orientations to takeovers. Second, although self-regulation may be appropriate for such specific institutions as the stock exchange, which has a state-backed monopoly, it has different effects when applied to the whole corporate sector. Our data on accountancy illustrates this.

Accountancy matters were central to all four case studies. The two relevant prosecutions so far have been unsuccessful, because the profession has failed to generate precise and unambiguous rules relating to true and fair financial reports. "Within certain flexible extremities, true and fair can mean very much what directors and auditors want them to mean" (Ryan, 1967). This statement by the NSW Commissioner for Corporate Affairs applies not only to Australia. In every capitalist country government has left it to accountants to generate the rules for corporate financial reporting, and everywhere the rules produced have been imprecise and inconsistent (Birkett and Walker, 1974; Zeff, 1972).

The inability of Cambridge's auditors to effectively resolve basic theoretical issues, to approach the audit systematically, and to ensure that accounts produced were consistent, is symptomatic of the profession's approach to financial reporting. There is, to use Weber's terminology, an absence of formal rationality. The lack of formal rationality ensures that in preparing accounts the profession is able to achieve substantive objectives rather than merely applying abstract rules, but almost invariably it is corporate controllers who determine the goals. Like rulers in Weber's ideal type of traditional patrimonial system, controllers of modern companies reserve the freedom to make decisions of accounting principle on a case-to-case basis, without being bound by the precedents they set. An emphasis on self-regulation in the accountancy sphere, therefore, has given company controllers maximum freedom to pursue their own interests.

So far, we have reviewed the case studies in the context of advanced capitalism. Australia exhibits some unique aspects. Sectors of its economy have frontier characteristics, with strong emphasis on speculation in periods of prosperity. The comparatively rapid growth experienced since World War II has amplified these tendencies (see Wild, 1978). Australia has a weak manufacturing base and most export earnings come from the primary areas of mineral resources, agricultural produce, and pastoral industries. The country depends heavily on the inflow of foreign capital and technology to maintain and advance standards of living, and like other countries on the periphery of world capitalism it has experienced what Clark (1975:54) calls "the dangers of dependent development." These include an extreme sensitivity to downturns in world capitalism and the constant threat that foreign capital will sweep aside local economic and political autonomy. The latter problem has been exacerbated by the spread of multinationals, and over the last three decades Australian governments have stepped up efforts to balance foreign capital by encouraging domestic production through tariffs, tax concessions, and export incentives.

Our data reflect many of these developments. MSAL, Cambridge, Gollin, and the Bartons were active in such frontier areas as minerals, land, and trade, which are of central relevance to the postwar Australian expansion. That major miscalculations by directors contributed to the failures of the first three of these groups highlights the degree of speculation involved. MSAL, Cambridge, and Gollin, moreover, were hard hit by the world recession in the early 1970s and the OPEC price rises. The collapse of these groups is evidence of the vulnerability of Australian-based companies competing against foreign corporations which can draw on far greater capital reserves. The sudden rise of all four companies—especially the Barton enterprises—in the boom conditions of the 1950s and '60s reflects the comparatively open and speculative nature of Australian capitalism, and indicates the weakness of traditional influences in modifying economic behavior. The Bartons' skillful exploitation of tax concessions on calls and options in oil exploration companies also illustrates that attempts by Australian governments to encourage domestic capital formation sometimes exacerbate speculation and exploitation. In some ways at least, the elements of instability which Marx detected in advanced capitalism are accentuated in the Australian context.

## CONCLUSION

In reviewing four recent special investigations into Australian companies from a perspective combining elements of Marx and Weber's ideas, we have attempted to show that such data are of central relevance for understanding advanced capitalist societies.

The material presented provides insights into the dilemmas and temptations confronting controllers of large corporations in a society where there are growing inconsistencies between the dominant ideology and actual relations of production. It also gives some indication of the ways these problems often are resolved, and shows how corporate controllers can exploit several distinct but interrelated power structures. First, in their relationships with the state, directors can exploit an emphasis on predictability in law and administration. Second, in relations with shareholders and other investors, a flexible system of financial reporting can be manipulated. Finally, in relationships with staff, senior company officers enjoy the authority which is inherent in top bureaucratic positions.

In reviewing data on company investigations it is virtually impossible not to be indignant at the inconsistencies between what some businessmen practice and what they preach, and at the way they bend norms, values, and laws to their own advantage. Like Weber, however, we contend that social scientists should set aside these emotions and attempt an empathetic or intuitive understanding from within *(verstehen)* of the corporate controller's situation and behavior. Only then will there be the possibility of clear understanding on a topic where, more than in any other area of contemporary criminology, research has been marred by the rush to judgment from without.

## NOTES

1. After seven attempts they secured bail of $40,000 for Alexander Barton and $30,000 for Thomas (Sydney *Morning Herald,* January 21, 1978:5). However, recent press reports indicate that despite their legal problems the defendants have been able to maintain a comfortable style of living (*Australian Financial Review,* December 4, 1978:38)

2. The term "money-market" describes the system whereby private companies lend one another their surplus cash. Usually, merchant banks act as intermediaries in these transactions. All loans obtainable on the money-market are short, or at best medium-term, and involve heavy interest repayments.

3. Note, however, that Aubert emphasized that the legislation he was examining may have been the product of political and economic developments distinctive to Norway in the postwar years, and he was well aware (Aubert, 1963) of the relevance of Weber to contemporary research in the sociology of law.

4. This helps account for the burgeoning of a professional middle class in advanced capitalist societies, and poses a significant challenge for Marxist theory. For an attempt to account for the professions within this tradition, see Johnson (1975) and Sutton and Wild (1978). The latter article considers the applicability of Johnson's framework to law and accountancy, and argues that it should be extended to accommodate ideas concerning rationality and authority.

## REFERENCES

ALBROW, M. (1975) "Legal positivism and bourgeois materialism." British Journal of Law and Society 2 January:14-31.

AUBERT, W. (1952) "White collar crime and social structure." American Journal of Sociology 58 (November):263-71.

——— (1963) "Researches in the sociology of law." American Behavioral Scientist 7 (December):16-20.

BENDIX, R. (1962) Max Weber: An Intellectual Portrait. London: Methuen.

BIRKETT, W. P. and R. G. WALKER (1974) "Accountancy, a source of market imperfection." Journal of Business Finance and Accounting 1 (Summer):171-193.

BOOTH, B. (1977) "The Minsec case." Delivered to the staff of the School of Accounting, University of New South Wales. (unpublished)

BURKE, M. (1976) "Fourth interim report of the special investigation of the Barton Group of Companies, together with a supplement." Paper No. 4, Parliament of NEW (Second Session).

CLARK, D. (1975) "Australia: Victim or partner of British imperialism?" In E. L. Wheelwright and K. Buckley (eds.), Essays in the Political Economy of Australian Capitalism 1. Sydney: ANZ Book Co.

DOMHOFF, G. W. (1967) Who Rules America? Englewood Cliffs, NJ: Prentice Hall.

GEIS, G. (1967) "The heavy electrical equipment antitrust cases of 1961." In M. B. Clinard and R. Quinney (eds.), Criminal Behavior Systems: A Typology. New York: Holt, Rinehart & Winston.

GOULDNER, A. (1955) Patterns of Industrial Bureaucracy. London: Routledge & Kegan Paul.

GROSS, E. (1978) "Organisations as criminal actors." In P. R. Wilson and J. Braithwaite (eds.), Two Faces of Deviance. Queensland, Australia, University of Queensland Press.

JOHNSON, T. (1975) "The professions in the class structure." In R. Scase (ed.), Industrial Society: Class, Cleavage and Control. London: Allen and Unwin.

MARX, K. (1971) Capital, Vol. III. London: Progress Publishers.

RAE, P. (1974) "Australian securities markets and their regulation." Report of the Senate Select Committee on Securities and Exchange. Canberra: Australian Government Publishing Service.

RATH, A. F., P.C.E. COX, and H. A. COLLUM (1977) "Report of inspectors investigating the affairs of Mineral Securities Limited, First Australian Growth and Income Fund, and Second Australian Growth and Income Fund, Vols 1, 2 and 3." Paper No. 123. Parliament of NSW, 1976-1977 Session.

ROBINS, B. (1978) "First return on Cambridge debenture stock." *The Australian Financial Review* February 3:26.

RYAN, F. J. (1967) "A true and fair view." Abacus 3 (December):95-108.

(1973) Minutes to the Attorney-General from the Commissioner for Corporate Affairs Concerning the Alexander Barton Group of Companies. Paper No. 38. Parliament of NSW, 1973 Session.

SANTOW, G.F.K. (1977) "Regulating corporate misfeasance and maintaining honest markets." Australian Law Journal 1 (August):541-582.

SELZNICK, P. (1966) T.V.A. and the Grass Roots. New York: Harper & Row.

SPENDER, J. (1977a) "Second interim report of an inspector appointed to inquire into certain matters concerning the affairs of Gollin Holdings Limited and other companies." Paper No. 127. Parliament of NSW, 1976-1977 Session.

(1977b) "Fourth interim report of an inspector appointed to inquire into certain matters concerning the affairs of Gollin Holdings Limited and other companies." Paper No. 163. Parliament of NSW, 1976-1977 Session.

(1977c) Fourth Interim Report of an Inspector Appointed to Inquire into Certain Matters Concerning the Affairs of Gollin Holdings Limited and Other Companies. Paper No. 163. Parliament of NSW, 1976-77 Session.

SUTHERLAND, E. (1949) White-Collar Crime. New York: Holt, Rinehart and Winston.

SUTTON, A. C. (1978) Company Investigations 1975-77. Sydney: The NSW Bureau of Crime Statistics and Research.

and R. A. WILD (1978) "Corporate crime and social structure." In P. R. Wilson and J. Braithwaite (eds.), Two Faces of Deviance. St. Lucia: Queensland University Press.

SYKES, T. (1978) The Money Miners. Sydney: Wildcat Press.

TAYLOR, I., P. WALTON, and J. YOUNG (1973) The New Criminology. London and Boston: Routledge & Kegan Paul.

WEBER, M. (1954) On Law in Economy and Society (E. Shils and M. Rheinstein, trans.). New York: Clarion.

WILD, R. A. (1978) Social Stratification in Australia. Sydney: George Allen and Unwin.

WRIGHT, K.M.B., P. R. CALLAGHAN, H. A. COLLUM, and J. H. RENNEBERG (1977) "First interim report by the Corporate Affairs Commission into the affairs of Cambridge Credit Corporation Limited and related matters." Paper No. 203. Parliament of NSW, 1976-1977 Session.

ZEFF, S. A. (1972) Forging Accounting Principles in Five Countries: A History and an Analysis of Trends. Champaign, IL: Stipes Publishing.

## ABOUT THE AUTHORS

EVA ASHMORE is a criminalist and investigator, and raised a family as well. She graduated with a B.A. in Society and Justice from the University of Washington in 1978.

MICHAEL BRINTNALL is Assistant Professor of Political Science at Brown University. Among his writings are publications on the politics of white-collar crime and the role of police in addressing white-collar crime. His research interests include public policy-making and evaluation research. Professor Brintnall received his Ph.D. from MIT. He will be on leave in 1980 at the Department of Housing and Urban Development in Washington, D.C.

W.G. (KIT) CARSON, a native of Ireland, studied at the Queen's College, Oxford and Churchill College, Cambridge. He is currently Senior Lecturer in Criminology at the University of Edinburgh, Scotland; and edited (with P. Wiles) *Crime and Delinquency in Britain,* has authored various articles on white-collar crime and the sociology of law, and is currently completing a book on the legal regulation of multinational oil corporations operating in the British Sector of the North Sea. Carson is co-editor of the *International Journal for the Sociology of Law.*

HERBERT EDELHERTZ, Director of the Law and Justice Study Center of the Battelle Human Affairs Research Centers in Seattle, Washington, received his LL.B. from Harvard University. Previous to his research activities with Battelle, Mr. Edelhertz was in private law practice in New York City, and directed nationwide federal prosecutions of a broad spectrum of white-collar criminal activities as Chief of the Fraud Section, Criminal Division, U.S. Department of Justice. Among published work written or co-authored by Mr. Edelhertz are: *The Nature, Impact and Prosecution of White-Collar Crime;* and *Public Compensation to Victims of Crime.*

GILBERT GEIS received his Ph.D. from the University of Wisconsin and taught at the University of Oklahoma; the State University of New York, Albany; and California State University, Los Angeles before joining the faculty at the University of California, Irvine in 1971. His recent research emphases have been in the areas of forcible rape, white-collar crime, victimless crime, and victimology. He was president of the American Society of Criminology in 1975-76. His best-known books are: *Man, Crime, and Society* (with Herbert Bloch), *White-Collar Criminal* (with Robert Meier), and *Forcible Rape* (with Duncan Chappell and Robley Geis).

COLIN H. GOFF, a doctoral candidate in the Social Ecology Program, Criminal Justice option, at the University of California, Irvine, is currently doing research in the sociology of law, specifically laws inimical to powerful interests and legal procedures. He is coauthor (with Charles Reasons) of *Corporate Crime in Canada: A Critical Analysis of Anti-Combines Legislation.* He has also published articles in the *Criminal Law Quarterly.*

EDWARD GROSS, a University of Chicago Ph.D., has taught at Washington State University, University of Minnesota, University of California at Santa Barbara, and is presently Professor of Sociology at the University of Washington. He is a past president of the Pacific Sociological Association, and was recently a Fulbright Fellow in Australia. His work ranges over the subjects of complex organizations and social psychology.

HUGH D. GROVE is Associate Professor of Accounting, School of Accountancy, University of Denver. He earned his B.S.B.A. and M.B.A. from the University of Michigan. He has published articles on not-for-profit performance evaluation; human resource accounting; extractive industry accounting theory; and taxation, financial accounting theory, financial auditing, and management auditing. He is an editor with Anton and Firmin of *Contemporary Issues in Cost and Managerial Accounting—A Discipline in Transition,* and has contributed articles to *Evaluation of Human Services Programs.*

ANDRE L HEUREUX is currently a candidate for a J.D. (1981), University of Washington School of Law. His emphasis is on the problems of unrestricted regional development and the role of local government: criminal law. His research at the present time is in two areas: (1) delineating the constitutional doctrines of pre-emption and preclusion as related to federal Indian law, and (2) historical comparison of the evolution of federal Indian law and the development of New Zealand law affecting the Maori.

MARY V. McGUIRE is a research scientist at the Battelle Law and Justice Study Center in Seattle. She earned her Ph.D. in social psychology at the University of Washington. She has taught courses in social psychology and in psychology and law at the University of Washington, and previously conducted research at Stanford University, Psychology Department, and at the Battelle Seattle Research Center.

MICHAEL D. MALTZ is Associate Professor in the Departments of Criminal Justice and Systems Engineering, University of Illinois at Chicago Circle. He is Chairman, Special Interest Group in Crime and Justice, Operations Research Society of America. His research interests include the development of new quantitative techniques useful in the study of criminal justice problems.

DONN B. PARKER has 30 years of experience in the computer field in technical, management, consulting, and research positions. He received a M.A. in 1954 at the University of California, Berkeley. He has spent the past nine years doing research and consulting on the subjects of computer-related crime and computer security, funded in part by the National Science Foundation and the Law Enforcement Assistance Administration, U.S. Department of Justice. Among his many publications are the books *Crime by Computer* and *Ethical Conflicts in Computer Science and Technology.* He has most recently completed an "Investigation and Prosecution Resource Manual" on computer crime for LEAA.

STEPHEN M. POLLOCK is Professor of Industrial and Operations Engineering, and Research Scientist in the Institute of Public Policy Studies at the University of Michigan. His general interest in the application of mathematical modeling techniques to a variety of problems has led to recent studies of criminal recidivism and bid-rigging. He has published and taught in other operations research topics, including decision analysis and search theory. He is currently an area editor of *Operations Research* and an associate editor of the SIAM *Journal of Applied Mathematics.*

CHARLES E. REASONS, a Ph.D. in sociology from Washington State University, is Professor of Sociology at the University of Calgary. He has published widely in criminology, law, and sociology. His most recent books are *Corporate Crime in Canada* and *Sociology of Law: A Conflict Approach;* and he is working on books on social problems and on occupational safety and health in Canada.

LAURA SHILL SCHRAGER began her sociological training at Washington State University where she and James Short did a research project on organizational crime. After receiving an M.A. in 1978, she entered the Princeton doctoral program. She is currently studying the context in which complex technological research is carried on and related policy decisions are made by analyzing the communication networks and belief systems of academic and corporate researchers, government officials, and public interest representatives who are involved in nuclear waste management and photovoltaics.

DONNA D. SCHRAM received her Ph.D. in psychology from the University of Washington and has been Research Director for Special Projects of the Washington State Juvenile Parole, Director of Research of the Seattle Law and Justice Planning Office, and Director of the Washington State Law and Justice Planning Office. She was a Visiting Scientist at the Battelle Institute, doing research on the police response to rape. She is now a private consultant, doing research on the impact of the new juvenile code of the State of Washington.

JAMES F. SHORT, Jr. is Professor of Sociology and Director of the Social Research Center at Washington State University. He has been Dean of the Graduate School, a visiting professor both in the United States and abroad, Secretary of the American Sociological Association, editor of the *American Sociological Review*, co-director of the research for the National Commission on the Causes and Prevention of Violence, and has authored or edited ten books and numerous professional articles. He has received numerous professional honors. His current interests are on the effects of income maintenance on crime and delinquency, organizational crime, and political implications of juvenile delinquency.

NEAL SHOVER (Ph.D., 1971, University of Illinois, Urbana) is Associate Professor of Sociology at the University of Tennessee, Knoxville. He is author of *A Sociology of American Corrections* and a number of articles on law, criminality, and official reactions to crime. His current research interests include gender roles and their relationship to criminality, the long-term social and psychological effects of criminal involvement during early life, organizational crime, and the regulatory process.

JAMES E. SORENSEN is Professor of Accounting, School of Accountancy, University of Denver. He received his B.S.B.A. and M.B.A. from the University of Denver and Ph.D. from the Ohio State University. He has published in the *Accounting Review*, *Journal of Accountancy*, *Decision Sciences*, *Financial Executive*, *Administrative Science Quarterly*, and the *Journal of Organizational Behavior and Performance*. Publications include "Reliability and Validity of Accounting Data," *Journal of International Accounting* (1976), and *Evaluation of Human Service Programs*.

THOMAS L. SORENSEN is Professor of Sociology at Arapahoe Community College in Littleton, Colorado. His research interests have focused on conflicts of professionals in bureaucratic organizations. He has co-authored articles which have been published in such periodicals as the *Administrative Science Quarterly*, *Journal of Accountancy* and *Decision Sciences*. His current research interests are in social deviance.

EZRA STOTLAND is Director of the Society and Justice Program and Professor of Psychology at the University of Washington. He received his Ph.D. in social psychology from the University of Michigan and has authored, co-authored, or edited articles on the psychology of white-collar crime, the investigation of white-collar crime, and psychological and organizational aspects of policing. He has also published books and articles on empathy, attitudes, identification, organization, mental health, and suicide. He has been President of the Society for the Psychological Study of Social Issues and the Washington State Association of Criminal Justice Educators.

ADAM C. SUTTON obtained a B.A. in philosophy and anthropology from the University of Sydney and is completing a Ph.D. on company crime at the University of New South Wales. His main research interests include the sociology of law, the professions, and bureaucracy. He has worked as a computer programmer for the New South Wales Government and as a research officer for the N.S.W. Bureau of Crime Statistics, where he has produced reports on company investigation and on the discipline of lawyers. He is presently Computer/Research Officer for the New South Wales Department of Corrective Services.

DIANE VAUGHAN received her Ph.D. in sociology from the Ohio State University in June 1979. Her research interests include organizational crime, victimology, complex organizations, sociology of gender, and sociology of life cycles. She is currently engaged in research on the social control of organizations as a postdoctoral fellow in the Department of Sociology, Yale University.

MARILYN E. WALSH holds an M.A. and a Ph.D. in criminal justice from the School of Criminal Justice at the State University of New York at Albany. She is currently a research scientist on the staff of the Law and Justice Study Center of the Battelle Memorial Institute's Seattle Research Center. Dr. Walsh is the author of the book, *The Fence—A New Look at the World of Property Theft*, as well as of numerous articles and reports concerning the theft and fencing of stolen goods, stolen property trafficking patterns, and investigative and enforcement strategies for combating organized theft activities. She has also co-authored (with H. Edelhertz) the book *The White-Collar Challenge to Nuclear Safeguards*.

RONALD WILD completed his Ph.D. at the University of Sydney where he was the Drapers' Company Commonwealth Scholar. From 1970-4 he was a lecturer in Anthropology, and from 1974-8 a senior lecturer in Anthropology, at the University of Sydney. He is presently Professor of Sociology at LaTrobe University, Melbourne. His other publications include *Bradstow: A Study of Status, Class and Power in a Small Australian Town* (1974), *Social Stratification in Australia* (1978) and papers on social stratification, community studies, ageing and corporate crime. He is currently working on books on community studies in Australia, and English and American comparisons with Bradstow.